ACTING AND STAGECRAFT Made Simple

The Made Simple series
has been created
primarily for self-education
but can equally well
be used as
an aid to group study.
However complex the subject,
the reader is taken
step by step,
clearly and methodically,
through the course. Each volume
has been prepared by experts,
using throughout the
Made Simple technique of teaching.
Consequently the gaining
of knowledge now becomes
an experience to be enjoyed.

In the same series

Accounting	German
Acting and Stagecraft	Housing, Tenancy and Planning Law
Additional Mathematics	Human Anatomy
Administration in Business	Human Biology
Advertising	Italian
Anthropology	Journalism
Applied Economics	Latin
Applied Mathematics	Law
Applied Mechanics	Management
Art Appreciation	Marketing
Art of Speaking	Mathematics
Art of Writing	Metalwork
Biology	Modern Biology
Book-keeping	Modern Electronics
British Constitution	Modern European History
Business and Administrative	Modern Mathematics
Organisation	Money and Banking
Business Economics	Music
Business Statistics and Accounting	New Mathematics
Calculus	Office Administration
Chemistry	Office Practice
Childcare	Organic Chemistry
Commerce	Personnel Management
Company Law	Philosophy
Computer Programming	Photography
Computers and Microprocessors	Physical Geography
Cookery	Physics
Cost and Management Accounting	Practical Typewriting
Data Processing	Psychiatry
Dressmaking	Psychology
Economic History	Public Relations
Economic and Social Geography	Rapid Reading
Economics	Russian
Effective Communication	Salesmanship
Electricity	Secretarial Practice
Electronic Computers	Social Services
Electronics	Sociology
English	Spanish
English Literature	Statistics
Export	Teeline Shorthand
Financial Management	Twentieth-Century British History
French	Typing
Geology	Woodwork

ACTING AND STAGECRAFT Made Simple

Derek Bowskill

Made Simple Books
HEINEMANN : London

Made and printed in Great Britain
by Richard Clay (The Chaucer Press) Ltd, Bungay, Suffolk
for the publishers William Heinemann Ltd,
10 Upper Grosvenor Street, London W1X 9PA

First edition, March 1973
Reprinted, March 1979
Reprinted, February 1983

British Library Cataloguing in Publication Data

Bowskill, Derek
    Acting and Stagecraft.—(Made simple books)
    1. Amateur theatricals
    I. Title   II. Series
    792′.0222   PN3155

ISBN 0–434–98574–0

Drama means action. Since there is no action without equal and opposite reaction, drama also means conflict—action, reaction and interaction in the doing of life.

Life, as we know it, means experiencing and communicating. Drama selects what is meaningful and presents it with style. It can be defined, therefore, as the imaginative communication of significant experience. It may make us laugh, cry, think or, indeed, all three at the same time. Above all it sets out to make us respond and, by practice, to become more responsive in general. This book invites you to respond.

Drama is essentially practical with an endless variety of forms, and the best way to learn about it is to do it—by seeing plays or performing plays; by joining a group or a class or by doing examples and exercises of the kind described in this book.

While the book is designed as a personal guide for the non-professional—during training, rehearsal and in performance—it can also be used in conjunction with, or as a basis for, group training in schools, colleges and further education classes, as well as for mixed, all-women and youth drama groups and companies. It provides valuable material and exercises for students proposing to take examinations in speech or drama leading to such qualification as A.D.B., L.R.A.M., L.G.S.M. and so on.

This book does not offer a package-holiday-type guided tour of drama and theatre. It may have some of the elements of a catalogue and suggest some particular tickets or special vehicles but, more importantly, it sets out to describe the terrain; to explain some basic map-reading techniques and to erect the occasional signpost. The journey of exploration and discovery must be taken alone. This book is intended to start you on that journey.

DEREK BOWSKILL

Acknowledgments

I should like to acknowledge the assistance I have received from the organisations contributing to the Appendices. In particular, my sincere appreciation is extended to Arthur Hodgson (Hon. Sec., Guild of Drama Adjudicators), Peter Husbands (Sec., Drama Board) and Tony Tuxford (Technical Sales Manager, Furse Stage Lighting). I should also like to thank my wife, Jill, for her help in general and for her particularly valuable contributions to the sections dealing with Movement.

For permission to reprint the various extracts in the book, grateful thanks are due to the following:

Geoffrey Bles (Publishers) Ltd for *An Actor Prepares* by Constantin Stanislavsky; Calder and Boyars Ltd for *Notes and Counter Notes* by Eugene Ionesco; Faber and Faber Ltd for *Waiting for Godot* and *Endgame* by Samuel Beckett, *The Sport of My Mad Mother* and *The Knack* by Ann Jellicoe, *The Maids* by Jean Genet and *The Cocktail Party* by T. S. Eliot; Macmillan London and Basingstoke and St. Martin's Press for *The Silver Tassie* by Sean O'Casey; Curtis Brown Ltd for *Blithe Spirit* and *Still Life* by Noel Coward published by William Heinemann Ltd; David Higham Associates Ltd for *Luther* by John Osborne published by Faber and Faber Ltd; Oxford University Press for *A Phoenix Too Frequent* by Christopher Fry; Methuen & Co. Ltd for *Serjeant Musgrave's Dance* by John Arden, *The Dumb Waiter* and *The Caretaker* by Harold Pinter, *The Fire Raisers* by Max Frisch and *The Quare Fellow* by Brendan Behan; Dr Jan Van Loewen Ltd for *The Women at the Tomb* (from *Seven Plays* Volume 1) by Michel de Ghelderode published by MacGibbon & Kee; Laurence Pollinger Ltd for *Sam the Highest Jumper of Them All* by William Saroyan published by Faber and Faber Ltd; Elaine Green Ltd for *Camino Real* as *Ten Blocks on the Camino Real* (a one act play) © Copyright 1948 by Tennessee Williams, as *Camino Real* (revised and published version) © Copyright 1953 and for *A Streetcar Named Desire* © Copyright 1947 by Tennessee Williams, both extracts taken from *Four Plays* by Tennessee Williams published by Secker and Warburg 1957; the Estate of the late Josef and Karel Capek and A. M. Heath & Co. Ltd for *The Life of the Insects* and *And so ad Infinitum*; A. D. Peters for *The Brig* by Kenneth Brown published by Methuen & Co. Ltd and *The Deep Blue Sea* by Terence Rattigan published by Pan Books Ltd; *In Camera* by Jean-Paul Sartre copyright © 1944 Editions Gallimard, Paris, translation by Stuart Gilbert copyright © 1946 Hamish Hamilton, London; Guardian Newspapers Ltd for an extract from the *Guardian* of 20th April, 1972.

I apologise for any omissions.

D.B.

INTRODUCTION

The theatre today is in a state of change. The rate of change, as in everything, is increasing. The symptoms of change can be seen in new styles of acting and production, as well as in new forms of writing and presentation.

It is not so long ago that the whole theatre movement was solidly traditional: traditional plays being produced by traditional methods on traditional stages. Professional and non-professional were mutually exclusive groups and music, song, dance, circus and cinema were separate art forms. There was no mixing, mingling or interchange.

Now the edges are blurred and the theatre is broadening and deepening its form and content. As it does so, embracing new material in a fresh way, it is creating new rules to meet changing attitudes and a conscious awareness of and interest in things social, moral, political and sexual.

The huge gulf once separating professional from non-professional no longer exists. The increasing responsibility and power of Arts Councils, Arts Associations, National Drama Organizations and Drama Advisers is fostering the growth of a co-operative approach to theatre arts.

In the theatre itself, plays touch hitherto taboo subjects. Forms of presentation are becoming more and more mobile. Relationships between actors and audiences are growing and developing—passivity from an audience and glamour from an actor are no longer enough in themselves.

Theatres and their stages are changing in size and shape. Theatre companies are taking to the streets and the beaches; playing in basements, pubs, clubs, cafés, restaurants and churches. Lunchtime theatres are now well established.

Innovation and participation are the new keynotes and the interested individual can no longer find a definitive set of rules to guide him. He is thrown back on his own responses and resources.

In these conditions of change, experiment and discovery, the non-professional holds a privileged position. Time, money, manpower and opinion are all on the side of the non-professional. He can innovate without restraint, experiment without fear and take whatever time is needed. The non-professional can set his own standards and his own priorities. His disciplines are his own and those of the theatre he creates. The discovery of such disciplines and the continuing expansion of the boundaries of the theatre is what this book is about.

Table of Contents

Made Simple   ACTING AND STAGECRAFT

CHAPTER ONE

ACTING AND LIVING

'I hold the world but as the world, Gratiano:
A stage where every man must play a part.'

The Merchant of Venice

'On the stage he was natural, simple, affecting;
T'was only that when he was off he was acting.'

Goldsmith on Garrick

The Self and Self-Images

Acting and living have much in common. Life frequently casts us into different roles; some pleasant—some unpleasant. When it does, we select the part of our personality that is most appropriate and use it, be it stern parent, loving wife, angry driver of motor car or satisfied client of a supermarket. Sometimes the selection is conscious and at other times we are completely unaware of it.

When the role pleases us, we are relaxed and operate smoothly. But when the role fails to match up to our own **self-image**, we become tense and uncomfortable. Sometimes we have to 'bite the tongue' in order to prevent a breakdown in communication; sometimes subtle flattery has to be used to ease relationships with a difficult colleague. Either way, we are not 'being ourselves'. Or, rather, we are being only one of our many selves.

The question of which self to choose occurs frequently—the first date with a boy or girl; a meeting with an old sparring partner in the local; an encounter with the new neighbours; a first visit to an expensive club; or an evening with the school Parent Teacher Association. The choosing of the self on these occasions—the way to dress, to move and to speak—is intended to oil the wheels and help everyone 'get on' together. The wider the range from which we can choose this 'self' and the more accurately we can make the choice the less likely are we to 'get off on the wrong foot'. A surge of interest in this **range of behaviour** and **sensitivity of choice** has shown itself in the United States with the massive growth of Encounter groups—all aiming at developing personal aids for group communication.

Some people are keenly aware of these aids; others have little knowledge of their existence and even less wish to learn—and that, of course, is their personal privilege. No such privilege exists for an actor. **Self-awareness** is the cornerstone of the art and craft of acting.

The differences between self-awareness and self-consciousness are examined in Chapter Nine. Here it is sufficient to remark that anything that can help an actor achieve flexibility and efficiency in the communication of experience is worthy of attention and study.

Experience, Expression and Communication

Basic communication of experience is not a complex or difficult operation. A baby screaming in a cot and a rock group in a sound and light show do it

1

extremely effectively. But although the baby's screams tell of significant experience they are not imaginative: and while the rock group's screams may be
unbelievably imaginative they seldom relate significant experience and drama
has been defined as 'the imaginative communication of significant experience'.
If an actor is to succeed, the form of his work must be imaginative and its
content significant. To achieve this the actor must have mastered the tools and
understood the techniques involved in the journey from inner, personal experience, through it's externalization into dramatic self-expression to it's organization into group communication and an act of theatre. Having mastered and
understood these tools and techniques he must exercise and service them—
just like a motor-car. Except that in this case he is his own engine, vehicle, and
driver combined into one integrated unit.

Unfortunately for many would-be actors, depth of personal experience and
sincerity of self-expression are no guarantee of efficient group communication.
I remember vividly the case of an experienced actor playing the father in
Chekhov's *The Proposal*. The production was being toured and after each
performance there was open discussion with the audience. The actor was
genuinely convinced he was presenting the father as a sympathetic character
and it came as a great shock to him that audiences had formed a most un-
sympathetic opinion. What the actor was experiencing inside himself was
denied by what he actually communicated. After many evenings of heated but
friendly discussion it finally transpired that it was the actor's use of his eyebrows that created this unwanted impression. Strict reappraisal was followed
by stricter re-rehearsal until actor and audience were finally sharing the same
character. Here, then, is an excellent example of the fine attention to detail
that every actor must give to the tools and techniques of communication.

These tools that are used in rehearsals and performance are no different
from the tools that we all use in everyday life. On stage they may be used in a
different way and may carry a greater charge. Nevertheless, the tools themselves remain the same. Breathing; bodily movement; facial expression and
explanatory gesture; the intonation of a sentence; the raising of an eyebrow;
the handling of a knife and fork—all are part of day-to-day living. Yet, for an
actor they are the delicate fingers of the spirit with which he reaches his
audience.

The Senses

It would be ludicrous to imagine an actor giving a performance without the
use of his five senses—yet they too are no different from the ones we all take
so much for granted in everyday life. True, there are occasions when the senses
come into their own, even in the most mundane of lives: heat from a kettle
makes an immediate impact; an unpleasant smell receives instant attention;
a blow from a hammer is speedily understood. At a less mundane level there
are few who have never paused to marvel at the sight of a particularly beautiful sunset or who have not noticed with delight the taste of an exciting new
drink. But in the main the senses are taken for granted and frequently abused.
The hearing that warns of approaching traffic; the early smell of leaking gas or
the simple sight of brick wall—all are essential but are often overlooked. The
attention we pay to our senses bears no relation to the use we make of them.
It is these much undervalued senses that an actor uses all the time. Unlike
most of us, however, he uses them sensitively tuned to concert pitch.

Imagination

An actor also needs imagination. So does any sensible individual if he is not to court disaster throughout life. It is not only experience that teaches us to step back from the wheels of a bus: imagination—**the intelligent prediction of future events based on a sensitive understanding and perceptive analysis of the past**—also has a part to play. By rearranging the known we can create the inner experience of the unknown.

Take the incident with the bus. The computer of the mind quickly transmits visions of terrified faces and broken bones; sounds of squealing tyres and ambulance sirens; the crowd pictured round the crumpled body. These sounds and sights may have been met originally in reality, in posters and paintings, on cinema or television screens, on gramophone records or on the radio. Whatever their source, they have been stored in the memory bank and the composite that is transmitted from it is accurately connected with the 'living moment' and the act of imagination occurs. We step quickly back—saved by imagination from tasting an unpleasant experience.

Body Memory

Most of our actions are directed by a combination of **memory** and **imagination**. The more we rely on memory, the more we stultify. The more we call upon imagination the more we grow as flexible, mature personalities. This use of memory and imagination is for most of us unconscious and unremembered —we rely on them, and underestimate their function, just as much as we do the senses. When an actor uses them he does so with knowledge and awareness —accepting his dependance upon them to communicate with an audience. He particularly relies on an efficient 'body memory'. For most of us this facility is used on the mechanical trivia of life and we are hardly aware of its existence. There is no special reason for us to consider it deeply or at length. Nevertheless, body memory underpins our waking lives and we should be just as much at a loss without it as any actor.

An actor makes many calls upon his body memory, not the least of which is to help him to get into a role as quickly as possible. The manner in which a certain character holds the handle of a tea-cup may be a sufficient trigger mechanism for one actor. All he needs is to make the specific position of the wrist, hand and fingers and the whole essence of the role will flood over him. For others it may be a way of sitting or walking; a certain tilt to the holding of the head; an angle for the left shoulder. Others may need more than these isolated specifics. They may need to recreate a set of mannerisms in the rhythm of lighting a cigarette; a whole style of walking; a total pattern of going through a doorway. Whatever the individual specific may be, **once it has been accurately recreated it will trigger off the total experience of which itself it is only a part**. Many actors use 'things', especially parts of costume, to help them recreate a role.

Normally, body memory is used to guide us through a series of physical manoeuvres that we cannot easily remember intellectually in their proper sequence—or, if we can, the sheer business of actually thinking them out so delays the action that it may well be too late when it is finally accomplished. Sometimes there may be an urgency to the situation—as in the use of the feet in driving a car; sometimes the action is repeated so many times that to think it out for every occasion would require minutes instead of the appropriate fraction of a second. Activities like knitting, needlework, lighting a cigarette, unlocking a door or using a typewriter all rely on body memory taking over and allowing the mind to continue unhampered. The actor uses this aspect of body memory to help him with quite a large part of his performance. The 'movement pattern' of the piece can be so set in his body memory that he can use the rest of his resources freely to make the experience rich and meaningful. The tennis-player does not re-think the physical relationship of his body to his racket before the execution of every stroke; neither does the actor work out which foot goes where every time he moves. His body memory keeps the main pattern continuing and the actor can pursue the task of making the actions significant. This is not to suggest that the actor should become an unthinking zombie or that there should be an aura of mechanical repetition about what he does. It serves only to underline that there are certain areas of the actor's work that should be **burned into his body memory with such intensity that no effort is needed for their recall—all effort being reserved for making those actions significant.** Seen in such a light, the actor's body memory serves a valuable purpose —that of freeing him to progress his role of interpreter. It's not **what he does** but **the way that he does it,** that ensures the communication of his performance.

The Persona: Emotion and Spirit

Although the actor may see himself as a flexible collection of identification possibilities with no fixed self-image, the tools he brings to his art are as rigid as his own persona. We are all what we are—all trapped in a prison cell called self. So is the actor. Fortunately there is a key to the door of this cell— the key of understanding and self-knowledge. Once the mind comprehends and accepts the rigidity of the personality's framework it becomes possible for the individual to function *apparently* without that frontier. The intellect can play the keys of the 'Mighty Wurlitzer of Self' to full effect only when the extent and range of that keyboard is comprehended and accepted. Much tension in the world at large (and much bad acting on the stage) is the direct result of frustrations created by an attempt to play notes that are not on the keyboard.

Happily, there is hope for growth and progress. It is possible, by the delicate and intelligent use of existing notes to create new and pleasing ones. It is only the obsessive search for new notes (at the oversight and expense of the existing ones) that prevents growth, creates inhibitions and sets up frustrations. A relaxed and easy use of known personality traits (existing notes or keys) with their many combinations and permutations, will provide the right free-wheeling conditions for flexible, expanding communication. The alternatives are strain or stagnation. The actor is gripped by this apparent paradox, as we all are. For the actor it means resisting the evils of type casting, yet acknowledging that all he can ever bring to the theatre is his personal testimony to the human condition.

There is a certain intensity of spirit in all personal and social relationships. From time to time this intensity has to be used at maximum force, but most of the time there is no need for such a charge. Everyday relationships can normally be taken at 'cruising speed'. For the actor there is no such relaxation. Although on stage he may never need a greater charge than he uses on occasions off it, he will need it for much longer periods and in addition there will be a large audience. In his private life it is unlikely that the actor will have to encompass a range of more than three or four people at any one time. From the stage he must embrace hundreds and the charismatic intensity must reach them all.

Emotion is closely related to this intensity of spirit. It is claimed by some that a life without the crests and troughs of emotion is a condition devoutly to be wished and there are those who throughout their lives pursue some nirvana of calm of mind, all passion spent. Certainly our social and educational systems seem intent upon such ends. But whatever our position, few of us completely avoid the grip of powerful emotions, and for many the very harnessing, expressing and communicating (or disguising, as the case may be) of those emotions can be a lifetime's task.

As they had in common a need for the re-education of the senses, so actor and individual have a need for the **re-education of the emotions**. In many schools and colleges what passes for educating the emotions is a long and drawn out exercise in discipline. It is possible to draw a parallel in plumbing. For the water supply to function properly there must be a **direct connection with the mains and a simple control at a local outlet.** This is normally achieved by the provision of pipes and hand-controlled taps. The system works easily and well. When we consider the emotional system we find little attention paid to the nature or function of the mains (and certainly no attempt to make a direct connection) but an obsession with the operation of the taps—with special training to keep them in the 'off' position. We learn to be expert with taps that are unconnected with the main. For the individual, this may or may not be a satisfactory situation. For the actor it is untenable and intolerable. The actor needs the full power of his emotional experience (the mains) and expression (the taps) at his immediate command and under his full control. This should give pause to those who believe the necessary hallmark of an actor to be a 'prima-donna' temperament. It is destructive for any actor to have an emotional charge that he cannot control efficiently, sensitively and completely.

This combination of senses, memories, imagination, spirit, emotions, mind and body is the sum total of the actor's tools and it makes for an unusual challenge: the self as performer and instrument. The instrument of the actor is his own being. It is true that the actor uses some skills that are not in highly developed use in the world at large, but they are still skills of communication —that is, skills of living—and although the actor has the artifact of a text, it is his job to render it transparent, if not invisible. Actor and text must be one.

Being his own instrument it is the essence of himself that he offers up for public perusal and appraisal. There is nothing to place between himself and audience—no contraceptive membrane to offer security.

It is part of the human condition to protect some small part of the self, confident that it will be immune from invasion or rape. The actor has no such armour. He is naked and alone.   ·

CHAPTER TWO

ATTITUDES AND APPROACHES

The Approach to the Text

Subjective or Objective?

The characterization that an actor offers on the stage—the 'finished product' as it were—is a combination of many ingredients, events and processes. One significant ingredient is the **actor's own assessment of the role** as it first appears to him on the printed page—an assessment that will persist through rehearsals and performances, unless some specific force occurs to bring about a change. This assessment is important to the actor because its influence comes to bear not so much on what he knows of the character but on what he *feels* about what he knows. The traits of the character can be drawn accurately and objectively from the text. The actor's emotional attitude to these traits is mainly subjective and often unconsciously created. He may be sympathetic or hostile; he may find it easy to identify with the character's use of language or he may find the movement and gesture pattern removed from his own experience. These personal responses will of course affect the actor's judgment on the role he is to play and upon the way he plays it. During performance he will offer **not only a character but also a commentary upon that character.**

All this is to the good. It is a proper part of the actor's task to offer comment and insight on the role. What is difficult, is to be aware of the attitudes from the moment they are created and thus to be able to make full and meaningful use of them. It is important that they should be made known at the earliest possible stage in rehearsals. I recall I was asked once to attend a dress rehearsal and offer whatever comment might be helpful. (It is almost impossible for an outsider, no matter how expert, to be helpful at dress rehearsals—but more of that in Chapter Seventeen.) One actor, using the full range of properties for the first time, drank the remaining 'tea' in his cup with a splendid flourish. I saw nothing particularly remarkable in it but it was singled out for comment by the director when the time came for post-mortem notes. It transpired that the director did not very much care for the splendour of the flourish. Discussion was pleasant for a few moments until the director said: 'But you see, he wouldn't behave like that!' This in turn led to a conference that lasted five hours.

I did not stay for the final outcome since the first few minutes showed that actor and director had worked through the whole rehearsal period in total ignorance of one another's feelings about the role in question. They had both made judgments on the character, each of which was reasonable and had justification in the text. There would have been no problem if their views had been known to each other in the early stages of the rehearsals. By a series of unhappy accidents there had been no catalyst to help expose this difference, not so much of opinion, but of emotional attitudes, until the dress rehearsal.

I saw the performance on the opening night. Neither actor nor director was in any way content—not even with details that before had been a source of pride. Each was beginning to see the rest of the previously undisclosed iceberg.

The audience was pleased with the individual performance in question and the production in general.

As mentioned above, it is part of the actor's task to offer personal comment and enlightenment on the role he plays. The place for objectivity is the laboratory, not the theatre. The scientist and academic may search for laws and definitions but the theatre knows few laws, and there is no such thing as a definitive performance. It is these variations on the unchanging text that make the theatre a place of such constant interest.

The actor's emotional attitude to the part he is playing—his 'feeling' for it—can influence his performance in many ways. The factors that go towards the creation of a character are considered at length in Chapters Eight to Twelve, and it is sufficient here to quote one example. Take the case of Macbeth.

Most English actors would approach this play with strongly formed emotional attitudes to the question of 'messy' or bloody murders.

Take the following lines:

'Is this a dagger which I see before me,
The handle towards my hand?'

and

'I see thee still;
And on thy blade and dudgeon gouts of blood,
Which was not so before. There's no such thing;
It is the bloody business which informs
Thus to mine eyes.'

The immediate and spontaneous reaction is unlikely to be completely free from prejudice. There are few of us capable of taking even the intangible manifestation of a blood-stained dagger without some rejection symptoms, and fewer who would be able to see the incident as one to be welcomed and embraced with impatient expectation. If the actor is to prepare his role thoroughly, he must, however, be able to try out such an attitude of mind and try it out without overtones of moral criticism. Only when he has added this attitude to his range will he be able to choose significantly which interpretation it is best to offer first to his director. The wider the range of attitudes the actor can bring to his interpretation, the more effective will be his final sensitive choice. To be able to clear the way for an examination of the state of mind of Macbeth at a time when he might have believed that murder, bloody or otherwise, was in no way remarkable—or if it was, then it was a stimulating and exciting event—will create a rich backcloth against which the actor can present those things that will most significantly illuminate the character of Macbeth and the total concept of the play.

Assessments

It is important that the actor should make as few rigid judgments as possible when first approaching the text—and of equal importance that the director should know of any that have been made. When this happens, any comment the actor makes on his role through the way he plays it, will at least be conscious and not spring from blind prejudice or unacknowledged emotions. The actor can make his strongest moral point in performance if he begins his work on the text and in rehearsal with an open mind.

When an actor is asked to play a part that is in itself unattractive from the personal point of view, he must ask himself how strong is his belief in the whole play and whether that can counteract his adverse feelings. Only if his faith in the whole play is unshakeable should the actor agree to undertake the role, otherwise he will find it difficult to commit himself entirely to the part he is to play. Even if he has reservations about his own role when considered out of context, the actor's commitment to each and every performance must be total. Sincerity, it is true, is not by itself enough, but without it the actor will in all probability become as sounding brass or tinkling cymbal. The reference is apt, since the actor has much in common with the priest—both are inter-mediaries between what endures and what is transient. Both aim to celebrate the joys and fears of the human condition—and both do it in public as elected representatives performing on behalf of the community.

In the performance of the ritual celebration of the human condition there can be no place for a 'take it or leave it' attitude. The actor must go out to his audience to touch their spirit. **It is his job to reach out to them—not theirs to struggle to contact him.** The actor must fight through whatever emotional smoke-screens the audience may put up, to ensure that he touches them with the real experience of what the play has to say —and often this can be a diffi-cult process. The more famous the actor, the more difficult it can be for him to pierce the defences of an audience orientated to appreciate his performance rather than to receive the experience of the play—and even more difficult at times for those left on stage when the famous actor has left it. Whatever the 'star' rating of the actor, it is essential that he should prevent the style of his performance from getting between the message of the play and the audience. This is more difficult than it sounds. Here, it is enough to suggest that the content should dictate the style—what the actor has to say governs the way he should say it—and without claiming that every play should have a great 'message', it can be said that every play must be about something, and it is about that 'something' that the actor speaks.

It may be possible to justify obscurantism in esoteric, minority sub-cultures, but **the essence of theatre is that it speaks to all men.** It can never truly be itself nor work at optimum level when this is not the case. The better the play the more it will communicate more deeply with more people. The unperformed test may be a beautiful creation, but as a work of art it achieves stature only in so far as it is able to affect the lives of the community for which it was written. The same standards apply to the actor; his task is to illuminate the human condition more brightly for more people. As a principle of art appreciation this may not be acceptable for poets, painters, or sculptors—though I believe it is—but for those who pursue the art of theatre it should be axiomatic, even though it is often conveniently overlooked. Theatre must approach people as they are, if there is to be any hope that they will be influenced by the plays performed. In this sense the audience is always right and although we may not agree with what was in Johnson's mind, nevertheless what he said of the theatre is relevant in it's implications: 'For we who live to please must please to live'.

Audience Reaction

It is not easy for an actor to accept that the audience is always right. It is sometimes too much of a temptation to pass judgment on audiences that have been adversely critical. To do his job properly the actor must constantly search for ways to be in close touch with those who were apparently unimpressed by the performance. It is too much of a flattering unction for the actor to claim 'you pays your money and you takes your choice'. In the theatre this is an easy way out. It is difficult for an actor to take rejection symptoms from an audience, since elements of personal reserve will arise to protect him from being 'hurt'. But there is no place for this personal reserve in the theatre. The only brakes on the actor's processes must be professional and artistic. This is the constant dilemma of the actor: the personal self must be protected from abuse while the professional self must use positively the reactions of those who found the work unacceptable. While he is on stage no question of personal defence must inhibit his giving out.

Giving Out and Taking In

Off stage the situation is quite different. During a performance the actor is 'giving out' in an intense manner. Even if the external manifestations of his role are relaxed and cool, there is an inner tension of effort.

Off stage he must be 'taking in' with a similar intensity. Not only does he need to 're-charge his batteries' but he also needs to be furnishing himself with the tools of his trade in a way that few other occupations require. Most jobs allow the necessary time for preparation and even additional training if needed. The actor has no such luxury. Rehearsals, where such preparation might be expected, are a time to organize his giving out rather than a time for taking in. He is taking in the play itself—but he will have neither the time nor opportunity for the general intake of refreshment that equips him for his job. This refreshment—a sensitive observation of the human condition at work and play—will occupy his time when, in theory, he is not 'working'. Drama school and rehearsal help him to channel specific areas of self for performance, but the creation of the self he must undertake at any time he is not rehearsing or performing. (It is true that some companies manage time for this creative 'taking in' during a rehearsal period, through improvisation classes and group work, but there is time only for marginal growth.)

In a sense it might be said that an actor's life on stage is easier than his life off it. During performance the attention of cast and audience alike is focused on creating an act of theatre. Off stage the actor is surrounded by the trivia of a complex, 'busy' world from which he must observe and choose that which will help him most to develop as a human being and as a communicator of human qualities. Chance enters the prepared mind and an actor's mind must be prepared to observe and select on all occasions. Rather like Azdac, in different circumstances, he must at all times be *'ready to receive'*.

Receiving and Perceiving

For the actor there can be no looking without seeing or listening without hearing. He must see and hear anything that will shed light upon the human condition. He must also cultivate the art of seeing without looking and hearing without listening. There are few people who do not change their mannerisms when they know they are being observed and, in the main, it is unselfconscious behaviour that the actor wishes to see. To be at such a pitch of sensitive awareness at all times is extremely demanding upon body and spirit alike—to say nothing of nervous energy. It can also play havoc with personal and social relationships as well as the actor's need to relax. It is self-evident that the more the actor takes in, the more he has to bring to his performance.

When he comes to this stage of the work, sensitivity in awareness will be joined by the need for sensitivity in the use of the actor's only means of expression and communication—his body. In later chapters the divisions of this working body are considered in detail. For the moment the three major ones are mentioned: body image; movement and gesture; and voice. All three areas need to be fit and flexible. There is great merit in Gordon Craig's outline of the perfect actor of the future as an 'ubermarionette'—suggesting as it does majesty in proportion and perfection in response.

An actor's roles will take him from the need for the grand, magnificent, theatrical language of the body in sweeping flow to the smallest, and apparently unremarkable 'naturalistic' gesture. Take the following scene, which must, in essence, have appeared in thousands of plays:

Mr X is talking to Mr Y. They are co-directors of a company and both sign cheques on the company's behalf.

MR. X: But I didn't sign that cheque. (*Lights cigarette*) You did.

Note that the stage direction does not indicate whether the actor is to use a match, a spill or a lighter; it is bald and needs it's nakedness covered. The examples on page 11 show how such an insignificant gesture can carry a charge quite beyond the normal expectation for such an everyday occurrence.

The examples are given in the form of exercises to aid clarity. It may also be appropriate for some of them to be used as such. If this is the case, readers are asked to take note of the following:

The Two-way Movement of Ideas and Action

There are two basic ways of approaching acting and they are valid whether relating to a teacher and the class or the director and his company in rehearsal. One approach outlines the dramatic experience to be communicated and leaves it to the actor to find his own means of expression; the second gives the actor a series of objectively described tasks—movements, words and gestures —and leaves him to inject them with meaning.

It is not suggested that one way is better than the other—both have an important part to play in building up an actor, his resources and his performance. There is no reason why both methods should not be used side by side. What is important is that students should never be in doubt as to which method is being employed. The following example shows the principle at work.

Using the first approach the students would be told to take a wet floor-cloth and wring it out until dry. Accepting personal variations, there will be sufficient similarity for the physical movements to be seen to be correlatives. Using the second approach the leader would demonstrate a movement of the hands that involved similar muscular tensions to the one in question, request the students to do exactly the same and then ask them what they had imagined they were doing.

The basic consideration these two approaches suggest is that the workings of the imagination and it's external manifestations are in fact a two-way reversible process. Provided the leader leaves plenty of opportunity for the end product to be 'open' and concentrates his attention on the **process**, then both approaches can do nothing but good. The important thing is for the students to come to understand that the process is two-way, with particular stress on their understanding that there is no such thing as a movement exercise that does not stimulate the feelings and the imagination. With some students the passages may be blocked or they may have a 'one-way' non-return valve in need of easing, but after a time they will discover how body and imagination mutually feed and stimulate.

The second approach is excellent in the beginning of creative work, when the end-product is for class consumption only. It is here that the idea of 'creation by accident—art by design' comes into its own. The student can be staggeringly surprised when he lets his body have free play in stimulating his imagination. By kinaesthetic accident he can open up whole areas of meaning in his work that mere thought or imagination could never have brought to light.

With regard to the exercises which follow, the student should be encouraged to try them without prior discussion as to their 'meaning' and consider what emerges in the **doing** of the exercise. The aim is to open up the student's mind to the significance of acts so small they are easily overlooked. **Discussion before doing will only ensure that the known is practised and the unknown left unseen and unexplored.**

The actual doing should take the student by surprise so that through the physical he obtains an 'accidental' imaginative experience. It is only by trying something at which he is inexpert and the significance of which is unknown to him that he will open up new areas of work to extend him usefully. The aim on all occasions should be to place the student on the frontiers of his own experience so that in terms of artistic expression and communication he is alone and partly lost in a shifting situation. The exercises listed below will achieve nothing as grand as the last few sentences suggest. The first step should be small and within the student's range the resultant experience will be similar in size. Nevertheless, the principle remains the same as for the most advanced and complex exercises.

MR X: But I didn't sign that cheque. (*Lights cigarette*) You did.

EXERCISES

(Each sequence should begin when the first sentence has been completed)

1. Match-box in pocket (or handbag, if preferred). Take out with one easy movement and hold in the same hand. Using the thumb of that hand only, open box. Take out a match without fuss and strike it alight first time. Watch it spurt to life, then speak with it still burning, looking at partner (actual or imaginary) while the two words are uttered.

2. Match-box lying on the floor. Kneel to pick it up and then repeat as in (1). Speak from the kneeling position.

3. As in (2), but stand to speak.

4. Match-box on table. Hand to a position over the box and held quite still immediately above it for as long as possible. Pick up box and repeat as in (1).

5. Repeat exercise (1) but look at lighted match while speaking last two words.

6. Repeat (1), but fumble when taking match from box.

7. Repeat (6), but *pretend* to fumble when taking match from box.

8. Take match-box from pocket. It falls to the floor. Ignore the fall and speak immediately it hits the floor. Without taking eyes from partner retrieve match-box and light match.

9. As in (8), but wait until the match is struck before speaking.

10. As in (9), but hold match-box still for as long as possible, looking at it. Then take out match and strike it.

11. Take match-box from pocket, hold in one hand and push container slowly open with the other. A match is selected but will not light. It is discarded. Another is selected—it will not light. It is discarded and the match-box is replaced in the pocket.

12. As in (11), but before the selected match is struck it is inspected and finally rejected. A second match is chosen and struck—it lights.

This series of exercises is, of course, neither definitive nor exhaustive but should give the student some starters from which to explore the beginnings of his own inner creative life and some of the complexities of communication. It could be useful for the exercises to be tried in the group situation so that actor and group can discuss their meaning: (*a*) to the actor, (*b*) to the group. Such discussions expose the intriguing differences between what the actor knows he felt as a result of the action and what he actually communicated. (If this method is tried the group should not know the action until it is performed by the individual actor. The group should also have a relationship where there is no question of competition between students; where there is total trust in a search for truth; and, above all, where permission to fail is taken for granted. If these conditions do not exist, it would be inadvisable to try the exercises since they would probably result in the demonstrative and extrovert, or inhibition, frustration and embarrassment.)

Inhibitions and a Way to Attack Them

Strangely enough there are many would-be actors who suffer from inhibitions which prevent them 'letting go' with their bodies, minds or spirits. Like giving up smoking, getting rid of inhibitions depends largely upon the individual's inner wish to do so. Helping the student wish his inhibitions to go is not within the scope of this book, and an expressed desire for it to happen is no guarantee that a real wish exists.

The foremost aids in helping the shy, tense, hesitant or otherwise inhibited actor are covered by the following chapter on Concentration and Absorption and by Chapter Six on Improvisation. It is in these areas that most help can be given. As part of such an approach, or as a ploy in its own right, it is a good idea for a shy student to go for an evening out, with an experienced member of the company, to places where they are not known, with the experienced member in full disguise for the street. This is not as outrageous as it may sound, since today, most stage make-up must stand the test of close inspection—especially in small arena theatres.

No doubt the experienced companion will take the obvious steps of using spectacles—dark or otherwise—unusual clothes and easily available false hair and wigs, so there will be little need for face make-up. The disguised actor should have little difficulty in demonstrating to his shy companion that the public appearance is painless and that fewer people than he thought look even *once*—never mind stare.

The point is to show the student how easy it is to get away with being 'another person' in public. His colleague will have behaved in a manner foreign to him without causing the slightest comment or raised eyebrow. On the second evening the roles are reversed and the companion merely helps the student retain confidence.

Journeys with a companion may need to be repeated before the student has sufficient faith to venture on his own. It is not likely to take long since the idea quickly catches on and intrigue and interest take over from inhibition. Results from this simple, enjoyable exercise are extraordinary; relaxation of tension, improvement in 'presenting' a character in class, and great strides in language flow. The combination of the undeniable 'fun' aspect of the exercise and the stimulus to reconsider the nature of acting, seems to help overcome the most severe inhibitions.

I first used this 'street' training for different purposes. It was quite by chance I found it had this special quality of releasing actors from some of their inhibitions. A further merit came with the building up of bonds within the company—bonds of trust that grew rapidly, and even overcame some personal antagonisms. The method is easy, inexpensive, instructive and enjoyable. The fact that it helps release inhibitions soon pales into insignificance and is forgotten in the involvement with the work—a fact that speaks for itself when considering it might be the prime aim. At the time of writing none of my actors has been accosted—and I have not been prosecuted. I wish the same good fortune to any group who decide to give the method an airing.

CHAPTER THREE

CONCENTRATION AND ABSORPTION

'. . . a mind forever voyaging through strange seas of thought alone.'

Wordsworth on Newton

'Which of you by taking thought can add one cubit unto his stature?'

Matthew

The Genuine and the Deceptive

It is a far cry from the authoritarian teacher's rudely shouted 'Think, boy, think', to a naked female in a Lotus position in the sensitivity class of an Encounter group. Such, however, is the range of methods used to improve personal and group concentration and absorption. The former method is happily dying out, while the latter, or its variations, are rapidly gaining strength.

Yoga

In the following chapter the influence of Zen Buddhism on approaches to educating the imagination will be considered. In this chapter it is interesting to note, in passing, the increasing effect of Yoga upon actors' training in concentration and absorption. Or, rather, the effect, in the main, of *pseudo Yoga*, since, in the main, teachers who use this approach select from the carefully graded stages of the Hindu discipline only those specifics that appear to appeal to the immediate and the expedient. This flirtation with selections from the lower levels of Yoga has brought sincere and sharp criticism from practitioners of true Yoga who see it as a perversion of the nature and purpose of the discipline and, as such, maintain it to be dangerous.

While there are many schools and teachers who use these supposed Yoga methods to aid concentration and absorption, there are more who channel them into specific areas of posture and breathing; some maintain that these are the only ways to gain mastery over the art of acting. Students are encouraged to believe they are pursuing the *igniis fatuus* of some mystical panacea of the theatre, while in fact they are being seduced into esoteric habits which are in no way related to the art of acting or the reality of living. To adopt such symptoms without proper reference to the nature or purpose of the originating cause is likely to lead only to misunderstanding and harm. This particularly applies to those methods of teaching breathing established upon the premise that inhalation and exhalation exist in, and are controlled by, some intangible 'second' or even 'third' brain—existing, if anywhere, near the solar plexus.

Unless teacher and student alike are going to explore thoroughly the Eastern ethos and culture that gave rise to the disciplines—or better, to study with a living master—I believe it wisest to approach concentration and absorption through methods that can be easily practised and readily understood. The principles and practice of the disciplines of Yoga should be left as a free choice to the student, made on relevant grounds, and not the shibboleth or reward of drama classes.

14

I am not opposed to a search for spiritual enlightenment, personal control and individual responsibility—merely cautious after seeing some of the superficial dabbling that is practised in the name of Yoga. The following quotation from Blake's *Auguries of Innocence* sums up for me many of the fruits of a fully functioning system of personal concentration and absorption.

'To see a World in a grain of sand,
and Heaven in a wild flower,
Hold Infinity in the palm of your hand,
and Eternity in an hour.'

Definitions

To be able to hold 'Eternity in an hour' is particularly relevant to any consideration of absorption. The condition of spiritual identification with a mystical unity—which is the aim of much meditation—has a lot in common with the state of absorption. Since the disciples of meditation claim it to be essentially different from concentration and since one does not necessarily need concentration to promote absorption (though concentration can lead to absorption) it would appear appropriate to consider some differences between two concepts which are often confused. Indeed, in many drama classes 'concentration' and 'absorption' are used as synonyms.

Concentration

Two similar technical definitions of concentration are a helpful starting-point:

'To increase strength by contracting the volume', and
'To increase the quantity in unit space.'

I find these definitions, drawn from physics and chemistry, immensely helpful when used in conjunction with a third:

'To bring together to one point.'

When thinking about mental effort and concentration most people have difficulty in considering anything but a vague and ill-defined emotional attitude with accompanying symptoms of physical tension and strain. The way in which we speak of the relief and exhaustion that follow periods of concentration supports this view. Recognition and awareness of concentration are, of course, immensely helpful when wishing to recapture it. This may seem an unnecessary and trivial point—if not self-evident and naïve—to some readers, but in my experience there are many people who have the utmost difficulty in being able to concentrate, even when they sincerely wish to and the subject-matter is of great importance to them. This, I have found, applies to those who are in no way emotionally disturbed (where the ability to concentrate is understandably impaired) but have lost, or have never found, the necessary talent or control to be able to arrange their thought processes to such a point of focus.

Absorption

Quite a lot of students who have not been able to concentrate, even when they have wished to, have, of course, often been absorbed by a thought or an event and have been misled into believing that they were in fact 'concentrating'. This brings us to an appropriate place for some definitions of absorption:

'Disappearance through incorporation in something else'.
'A sucking in of fluid, light or nutriment'.
'A loss of identity in'.

Once again there is a combination of ideas drawn from other disciplines—and once again I have found them helpful.

Interaction of Concentration and Absorption

At first glance it would seem that the **ability to concentrate is under the control of the individual** concerned and that it can be exercised, or otherwise, at his discretion. Personal will-power or wish or need are not, however, able to control the presence or absence of absorption. It appears to come and go under its own impetus and is much more in the nature of a 'gift'.

There is little doubt that absorption can often follow concentration, but no evidence that even the most intense concentration will guarantee absorption. From my own experience and from what students tell me, one of the major differences between concentration and absorption is that the former carries with it real personal effort and considerable self-awareness—while absorption is effortless and unaware.

From the way interruptions—visual, aural and tactile—can easily disturb a student who is concentrating and can have no impact on the same student when he is absorbed it would seem that the former has all the attributes of cycling up a hill while the latter is more like free-wheeling down one. The crest of the hill to be overcome—the 'hump'—seems to be that of **interest**, if not even self-interest. Unfortunately, our education system tends to overvalue the virtues of concentration and underestimate the importance of absorption so that many students have an unhappy background of experience in these areas. Society, too, for entirely different reasons, is mobilized against absorption and encourages a constant succession of fads and fancies—mainly concerned with the commercial exploitation of passing sensation.

Difficult Students

There are many students, however, who wish to learn how to concentrate and become absorbed in what will help them as actors, but who find it difficult to do so except in quite short time-spans. Indeed, if their own assessment is accurate, some of them find it impossible. Since the motivation is right it is not too difficult to help this group.

A group that is much more difficult to help is one made up of, or containing, those who appear to have a keen interest in the theatre but unfortunately also appear to have no wish to learn how to concentrate upon anything. In passing, I would say that individuals in this group have more of an interest in themselves. They have the pride of themselves in the art, rather than the pride of the art within them. They appear to wish to learn the 'art' of acting and the 'mystery' of the theatre only if it can be accomplished without mental effort and without the rigorous discipline that accompanies concentration.

What follows is, I know, a personal opinion—supported by many prejudices and subjective value judgments—but I have found it wisest and most rewarding to all concerned not to work with students from this group—not because of difficulty with individual students—but because theatre arts require a high level of group concentration. More is said later about group work. It is sufficient here to point to the difficulty in attaining group concentration and sensitivity if any one member of the group is not fully prepared to search after his own.

I believe this question of the individual's preparedness to work towards high standards of concentration and absorption is a crucial criterion in accepting or retaining a student in a drama class or theatre group. I believe it wisest and most fruitful to be ruthless and exclude those who do not meet the necessary standards of preparedness. It is, of course, a matter of personal decision. I can only urge my view—and to those who differ, wish only the best of good fortune while uttering the well-worn phrase—'on your own head be it!!'

Starting from Real Interests

From what has already been said about concentration and absorption it will come as no surprise to the reader that I recommend that students be approached through ideas, events on things that **actually interest them**, either as individuals or, preferably, as a whole group working together. Whether the students are professionals in rehearsal, professionals in training, amateurs at an evening meeting or children at the top of a primary school it is essential that their genuine interests are used. The more explicit their interest in the activity the more possible it will be to approach it with the explicit intention of training powers of concentration. It is likely, for example, that professionals in training will accept such an overtly stated aim more readily than will members of a semi-social group. If topics which already have an appeal to the students are used it will be much easier to engage their commitment immediately and so move quickly into areas of deep absorption. Variations on these personal topics will later be acceptable as targets for the focusing of concentration. But all the time the aim is to gain the willing consent of the students to the exercise. Some effect can be gained through a paternalistic or authoritarian approach, but worthwhile permanent results stem only from freely given consent.

Topics which actually interest the students will vary as much as their age and condition. In any case, at this stage, the subject-matter and its form of expression (words, pictures, sounds, music, etc.) are of little consequence compared with the absorption that stems from their use. The students should feel that they are *free to become absorbed in whatever they wish.* **Certainly no judgments should be made about content**—*there should be no feeling of shame or guilt.* If the form is too noisy to permit full absorption to the rest of the group the students themselves will make the point well enough, and that in itself will reinforce the purpose of the exercise.

If the subject-matter and forms of expression that promote the searched-for absorption are not important, the feelings that go with it and an awareness of it certainly are. It is these qualities that need to be exposed and made manifest. The students may have no common yardstick to judge absorption levels and it is important to clarify this area, and the language that can be used about it. It is difficult to talk easily, exactly and lucidly about personal inner experiences.

Once an absorbed atmosphere has been obtained within the group, the leader should test its efficiency by creating a number of distractions—visual, aural or tactile. For some of the students it will take little to disrupt their absorption completely—for others it will take more even to disturb it. It can be fascinating and fruitful if the distracting noises are played back later so that students can recognize precisely how many and which noises filtered through absorption into awareness. Many of them will be amazed at the strong barrier that protects them from disturbance when their absorption is working fully.

In this area of work, as in anything creative or artistic, the only yardstick the external observer has of the intensity of the individual internal experience is its outward expression. There is frequently a vast differential between these. If the work begins with the students' genuine interest it will be much easier for him to make an honest response and assessment to the quality of his own concentration and absorption. This in turn makes it easier to progress, discuss and assess what has been done.

Diagnosing this differential between experience, expression and communication is a crucial task for the tutor and a difficult one for the student. For them both it is surrounded by traps, pitfalls and difficulties. For these reasons, if no other, it is essential to start with exercises that are based upon the reality of the students' interests. It is then so much easier to build up an atmosphere of common understanding and trust.

Practical Approaches

The first exercises should, therefore, be those hinted at above; the students are asked to involve themselves in any activity that interests and absorbs them. Once this has happened they are challenged in their absorption to withstand from the tutor an onslaught on their senses.

They are then asked to become more conscious of their powers of concentration and to harness them to help overcome the forces attempting to destroy their absorption.

The first stage is not really conscious. The second is in using the will and powers of concentration.

It should not take long before it is possible to move from the completely individual approach, to one in which the whole group has been able to find a common experience to unite their absorption. A useful approach with a group of young adults is to choose a piece of music from their subculture that has some complexity in rhythm or harmony and ask them to identify with a part that requires some real listening for them to isolate and recall it. When this step has been achieved it brings with it the bonus of uniting the group in a special way that will prove to be of inestimable value as the exercises grow in difficulty.

This subculture music is, of course, only one way in. There are many others and they will automatically be dictated by the individual personalities of the students.

A simple challenge is to use two sound stimuli—both of which are of interest to the student—place him equally between the two and get him to switch his concentration from one to the other. His next exercise is to balance his concentration equally between the two. When complete mastery of this technique has been obtained—and the student must test himself fully in this—he can add the complication of a visual stimulus—with or without its own sound source —and continue along the same lines. (If the visual stimulus is a television screen, an intriguing exercise is to use the TV picture but have a separate sound-track on tape and switch the concentration from aural to visual, and later try to resolve the two contrasting stimuli. Not only does it tackle the concentration/absorption training area well, it also stimulates the imagination. The mind truly boggles at some of the rationalization that has to occur before the resolution can come about. This, however, seems to be part of the interest.)

There is a third step that may be usefully taken before moving to exercises explicitly concerned with acting: that is to provide the group with a series of objects not likely to be interesting in their own right and give them the same kind of challenge as in the previous examples. Concentrate first on one; then the other and finally on both together. The chosen articles should range from the sensational and extraordinary to the mundane—the aim being to suggest that **any actor must be able to charge and illuminate the apparently unremarkable with such intensity and brilliance that its unique and vibrant significance can be recognized and understood.** In this context the 'apparently unremarkable' is only valid as a concept before the students have been through the particular experience. Once the training has done its work the students should find it difficult to consider anything 'unremarkable'. Thus it will be possible to move from the huge image cast by a coloured slide to a match chosen at random from an unused box.

The methods suggested above are all part of a unified approach which starts with the students freely given interest. The next exercises follow when the initial stage has been consolidated.

EXERCISES

The first comes from the 'Master'—Constantin Stanislavsky. In *An Actor Prepares* there is the story of the director and the actress, Maria, and their involvement with the lost pin.

" 'Let us give a new play,' said the Director to Maria, as he came into the classroom today.

'Here is the gist of it: your mother has lost her job and her income; she has nothing to sell to pay for your tuition in dramatic school. In consequence you will be obliged to leave tomorrow. But a friend has come to your rescue. She has no cash to lend you, so she has brought you a brooch set in valuable stones. Her generous act has moved and excited you. Can you accept such a sacrifice? You cannot make up your mind. You try to refuse. Your friend sticks the pin into a curtain and walks out. You follow her into the corridor, where there is a long scene of persuasion, refusal, tears, gratitude. In the end you accept, your friend leaves, and you come back into the room to get the brooch. But—where is it? Can anyone have entered and taken it? In a rooming house that would be altogether possible. A careful, nerve-racking search ensues.

'Go up on the stage. I shall stick the pin in a fold of this curtain and you are to find it.'

In a moment he announced that he was ready.

Maria dashed on to the stage as if she had been chased. She ran to the edge of the footlights and then back again, holding her head with both hands, and writhing with terror. Then she came forward again, and then again went away, this time in the opposite direction. Rushing out towards the front she seized the folds of the curtain and shook them desperately, finally burying her head in them. This act she intended to represent looking for the brooch. Not finding it, she turned quickly and dashed off the stage, alternately holding her head or beating her breast, apparently to represent the general tragedy of the situation.

Those of us who were sitting in the orchestra could scarcely keep from laughing.

It was not long before Maria came running down to us in a most triumphant manner. Her eyes shone, her cheeks flamed.

'How do you feel?' asked the Director.

'Oh, just wonderful! I can't tell you how wonderful. I'm so happy,' she cried, hopping around on her seat. 'I feel just as if I had made my début . . . really at home on the stage.'

'That's fine,' said he encouragingly, 'but where is the brooch? Give it to me.'

'Oh yes,' said she, 'I forgot that.'

'That is rather strange. You were looking hard for it, and you forgot it!'

We could scarcely look around before she was on the stage again, and was going through the folds of the curtain.

'Do not forget this one thing,' said the Director warningly, 'If the brooch is found you are saved. You may continue to come to these classes. But if the pin is not found you will have to leave the school.'

Immediately her face became intense. She glued her eyes on the curtain, and went over every fold of the material from top to bottom, painstakingly, systematically. This time her search was at a much slower pace, but we were all sure that she was not wasting a second of her time and that she was sincerely excited, although she made no effort to seem so."

1. (*a*) Act out Maria 'acting out' as in the first part.
   (*b*) Act out Maria 'doing' as in the second part.
   (*c*) Conduct an individual search for an actual placed pin.
   (*d*) As a group conduct a search for several placed pins.
   (*e*) As a group *act out* the search for several placed pins.

(In parts (*c*) and (*d*) it is of course necessary for the tutor to have placed the necessary 'lost' objects in suitable situations before any of the students arrive for the class).

2. Individually each member of the group is given the following challenge: 'No matter what happens—you are not to laugh or smile in any way'. It is then up to the rest of the group to make the student do precisely what he has been told not to. (Physical contact may or may not be allowed by the tutor—it is best the rules should be devised and agreed locally. It is likely that the question of *fairness* will arise after one member of the group has succeeded in making the subject laugh by *cheating*. All this is a proper part of the training and will do nothing but good in establishing group trust and sensitivity. The tutor may feel therefore that it is not necessary to issue any 'rules' before the exercises begin, allowing them to grow during play. The students know in any case that every 'unfair' act structures itself into the routine and merely builds up the difficulties through which the exercise is progressed).

3. (*a*) In the face of constant distraction from the rest of the group, try to read aloud with full understanding the following two passages. (The distrac-

tions from the group should cover the full range from the previous exercise—
unexpected abrupt noises; continuing noises getting louder; changing lights;
personal confrontations, etc.).

LEWIS CARROLL

In winter, when the fields are white,
I sing this song for your delight—
In spring, when woods are getting green,
I'll try and tell you what I mean—
In summer, when the days are long,
Perhaps you'll understand the song:
In autumn, when the leaves are brown,
Take pen and ink, and write it down.
I sent a message to the fish:
I told them 'This is what I wish'.
The little fishes of the sea
They sent an answer back to me.
The little fishes' answer was
'We cannot do it, Sir, because—'
I sent to them again to say
'It will be better to obey.'
The fishes answered with a grin
'Why what a temper you are in!'
I told them once, I told them twice:
They would not listen to advice.
I took a kettle large and new,
Fit for the deed I had to do.
My heart went hop, my heart went thump;
I filled the kettle at the pump.
Then some one came to me and said
'The little fishes are in bed.'
I said to him, I said it plain,
'Then you must wake them up again.'
I said it very loud and clear;
I went and shouted in his ear.
But he was very stiff and proud;
He said 'You needn't shout so loud!'
And he was very proud and stiff;
He said 'I'd go and wake them, if—'
I took a corkscrew from the shelf:
I went to wake them up myself.
And when I found the door was locked,
I pulled and pushed and kicked and knocked.
And when I found the door was shut
I tried to turn the handle, but—
There was a long pause.
'Is that all?' Alice timidly asked.
'That's all' said Humpty Dumpty.
'Good-bye.'

CRITIQUE OF PURE REASON—INTRODUCTION
EMMANUEL KANT

Of the Difference between Pure and Empirical Knowledge.

That all our knowledge begins with experience there can be no doubt. For how is it possible that the faculty of cognition should be awakened into exercise otherwise than by means of objects which affect our senses, and partly of themselves produce representations, partly rouse our powers of understanding into activity, to compare, to connect, or to separate these, and so to convert the raw material of our sensuous impressions into a knowledge of objects, which is called experience? In respect of time, therefore, no knowledge of ours is antecedent to experience, but begins with it.

But, though all our knowledge begins with experience, it by no means follows that all arises out of experience. For, on the contrary, it is quite possible that our empirical knowledge is a compound of that which we receive through impressions, and that which the faculty of cognition supplies from itself (sensuous impressions giving merely the *occasion*), an addition which we cannot distinguish from the original element given by sense, till long practice has made us attentive to, and skilful in separating it. It is, therefore, a question which requires close investigation, and is not to be answered at first sight— whether there exists a knowledge altogether independent of experience, and even of all sensuous impressions? Knowledge of this kind is called *a priori*, in contradistinction to empirical knowledge, which has its sources *a posteriori*, that is, in experience.

(*b*) When the exercise has been tried with some element of success, the students should try to commit to memory as much as possible of one of the pieces—working against the clock, with similar group distractions (1½–2 minutes is about the optimum time).

I have found it important for the individual students to go straight on to their second piece *immediately* after his first, rather than going round the group with each.

A useful manoeuvre is to use the Kant first for the reading and the Carrol first for the committing to memory.

4. Following the previous work on solo concentration and group disturbance the next exercise should provide a useful bridge between purely personal work and theatre expertise.

(*a*) Two students of the same sex try to undertake a discussion in which one of them argues a specific case or proposition and the other tries to understand it fully—sometimes by asking questions. The rest of the group offer the kind of disruption they have used in the previous exercise. (If this 'logical' discussion is too big a step for the students to take, then one partner can give a set of instructions to the other. Understanding can be tested by the second student performing the tasks that he has been set, or, alternatively, repeating the information he has been given. Obviously the tests have a more effective 'bite' if the subjects used are entirely new to the student concerned. For example, they may give directions to get to a house in an area the student does not know, a simple technique in fly fishing, or a description of human blood circulation).

(*b*) A male and female student act out one of the more intimate duo scenes from *Romeo and Juliet* while the rest of the group take on the characters of by-standers. It may be good to try the exercise first with the rest of the class interrupting in their own characters as in the previous exercises, following this with the addition of characterization. The roles they play can vary from fish-wives and drunken sailors, to cynical wits, to angry members of a queue venting their wrath upon the hapless pair, to over-happy members of marriage celebrations. The aim is still the same—to offer the two students a chance to try their skill at shutting out the rest of the world while pursuing their own experience.

(*c*) The next sequence is similar to (*b*) above. It is written, however, for performance as it stands and will accept a variable cast. The scene is taken from *Romeo and Juliet* and is set in a ballroom—it is a truncated and adapted version of the play. The interruptions in the text come from actors who 'surround' the young lovers while they are 'frozen' in the first intensity of their infatuation. It can be played effectively with only three characters, but can also accommodate a crowd in a dance-hall—the scene being played against a backcloth of dancers and intrigued onlookers. The key is still the same—the success of Romeo and Juliet in fighting any break in their absorption with one another. (This scene is taken from the end of a play of mine written for open stage and audience participation: *Woman   Angel of   ?*)

ROMEO AND JULIET—A DANCE OF DEATH

The scene is set in a ballroom, dance-hall, discotheque or equivalent. The action takes place during one interrupted dance sequence. The whole cast—except where specially indicated—take part in the dancing; as does the audience—or as much of it as is prepared to! All the lines from the play are therefore dropped into a dance environment. The co-operation of the cast/audience is required in the speech sequences and their sensitivity will determine whether there is active physical and vocal participation or whether they will 'freeze' into onlooking statues.

The cast is as follows:

ROMEO *and his friends*
JULIET *and her friends*
MERCUTIO
NURSE
TYBALT
PRIEST

All the players should be dressed in a distinctive manner which links them together—through design, pattern, colour or cut. Music is played for a dance. The players approach the audience inviting them to dance. (This can be done from the moment the audience first enters, so that gradually a dance-hall atmosphere builds up.) When the social temperature is such that most people are feeling free and relaxed, the music should end abruptly—it should be in the middle of a number and the middle of a phrase and should be switched out not faded—and the text begin. The men travel throughout the members of the dance speaking deliberately about the women/girls that they meet. When Romeo speaks it is of Juliet who is distanced as much as possible. This distancing is important on two counts: between them they can embrace in this first

speaking virtually the whole audience and must of course, speak across them
—this sets the style for the rest of the presentation. During the following dance
sequence Romeo and Juliet approach one another across the full length of the
'dance-hall'. They are surrounded by dancers and their progress is not easy—
in order to achieve these two effects they must be properly distanced in the
first place.

DANCE

MAN 1: This is that very Mab
  That plaits the manes of horses in the night
  And bakes the elf-locks in foul sluttish hairs.
MAN 2: Which once untangled much misfortune bodes.
MAN 3: This is the hag, when maids lie on their backs,
  That presses them and learns them first to bear.
MAN 4: Making them women of good carriage.
ROMEO: This is she doth teach the torches to burn bright!
  It seems she hangs upon the cheek of night
  As a rich jewel in an Ethiop's ear—
  Beauty too rich for use, for earth too dear!
  Did my heart love till now? Forswear it, sight!
  I ne'er saw true beauty till this night.

DANCE

JULIET: Although I joy in thee,
  I have no joy of this contract tonight.
  It is too rash, too unadvised, too sudden;
  Too like the lightning, which doth cease to be
  Ere one can say 'It lightens'. Sweet, good night!
  This bud of love, by summer's ripening breath,
  May prove a beauteous flower when next we meet.
  Good night, good night! As sweet repose and rest
  Come to thy heart as that within my breast!

(ROMEO *and* JULIET *remain absolutely still in their embrace while the priest
speaks. He addresses them and the audience of surrounding dancers*)

PRIEST: These violent delights have violent ends
  And in their triumph die, like fire and powder,
  Which as they kiss consume. The sweetest honey
  Is loathsome in his own deliciousness
  and in the taste confounds the appetite.
  Therefore love moderately. Long love doth so.
  Too swift arrives as tardy as too slow.
ROMEO: O, wilt thou leave me so unsatisfied?
JULIET: What satisfaction canst thou have tonight?
ROMEO: Th'exchange of thy love's faithful vow for mine.
JULIET: I gave thee mine before thou didst request it.
  And yet I would it were to give again.

ROMEO: Wouldst thou withdraw it? For what purpose, love?
JULIET: But to be frank and give it thee again.
  And yet I wish but for the thing I have.
  My bounty is as boundless as the sea,
  My love as deep. The more I give to thee,
  The more I have, for both are infinite.

DANCE

ROMEO: If I profane with my unworthiest hand
  This holy shrine, the gentle sin in this,
  My lips, two blushing pilgrims, ready stand
  To smooth that rough touch with a tender kiss.

(ROMEO *and* JULIET *ignore* TYBALT *completely—it is as if he were not there. There is of course sufficient pause and stillness from them to enable the* TYBALT *lines to take their place.* TYBALT *addresses* ROMEO *and* JULIET *and also the surrounding audience of dancers*)

TYBALT: This, by his voice, should be a Montague.
JULIET: Good pilgrim, you do wrong your hand too much,
  Which mannerly devotion shows in this.
  For saints have hands that pilgrims' hands do touch,
  And palm to palm is holy palmers' kiss.
TYBALT: What, dares the slave
  Come hither, covered with an antic face,
  To fleer and scorn at our solemnity?
ROMEO: Have not saints lips, and holy palmers too?
JULIET: Ay, pilgrim, lips that they must use in prayer.
TYBALT: Now, by the stock and honour of my kin,
  To strike him dead I hold it not a sin.
ROMEO: O, then, dear saint, let lips do what hands do!
  They pray: grant thou, lest faith turn to despair.
TYBALT: This is a Montague, our foe.
JULIET: Saints do not move, though grant for prayers' sake.
TYBALT: A villain, that is hither come in spite
  to scorn at our solemnity this night.
ROMEO: Then move not while my prayer's effect I take.
                  (*He kisses her*)
TYBALT: 'Tis he, that villain Romeo.
ROMEO: Thus from my lips, by thine my sin is purged.
JULIET: Then have my lips the sin that they have took.
ROMEO: Sin from my lips? O trespass sweetly urged!
  Give me my sin again.
                  (*He kisses her*)
TYBALT: Patience perforce with wilful choler meeting
  Makes my flesh tremble in their different greeting.
  I will withdraw. But this intrusion shall,
  Now seeming sweet, convert, to bitterest gall.
                (TYBALT *leaves them*)

NURSE: Madam, your mother craves a word with you.
ROMEO: What is her mother?
NURSE: Marry, bachelor,
    Her mother is the lady of the house,
    And a good lady, and a wise and virtuous.
                            (ROMEO *leaves them*)
JULIET: What's he that follows here?
NURSE: I know not.
JULIET: Go ask his name. If he be married
    My grave is like to be my wedding bed.
NURSE: His name is Romeo, and a Montague,
    The only son of your great enemy.

DANCE

MERCUTIO: Tybalt, you ratcatcher, will you walk?
TYBALT: What wouldst thou have with me?
MERCUTIO: Good King of Cats, nothing but one of your nine lives.
    That I mean to make bold withal, and, as you shall use
    Me hereafter, dry-beat the rest of the eight.
             Dramatic Dance of Fight—Through the dancers
                    (*Mercutio is killed*)
ROMEO: Now, Tybalt, take the 'villain' back again
    That late thou gavest me. For Mercutio's soul
    Is but a little way above our head,
    Staying for thine to keep him company.
    Either thou or I, or both, must go with him.
             Dramatic Dance of Fight—Through the dancers
                    (TYBALT *is killed*)
JULIET: My only love, sprung from my only hate!
    Too early seen unknown, and known too late!
    Prodigious birth of love it is to me
    That I must love a loathed enemy.
NURSE: What's this, what's this?
JULIET: A rhyme I learnt even now
    Of one I danced withal.
    Art thou gone so, love-lord, aye husband-friend?
    I must hear from thee every day in the hour,
    For in a minute there are many days.
    Oh by this count I shall be much in years
    Ere I again behold my Romeo.

DANCE

ROMEO: Farewell
    I will omit no opportunity
    That may convey my greetings, love, to thee.
JULIET: O, thinkest thou we shall ever meet again?
ROMEO: I doubt it not; and all these woes shall serve
    For sweet discourses in our times to come.

JULIET: O God, I have an ill-divining soul!
  Methinks I see thee, now thou art so low,
  As one dead in the bottom of a tomb.
  Either my eyesight fails, or thou lookest pale.
ROMEO: And trust me, love, in my eye so do you.
  Dry sorrow drinks our blood.
  Adieu, Adieu!
JULIET: What if it be a poison which the Friar
  Subtly hath ministered to have me dead,
  Lest in this marriage he should be dishonoured
  Because he married me before to Romeo?
  O, look? Methinks I see my cousin's ghost
  Seeking out Romeo, that did spit his body
  Upon a rapier's point. Stay, Tybalt, stay!
  Romeo, Romeo, Romeo,
  Here's drink. I drink to thee.
ROMEO: A dram of poison, such soon-speeding gear
  As will disperse itself through all the veins,
  That the life-weary taker may fall dead
  And that the trunk may be discharged of breath
  As violently as hasty powder fired
  Doth hurry from the fatal cannon's womb.
  O here
  Will I set up my everlasting rest
  And shake the yoke of inauspicious stars
  From this world-wearied flesh. Eyes, look your last!
  Arms, take your last embrace! and, lips, O you
  The doors of breath, seal with a righteous kiss
  A dateless bargain to engrossing death!
  Come, bitter conduct, come, unsavoury guide!
  Thou desperate pilot, now at once run on
  The dashing rocks thy seasick weary bark!
  Here's to my love! (*He drinks*) O true Apothecary!
  Thy drugs are quick. Thus with a Kiss I die.
    (ROMEO *remains standing—all the men in the cast go through the*
    motions of dying from poison)
JULIET: I will kiss thy lips.
  Haply some poison yet doth hang on them
  To make me die with a restorative.
    (JULIET *remains standing—the other women in the cast die from poison*)

(*The following lines emerge slowly and quietly from a humming that has started*
from the poisoned bodies 'dead' on the floor. With the humming they slowly rise.
The words are to be chanted—Gregorian style—by the full cast except ROMEO
and JULIET. *The line divisions suggested seem to be the best for this purpose.*
'Natural' choral speech from the cast takes over with the line 'Romeo, there
dead, . . .')

These violent delights have violent ends and in
their triumph die. // Like fire and powder,

Which as they kiss consume. // The sweetest honey
Is loathsome in his own deliciousness //
And in the taste confounds the appetite. //
Therefore love moderately. Long love doth so. //
Too swift arrives as tardy as too slow.//
Romeo, there dead, was husband to that Juliet;
And she, there dead, that Romeo's faithful wife.
A glooming peace this morning with it brings.
The sun for sorrow will not show his head.
Go hence, to have more talk of these sad things.
Some shall be pardoned, and some punished.
For never was a story of more woe
Than this of Juliet and her Romeo.

DANCE

(There is much slower, quieter music for the cast to escort ROMEO *and* JULIET *off. There can be a return to the previous style of music—with or without the cast—as taste requires.)*

5. (*a*) Once the confrontation between the sexes has been overtly made, as in Exercise No. 4, work on concentration and absorption can proceed to what I call the 'sex ball game'. The game is played in a chalk circle or a ring marked with chairs or equivalent with spectators at the ringside. There are two players to each team and they should be either two men *v.* two women, or a man and woman in both teams. The aim is for the teams to keep possession of a ball, which is thrown in the air in the usual way by a referee. 'Keeping possession' is, however, metaphorical as well as literal. The idea is that the possessors of the ball should concentrate upon it so much that nothing the other team does is capable of interfering with it. At any one time one of the team will actually handle the ball and the other will 'protect'—('*protection*' going to whatever lengths the referee will allow, but no more and no less than what is allowed in '*attack*') I have found it best not to allow sheer strength to win— although touching does play a large part in the game. A goal is scored by gaining possession of the ball or distracting the team member so that he loses concentration and 'gives up' the ball. (Laughter is a frequent sign of defeat.) If, however, a team manages to keep the ball for more than thirty seconds they are deemed to have scored a goal. The game can be played to a score of, say, the best of five goals or against the clock for, say, three minutes. The role of the onlookers can be whatever the group or the referee wish. I have found it useful to have them encourage from the sidelines in the usual manner, adding to the challenge of the situation and giving more bite to the game.

(*b*) This is a similar exercise requiring the student to retain possession of an article (clothing, an umbrella, a hat or a book) in the face of constant distraction and challenge situations from the group. It is best played in a circle with the student in possession in the middle and the rest doing their best to assist one another in breaking the student's concentration and also outwitting him so that a member of the rest of the group can 'take' the article without any effort. Although it is less complex than the previous exercise, it is more difficult. I have found it fits better into the pattern of training after the 'sex ball game' rather than before it. The same rules apply with the same embargo on brute force to gain or retain the article.

6. (*a*) The students sit comfortably on a chair or on the floor—the exact place and position do not matter but they will be there for some time and will need their hands free.

With one finger each student finds a rough surface that interests him, and it is best if he does it without looking. In fact the exercise often starts best if the students work with eyes closed.

When he has found the surface—it may be on his clothes, the chair, the floor—he explores it until he finds approximately a square inch that interests him particularly. When he has done this—and there is no point in proceeding until the interest is genuine, no matter how long this may take—he begins to concentrate upon that square inch until he is no longer conscious of anything or anybody in the room or about his person. This search for being completely '*lost*' in the tip of the finger may take take a long time and it may be necessary to stop the exercise more than once to reinforce ideas. It helps many students to know they are sharing their difficulty with others—especially if some have experienced the sensation but lost it after only a few seconds. *Becoming lost* is often a breakthrough for many students and some of them need the opportunity to discuss it with friends or neighbours—anyone who is prepared to listen. The leader should be prepared for such a social explosion. There is little point in trying to stop the loud and busy chatter, since many students will be discussing their first real experience of being totally absorbed in a tactile sensation. They should, however, be encouraged to pursue the experience as soon as possible after such a break. It is useful to draw the students' attention to the explosion following the exercise. Their awareness helps them understand the nature of the experience and also keep the social interchange to a minimum.

The main aim at this point is to help the student gain control over his concentration to prepare for absorption to 'come' through tactile sensation. Any flow from concentration to absorption seems most effective when applied to tactile exercises. Only when the student has gained sufficient skill in controlling the tactile experience described above *at will* is it appropriate to move on to the next stage.

(*b*) The exercise in (*a*) is repeated with the finger-tip of the other hand on a smooth surface.

Once concentration/absorption is established with the different surface—and this should be quicker—the leader should arrange for a number of interruptions intended to break it. The purpose is to ensure that the student has reached the right level of control before moving on. The interruptions should come in the shape of sounds or lights or touch and can be short or long as required. Students should have the ability to resist these intrusions and retain a high level of work before the next step is taken.

(*c*) Still in the original, comfortable position the student places his finger-tips one on the smooth and one on the rough surface. The aim now is to move the finger-tips at the same time—still using no more than a square inch—and to change the focus of concentration from one to the other as soon as total absorption is achieved. The switching of focus should continue long enough to give the student plenty of experience of 'moving' his concentration. He should be encouraged to note the 'fading' of one image as the other takes over. This shifting of the focus is crucial and plenty of time should be allowed for it to work. Later the students will undertake similar exercises with an abstract focus and it will help if they have fully explored the concept without undue strain. It is important to keep both fingers moving throughout the exercise— there will be a tendency for the one not in use to remain still and this takes the exercise back a stage.

It will help the student's understanding of the process if they repeat the exercise a number of times with eyes closed and later open them. (There is a lot to be said for working with eyes completely closed *until this stage*—but leaders may not feel this to be necessary or appropriate.) The exercise works well in three different stages: (1) eyes closed; (2) eyes open but not looking at the fingers; (3) looking at the fingers concerned. A further step when the group has built up sufficient trust, is to look at the hands of other students and then eye to eye. (Leaders may feel this step is best taken after some of the following exercises have been used.)

(*d*) The student should now focus his concentration on both moving finger-tips. The aim of the exercise is to demonstrate the lowering of intensity when the concentration is on the two finger-tips together. It may be of interest to combine some of the foregoing stages before moving on. Consideration and exploration of this lowered state of concentration will appeal to some more than others—in this, as in most exercises, it is best to allow the students to work at their own rate and not impose a series of time stops. At first there will be considerable variation in their time-spans, but later these will come together as group sensitivity grows. Allowing the students to find their own mean rhythm will aid the process and the students' awareness of it. It is best to let the students feel the development has occurred *apparently without effort*— or as a by-product of something else—rather than to encourage them to search for it. Most learning is best undertaken by discovery—and discovery is less real when a student already has in his mind the concept for which he 'discovers' an objective correlative.

(*e*) Having explored concentration and absorption in a defined area of touch, the next step is to provide the challenge of another of the senses. Listening is added to the previous exercises. (For the work to be at optimum level it may be worthwhile to spend time on the exercises on listening described on pages 54–55. If the students are not aware of the difference between **listening** and **waiting to speak** or are unaware that it is possible to **listen yet not hear**, it is unlikely that the present exercise will work as it should.)

The students should start with one of the previous touch exercises and add to it a similar intensity in listening. As the focus of concentration was changed before from finger to finger, now it is changed from touching to listening and from listening to touching—with one or both fingers. When the process has been consolidated—and this may take some time—the students should be given practice in focusing on the two areas of touch, rough and smooth, and on listening as well. They will begin to realize the difficulty of concentrating intensely on three such simple things, and this is usually a great step forward.

Local circumstances will dictate how necessary it is to provide sounds. There may be enough differing noises in and out the room for there to be no need of any addition. The leader should be prepared with a number of instruments to make sounds that are continuous or with long periods of reverberation. Simple music should also be available.

The combinations and permutations of listening and touching with eyes open or closed are such that each student should be able to find a pattern that is intriguing and meaningful.

(*f*) When (*e*) has been fully explored and consolidated it will be time to add exercises for looking and seeing from pages 52–54. These exercises are different from the opening and closing of the eyes referred to above—where they are only important in drawing the students' attention to the specific challenges. They are added in their own right to offer further complexities in a rigorous and complicated programme. The student will be using two finger-tips for touch plus listening and looking—separately or together. By this time the student should be quite expert in switching the focus of his concentration but it will still be a challenge to work with different combinations and he will need time to master rearranging the combinations with optimum efficiency.

(*g*) Now the students begin to make sounds of their own. They will probably begin quietly and this is helpful to the individual student as well as his immediate neighbours. For the exercise to succeed the sounds must not build up a high level of noise or no student will be able to profit. There are textures to be explored; sounds to be made and others listened to; and visual images to be accommodated. The possible combinations of concentration and perception will offer even the most aware and skilled student a continuing challenge.

7. A different way to begin concentration sessions is for the students to balance on one leg, keeping the rest of the body absolutely still. It is unlikely there will be many who can achieve this without considerable effort. Once there is a reasonable level of success, the students should repeat the exercise with eyes closed—this will require intense concentration and co-ordination. The same process can be tried with balancing a book on the head. The students might even try to balance the book on the head, standing on one foot, *with eyes closed*.

The aim of the balance work is to give the students an exercise requiring a high level of concentration without drawing attention to the fact. I have found it helpful, when working with professionals in particular, to be able to turn to this sort of exercise as a relaxation. There is never any problem in getting actors—or athletes—to do balance exercises—the primary objectives being obvious—and the spin-off merit of training concentration comes unconsciously.

In secondary schools there are similar virtues. I have heard frequently during balance exercises: 'Stop it! You're putting me off!' to some irritating neighbour about to make the student concerned burst into laughter. This kind of spontaneous remark is an indication of a young student becoming aware of his powers of concentration. Rather than a disruptive interruption it is more a signpost of progress.

8. The students sit in a circle on the floor and after some preliminary exercises to attune to listening intently (see Chapter Six) they make sounds that only they can hear. The sounds may be made by any part of the body—a clicking of finger-nails or the scratching of hair or voice sounds. It is likely that the exercise will promote too much sound at first. If they have become expert in the art of listening they will be able to hear much more from their near neighbours than they expected. Correcting this will help drive them back into themselves, which is one of the arts of learning concentration and absorption. When the right sound level has been reached they begin speaking to themselves in whispers. Once again this is the kind of exercise which will help

them to retreat into their inner selves, mainly out of inhibition, since there are few who can take the idea of conducting a conversation with themselves without some kind of mild self-consciousness. This will work in favour of the exercise.

When the whispered conversation is established and they can hear themselves without hearing one another the leader should move round the group listening intently—and physically close—to the students. This gives them an additional challenge—different from the collective 'ear' of the rest of the group. If the exercise is working well the leader should just be able to hear when his ear is very close to the student.

The next step is to make the whispering loud enough for two or three near neighbours to be able to hear. The students then have to whisper at the right level, listen to it and at the same time listen to their neighbours. It is useful to check after the first few minutes that the students have actually heard correctly what was being whispered around them. Generally there are sufficient misheard words and ideas to make the retelling an amusing experience.

9. This exercise provides harmless fun as well as requiring intense concentration. The students sit in a circle, preferably on the floor, and undertake the following tasks while saying out loud a nursery rhyme they know well. The exercise works only when the rhyme is known well enough to be repeated without much thought and effort.

(a) Add up a list of numbers and give the total. (The list should not be too long or too difficult. The leader uses 'flash cards' with the individual numbers on them. After a time the speed of showing the cards should increase. Then, quite difficult in fact, the leader can give the numbers orally while the student is still saying his rhyme out loud. As a variation the student can write down what is being said or shown and later do the addition—all while saying the rhyme aloud. These variations apply equally to the following tasks):

(b) Do simple multiplication.

(c) Create a grocery list with prices and totals.

(d) Intersperse the lines of the rhyme with the spoken names of the rest of the group—keeping a strict and preferably speedy rhythm with rhyme and names.

(e) Write a list of the names of the rest of the group.

All the exercises can be done individually by the members of the group or at the same time. If the latter there is the possible variation that they all say the same rhyme *or* they all say a different one. Generally there is a high level of amusement and social, excited noise—all of which add considerably to the point of the exercise!

10. As suggested earlier there is a strong link between imagination and concentration and absorption. The following stages in a rather long exercise train the imagination as well as the other two powers.

(a) The students are given as much time as they need to find something in the room that interests them. (It is important it should genuinely catch their interest as they are going to spend a long time with it. Although it is true that 'everything is interesting', for this exercise some things will be more interesting than others). If the students do not know the room the exercise will also provide a useful opportunity for them to get to do so—and this will take time. If, however, they know it well, familiarity may have bred disinterest and it could be appropriate for the leader to offer suggestions as to where they might begin their search. Such an injunction should be unnecessary—but students tend to feel they 'have been there before' and may need help to rediscover the room, its fixtures and fittings. One instruction is important: they should find an object they can get close to and stay with easily.

(*b*) When the object has been chosen the students should look at it from far away; close up; above and below—from as many different angles as possible. If polaroid cameras are available they should be used by the students.

(*c*) From this stage it is important the students should not speak to one another and should move as quietly as possible. They explore the object through touch. Not only fingers and hands but noses, elbows, cheeks, feet and the palms of the hands, etc. It is likely that this part of the exercise will take a long time.

(*d*) The students now listen to the object. It may have its own noise already —a clock or water-pipe for example. If not, the students listen for the noise it *should* have. (In one sense it is a drawback if the object has a noise since this may limit the range of imagination.) In any case there is plenty of opportunity for the students to listen 'for' as well as 'to' their object. Having listened 'to' and 'for' the noises the students then create a variation of noises by touching, smoothing, scrapping, tapping, etc.

(*e*) The students return to looking at the object from different positions in complete silence. Once again the use of polaroid cameras is to be recommended.

(*f*) The period of quiet contemplation in the previous exercise will prepare students to take the next step. (I have found the exercise to go wrong when I have rushed the early development or not allowed long enough for looking again after the noise-making.) The students breathe upon the object in as many ways as they can contrive. The aim is to bring the students to more personal terms with the object—and this certainly happens when the breathing is close and warm. Plenty of time should be allowed for this, not only in its own right but also to prepare the way for the next stages.

(*g*) From as many different places as possible the students smell the object.

(*h*) The students taste the object.

(*i*) Return to looking—particularly from afar—recalling the qualities explored through the other senses. This return to looking should give a deeper insight into the quintessential quality of the object. It should also afford an opportunity to build up a large composite view of the object—a view that will be needed in the next stages of the exercise. This revaluation and re-orientation is crucial for the next steps to work properly.

(*j*) The students talk to the object—from near and far—using their own language at first. As the exercise develops they should create replies in the object's language and then talk to it in that language. The leader should watch carefully for any break in absorption, since some students may find it difficult to undertake the exercise easily and others may be distracted by the interesting noises made around them. It is important to help those who lose absorption regain it quickly. The leader may instruct the students to keep close to their object for some time and to talk in whispers, encouraging them individually to move away slowly when he can see they are ready.

(*k*) The students grow into *being* their object—moving in close to identify—

as if the voices had gradually hypnotized them into such growth. This is the key stage in the exercise—*since the identification will be the physical embodiment of their absorption.*

(*l*) When the identification has reached full intensity the students move as combined person/object—fully absorbed and belonging together. Diagnosing the success of the exercise is not easy—some students may be able to reach a fully absorbed identification with no change in the way they look or move. Many students, however, will succeed in creating alarming physical attributes and the leader will assess whether these are sufficient and necessary to the state of absorption.

(*m*) The moving objects speak in their own tongues—which may, of course, be English.

(*n*) The moving, speaking objects meet, relate and communicate. By the time this stage has been reached the students' imaginations may create a number of intriguing, spontaneous group situations. These situations should be allowed to develop and burn themselves out, otherwise the students will have built up too strong an inner charge to be left without release. I have found it best to encourage the group work to continue until the absorption of some students begins to fail. Then draw the exercise to a close.

A period of relaxation is wise after this series which should be progressed in one session. The exercises can use a tremendous amount of nervous and physical energy, lasting as rich, ongoing experiences for more than two and a half hours.

CHAPTER FOUR

IMAGINATION

'These deeds must not be thought
After these ways; so, it will make us mad.'

Macbeth

'We carry within us the wonders we see without us.
There is all Africa and her prodigies in us.'

Sir Thomas Browne
Religio Medici

Definition and Purpose

In Chapter One I suggested imagination was the 'intelligent prediction of future events based on a sensitive understanding and perceptive analysis of the past'. I also suggested its function and purpose in the world at large was protection from bodily harm. In theatre arts, its function is to protect and educate the spirit and in this it is no different from other artistic activities speaking as it does to the inner self.

But not all the traffic of the imagination is as intensely loaded as this might suggest. The following brings a different view.

Take memory of a train journey.
Add more memories: wind on the face;
an aerial photograph of New York;
a sheepskin rug and standing in a cold shower.
Combine them. They can create
a lively image of flying over New York
city on a magic carpet in a rainstorm.

Combining memories of everyday events and objects to create a child-like fantasy, stretches the mind and exercises the imagination, but not to their limits. Few of us would find it difficult. But for many actors beginning training, it is a full extension of their powers. Their progress to a full flowering of a lively and far-ranging imagination can be exciting—if sometimes slow and drawn out.

Zen

At some remove from the child-like are exercises which can stimulate the imagination for a life time without losing potency. Many of these have their ancestry, if not their origin, in the Rinzai sect of Zen Buddhism. (I am not suggesting a place for Zen in theatre training—although at the feet of a master it may bring concomitant merits—merely pointing out some parallels which seem interesting and relevant.) Two of the koan used in Zen will demonstrate the necessary stretching of the imagination. The first is a question: 'A girl is walking down the street. Is she the younger or the elder sister?'
The second is a well-known challenge: 'Recall the sound of one hand

35

clapping.' Question and statement alike require the student to exercise his mind on levels where rational thought will no longer help him. On a first encounter with such irrationality the student may despair. After some effort he may discover his imagination working in a previously unknown way.

An apparent passion for **incongruity** and **irreconcilable irrationals** is one area of imagination training which has common ground with Rinzai Zen. Another is the interest and importance attached to the **experiential** and the **spontaneous.** For example, the proper response to the question about the girl walking down the street is not to talk or think about it, but simply to do it—to become the girl. There is virtue in all three aspects but in an actor's early training **doing is more crucial than talking or thinking.** Since the irrational, the experiential and the spontaneous motivate much of the training I advocate for the imagination, it is interesting to note the compatibility with Zen, which according to the 79th edition of *Pears Cyclopaedia* is 'something . . . that is not a religion, has no doctrine, knows no God and no after-life, no good and no evil, and possesses no scriptures but has to be taught by parables which seem to be purposely meaningless.' I know no better description of theatre.

Concentration, Absorption and Sensory Perception

This chapter is deliberately placed between that on concentration and absorption and the next chapter dealing with the senses, because I have found liberating the imagination improves the quality of absorption and concentration. Improving sensory perception may do the same and increasing powers of concentration frequently stimulates the imagination. Imagination, sensory perception, concentration and absorption are closely linked and it is sometimes difficult to separate them. Certainly one problem in group work is that the students benefit from individual and different starting-points. The previous chapter suggested some ways of dealing with the situation. Many of those exercises stimulate the imagination and many use a tactile starting-point. Little reorientation is needed for them to be used in conjunction with this chapter.

Spontaneity

An important factor in training the imagination is the students' ability to use their **immediacy technique,** that is their personal level of spontaneity. I have met few students in whom the spontaneity factor is absent or dead. But I have met many with it almost atrophied. Some had been so conditioned from childhood that they were unaware of their spontaneity and some had it under such control that its first murmurings were quickly diagnosed and successfully treated—that is, blocked for ever.

The unaware are easier to deal with than the blockers. For the former it is a source of joy to discover the capacity to make direct responses—even to the most simple stimuli. They discover, too, that these spontaneous responses are easier than carefully considered ones and are imaginatively richer and fuller as well. They discover spontaneous responses to be happier experiences than they thought. Those who block are not so pleasant or simple to deal with. Carefully considered reasons are given for controlling spontaneity—reasons such as morality, religion, compassion, politeness and social etiquette. It is not always easy to deal with these criticisms without losing the student, and sometimes this is the best solution. But there are many students who block through fear, or the lack of a suitable self-image. The most common reason for rejection is that any form of immediate response or spontaneous expression is indulgent and unnecessary—and, what is more, inconsiderate to others.

In this area of training strict authoritarianism can work Those willing to try are easy to help but for those who continue to block I have found no alternative to throwing them in the deep and hoping they swim. For those who stand on the brink an authoritarian voice is most helpful—pushing them in or startling them into jumping themselves.

It is not suggested that spontaneity always produces meaningful results— merely that creativity cannot come about without it. Untempered immediacy or over-heated spontaneity can be destructive and the wise leader is aware of this and plans his sessions accordingly.

Creativity

Spontaneity begets spontaneity: one creative act leads to another and a chain reaction—the creative process—is under way. At first the creative urge of the inhibited will show itself clearly, if hesitantly, in acts of expression that last for no more than a few seconds. It is important that these students have a proper atmosphere of sympathetic flexibility and are given time to develop. Creativity moments of insight—needs a free flow, not too hampered by clocks or rigid instructions. These moments of insight will eventually lead to a state of heightened awareness—the best breeding-ground of creativity.

These first genuinely creative acts will be hesitant, inaccurate and vaguely directed. This is a desirable state, since the student will be taken unaware by the explosion of what was previously secure. For the newcomer to spontaneous work, the creative moment will appear as a strange world with unrecognizable boundaries. **During the moment of creativity he expands into this new world, touching upon idea after idea until he is exhausted and returns to actuality.** His memory of much of the experience will be vague and ill-defined—but some will be recalled with clarity, and later be fined and refined until ready to be expressed and communicated.

When confronted with a new vision of the world or our place in it, many of us reject it out of fear of the unknown. Or, if we do not entirely reject it, we reshape it until it becomes recognizable and no longer a danger or threat. **Imagination enables us to cut through the probable, achieve the possible and glimpse the unattainable.**

Permission to Fail

Theatre training offers a privileged opportunity denied to the outside world —permission to fail. It is an interesting paradox that an actual physical deed of little significance to the individual who commits it, may prompt society to respond with the full weight of its authority while paying little heed to those deeds of the spirit that have a lasting impact. Take the case of a small boy who throws a stone through a window; it is likely he will be punished in some physical manner. There is no guarantee he will gain anything from the deed or resultant punishment. The deed may have been so speedy as to deserve the label 'trivia', in terms of the boy's experience—except for society's attitude. If the boy could have been given the opportunity to understand the act of throwing—and its possible consequences—through a creative experience, his spirit would have been permanently scratched. **By the poetic doing of the stuff of life he could have experienced and learned more in an hour's intense workout**

than in a hundred actual events. While it is true that all we learn from experience is that we learn nothing from experience, we can learn anything and everything from creative imagination.

Permission to fail in a drama class means we can try out our personal watersheds of *bricks through windows* knowing we shall be repaid in a coin we have used—and not the potential trivia of actuality. Permission to fail means no premature, presumptuous value judgments being made on early explorations. If the student is to expose his tender, inner life he must be sure he is not going to expose it to attack. We are all vulnerable, and none of us will dredge out secret hopes and fears if there is the possibility of them being the subject of scathing comment or mild derision—clichés and stock responses will be performed as a defence. None of us wishes to be hurt and the drama class must protect students from the intrusion of unnecessary judgments—complimentary or otherwise.

Direct Responses

The first step in educating the imagination is to encourage the student to respond with spontaneity. This will allow the subconscious to explode into imaginative experience. The student will come into direct confrontation with something genuinely new, either in himself or the world outside—a new experience in itself or an insight into an old experience that makes it new. Either way it will put the student off-balance momentarily and moral values and rational judgments will be irrelevant and invalid. The process may take only seconds but the student needs a sympathetic atmosphere and permission to fail, so that he can **accept the experience for what it is and achieve a method of expressing it.** *Not until later should he be encouraged to consider what the experience meant in personal, social, moral or religious terms.* A danger lies in wanting to make these judgments as soon as possible—to help keep life secure and tidy. Unfortunately this truncates the experience and disguises it in well-worn garments or bends it to fit a well-ordered pattern, destroying its validity by siphoning off the significance with clichés and stock responses.

Some of these stock responses can be avoided by limiting discussion to an absolute minimum. In the early stages of training I suggest no discussion at all. I have found imaginative, creative work is not helped but hindered by it. The place for discussion comes later, when the students are communicating experience and not creating it. Discussion, practice and preparation block direct responses—consolidating the prejudices that imagination and creativity attack. All three may amend what *has been* created, the better to express and communicate it, but I have found them a drawback to the creative and imaginative processes.

The following exercises offer a step-by-step journey from the simple beginnings of spontaneous responses to the more complex workings of the released imagination.

EXERCISES

1. (*a*) The student blows up an ordinary balloon. The aim is to burst it by blowing, without being taken by surprise—to estimate exactly when the balloon will burst. It can be individual, with a partner or in a group since anyone can try to decide the moment of bursting. The exercise is good fun and, as

such, is a useful starter. The fun element brings quick and lively interest which aid concentration. A bellows-type aid may be used, but blowing by mouth adds to the nervous energy and general excitement.

(*b*) An exercise which apparently tests reflex actions through harmless fun, uses the 'anti-breathalyser' machine, once popular in hotels and public-houses. The participant watches red, yellow and green lights and tries to retrieve his coin before, falling under gravity, it passes a certain mark. When played under appropriate social conditions with alcohol for prizes or forfeits the exercise does its work by stealth with much enjoyment all round.

(*c*) This also exercises the spontaneity factor through a game. It can be played individually, with a partner or in a group. The player bounces a ball against a wall or to the others. The challenge lies in using a ball that bounces asymmetrically—they can easily be obtained from toy or sports shops.

2. (*a*) An exercise which falls half-way between the 'fun' type above and the more orthodox uses an ordinary oil, air or water lamp. The lamps are electric and feature large bubbles which change shape, rise and fall within a glass case. The bubbles are controlled by the heat from the light.

The students can work in groups, pairs or individually. There are two parts to the exercise: the first consists of watching the bubbles and accompanying their movement with words and sounds—the vocalization can take any form—on a strict one-to-one basis. The second consists of accompanying the bubble movements with body movement. It is possible to combine the two parts and to move from solo to group work quite easily.

(*b*) This is a development of Exercise 2 (*a*). It uses a simple slide projector positioned to give an image at least four feet high. The students make slides—individually, in pairs or groups—using oils, water, spirits and dyes. Slides for this purpose consist of two thin glass plates in a plastic frame with the 'mixture' between the plate. When the slides are placed in the projector, gravity and heat from the projector keep them moving. It is less smooth and more surprising than with the electric bubble lamp. The size of the image and the bold outlines of colours provide a dramatic stimulus. The exercises are the same as in 2(*a*).

3. (*a*) For this exercise the students need blindfolds and a good working space. (The use of a blindfold is recommended—certainly in the early stages of training—because the urge to open the eyes is often too strong for students to resist, and frequently they are opened by accident. Even a momentary break from the blindness destroys the proper build up of the exercise.) The blindfolds are put on and the students stand quite still. At a given signal they jump into the air, landing in the most twisted position they can manage. The purpose of the blindfold and the jump (it is essential both feet leave the ground) is to make the landing position accidental. It is almost impossible to plan the body position on its return to the ground. Although this does not itself exercise spontaneity it prepares the way and stimulates the imagination.

When the students are in their twisted positions the leader ensures they keep absolutely still while he explains the next stage. His manner of speech is strict and intense.

(*i*) The students concentrate on the separate parts of the body for three or four minutes. As they become aware of discomfort in any part the leader mentions it to capitalize their unease. This is a deliberate move to build up a hostile impatience at being kept in the position for so long. This will later help them explode into action—using their 'hostility' to push them into effective spontaneity.

(*ii*) The students consider what they would feel if they were permanently as they are—how would they move; how would they 'utter'; what sounds would they make. The leader's mode of speech continues to be severe.

(*iii*) When group energy has built up sufficiently the leader 'drives' the students into movement and sound. They become the creatures they have been thinking, feeling and physicalizing. The pent-up energy will guarantee an immediate, spontaneous response to the sheer opportunity to move. The students will be so enthusiastic to be free, they will let the impulse lead them into creativity. (It is useful to have sounds and music available. With experienced students the coincidence of the twisted positions and the sounds will be enough to stimulate them into physical work. For the less experienced the use of sounds and music will supplement the leader's voice and build up the wish and need to move.)

(*b*) Another exercise providing 'fun' also makes use of a blindfold. The working area is prepared in advance and provides a maze of contrasting noises, textures and things. Objects hanging from the walls and ceiling have unusual textures and make peculiar noises. The floor has contrasting patches—rough, smooth, slippery, noisy, etc. Tables have instruments and objects which are strange to touch and make interesting noises when moved.

The students are led singly or in small groups through the maze, being left to themselves as much as possible. They should not spend too much time identifying the various stimuli or the investigation will defeat the point of the exercise. They should be moved on, if necessary, as soon as any one object begins to lose its impact.

4. An exercise which seems to be frightening to students at first, but later grows into an area of considerable interest is one which uses a tape-recorder placed in a sound-proof or well isolated room to ensure the student will feel protected. The student is left alone, for no longer than an hour. The instruction is simple: 'Talk to yourself—or the tape-recorder'.

The first ten minutes can sometimes be disturbing for a student—but a relationship does build up and the flow of ideas and language can be a surprise to everyone—including the student. The isolation of the method seems to liberate the imagination in an unusual and powerful way. The student may be instructed to erase *nothing* on the tape. With hesitant students this can be an inhibiting factor, and while it offers illumination of the process of the imagination at work, it is not a vital part of the sequence.

5. The following exercise stimulates imagination and improves language flow. The students sit in a circle. The game is simple: to tell a story as a group, with each member contributing an agreed number of words at his turn. The first time round each student may speak one word only; the second time two; the third time three and then into phrases, etc. This can be varied by the students adding a new character, place or object to the story at each turn— when there would be no limit to the number of words.

As the students become more expert the game can be developed by the leader adding variations: 'Advance'—'Retreat'—'Expand'—'Stay put'—to which the students respond by taking the story forwards, backwards, filling in, etc. The movement from turn to turn can progress from going round the circle in order, to jumping across it at the leader's instruction.

The game can be further varied by using a spinning bottle in the centre of the circle. Each student spins the bottle and while it is moving tells his part of the story. When the bottle stops, the student to whom it is pointing starts it spinning again and continues the tale where the previous student left it. The exercise tests powers of concentration and co-ordination as well as imagination and language flow.

6. Story-telling is used in a different way in the following series of exercises.

(*a*) From a collection of pictures and photographs the students select three. They show them to the group and tell a story which unites them. The time allowed for preparation should depend upon the experience of the group but the aim should be to progress towards immediate story-telling. After a little experience the students should no longer be allowed to choose their own visuals but have them given to them a few seconds before they start the exercise.

(*b*) Sounds are now introduced into the exercise. At first they should be played to the student before he begins the story—after a little practice they may be played at any time during the telling at the direction of the group leader. The sounds can be produced by a tape-recorder or by the group and should include abstract noises as well as easily recognizable ones. A variation of this method requires the student to make his own noises—the directions coming from slips of paper issued to him by the group.

A useful technique is to allow the students to have the visuals for overnight preparation but without being told of the number or nature of sound interruptions that will come during the actual telling. In this way the students soon discover that over-rigorous preparation of one story line is bad preparation and their best method is to devise as many story lines as possible—thus enabling them to accept more readily whatever sounds may be given. In this way they are encouraged to keep a flexible approach to the given visual material and begin to see more easily the infinity of relationships their imagination can achieve within the compass of three photographs.

(*c*) The next step is to use this story-telling with sounds and visuals as a basis for group play-making. The individual student is given the visuals and sounds before the exercise and the aim should be to keep this preparation time to a minimum. As the student tells his story the rest of the group play it out simultaneously. This presupposes some experience of group work and a reasonable level of sensitivity and spontaneity. For story-teller or group to be too slow and hesitant would build up frustrations and defeat the point of the exercise.

An advance from this stage is for the story-teller to be given the aids at intervals during the telling so that he has no time for preparation. A final step is for each of the students to tell part of the story—taking over their part at the introduction of a new sound or visual. This stepping in and out of roles, yet keeping the narrative and the playmaking on an unbroken course, tests imagination, spontaneity, absorption, intellectual control and group sensitivity at the same time. Because of its complexity, it is best kept for groups with some experience and expertise who have built up a good measure of internal trust.

It will be noticed that the story-telling exercises all involve external stimuli. This is an attempt to ensure the students are extending their imaginations, since without these externals story-telling tends to exercise language flow without stretching the imagination—the content being easily arranged, self-selected material drawn from the front of the memory. The use of externals extends the exercise beyond this.

7. Images projected from slides can be a most effective stimulus to the imagination, especially if they are very large. The very size of the image has a powerful effect on the student.

The first step is for the image to be projected on a wall or large screen and the students squat close to it and absorb themselves in it. In the early stages it is helpful to have sounds and/or music available on tape, as this will encourage absorption. The students should be dominated by the image and left to lose themselves in it. With some groups this will lead automatically into action, with the students pursuing their thoughts into expression and communication. Others may need starters to help them. Some groups may benefit by talking to one another about their ideas as they come to them—explaining the strange sights they can see in the image.

Shadow play may emerge with some groups and although it may begin at a shallow level, it can quickly grow into significant areas. The leader should not be tempted to stop the child-like enjoyment there might be in the fun of the shadows—it is often the doodling that precedes meaningful creativity. It can also lead easily into an area that can absorb and engage the students deeply. The original attempts to create shadows will probably be through the use of fingers and hands. This should be encouraged to grow so the students use other parts of the body, and as soon as possible, stand in the beam casting the image. When this happens it will not be long before someone sees the effect of the images when they are projected upon the intervening bodies. This effect is more telling if the image falls upon white shirts or trousers, and even more so when it is bare flesh. The leader may find it necessary to call the students' attention to what is happening—but it is best if they can discover it for themselves.

The combination of becoming lost in the large image, talking about the shapes and objects that can be found in it and seeing it projected upon clothing and bodies—moving or still—will soon stimulate even the very slow into imaginative experience. Some will prefer to talk and some to do, and the exercise can accommodate both simultaneously.

The content of the slides can be anything from holiday snaps, close-ups of flowers, animals to abstracts. Variety can be added by projecting the images on to moving sheets, handkerchiefs, the floor, the ceiling—especially the corner cornice. Even the most simple snap of the face of a cat or dog becomes fresh and wonderful when seen in such ways.

Individually, or in the group, the students can make their own accompanying noises to create a sound environment for the image. It is likely that some students will enjoy adding the sounds while others move in the light—guided and helped by the spontaneous noises.

An interesting variation, not necessarily involving action or movement from the students, is for them to add different sounds to accompany the image— noting the change in impact when the sound changes. The leader may wish to prepare a tape to demonstrate this change with contrasting pieces of music. The students may be encouraged to begin with the following sequence: whistling—humming—finger-clicking—laughing—moaning—slow hand-clapping. If they wish to develop the idea they can be divided into groups and 'orchestrate' their sounds.

I have found these exercises, in various combinations and permutations, open a new world of imaginative experience that engages the students over a long period and fruitfully feeds their creative processes.

The exercises can also be usefully employed with ciné films. This adds the element of spontaneous reaction and can be a real challenge.

8. The visuals used in Exercise 6 (*a*) can be put to a different use in an exercise that encourages the student to allow his absorption to lead him into imaginative thinking and feeling. The leader may wish to use taped sound as a background additional stimulus.

The students are in groups of five or six. They lie on their stomachs in a circle with their heads to the middle, fairly close together. In the space in the circle the leader puts a photograph. It should be preferably larger than twelve inches square and be abstract enough not to have an obvious frame of reference or viewpoint. The students concentrate on the photograph long enough to become lost in it and then speak quietly aloud their thoughts and feelings about the picture. They are told to talk to themselves so that the others can hear—but not to address the others, ask questions or actively listen. The group will build up a montage of words and phrases that all will hear and slowly the individual thoughts and feelings will build into a group statement. Generally, I have found the element of shyness in most students is effective in controlling the sound at the optimum level without the need for the leader to intrude. It is important that the sound should not carry beyond the circle and the students focus on themselves.

The release of imagination and language flow is encouraging to the quieter student, who can often find a happier starting-point here than in other more physical exercises. Alternatively, I have found the exercise to be very useful as a stimulus to dramatic dance. The students continue their talking about the photograph and, keeping their eyes fixed exclusively on it, stand and slowly and quietly put into action what they are thinking, feeling and saying. As a development, the students can also make the sounds they feel are suitable for the picture, and use those as a basis for their movement work.

9. A variation from the photographs used in the previous exercise are line drawings in the style of the illustrations on pages 44 and 45.

The essence of the line drawings lies in their non-explicit, non-specific meaning. They are mainly abstract with only a suggestion of meaning. The students project into the drawings their own thoughts, feelings and meaning. They can be used individually, with a partner or in small groups, as a basis for discussion, dramatic dance, play-making and character building. On the first two or three occasions the leader may wish to prepare some line drawings himself. Later, the students can make their own on thin card, shuffle and distribute them round the group. A development from the line drawings is for the students to make matchstick men or monuments and also to use charred paper and matchsticks stuck on to black or white card and then sprayed with lacquer or paint from an aerosol. If polaroid cameras are available the photographs of these creations can be used in a similar way.

10. The students collect pictures, sketches and photographs to make a collage. Suitable material for this can be found in magazines and many of the weekly colour supplements. The theme or title for the collage could relate to emotions, moods or characters. The students are told that they are going to use the collage as a basis for creating a dramatic character. When they have

made their final selection of material they are told to divide it into two more or less equal parts—one part containing the more attractive and useful material and the other, the less. When this selection has been made the students **discard the more attractive material**. The rest is used as a basis for the creation of a character. They should be encouraged to discuss, write, sketch and paint about the elements of their collage that suggest a suitable character-ization. The exercise may be undertaken individually, with a partner or in small groups.

11. This exercise will appeal to students and leaders who are technically minded. Two tape-recorders are required and they are placed well apart (six feet between the two is a good starting position). The tape is placed on the feed spool of the first tape-recorder and the take-up spool of the second. The first recorder is placed in the record position and the second tape-recorder in the playback position. A microphone is plugged into the first tape-recorder and the student begins to speak about any subject that interests him. Depend-ent upon the speed of the recording and the distance between the two tape-recorders, after a short interval the student will hear his own words coming back to him from the second tape-recorder. As soon as this happens he is involved in an intriguing and complex exercise of imagination and spontaneity in keeping his conversation going. The leader may find it helpful to suggest titles or subjects to the student.

When the students have had some individual experience in the exercise it is possible for two or three students to use the microphone together.

12. As a stimulus to the imagination in its own right and as an accompani-ment to the previous exercise the students might find it interesting to listen and respond to a record made by John Cage and David Tudor called 'In-determinacy' (this is a Folkways record FT37–4). The record contains an interesting combination of words, songs and music. As a follow-on the students may wish to create something similar using tape-recorders.

13. The next exercise takes the students into an area of improvised play-making. The usual basis for such exercises is a fairly full description of place, character, time, activity, etc. and frequently time is given for preliminary preparation and discussion. In this exercise the students are given details of only one of those before the exercise begins. For example 'You are all digging a hole with a spade'. As soon as the instruction is given the students immedi-ately respond by putting the instruction into action. No time is given for preparation. The essence of the exercise consists in the students working together to resolve the conflicts that they will have themselves created by being involved in digging a communal hole but with no common purpose. Some may be up a mountain, some may be in a pit. For some it may be a relaxing afternoon in the garden and for others an exhausting day in the desert. Another example—the leader may say 'You are all in a very depressed state of mind. You are meeting together—now'. Once again the students put the suggestion into action immediately. Once again there will be conflicting details of time, place and activity.

The point of the exercise is not to explore dramatic depths in an agreed group endeavour but, by challenging the imagination and spontaneity of the students, to spark off unexpected ideas and responses. It is important that the leader gives to the students as little direction as possible in his opening state-ment. The chances will be then much stronger that the students will have to wrestle to make rational the conflicting and often mutually exclusive components that have been created by the group.

14. The students sit in a circle and one of them goes into the middle and begins some occupational or dramatic action. Sometimes there is no need for speech in the early part of the exercise but the students should be told that it is an essential requirement later. The students forming the circle go into the middle to join the student already there the moment they see a possibility of adding to the dramatic situation. In the early stages of the exercise it will probably be best to restrict the number in the circle to no more than five. When the students have had some experience of the exercise it can build to contain the whole group.

The exercise requires that the students are able to recognize a moment that is suitable for their entry. Having recognized such a moment their imagination and spontaneity will be tested in doing something about it. Students will soon come to recognize **unnecessary interruptions and additions** and to differentiate between those and events or characters that progress the exercise.

15. This exercise should be used at a time when the students are working upon creating a character over a period of days or weeks. The students sit in a circle in a group of seven or eight. The rule of the game allows only two, three or four students in the circle at any one time. It is probably easiest if the first time the exercise is used the number is restricted to two, progressing to three and four as the students gain expertise. The aim of the exercise is to keep a situation or storyline continuing smoothly while the individual characters in the scene move in and out frequently and quickly. The students keep their character throughout the exercise and movement in and out of the circle is achieved by 'tagging'. The skill comes in the way the students handle their exits and entrances. It is likely there will be many comedy situations at first and this should be allowed, perhaps even encouraged, as it helps engage the students' interest and keep the exercise moving speedily. However, leaders may find it wise to place an embargo upon comedy after the students have had reasonable experience in making the exercise work.

Imagination, spontaneity and sensitivity are all being exercised simultaneously. There is also the need for the students to be fully absorbed and concentrated so they do not lose their grip upon their characters. Needless to say the additions, intrusions, exits and entrances must add significantly to the dramatic activity in the circle. The addition of near 'business' is not only useless but also destructive.

In Conclusion

The purpose of the foregoing exercises is to train the imagination so that it operates efficiently and easily. It is the student's task to ensure that when his imagination is working well he uses it properly and with an appropriate discipline. The function of the imagination is to illuminate, not to confuse. The student should exercise control over its use in the same way as he would use a tap to regulate the flow of water from the mains. Just like a water supply, the student's imagination will be useless to him if there is no regulating control or no connection to the mains supply.

In the definition of drama as 'the imaginative communication of significant experience', the word imaginative refers to the actor's efficiency in actually getting through to his audience. The phrase 'It's not what you do but the way that you do it' may be a cliché but an actor's quality and style—his 'way'—reflect his imagination and the use he makes of it. The best of actors gets through to the largest number of people in the broadest and deepest manner. Some actors are able to get through to a large number but without casting much illumination on the human condition. Others may be able to cast intense illumination but only for a small number of people with a very special viewpoint. An actor's aim must be to achieve optimum effect in combining the depth of experience he communicates with the number of people that he communicates it to. An actor's imagination is of no use to him unless he can select what will enable him to communicate to his audience more efficiently. In the theatre, as in any other art form, there is no room for waste.

Just as some members of an audience are affected more by what is heard than by what is seen, so are many actors. The preceding exercises combine the two kinds of stimulus. It is important for leaders to know that some students will be more stimulated by what they see than by what they hear but for others the process will be the opposite. In exactly the same way there are some students who have a most active visual imagination while their aural imagination is slow and insensitive. Group work will soon show which students respond best to which kind of stimulus. In the early stages of training it is best to offer a combination of the two kinds of stimulus so that no student is left completely at a standstill. As the student's experience grows so should he be prepared to respond to the challenge of training whichever is his weaker ability.

Implicit in all the exercises is the suggestion that the best stimuli leave unstated something that is important and significant. In any useful stimulus to creativity there must be that which is left unsaid and unexplained. The material will, therefore, tend to be abstract. It is better for it to be totally abstract—containing no single specific that can be accurately validated—than it is to be totally explicit. Nothing inhibits the imagination so much as that which is understood or that which can be fully explained.

CHAPTER FIVE

THE SENSES

The System at Work

Everything we experience comes to us through our ability to receive messages via our senses. Without our senses we can experience nothing, express nothing and communicate nothing. Through our senses we are informed of the real world and kept in touch with it. Our senses tell us of change in our environment. They guide our journey and help model our lives. They make up the most complex broadcasting and receiving apparatus that we shall probably ever meet. All over our body are organisms highly sensitized to special stimuli and capable of transmitting exact messages. Their jobs are separate and mainly exclusive. We see with our eyes and taste with our tongues. We cannot tell how hot it is by listening nor can we trace the smell of leaking gas through our eyes.

Most of us spend our daily lives using our senses in a generalized and unselective manner. It is not until we are faced with the loss of one of our senses that most of us think very deeply about their selectivity and separateness. For an actor such considerations are essential. He must learn what they can do separately and what they are incapable of doing. He must take careful note of how they combine together to increase his awareness of the world. He needs to know how his sensory receivers pass on stimulus to him. He also needs to know something of the way he interprets this message once he has received it. Pure sensation, like pure movement, is very unusual. Whenever we see or hear anything, just as whenever we move, it is unusual if it is not associated with some meaning, purpose or emotion. We may see with an eye similar to a camera but we perceive, that is **understand and make sense of the message**, with the eye of a person. Similarly we hear not with the ear of a tape-recorder but with the ear of a man.

Reception and Perception

Although the messages we receive may be susceptible to scientific diagnosis and reduced and broken down to unit stimuli, whatever we make of those messages depends upon who we are. We see not what is there but what we can see. We hear not what is there but what we are able to hear. At any one moment our perceiving is conditioned by our lives to that moment. All our previous sensory experiences, our parental background, our education, our prejudices, wishes, hopes, fears, and feelings of the moment all govern what we make of what our senses tell us.

The major elements that govern how we interpret sensory messages are as follows:

    (i) Our personal hopes, fears and ambitions.
   (ii) Our previous sensory experiences.
  (iii) The environment of the event.
  (iv) The essential nature of the sensory message.

Readers may disagree with the order in which these elements are placed. There is much to support the view that for an actor the above priority is correct. It is important in an actor's training that the four elements above are rearranged as much as possible. Not only does this accustom him to change but it also helps him to create with sensitivity and recreate with insight.

We are all susceptible to our emotions and instincts. We are all influenced by our own enthusiasms and our wish to please and be pleased. Perhaps actors are more influenced by these things than other people. This is important, since these qualities, while not changing the nature of the messages we receive through our senses, do influence the total meaning we draw from them. An actor needs to understand the importance of this conditioning. It is not suggested he should try to change his essential personal make-up but to become keenly aware how he himself sifts sensory evidence. We are all self-selective in what we meaningfully receive from our senses. The more an actor is aware of this the more flexible will he be in his training. For a fuller description for these processes at work see the companion volume *Psychology Made Simple*.

Seeing and Hearing

More than any others these two senses enable us to relate and communicate with one another.

We 'see' when light waves come through the pupil of the eye and then through the lens. They are focused on the retina and from there passed on as messages. The retina is sensitized for two different kinds of seeing. It has **rods** which are used for low-level and colourless vision. It also has **cones** for higher levels of light and colour vision. It is not necessary to go deeply into the subject here. Most of us are readily aware that it is not possible to transfer immediately from night vision to daytime vision. Readers may care to note that cones are positioned towards the centre of the eye. An experiment will clearly demonstrate this. Get a friend to hold a coloured object about three feet from the eye to the side. Concentrate on it without moving the eyeball. You will be able to identify it but not see its colour.

The three parts of the eye—**pupil, lens** and **retina**—are similar to the three major parts of the ear. There is the **external ear** which catches the sound waves and may be equated with the pupil. The **middle ear** arranges and focuses them rather like the lens and the **inner ear** actually receives the sensory stimulus—like the retina.

The human ear cannot discern all sound-waves that are made. Generally speaking we are able to 'hear' sounds within a vibration frequency between 25 per second and 20,000 per second. Dogs and other animals can hear higher frequencies than this.

That many of us do not use our ears efficiently is well known. One needs only to talk to a blind person about what they hear to understand this. Even closing our eyes for a few minutes informs us of the many sounds around us that we usually do not select to hear. The exercises at the end of this chapter attack general habits of **looking without seeing and listening without hearing**.

Taste and Smell

Generally speaking these two senses are always associated. In everyday life when we refer to a taste we are generally referring to a combination of taste, smell and texture in the mouth.

Both taste and smell are chemical senses. Basic tastes are as follows: bitter; metallic; salty; sour; sweet.

Basic smells are as follows: burning; flowers; fruits; putrefaction; spices.

The above classifications in taste and smell are by no means exclusive or objective. They are a useful indication of basic classifications.

Feeling

Most of us have played games when a person is blindfolded and told that he is going to be touched with a hot iron. He is in fact touched with a piece of ice. Much confusion and fun normally results.

The feeling senses—classified under touch in the classical definition of the five senses—can be divided into the sense of **pressure, heat and cold,** and **pain.** Areas sensitized to these separate feelings cover the whole of the body. The places where we are kissed, tickled, or smoothed gives some indication of this planning.

Balance

The classical definition of man's 'five senses' did not include a reference to a sense of balance. An ability to stand and walk maintaining a vertical and balanced position is essential for everyday living. It is even more important to an actor. It is particularly important to an actor in the 1970s who may be required to live, move, dance and have his being in all kinds of unusual circumstances. The actor of today needs to be much more of a dancer than he has done in the recent past. The simple ability to turn quickly for a period of time without going dizzy is obviously useful to him.

Body Image

Like the sense of balance, the sense of body awareness has only recently been added to the previous five senses. It is obviously of great importance to an actor, sportsman or dancer, to be sensitively aware of what is happening to his body. He also needs to be able to control his body shapes through muscular co-ordination with great accuracy. Proper muscular organization and kinetic awareness are essential to him.

If an actor is to work efficiently he must be able to receive what his senses tell him with accuracy. He must also be able to perceive with more than ordinary sensibility what those messages mean. He must be able to arrange them into useful forms. He also needs to know exactly how he is working upon the senses of his colleagues and his audience. The following exercises are all aimed at increasing the sensitivity of the actor's sensory receiving stations. They also aim to improve his ability to **make sense of what his senses tell him.** They set out to help him become a more efficient receiving and broadcasting organism. The more he takes in with his senses the more information he will have available to communicate. The more he makes sense of that information—the more he perceives—the more he will be able to communicate with rich purpose.

EXERCISES

The exercises should form a **regular part** of an actor's approach to his work. They will be useful to him whether he is in training or in work. They are not set as once and for all goals that will work like a panacea. Approached with concentration and pursued with diligence they will reward the student with a slow but regular growth towards increased sensitivity and sensibility.

Looking

1. Look around the room and choose a special line or shape. Choose a straight line, a square, a circle, an oval or a right-angle, etc. Find other shapes similar to the one you have chosen.

2. Look around the room and choose an object such as a cushion, a table-lamp, a chair back or an ornament. See how many shapes it contains. See how many other objects in the room echo the shapes in the one you have chosen.

3. Walk around the room drawing the shapes of the objects you can see with your hands in the air. Do this first with the fingers on a small scale. Then do it with one hand on a larger scale. Finally use both hands on a very large scale.

4. Walk around the room looking at it and its contents through a mirror.

(*a*) Use both eyes to look into the mirror.

(*b*) Place the mirror on the left-hand side of the nose at right-angles to the face and close the right eye. By walking around the room and changing the angle of the mirror select specific views that interest you.

5. Make a camera viewer with a piece of card or the hands as shown in the figure below and view the room, selecting shots that are angular; curved; pleasing or ugly, etc.

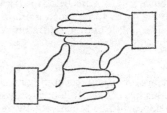

6. Look around the room to see the relationships between the objects in it. For example: a table-lamp and a table; a telephone and a clock near by; an armchair and its cushion; a kitchen chair and a neighbouring chair. In your imagination give them life—even personalities—of their own.

(*a*) Discover and analyse their interrelationships.

(*b*) Change their positions and create new interrelationships.

(*c*) Speak out loud the thoughts and feelings that stem from their inter-relationships.

(*d*) Work with a friend, each of you identifying with one object.

7. Go into a room for a short period (30 seconds to 2 minutes) then leave.

(*a*) Make a list from memory of the contents of the room.

(*b*) Make a sketch from memory.

(*c*) Return to check.

8. Choose a room with large windows and go into it from time to time during the daylight hours. Note particularly the changes in atmosphere brought about by the differences in lighting. Make rough sketches of the changes you see in shapes, light and shade. When you have sketched a number of these repeat the exercise using different available light sources—for example a standard lamp, a table-lamp, an overhead lamp.

9. Using the same room (or a different one if you prefer) take a torch with a

narrow beam and look round the otherwise darkened room. (An ordinary flash-light with the lens covered by a mask with a pin-hole in it will be satisfactory). Select small areas and specially consider their emotional and dramatic impact.

10. Go into any room and look at special sections of it. For example: wall by wall or corner by corner. Look at them from different angles. Consider what dramatic and emotional significance they have. Work out what dramatic situations you feel spring from these areas. Then create other scenes that you feel are particularly suitable.

11. Look carefully at the faces of your friends (also people on buses, in restaurants, photographs and magazines, etc.):

(*a*) Write a description of the essential message that the face is expressing.

(*b*) Make rough sketches of these expressions.

(*c*) Reproduce them with your own face with the aid of a mirror.

(*d*) Try these exercises with a friend, each of you using constantly changing expressions.

12. Watch people at work and play.

(*a*) Write detailed descriptions of some of their movements. Make your descriptions as full and as accurate as possible.

(*b*) Check your descriptions by working with a partner and performing each other's descriptions.

(*c*) Make matchstick sketches of some of the more interesting positions you noticed.

(*d*) Make some of these sketches three-dimensional by using pipe-cleaners, matches, etc.

(*e*) Recreate some of these positions with your own body. You may find it helpful to work with a friend and/or a full-length mirror.

13. Walk round a garden and choose a small area—no more than one or two inches square. In that area see how many different shapes, colours, things alive and dead you can see. Try this with flowerheads, the inside of a rose, the soil and the grass, the bark of a tree, etc.

Try the same exercise in the street, on walls, pavements, seats, the gutter, wastebins, etc.

(*a*) Write descriptions of what you have seen.

(*b*) Make sketches.

(*c*) Create with your body some of the shapes you have seen. (Some of these you will be able to do at the same time as looking. Some you will prefer to try later.)

14. Look at a room, a car, the inside of a bus, or a group of houses, dividing what you see into colour blocks. Discover where these blocks of colour contrast with one another and where they echo one another.

15. Choose a mechanical object such as a clock, a typewriter, a car engine or a record-player. Find as many examples as you can of mechanical movement that you can easily inspect. Look at the different patterns of movement and the interrelationships. Look at them closely when they are moving and when they are still.

(*a*) Write about what you see.

(*b*) Make sketches.

(*c*) Recreate the movements with your own body. (You may prefer to try this last exercise with a friend.)

16. Watch people at work to discover their repeated movement patterns. For example bus conductors, traffic-wardens, a lame man, people going through a revolving door, driving a car, riding a bicycle.

(a) Make matchstick sketches of various stages of their movements.

(b) Repeat these movements yourself.

17. Watch people on the television screen and try to mirror their movements and actions—their hands, feet and legs, faces, etc.

18. In a group of, say, six choose a lemon from a sack containing one for each person. Look at it for as long as you need to be able to remember it. Replace the lemons in the sack. Shake them about and then try to identify your original lemon.

In most of these exercises the use of a polaroid camera will be of great assistance.

Listening

1. Go round your own house or place of work (anywhere you know well).

(a) Stand still in different places. Close your eyes and listen.

(b) Move around as much as you can in safety with your eyes closed, listening carefully.

(c) Get a friend to help to take you to less well-known spots and repeat the exercise.

2. With your eyes closed get a friend to go with you for a walk, a bus, train or car ride, etc. Go to different environments and let your friend guide you, *while you keep your eyes closed*, listening intently. (You may prefer to use dark glasses to prevent drawing attention to having your eyes closed.)

3. Create a reproduction of the sounds of everyday life, and later more unusual and difficult sounds. For example: a telephone ringing, a telephone being dialled, a clock, a typewriter, a car exhaust, an aeroplane, a motorbike, the sea, the wind, wood burning, paper rustling, etc. Do these exercises:

(a) with your own body.

(b) with your own voice.

(c) with objects found in the room.

(d) with things found in the garden.

Repeat the exercises with a friend and then in a group.

4. With or without the aid of a tape-recorder, individually or in groups, create a number of sound montages. For example: a circus, an airport, a fairground, city life, the beach in summer, etc.

5. Listen to different sounds, voices and music. Repeat their melodies, their textures and their patterns. Try these:

(a) with your own voice.

(b) with your own body.

(c) with objects found around the room.

6. Make as many different sounds as possible with:

(a) one hand by itself.

(b) two hands by themselves.

(c) hands and objects found around the room. (Experiment with the pitch of clapping with two hands. The range you can achieve is a very large one.)

7. Listen to different sounds, voices and music and, by using your imagination, give them different qualities and emotional and dramatic overtones

from their original ones. Create sounds of your own and treat them similarly. Experiment particularly with whistling, drumming and clapping.

8. In groups of people—in class and out—listen for the sounds of:

(*a*) your own breathing.

(*b*) other people's breathing.

9. (*a*) Listen to a piece of music for all those sounds, textures and patterns that are not part of the main rhythm/melody. A stereo tape-recording or record with widely separated channels can be very useful.

(*b*) Accompany some of these sounds with body movement, vocally and with percussion, using hands and objects around the room.

10. With your eyes closed get a friend to make a sequence of noises.

(*a*) Respond to them in terms of your inner dramatic and emotional reactions.

(*b*) Write down your responses.

(*c*) Listen to the sounds again and try to identify their causes.

11. With a friend or in a group hum, sing, clap and whistle:

(*a*) Keeping together with the same melody.

(*b*) Building to a climax.

(*c*) Building to a climax and down again. (Try to come down from the climax with as much sensitivity and discipline as rising to it.) Do these exercises with your eyes open and closed.

(*d*) Repeat the exercises with each individual using a different rhythm and different melody.

12. Use sound sequences similar to those in the previous exercises as a basis for:

(*a*) improvisation.

(*b*) play-making.

(*c*) a scene from a play.

13. Take the following dialogue and play against the sounds mentioned:

A 'I've never been here before.'

B 'What's that?'

A 'I've never been here before.'

B 'Nice—isn't it?'

A 'I find it strange . . . No, that's not the word . . .'

B 'Not strange?'

A 'No . . . more, what you might call . . . sinister.'

B 'How sinister?'

A 'Well, perhaps not quite sinister . . .'

B 'Uncomfortable?'

A 'Yes. Yes, that's it. Uncomfortable. Yes. Uncomfortable.'

B 'I don't. I find it pleasantly relaxing—just to be here. Pleasantly relaxing.'

Sound backgrounds to accompany the above dialogue

1. Waves on the shore.

2. Jungle cries.

3. Heavy machinery—loud.

4. A tap dripping.

5. A 'palm court' orchestra.

6. A single drum.

7. Whistling—half-way between human and wind.

Smelling

1. Choose small areas in a room, the garden and the street and examine them closely for their different smells.

2. With a friend make a guided tour, with your eyes closed, of contrasting environments.

3. Rub different surfaces with your fingers and hands and then smell them.

4. Smell the parts of your body.

5. Smell the parts of your friends' bodies.

6. In a group identify one another by smell.

7. Identify objects, food and drink by their smell. Get a friend to give them to you and keep your eyes closed. (Note the apparent difference in smell with your eyes closed and later opened.)

8. Play the 'objects on a tray' memory game using small impregnated sponges or bottles. Try this with a friend or in a group.

(*a*) Write about the smells.

(*b*) Draw an impression of them using first of all black and white and later colour.

(*c*) Create a dramatic character for each of the smells.

9. With a partner share the experience of smelling a particular object while discussing it and the dramatic impact it has. Then create a character from it. In the first instance it may be helpful to use strong smells like smouldering rags or fish and chips.

10. Read through some of the scenes in Chapter Eight. While reading:

(*a*) imagine a special smell.

(*b*) actually smell one of the objects from (8) above.

11. Write down a list of easily available smells.

(*a*) Create them in your imagination.

(*b*) Check against actual sources.

12. What is the smell of broken glass?

Tasting

Try all the exercises under the previous section substituting taste for smell.

1. Eat a meal with your eyes closed.

2. Try the 'margarine and butter' game. Later use different sandwich spreads.

3. With many foods and drinks concentrate on the differences, between touch, taste and smell. (Consider the texture in your hands as well as on lips, teeth and tongue.)

4. Describe a special taste in terms of smell; a special touch in terms of taste and a special smell in terms of touch, etc.

5. Create settings for scenes based upon a strong taste (salt, vinegar, blood, sugar). Create characters from those tastes. With a friend, or in a group, bring the characters to life in the settings you have created.

Touching

1. Find your way about a room you know well exclusively by touch. Eyes closed.

2. Find textures and temperatures that match one another:

(*a*) in the room.

(*b*) in the garden.

(*c*) in the street.

Try these (i) with eyes open and (ii) with eyes closed.

3. In a group identify your friends, exclusively by touch. Eyes closed.

4. With a friend identify objects on a tray with eyes closed.

(*a*) Make a list from memory.

(*b*) Write about your responses as you remember them.

(*c*) Try to identify the objects.

5. Individually, with a friend or in a group, handle different objects and talk about their texture and temperature. With your eyes closed and then with your eyes open:

(*a*) describe the textures.

(*b*) describe your reactions.

(*c*) find somewhere on your body or your friend's that feels the same or similar.

(*d*) try to identify them (use 'abstract' objects—a stone, a piece of wood or metal, wool, leather, silk, etc. Later use 'real' objects—a shoe, a safety-pin, a cigarette, a saucepan, a brillo-pad, etc.).

6. Tickle yourself using:

(*a*) only your hands.

(*b*) a feather or similar object.

Let a friend do the same for you. Try the exercise in groups with eyes open and closed.

7. Hold one hand with another trying to communicate different messages from one to the other. Contrast gripping, tapping, smoothing, scratching, etc.

8. Try the previous exercise with a friend. Later discuss your feelings.

9. With a friend (and later in a group) communicate exclusively by touch. You may wish to develop this exercise and create a new language where there are no words—only touch.

10. In a room, the garden, the street or the beach walk about in bare feet noticing the changing textures of the surfaces. Touch them also with the fingers, elbows and other parts of the body. With a friend go over the same surfaces keeping your eyes closed.

11. In groups keep in touch with at least two other people all the time. Agree on the kinds of touch you will use—light, heavy, slow, fast, etc. Try the exercise with eyes closed and later eyes open.

12. Play some of the scenes from Chapter Eight, concentrating on using touch with:

(*a*) both characters touching one another all the time.

(*b*) one character touching the second all the time.

(*c*) one character trying to avoid being touched by the other but not succeeding.

13. Play the dialogue from Exercise 12 under 'Listening' above in the same way.

14. Try Exercise 1 of this section using different kinds of gloves: leather; thin cotton; young children's glovelets, etc.

15. Blow on your own hands. Do this in as many different ways as you can

discover. Blow on different parts of your body. Share these experiences with a friend or in a group. Also with a friend or in a group play blow football with a ping-pong ball, a feather, a piece of paper, etc.

16. Handle a number of different objects. Recreate the movements of handling them and imagine the sensations as accurately as possible without using the objects.

17. Practise a number of occupational mimes. Try these with a friend at the simple level of:

(a) Can you tell what I am doing?

(b) The friend joining in the activity without being told what it is. Try this later in groups.

18. Carry an empty suitcase from place to place. Then fill it or partly fill it with heavy and light articles. Lift it to a high shelf. With eyes closed change the objects in the suitcase and pass it to a friend or round a small group. Recreate the movements accurately without using the case.

Balance

1. Stand quite still for as long as possible.

2. Stand still with one foot off the ground. Do this for as long as possible and then change feet. Later move hands, arms, knees and then trunk, slowly and as far as possible away from your centre of gravity—still retaining balance.

3. Try Exercises 1–2 with a book on your head.

4. Try Exercises 1, 2 and 3 with your eyes closed. (It is useful to try this exercise with a friend near by—just in case.)

5. Spin round in circles: (a) by yourself; (b) with a friend. Then repeat the spinning with a visual 'fix' on one spot like a ballet dancer.

Body Image

1. With a friend or in a group adopt a special body position. Relax from it and then repeat it exactly. Get your friend or the members of the group to check your accuracy. (A polaroid camera is particularly useful for this exercise).

2. Recreate the body position of a friend who is specially posing. Get others to help you check. Try it in front of a large mirror.

3. For a full working day walk with a constant limp or keep one arm absolutely stiff.

4. Isolate one part of your body (a leg, arm or hand) and restrict its movement. It may be desirable to bandage the particular part of the body in position. Keep it immobilized throughout a whole day.

5. If you are right-handed, become exclusively left-handed for an hour or so (or vice versa).

If the exercises are to succeed properly they must be conducted regularly and with concentration.

CHAPTER SIX

IMPROVISATION

Definitions and Descriptions

Chambers' Twentieth Century Dictionary in its revised edition offers the following definitions of improvisation:

'to compose and recite, or perform, without preparation'
'to bring about on a sudden'
'to make or contrive offhand or in an emergency'

and for the word 'offhand' there is this:

'without study: impromptu free and easy;
ungraciously ourt or summary'

To many people the word 'improvisation' means the use of a do-it-yourself kit of third-rate materials left over from the bargain counter of a make-do-and-mend jumble sale. It covers many activities—from running repairs during a motor-car rally to kitchen plumbing.

In drama, improvisation covers a multitude of approaches. At this juncture it will suffice to describe it as follows. The students are generally in a class situation and frequently in a hall or studio/workshop. They may be with partners or in small groups. The students will be presented with an idea, challenge or stimulus which motivates them to move and/or speak (very probably *behave*) with an *element of spontaneity*. The activity is very similar to *acting*—but without *set moves or texts*. It should be marked by *absorption, sincerity and significance*.

It may be appropriate to use left-over trivia when making urgent, temporary repairs to a motor-car, but it is by no means appropriate to use them in a drama class. Unfortunately the left-over trivia of living are often the main material in many improvisation classes. They are the bus queues; coach parties; waiting-rooms and cocktail parties—'and now be a butterfly'—'and now be a tree'—all situations frequently used to involve students in dramatic activity. Without proper purpose these become meaningless and are too often supported by insignificant specifics—drinking tea; laying a table; eating a meal; being served in a shop; knitting.

It took the combined genius and theatrecraft of Chekhov and Stanislavsky to illuminate universal significance by the dim light of the specifically mundane. Many of the prompt copies of these productions contain detailed notes about 'combing the hair'; 'filing the nails'; 'lighting a cigarette'. Undoubtedly tremendous care went into the choice of these activities and even more into their realization, rehearsal and execution: and this from men of genius working with a superbly trained and talented company. The challenge of injecting an ordinary event with extraordinary meaning should be approached with care and preparation—not offered to students as a regular diet. The student in an improvisation class needs spiritual sustenance and stimulus to feed him. The mundane will drain his resources and leave him bored and listless. If he is a creative and imaginative student he will be exhausted and frustrated— empty and cheated.

When embarking upon a journey of self-discovery it is no help to have eyes bandaged and ears plugged—as they can be by such trivia. It is at the end of his journey that the student will be able to see the universe in a spent match— in the meantime **to commit him to another boring bus queue will merely perpetuate the weakness of perception and insight that improvisation should be correcting.**

To Perform Without Preparation

Students should feel they are performing without preparation, but a well-chosen improvisation will call upon all their previous experiences and the result will only seem to be unprepared. I have seen many improvisations preceded by specific preparation—very often discussion. This does nothing but inhibit the creative process by arranging action and reaction; event and response. By the time it comes to 'do', nothing is left but a tedious working over pre-planned externals—the experience having long ago lost impact and significance. The only preparation needed is their experience of life to that moment in class and a readiness to trust and express it.

This suggests that improvisations start from where each individual student finds himself, but unfortunately, this is contrary to my personal experience in watching many improvisation classes. The large majority begin with group work related to a **theme.** I have no objection to group work or themes as such. My concern is with those individual students who are not ready to work creatively in a group, and with themes that carry insufficient charge to offer them engaging, impelling specifics with which they can readily identify.

The provision of proper stimuli is the major responsibility of the leader. When the stimulus is right, the student will respond in a natural way and create his own beginning position—his own platform. He will have to identify, relate and react. His creative expression will mirror his inner response and he will move towards effective and imaginative communication. This occurs only if the student is challenged where he actually is. If he is required to occupy some non-existent no-man's-land between himself and the leader there will be no need for a genuine response—both parties being content with clichés or outworn gestures. It is when the inner reality of his personality is touched that the student will need to make a direct response. It follows, therefore, that the leader must be able to understand and sympathize with the actual position of any student at any one time. It is not always easy for an adult leader to accept and use, for example, the interests and motivations of an adolescent male. For many of these young men it is a time of violent emotional relationships and sexual growth—neither of which is easy to accommodate in the confines of an orthodox class situation. Nor, for that matter are the insecurities of the ageing spinster, the worried wife or the anxious student.

If the student is to be involved in improvisations (and relationships) that stimulate his urge to expression and communication, **the content must be charged with symbols he will immediately recognize and wish to pursue.** Then, he will *respond naturally* and *appear to perform* without preparation.

To Bring About on a Sudden

If the catalytic agent chosen by the leader for improvisation has been well selected, the student will find it not only natural but also necessary to make a **sure and swift response**. There will be no question of working out what he feels or thinks about it—suddenly he will be in the grip of an experience that is highly charged. His response will be immediate and the expression will come out 'all on a sudden'. The student will not have intended it nor will he have thought about it. It will be perfectly natural and he will say or do something about it. All this will culminate in what the Americans call 'coming on strong'. Certainly it is strong, immediate and direct—'all on a sudden'.

In an Emergency

The function of all learning is to extend the frontiers of experience and the most important function of improvisation is to extend the frontiers of the personality in action. In the world at large there is seldom an opportunity to experiment in moments of crisis—usually the demands of the situation require us to respond with a reliable gesture or well-tried action. There is seldom room to manoeuvre. Although the crisis may be natural and actual there is no guarantee it will be 'real'. Real in the sense of 'living in the psyche' strongly enough to prevent future shocks from reactions that are not thoughtless and unorthodox. Improvisation, being artificial, can provide inner experiential reality without the embarrassment and potential danger of natural, external actuality. In an improvisation a student attempts to outline the contours of his soul and define its role in his condition of being. If his efforts are to bring worthwhile rewards, he must **live and act at risk**. He must reject the known in advance in favour of the unpredictable and the imponderable. In order to grow he must respond freely and in faith. Later he will contemplate with an open mind. The more there is **thought before action** the further will that action be **removed from the frontiers of his experience**. It will have retreated to a firmly entrenched position in the centre of his memory.

Improvisation offers the opportunity to experiment 'for real' without the encumbrance of external actuality but with the guarantee of burning the experience meaningfully into the spirit. It is, of course, the justification of any art form: that poetic reality is more telling and enduring than actual, natural experience—and the art of improvisation works on the human condition at large and in action.

Offhand

Improvisation's method helps the student explore the human spirit in crisis and at its frontiers—its purpose ensures, through proper practice of the real experience, that actuality can be dealt with in a freer and easier way. Improvisation does not lead students to live in a continual state of crisis but helps them, by grasping the nettle of extremity, deal in a relaxed and free-wheeling manner with the issues and events of everyday life. Having struggled and wrestled with one's own persona, and others, in conditions of strain and tension—at the same time learning—one can react with more maturity to the strain that some personal and group relationships bring with them. Practice at the frontiers helps the student bring greater perception and insight to the more mundane, central, events of living. Not only does this improve efficiency in such traffic but it also brings the rewards of deeper and wider appreciation of the universal relevance of the particular circumstances.

Improvising or Exercising?

It is important to differentiate between improvisation and the similar, often confused areas of acting exercises and play-making. Acting exercises train specific abilities and skills in the vocal and physical make-up of a student. Playmaking often uses these skills and, by placing them in varying combinations and situations with different partners and groups, shapes memory and imagination to give dramatic energy a pattern. Neither play-making nor exercise necessarily challenge the student in his private inner self. It is this territory that is the proper concern of improvisation.

Acting exercises and play-making offer the student an opportunity to practise all the elements that make up his persona—bodily movement, speech, gesture, the 'look in the eye' and the 'touch of the hand'—all important characteristics in defining the identity of the student, stating who he is; what he is and what he can do. No matter how much imagination and wisdom the leader may bring to his task, nor how much enthusiasm and spontaneous response he may achieve from the students, if the exercises are to succeed they will be proscribed by the security of known talents, operating in known conditions. They take the actual abilities of the student—perhaps practise them in known situations or *in vacuo*—and proceed to operate them in a 'new' situation.

Since the aim is to exercise specific abilities and skills—rehearsal to improve performance and ease of operation—it becomes clear that while there is a common element with improvisation, there is also a quintessential difference. Acting exercises and play-making encourage growth by exploring the expertise of the known. Improvisation stimulates creativity by structuring a situation that is new to the student and in which he is basically insecure; a situation in which his prejudices are irrelevant, his memory of no purpose and his learned skills inoperable. This is why it is important that the education of personal skills and group play-making should go hand in hand with improvisation. The student needs personal security before he can relax sufficiently to permit improvisation to do its work. He must have enough confidence to travel alone into a world that improvisation describes and defines as it creates it. When improvisation is working at optimum level, the student is in complete solitude and his creative imagination takes him into a living dream. All barriers are down and, momentarily at least, the student has cut through the miasma of the probable to experience the possible—buoyed up from time to time by views of the miraculous and glimpses of the impossible. Ionesco has this to say:

'The free development of the powers of imagination must not be restricted. There must be no canalization, no directives, no preconceived ideas, no limits. I believe a genuine work of art is one in which the initial intentions of the artist have been surpassed; where the flood of imagination has swept through the barriers or out of the narrow channels in which he first tried to confine it: extending beyond messages, ideologies and the desire to prove or teach. This absolute freedom of the imagination is called escape or evasion by the gloomy critics of our time, whereas it is true creation. To make a new world is to satisfy the insistent demands of a mind that would be stifled if its needs were not fulfilled.'

Change

It is one of the functions of improvisation to help the student get away from the dull, the routine and the cliché. If the student is to create new and rich dramatic experiences, or to offer new insights into them, he must be ready to leave behind the probable and excavate from within his own resources the unexpected. Dealing with this unexpected can cause problems. For one thing, it means dealing with change and the possibility of change. The twentieth century is remarkable for the changes that have occurred in its first seventy years—many more, and more wide-ranging, than in any previous century. The rate of change is also accelerating. It is important for the students to come to grips with this phenomenon. Change, and the rate of change, in our ways of living are reflected in the microcosm of the theatre. The good student will, therefore, equip himself to live in a changing society by practising innovation. This practice in innovation should cover movement habits, clothes, speech, make-up and all these aspects of behaviour that the student generally accepts as being unchanging.

Improvisation to Performance

Improvisation enables the individual student to break new ground in his personal experiences within a secure environment. It is a kind of emotional and experiential limbering. In group work and in rehearsal it enables the group to discover new responses to the material on which they are working. Many groups take improvised techniques much further and through them create the material that they are to perform. At a first examination this seems an attractive proposition. It is however much more difficult than it appears. To create the inner experience, shape its mode of expression and organize it so that it will communicate effectively with an audience is an art which few actors are able to achieve.

Even the famed historical companies—for example the Commedia dell'Arte —used a basic theme and format as a basis for their improvised performances. For a group to undertake the creation of such material from its early strugglings to final finished performance is not easy. A frequent additional complication is that many such groups wish to work without the aid of an external director or leader. To achieve the combination of creator, actor, performer, director and writer at one and the same time makes many more demands than many groups anticipate.

Flexibility

In individual and group training as well as rehearsal the function of improvisation is covered generally by the term 'limbering'. In performance its function is to enable the actor to give a **free-wheeling flexible response to the audience's reception of his performance**. This is a reflection of change. A change in the attitude of the theatre-going public over the past fifty years. Changes brought about quite naturally by deeper social movements. As in English social and political life there has been a move towards a greater involvement of members of the public, so has there been with audiences in the theatre. It is no longer satisfactory in either sphere for the figures of supposed superior beings to be allowed to live out irresponsible lives while the rest of the community support them in an unchanging, unchangeable ritual. There are signs of a very clear wish for audiences to be more deeply and liberally associated with the dramatic action on stage. The time is not yet ripe for full participatory theatre although moves in this direction are to be seen.

From the beginnings of the theatre with the Greeks the figures represented upon a stage have been moderated from irresponsible deities to responsible God figures through major kings and leaders to idols and great men. Today is the day of the common man and the symbols used upon a stage are now common symbols. There is no longer a vertical relationship between actor and audience; it is now almost horizontal. The relationship has much more in common with the Victorian music-hall artist and his audience than with the removed and worshipped actor of the 1930s. Audiences are now expressing a need to be able to identify with the actors in a way that is real for the audience. Previously it was sufficient for them merely to receive. Now they need a more egalitarian relationship.

Without discarding artistic standards or necessary disciplines the actor must be able to respond to his audience dynamic. A dynamic which expresses itself in immediate terms in the theatre but also in a more diffuse manner in the plays and acting styles it demands. This is not to suggest that an actor should be completely at the mercy of the whims of an audience nor to deny that actors have always adjusted to the needs of a particular performance. It means the actor must take careful note of the movement toward the act of theatre being more co-operative than before. Improvisation clearly helps an actor prepare for this in his performance.

Practical Approaches

An actor who can give a totally improvised artistic performance in public is a very rare artist indeed. The exercises that follow are not intended for such a purpose. They are aids to individual and group training that will improve flexibility of personal resources and communication expertise.

Many of the exercises previously outlined will be suitable for work in improvisation. But the aims will be different. Improvisation needs concentration, absorption, imagination and spontaneity all to be working efficiently before it can achieve proper success. Improvisation takes over where many of the previous exercises left off. For example, the exercises where the student uses make-up and costume in the street, on buses, in restaurants, etc., would now be taken more deeply into the realm of the creation of a character. Whereas before, the student was enquiring into the nature of his own spontaneous responses, he will now be exploring the possibilities that the dramatic character —complete with suitable make-up and clothes—enable him to bring about.

The student may find it easier to begin the exercises in the security of the drama class, but the improvisation will not begin to bite until the student carries through the results of what he initiates. This particular method of improvisation does not depend exclusively upon make-up and clothing. The student can create new ways of moving, standing, talking, etc., all of which will achieve the same result. The creation of a new voice or a new way of moving which the student lives with for forty-eight hours will offer him many challenges. For example, if a student chooses to move in the manner of a much older or a crippled person he will find there is a world of difference between experiencing and expressing this in a drama class and actually crossing a busy street. Students find this combination of the imaginative and the actual gets through with telling impact.

An exercise which takes the same principles into more advanced work is the 'nothing but the truth' or 'nothing but lies' game. Here the student pledges himself for, say, eight hours to tell nothing but the absolute truth. Or alternatively to respond to every statement or question with an untruth. When the game is played with rigid application of discipline it is more difficult than most students first think. A similar exercise involves the student in using a behaviour characteristic that is unusual for him—overweening pride; constant fear and anxiety; intense humility, etc. With these exercises the student is not using the vehicle of a dramatic character, but his own personality. The exercises throw him back upon his inner resources—usually unexposed—and the student will need to dredge from them a completely new set of responses if he is to undertake the exercise properly.

What is learned from the exercises is readily transferred to the group or class training situation or rehearsal. (More is said about the use of this method in group rehearsals in Chapter Fifteen.) The techniques can be used with or without the assumption of a dramatic character; in class, group or social situation. They should also be used within the security of the private bedroom or bathroom. In the early stages the student will be freer to give full rein to whatever his imagination suggests when he is alone. It is important that he should hold nothing back, no matter how ridiculous or bizarre it may appear. He is journeying a long a road that will lead him to rich creation through much that is accidental. He should capitalize upon this accident and see it through to its full conclusion. Real inner experience, personal expression and creativity come frequently by accident. The art and discipline of communication come by design and selection at a later date. It is harmful to the student's creative process to become selective too soon. A good motto is **'creation by accident—art by design'**.

EXERCISES

1. The students are given a selection of masks, make-up and items of clothing. Individually, in pairs or as a group they select what they need and use it in whatever way they wish. It is important that the students have as much privacy as they need during this preparation and no access to a mirror. The exercise can progress in one of two ways.

(*a*) The students go before a full-length mirror individually. They look at their reflection for a moment or two and then bring their responses to life. As each student leaves the mirror, so there will be more opportunities for interaction if the work is being progressed with a group. Although the exercise works very well on an individual basis, dramatic dynamic builds up more effectively when the students have partners or are working in a group.

(*b*) When instructed by the leader the students begin to mix and mingle. They will build up their responses and characters as a result of what other people say and do. They will be using the other students in the group as they used the mirror in (a) above.

2. The students are presented with a surrealist painting or piece of writing. They study it as a group and, when they are ready, bring to life their individual interpretations of the sounds, actions and characters that are suggested by the stimulus. This exercise works equally well with the students working with a partner.

3. The students work in pairs. One of them has a collection of objects and pictures which at intervals he shows to the other. The second student responds by creating sounds, actions and characteristics as they are suggested. The exercise works similarly to the word association game and continues to build until the student has created a working character with a life of its own.

4. The students work with a partner or in a small group. The students may wish to make sounds or to speak, and, while they should not be discouraged, this is not essential.

(a) The first part of the exercise is for the students to respond spontaneously in dramatic dance to previously unheard music. They should work together as a group and attempt to combine dramatic continuity with free responses to the music. It is important that the music provides an exact discipline for the students' work. The exercise is pointless if only the first fifteen seconds of the music is actually heard and used.

(b) After some experience of the previous method, the students divide into two groups and one group creates the music and sounds to stimulate the dramatic dance of the other. This has the additional advantage of a sensitive two-way movement between the two groups.

(c) A useful introductory exercise which can be used individually is to 'conduct' a piece of music from a record or tape. Once the idea of responding on a one to one basis has been established the student can progress into dramatic dance or character creation.

5. The students are now involved in using a text. The extracts should be short enough for the students to get to know them well without much difficulty. The scenes are then played in many contrasting ways. The students should not be limited in their interpretations by trying to justify what they do in terms of the full context of the play. The creation of incongruity by a radical alteration of the characters or the setting in which they find themselves will offer good opportunities for new insights.

The first and third scenes from Act I of *Macbeth* might, for example, be played in the following ways:

(i) Nursemaids with prams in a park.
(ii) A bridge party.
(iii) Business tycoons.
(iv) A military briefing.
(v) The insane.
(vi) A mannequin parade.

It will be quite impossible to justify some of the above in terms of the full play. The justification comes in exposing, in a fresh way, the inner meaning of the text. The students are forced into making new responses to material that they feel they know very well.

The foregoing exercises encourage the habit of innovation. They make it easier for the actor to get away from the orthodox and the cliché. They help him to face change more readily and to create and come to grips with something new and something fresh. Through the exercise of his imagination and spontaneity anything and everything becomes accessible to him. Here he can free-wheel and limber as long as he needs.

The method of improvisation can also be used in other ways. It can assist the creation of atmosphere; character building; timing, rhythm and style. When these are the objectives of the exercises the leader needs to outline with more detail and accuracy the content and style of the material he is going to offer. The student will be concerned more with trying out new modes of expression than with creating fresh inner experiences. Spontaneous reactions will still be important but a deeper absorption in a more restricted area of inner experience will enable him to practise varying the methods he uses to express it.

Improvisations leading to the production of a text belong to this category. Here again the leader will give more detailed outlines and allow more time for absorption before the exercise begins. Even at this stage the avoidance of preliminary group discussion is recommended as is the repetition of an improvisation. Many groups feel a need to 'polish' their improvisations. This tends to encourage a search for exact recall and the outcome is a mere rehash rather than a true step forward. It is better that the students should be allowed sufficient time within each improvisation to explore their aims fully rather than to attempt to improve by repetition. This regurgitation seems to appeal most strongly to the insecure and the uncreative—those in fact who need the essence of improvisation most. Rather than go over the old ground again and repeat it with many inaccuracies it is better that a fresh improvisation should be set and the subject attacked from another angle.

The following suggestions might prove useful starters. In each, the students provide the main motivations.

1. A group trying to move in **absolute silence**. Speech is not permitted.
2. A group of people speaking in whispers.
3. A group with one person crying.
4. A group with one person laughing.
5. A group with one person who is blind.
6. A group with one person who is deaf and dumb.
7. A group waking up to find themselves in a different place from where they went to sleep.
8. A group lost—jungle, ice cap, mountain—in which everyone is attempting to be in charge.
9. A similar group where no one will take charge or make any decision.
10. A group whose members are always asking questions of one another. Few (if any) answers are given.
11. A group with only one person working.
12. A group with only one person not working.
13. A group in which everyone suspects one other person of being a spy.
14. A party at which everyone is a gate-crasher trying to conceal the fact.
15. A conference where everyone is covering up their complete ignorance of the events and the subject-matter.

Once the students have some experience of making the improvised exercises work the leader can add new instructions at any time during the progress of the scene. For example:

1. The lights go out.
2. The sun goes out.
3. The ceiling begins to come slowly down.
4. Everyone goes blind.
5. The smell of gas is detected.

Similarly, by previous arrangement with an individual student, he (or she) at a signal from the leader suddenly:

1. faints.
2. laughs.
3. becomes afraid.
4. becomes anxious.
5. begins to take the furniture away from the room.
6. gives away money.
7. hysterically weeps.
8. begins to get undressed.

In Conclusion

It is appropriate for this improvised method to be used at any time when working on a text. More is said of this later. The leader will use his discretion when making cross-references to a text, but there is a danger. When an actor constantly uses improvisation to illuminate his approach to a character or a text there is the possibility that he will create an inner world which will be meaningless to an audience. **It is easy for an actor to create a frame of reference that becomes so much a part of his approach that he overlooks the fact that the audience is in ignorance of it.** This danger is often prevented if the leader uses improvisatory techniques as a method of building up the actor's resources **before he approaches the text.** This does not preclude the actor from following a liberal and flexible approach. It merely ensures that he will not begin to inhabit a private world of esoteric symbols that will mislead and confuse his audience.

There are many widely divergent approaches to improvisation. One constant factor, however, is that the leader himself is also improvising when he approaches his group. The gifted and sensitive leader knows this and capitalises it. His aim in approaching a group this way is to get in touch with their feelings and imaginations as efficiently as possible. He will then be able to lead them more accurately. Similarly, the aim of any improvisatory technique he uses is to put the actor in touch with his feelings and his imagination. This is the first stage.

The second stage is to improve the actor's ability to release his imagination and his emotions at the right time; in the right place; in the right way. Improvisation puts the actor in touch with the emotive and imaginative and dynamic he needs to relate with an audience. His artistic discipline and selectivity allow him to do that with optimum efficiency.

Above all students and leader alike must be aware of the need for growth in improvisations. There is a very real danger that group work can stand still while the students enjoy their new-found expertise. This marking time instead of marching ahead in improvisations can be useful from time to time. It encourages confidence and a feeling of security. When it is overdone it is merely indulgent.

After any improvisation session the student should ask himself the following: Has this broadened or deepened my inner experience? Has it prompted me to more fluent expression? Has it enabled me to communicate with greater accuracy and sensitivity? When the answers to these questions are 'No' the time has come to think again about the method and content of the improvisations.

CHAPTER SEVEN

BREATHING AND RELAXATION

Breathing to Speak

One of the main tools of an actor's trade is his voice. The way he is asked to use it may vary from time to time. Mannerisms come and go. For example, the 'voice beautiful' was very popular not long ago. It has now gone out of fashion. There is no longer a serious bar, as there used to be, to an actor with a regional accent. Nevertheless, the more flexible an actor's voices the more he will be able to use it for maximum impact in performance.

In order to use his voice at all a person needs breath. Since an actor has special requirements of his voice—few of us need to address large gathering in specially adapted voices very often—he must also make special demands upon his breathing. He must organize it to meet the peculiar needs of theatre performances.

Conscious and Unconscious Breathing

Normally we breathe in and out without conscious effort. From the minute we are born to the minute we die it is usually natural and automatic. We become aware of it only when we have certain special calls to make upon it, or have some disability such as a cold or asthma. If we have unexpectedly to run to catch a bus or a train our breathing makes us aware of its presence. Generally, such changes in breathing to meet specific circumstances are regulated without our conscious effort. It is only afterwards that we take note of them.

When asleep or at rest we need little breath. For running, athletics and energetic games we need a lot. We meet these differing needs by breathing in different ways. Running a 100 yards race requires different breathing from a long-distance cross-country race. Most of the time we can rely on our natural body mechanisms to make the appropriate changes. An actor's needs are more sophisticated. He must balance his athletic demands against his need to speak at all times with maximum efficiency and control. No actor can hope to give an acceptable performance if he is constantly out of breath.

The Natural Process

The natural process is for the muscles, after producing extra carbon dioxide, to send an appropriate message to the respiratory centre of the brain. Breathing is adjusted accordingly—after the event. On many occasions the natural process is perfectly satisfactory and acceptable for an actor in performance. But it is not always so.

An Actor's Needs

An actor's breathing must be organized not only to meet his athletic demands but also to meet his aesthetic requirements for voice and speech. In these circumstances he cannot afford to wait until after the event. He must organize his breathing in readiness for his needs.

In everyday life deep and correct breathing can aid good posture and keep the body in good tone. It can also help build up powers of concentration—a virtue particularly useful to an actor.

In addition to the normal breathing requirements of everyday life, an actor has two factors to meet. First, the athletic demands of his profession may call upon him to use the **energies and disciplines of a football player or professional dancer.** Secondly, his breathing must serve voice production and be **properly available and under full control.** It is this second requirement that is the major concern of this chapter.

Respiration

Respiration is the process of drawing air into the lungs (breathing in or inspiration) and expelling it (breathing out or expiration). This enables the interchange of gases between the air and the blood. The blood absorbs oxygen from the air by means of haemaglobin in the red corpuscles and carries it to all parts of the body. After giving up the oxygen, the blood absorbs the carbon dioxide excreted by the tissues and carries it to the lungs to be exhaled.

Inspiration

Inspiration is a muscular effort. The diaphragm, which is a dome-shaped muscle arched upwards into the chest, contracts and becomes flattened, making the chest longer. The muscles between the ribs (intercostal muscles) also contract, elevating the ribs in front and making the chest wider and deeper. The lungs—being elastic—expand and fill the space, the air rushing down the trachea to fill them as a sponge fills when it is allowed to expand under water. The air enters the nose or mouth, passing into the windpipe and through the vocal chords in the pharynx.

Expiration

Expiration requires no effort. It may be described as passive since the elasticity of the lungs naturally tends to empty them so they may return to their unextended position. The bones of the thorax tend to return to their normal position similarly.

At rest the normal rate of breathing is fifteen to eighteen breaths per minute.

The Need for Relaxation

Most breathing is natural and unconscious. When specially concentrating upon it there is a tendency to tense muscles unnecessarily. This is a harmful process for voice quality. It is also a waste of effort. The more relaxed the rest of the body is, the more effortless and efficient will be the breathing.

Many students quite unthinkingly and unknowingly tense their necks and shoulders when practising breathing exercises. Some screw up their faces or clench their fingers. Such tensions inhibit easy and proper breathing. They also make voice production difficult and strained. Worst of all, they build up nervous tension. A vicious circle is quickly established and is difficult to break.

EXERCISES

Here are some suggestions to help you achieve full relaxation. If you wish you can incorporate them into the breathing exercises that follow.

1. Lie down on your back. Imagine you are on a cloud, a bed of foam or in

a warm bath. Move your limbs slowly and easily. Move them in slow motion. Try to achieve a floating sensation. The more you imagine you **feel** you are floating the more relaxed you will become.

2. Imagine you are standing in a warm shower. Feel the sensation of the warm water spraying on your limbs and running down your body. Concentrate on different parts of the body from time to time. Try to achieve the same floating sensation as before. (For the exercises in both 1 and 2 you may care to use real baths, showers and foam cushions as starters. For example, it will help you recall the floating sensation if you practise by letting one hand and wrist 'float' while you are in a bath.)

3. Lie down on your back and tense your muscles one by one. Tense them until you **just sense discomfort**. Then let them relax. Enjoy the feeling of release. The more you stiffen and tense the muscles, say in the left hand, holding them until they ache, the more you will achieve an enjoyable reflex relaxation.

4. Lie down on your back. Using the back of the head and your heels only, arch your body upwards away from the floor. Push and pull as if your stomach were being hauled to the ceiling. Breathe in as you commence your stretch and hold your breath and position as long as you can. When you can retain it no longer finally collapse and breathe in. The relief will encourage full reflex relaxation as in 3 above.

5. Sit quite still in a comfortable position with your eyes closed. Hum quietly to yourself. As you hum slowly rock yourself to and fro or from side to side. Repeat the exercise with a friend or in small groups.

6. Sit quite still in a comfortable position with your eyes closed. Stroke one hand gently with the other. Then stroke other parts of your body. Concentrate upon the tactile sensations and enjoy them. Repeat the exercise with a friend or in small groups.

7. In a small group let one person lie down while the rest of the group perform on him the exercises in 5 and 6 above.

8. As a separate exercise, or incorporated into the previous three, concentrate all your thoughts upon a piece of endless black velvet.

9. Sit or lie down in a comfortable position. Imagine your body, especially your veins and arteries, to be filled with brittle gritty substances. Imagine these substances being slowly changed for mercury; for warm milk; for your own blood. Enjoy the sense of well-being that comes over the body as your imagination takes over. Go with the feeling and relax into the sensations. Continue the changes and transformations until you are *nothing but gently flowing liquid*. As a starter for the exercise imagine you are a snowman melting in the heat of the sun or a lump of sugar slowly dissolving in a warm liquid.

10. Isolate a part of your body—a hand or a foot at first—and completely relax it. Get a friend to check the relaxation for you by shaking the part of the body concerned. Make sure it responds like a piece of dead wet fish. Continue with other parts of the body.

11. Check the muscles of your body separately for the contrast between tension and relaxation. Approach the exercise in a technical manner. Be as objective about it as possible. Get a friend to help you. Later increase the range of contrast between tension and relaxation.

12. Stand quite relaxed and still. Use as little effort as possible to keep you comfortably upright. Mentally check on the state of tension and relaxation in all your muscles. When you are confident you are as relaxed as you can be

without falling down, begin to relax slowly from the head downwards. Let the muscles go—head, neck, shoulders, trunk—until you are bending forward with your arms hanging to the floor. Stay in a relaxed position for a moment or two. Raise yourself to an upright position again slowly and with as little effort as possible. When returning make sure you hold your shoulders in the proper position with full relaxation. It will help to have a friend to guide and check you through the exercise.

In all the exercises *mental relaxation is just as important as physical relaxation*. Relaxation is a condition of the body. It is also an attitude of mind. Remember there is a constant flow between mind and body. Use it. Let your body help your mind relax and let your mind help your body. It is all under your control.

Warning: After relaxation exercises do not try to come to or move about quickly, too soon. You will find it helps to use the 'cat' exercises described in Chapter Nine.

Breathing

The following breathing exercises should be practised every day. There is much to be said for little and often. It helps you get into the right habits and there is less danger of over oxygenization than if you try to cram them all into a twice-weekly session. Try the exercises for just a few minutes at first. When you feel you are succeeding in the objectives, increase the time you allow until you are exercising for approximately fifteen minutes a day. These fifteen minutes should include a proper time for relaxation. **In all the exercises make sure you maintain the fully relaxed qualities you will have achieved from the previous exercises.**

1. Breathe in and out to a count of two seconds. Increase the second count to five—ten—twenty—twenty-five—thirty—forty—sixty seconds. Do not try to progress too quickly. This will only do harm. Do not allow yourself to become uncomfortable in any way. Increase the time you allow for the exercises a little each day.

Breathe:
(a) in through the nose—out through the nose.
(b) in through the mouth—out through the mouth.
(c) in through the mouth—out through the nose.
(d) in through the nose—out through the mouth.
Be aware of the sensation as it passes through your nose and mouth.

2. Once you have established full control in the exercises in above:
(a) Breathe in quickly and out slowly.
(b) Breathe in slowly and out quickly.
(c) Breathe in quickly and out slowly—holding the breath from time to time when expiring. The first time hold your breath only once and for a few seconds only. Then twice, then three times, etc. Each time hold your breath for a longer period.

3. Breathe in fully. Check for relaxation ensuring there is no unnecessary tension. Hold your breath for long as possible without discomfort.

Breathe out fully. Check for relaxation and hold breath for as long as possible.

Check both of these exercises with a watch with a second hand.

4. Stand easily and breathe deeply. Check your rib movements by placing your open hands on the sides of your ribs as you breathe. Your ribs should force your hands upwards and outwards. You can achieve considerable movement in this exercise. There should be enough movement to be readily discernable in a mirror and for you to feel easily. Get a friend to check the movement for you. (This exercise can usefully be performed in pairs—each holding the other's rib cage while checking on the movement during breathing.)

5. Lie down on your back and repeat the previous exercise.

6. Pant like a dog and check your muscle movement by placing your open hand just below your breastbone. Don't rush the exercise—try just a few pants at first. Later you should practise for longer.

(a) Breathe in and pant with the lungs full of air:
    (i) standing.
    (ii) lying down.
(b) Breathe out and pant:
    (i) standing.
    (ii) lying down.

Make sure you have full control over the panting. In particular, become aware of how much noise you make and how much you wish to make. Try the exercise making a lot of noise. Later repeat the exercise in absolute silence. Get a friend to help you check the muscle movements.

Warning: Do not overdo the exercises. Approach them with care and continuity. Try them gently and slowly at first. Progress your efforts with caution. Stop at any sign of discomfort.

CHAPTER EIGHT

VOICE AND SPEECH

Speech as the Basis of Living

Language is the basis of our civilization and even in these days of nearly total national literacy, **speech is still the most common and most telling form of language.** Speech is the basis of our everyday life and the form of communication to which we turn most readily and most often. We do not need to imagine being dumb to realize the significance of speech in our day-to-day lives. This significance is increasing every day as technical methods of reproducing the sound of the human voice take over many functions previously provided exclusively by the written word.

Contemporary psychologists maintain that language conditions, if not actually creates, our perception. Without language, they claim, we should live in an entirely different, unrecognizable world. Without speech, they further claim, we should be denied most of the everyday experiences we take for granted and easily express. While these views may appear to some to be extreme, there are few who will deny that words, especially when spoken, occupy a central position in our lives.

The Importance of Effective Speech

Good speech engages the interest of the listener straightaway. It often attracts listeners. It commands attention, not by shouting, ranting or rhetoric —these can soon become wearisome—but by simply being good speech. Furthermore, it can be easily understood. Good speech makes even the most complex concepts appear simple. It eases interpersonal relationships and understanding by its efficiency and courtesy. Listeners are always impressed when they know the speaker cares enough to take their needs into consideration.

No vocal mannerism or speech defect should interpose itself between speaker and listener. Any special consideration of style should have the express purpose of making meaning clearer. Style should support the content, making it more effective; it has no other purpose. There is no place for a voice which, no matter how beautiful, draws attention to itself. A style of speech or mouthing which is noticeable or remarkable is either ostentatious or indulgent. It defeats the proper purpose of good speech, which is **fluency of personal expression leading to growth of mutual understanding.** Any mannerism which siphons off the interest that should be focused on content is no aid to speaker or listener.

'It's not what you say, but the way that you say it' is a cliché, which, however naïve, contains an important truth. The style of speaking is the key to full understanding—and full understanding is the aim and purpose of good speech.

If these considerations are important and significant in the traffic of everyday life, they are crucial and quintessential to the actor's craft. No amount of panache, embellishment or pyrotechnics—even if superbly attractive in their own right—will serve him unless they are accurately and nicely put to service.

The Importance of Listening

Many functions and organisms go to make up the spoken word—breathing, voice production, articulation and the enabling body mechanisms. Perhaps transcending all of these, for the actor, is the ability to **listen with concentration and hear with understanding.** In the world at large, listening is often replaced by waiting to speak. One has only to watch the expressions on people's faces as they talk in a group to see this clearly in action. Many are listening merely to pounce upon the first opportunity to speak themselves. An actor needs to listen with more than average attention so that he can store up all he hears for future reference—the tiniest nuances as well as more dramatic, flamboyant styles. It might be said that an actor speaks as well as he hears and that he hears as well as he listens. In a sense he speaks with his ears. The more sensitively he listens, the more effective can be his speech.

Practical Approaches

Before you begin work on the exercises at the end of this chapter, accustom yourself to listening carefully to the way people use their voices. Take advantage of all the quiet opportunities you have to listen unobserved—in bus queues, supermarkets, hotels, restaurants, trains, etc.—and **listen without looking** at the people concerned. The way people look, the way they dress and use their bodies all help to create an impression of voice before a word has been spoken. Get used to isolating voices and drawing conclusions exclusively from what you hear.

Practise listening for different, distinct qualities. Listen for the way style is suited to content. Listen to how parents talk to their children and compare this with the way they talk with one another. A good place to try this is a supermarket cash-till queue where mothers are frequently involved in talking to children, friends and assistants at one and the same time. Listen to people ordering drinks at a bar and bus conductors asking for ticket money.

When you have tried listening in some of these situations and your ear is attuned to selecting conversation, become more discriminating. Pay special attention to the **volume and texture** of the voices. Pick out the differences in the way people use **pause.** Make a note of the times when you think the pauses were caused by shyness, lack of the right word or were used for deliberate effect. Listen for **variety in pitch and tune.** Listen for **changes in speed and rhythm.**

Generally, these qualities are combined with facial expression and body image to create an overall impression. Listen carefully so that you can isolate the individual characteristics as you hear them. Bring a new ear to the way you listen to the radio and telephone calls. After a concentrated session listening to voices on the radio, listen to television programmes with the picture turned off. This will help give an insight into the way we 'speak' with our bodies and often allow the voice to remain under-used.

Relaxation and Control

In the last chapter the major aim was to help you achieve relaxed and efficient control over breathing. Relaxed and efficient control over voice and speech is the aim of this chapter. There will be no attempt to encourage the assumption of a special voice or peculiar mouthings. Rather, the **growth of awareness of voice and speech and the journey towards maximum flexibility will be stressed.** Good breathing and the relaxation of all muscles not actually needed are basic essentials, and sensitive control makes for their effective use. For example, if the muscles are too relaxed, the voice will become breathy, rough and apparently hoarse; if they are too tense it will become thin, tight and strained. In either case it will not be easy to listen to and neither speaker nor listener will gain much pleasure from it. The human voice is such a marvellous instrument that its capabilities make even a Stradivarius seem coarse by comparison. Its use should be a joy and pleasure—combining efficiency and artistry in a satisfying whole.

The Vocal System

The full details of the component parts of the larynx, their function and the related complex muscular system are best left to a specialist. Interested students will be able to research for themselves in the anatomy sections of appropriate literature. Since we are concerned with the proper use of the organs of voice production and articulation it will be helpful, however, to know the basic facts.

Vocalization

The vocal cords, situated in the larynx, are the vibrating agents which actually produce the sound of the human voice. They are delicate muscles, covered with mucous membrane and run along the sides of the larynx from front to rear. Imagine the top of a bottle with a balloon stretched tightly over it with a slit across a diameter and you will have a rough idea of the lay-out. During breathing the two vibratory edges are kept apart. During inspiration they form a wide 'v' and during expiration a narrow one. When actually making voice—vocalizing or phonation—they are approximated and the breath passing through activates them. (The principle of causing sound-waves by using a vibrator will be well known to most readers. The plucking of an elastic band is one example and the comb and paper mouth organ is another.)

In the same way that the strings of a piano or a violin make different sounds dependent upon their length and tension, so do the vocal cords. The muscles controlling these cords can move them up or down, lengthen or shorten them, separate or bring them together and relax or tense them. These processes control the creation of sound and its pitch.

The more tense the vocal cords, the higher will be the pitch. More breath pressure will be needed to separate them, pass through and initiate the vibrations. A simple experiment with a rubber-band will substantiate this. The tighter the rubber-band is stretched, the more effort is needed to vibrate it.

Breath making the vocal cords vibrate will create the sound—the basic vocal tone—but two other processes must occur before it becomes fully developed speech. These processes are **resonation** and **articulation**.

Resonation

A tuning-fork when struck and allowed to vibrate freely makes little sound. If the base of the fork is placed upon a resonator—a table-top or a piece of stiff card on top of a tumbler—the sound is amplified and made easily accessible to the human ear. The human resonators are mainly the cavities in the mouth, nose and throat. The more available these cavities are made, the more the voice can be resonated. The effect of the closure of some of these, due to a cold for example, is well known.

Articulation

When the voice has been produced and satisfactorily amplified, it is treated and shaped to create the many different sounds that make up speech. This process is known as articulation and is achieved in the main by the lips, tongue and teeth. Without properly working organs of articulation it is impossible to create effective speech. Flexibility and control are the main qualities to aim for. Exercises for voice and speech set out to improve these qualities or to practise and make use of them.

The diagram opposite will help to make clear the functions of the main organs of voice and speech.

All speech sounds are divided into two categories: vowels and consonants. Vowels are sounds which continue. Their formation may be amended by the speech organs but their progress is unimpeded. Consonants are sounds created by the interruption of a vowel by the organs of articulation.

Vowels

There are three kinds of vowels.

Pure vowels are made by the speech organs remaining in the same position throughout the creation of the sound. These are called **monophthongs**. An example of a pure vowel sound is 'oh' as in **low** or **toe**.

Double vowels are made by the joining of two pure vowels. These are called **diphthongs**. An example is 'oi' as in **voice** or **moist**. The two pure vowel sounds combined are the 'aw' as in **port** and the short 'i' as in **sit**.

Triple vowels are made by joining three pure vowels. These are called triphthongs. An example is 'ure' as in **pure** or **cure**. The three vowels sounds combined are 'i' as in **sit**, 'o' as in **cook** and 'er' as in **herd**.

The main pure vowels are as follows:
1. **OO** as in **who**, you, do, too, shoe.
2. **OH** as in **so**, no, toe, snow, blow.
3. **AW** as in **talk**, walk, law, port, caught.
4. **AH** as in **far**, car, part, cart, shah.
5. **ER** as in **hurt**, curt, pert, bird, fern.
6. **AY** as in **fade**, mate, cake, state, gape.
7. **EEE** as in **feet**, peat, meat, sleep, tea.

The main pure vowels are all long. The other pure vowels are shorter. These **subordinate pure vowels** are as follows:
1. **oo** as in **book**, put, cook, took, could.
2. **o** as in **hot**, cot, got, pot, not.
3. **u** as in **cut**, truck, fun, gun, bud.
4. **a** as in **cat**, pat, sad, hack, mad.
5. **e** as in **set**, pet, men, then, let.
6. **i** as in **lip**, pip, pit, did, pin.

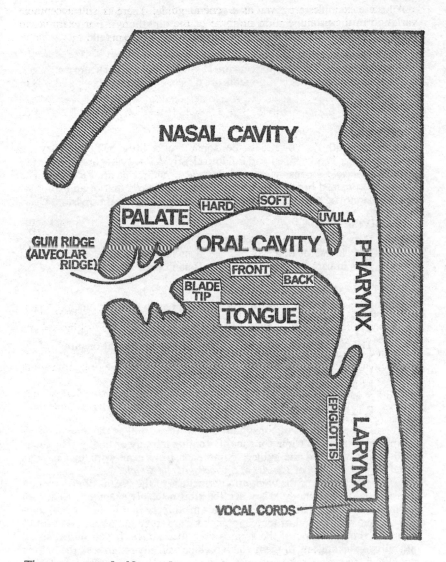

There are **seven double vowels:**

1. **air** as in **pair**. The components are **a** as in **pat** and **u** as in **cut**.
2. **ew** as in **dew**. The components are **i** as in **did** and **oo** as in **who**.
3. **I** as in **why**. The components are **u** as in **cut** and **i** as in **did**.
4. **ow** as in **how**. The components are **u** as in **cut** and **oo** as in **who**.
5. **oi** as in **boy**. The components are **AW** as in **talk** and **i** in **did**.
6. **ear** as in **fear**. The components are **i** as in **did** and **u** as in **cut**.
7. **oor** as in **poor**. The components are **oo** as in **book** and **u** as in **cut**.

All these examples are given as a general guide. There is still acceptable variation in the pronunciation of some of the diphthongs. For example, in number 5 above o as in hot is often preferred to the AW as in talk.

There are **three triple vowels**:

1. **ure** as in **cure**. The components are **i** as in **did**, **oo** as in **book** and **u** as in **cut**.
2. **our** as in **power**. The components are **u** as in **cut**, **oo** as in **book** and **u** as in **cut**.
3. **ire** as in **fire**. The components are **u** as in **cut**, **i** as in **did** and **u** as in **cut**.

Consonants

Compared with the vowels, the consonants offer little difficulty. They are easily recognized and defined and fall into clearly defined categories. There are **voiced** and **unvoiced** consonants and there are **continuants** amd **plosives**. The latter are so named because their major characteristic is that of an explosion and they cannot be continued. The following table will make the divisions clear.

PLOSIVES

Voiced:		Voiceless:	
D as in **dog** or god		**T** as in **toe** or hot.	
G as in **god** or dog		**K** as in **king** or pick.	
B as in **back** or cab		**P** as in **pack** or cap.	

CONTINUANTS

Voiced:		Voiceless:	
DJ as in **jaw** or budge		**CH** as in **chew** or much.	
Z as in **zebra** or buzz		**S** as in **see** or bus.	
ZH as in **measure** or closure		**SH** as in **shoe** or wish.	
TH as in **though** or with		**TH** as in **thought** or pith.	
V as in **very** or save		**F** as in **ferry** or safe.	
L as in **love** or all			
M as in **male** or lame			
N as in **nail** or lane			
R as in **Roger** or Harry			

There are other variants of consonant formation as well as the many combinations of double and triple consonants coming initially or finally. The interested reader will find the subject comprehensively dealt with in Chapters Seven, Eight and Nine of *The Art of Speaking Made Simple*.

Proper production of the voice and correct use of the organs of articulation are essential to everybody. **They are the vital machinery that makes speech possible.** It is what an actor does with this machinery that is the crucial question for him. At the end of the chapter there are some limbering exercises to help with the formation of the sounds described above. If you find unusual difficulty in tackling any of them you would be well advised to seek the help of a qualified teacher of voice and speech, since the rest of the exercises concentrate on helping you to use the machinery—your organs of voice production and articulation—in situations that relate to acting, rather than *in vacuo*.

Rhythm

Rhythm, like a gentleman, is probably more easily recognized than defined and manifestations of its presence or absence are universal and omnipresent. Rhythm surrounds us every minute of our lives. It influences us daily, monthly and annually through the movements of the universe and the changing pattern of day, night and the seasons. It is present in our cornflakes packets and our daily papers, the layout of motorways and supermarkets and in the movements of buses and football crowds. In individuals it is present in the sense of body image. It inhabits the whole range of body movement, from the total involvement of running or dancing to the detail of striking a match or filing a fingernail.

Rhythm is that flow and movement, or the appearance of flow and movement, sufficient and necessary to give a natural impression of life and vitality.

With expert dancers and athletes the **actuality** of the movement is obvious. In paintings and sculpture, trees and rock formations, it is the **appearance** only that informs the object with its rhythm.

In music, speech, song and dance, rhythm stems from the basic pulse of the heart. All four activities are extensions of abilities we need in order to survive as efficient animals. In their less sophisticated forms they enabled us to exist and continue existing as the human race.

In all animal life abnormality in rhythm draws attention to itself. Total lack of rhythm suggests complete weakness or death and over-active rhythm suggests lack of control—even panic. The natural result is the same in either case. The abnormality of rhythm marks its owner as an easy victim and invites attack from any nearby preying enemy. Even in the sophisticated life of a big city, an abnormality in the rhythm of personal movement draws attention to itself. It still suggests vulnerability, if only social.

Because of the continuing action of heart and lungs, everyone has an instinct for natural rhythm. Some may be more aware of it than others but it is present in every living soul. The instinct can be developed or allowed to lie dormant. The ability to improve the sense of rhythm lies within us all and is not, as many pundits claim, one of those things that you happen to have or not to have.

Time-beat, Pause and Climax

In effective voice and speech, the elements of rhythm are time-beat, pause and climax. The danger of attaching too much importance to the mechanical element of the first of these cannot be overstressed. Regularity of beat or stress is obviously significant in the creation of rhythm but the **regular repetition of a simple sound is no guarantee of vital flow.** Concentrate your attention on the pulsating beat of the heart action. Its inner charge of life will guide you well to the use of rhythm in effective speech. It is that rhythm, with its underlying pulse beat, that you should aim to echo in using your voice. The heart beat reflects the needs of the rest of the body and its regularity is affected accordingly.

The elements of time-beat, pause and climax as they combine to create rhythm in speech can be divided into two major parts: the **energy and strength** that go to create the volume of sound used and the **rate or speed** at which those sounds are delivered.

The strength or volume of the sound can be heard at work in two ways:

Accent

The variation of strength of volume within any word of more than one syllable. For example, **ea**sy, **di**fficult, im**po**ssible, **pro**bable, proba**bi**lity, **thea**tre, mu**ni**cipal. Most words have an accepted form of accent but there are some where variation is proper: **adult** or ad**ult**, **finance** or fin**ance**. There are those words where the stress varies from noun form to verb form. When used as a noun the accent falls on the first syllable and on the second when used as a verb. For example, **rebel** and re**bel**.

There are also those words which respond well to unusual accent or pronunciation, wringing a special emotive response from the listener: **lunatic** is usual, lu**natic** will startle; **leisure** is usual, lee**sure** will intrigue.

A comprehensive survey of the art and craft of pronunciation will be found in Chapter Eight of *The Art of Speaking Made Simple.* The examples quoted are sufficient to show the fertility of material available to an actor in the matter of the internal accents of words.

Whatever unorthodox pattern you may try out in training, rehearsal or performance you must be able to justify. An unorthodox interpretation, with unexpected accents, may succeed. It should be firmly based upon purposeful intent and not irrational whim or obsession with novelty.

Emphasis

Not only are there variations of stress within words themselves, but also within phrases and sentences. This kind of stress pattern has two functions: to make sentences **move easily and with a swing**; to give **additional meaning and emotive dynamic.**

A sentence needs an attractive stress pattern to make it easy to listen to. In the chapter on the senses, it was pointed out that they are particularly attuned to detecting *change*. An unstressed sentence will gain attention of neither ear nor owner.

Consider the following sentence: 'I know what you mean when you say you see red'. There are many possible stress patterns that will make it acceptable and comfortable to listen to but not bring a radical variation of meaning. For example:

'I **know** what you **mean** when you **say** you see **red**'.
'I **know** what you mean when you say you **see red**.'
'I **know** what **you mean** when you **say** you **see** red.'

Practise the sentence using equal stress on every word. You will discover how difficult it is to abolish stress (and also variation in pitch). You will discover how unnatural and unattractive the sentence sounds. When you say the three stressed sentences you will find you tend automatically to include a variation in pitch. The three examples do not radically change the meaning of the sentence. They merely make it easier to listen to.

Conscious changes in stress patterns are mainly used to create a particular meaning. Consider the following:

'I know you like your red shoes.'

A normal stress pattern for the sentence would be:

'I **know** you **like** your **red shoes**.'

Different stress patterns give a wide range of specific meaning. For example:

'**I** know you like your red shoes' (implication—the speaker knows but others may not).
'I **know** you like your red shoes' (special affirmation of speaker's knowledge)
'I know **you** like your red shoes' (listener may like them but others may not).
'I know you **like** your red shoes' (the listener's liking may not be sufficient justification for the situation).

'I know you like **your** red shoes' (but not necessarily the red shoes of others).
'I know you like your **red** shoes' (but not necessarily those of other colours).
'I know you like your red **shoes**' (but not necessarily other red garments or objects).

Spoken English is so flexible that the examples may be combined to give almost endless variations of subtle implications. The following is an extreme case of bending the meaning of a simple sentence in the combined use of stress and pitch:

'I **like** your book' spoken with a regular falling pitch through the sentence makes a direct statement of affirmation.

'I—**like** your **book**' with a rising inflection on the 'I' and a further rise in pitch for the following three words and a sharply rising inflection on the 'book' will suggest the exact opposite of the meaning of the written words.

Pause

The last example leads from stress in creating rhythm to timing. The pause between the 'I' and the 'like' has a distinct part to play. (Although something of the impact and meaning can be achieved without a pause.) The **length** and **amount** of pauses a speaker uses, govern, more than any other single factor, the rate of his delivery. It is true that the variation in the length of vowel sounds also affects the rate of delivery and this will be discussed later.

The pause is a most effective aid to speech communication. It has two main functions: to ensure the words are **properly audible and intelligible**: to increase their **emotional impact**.

Time must be allowed for an audience to assimilate words and digest their meaning and the length of pause will vary with circumstances. Many factors play a part: the mood of the audience; the size of the audience; the shape, size and acoustics of the hall and the natural pitch of the speaker's voice. Whatever the prevailing conditions, **a minimum pause is required between words and phrases if meaning is to be properly communicated—unless there are sufficient and necessary artistic reasons to justify a faster delivery.** Even so, such a pace should be used infrequently and with discretion. Whatever the initial impact, it is wrong to sustain such a pace since it will prevent comprehension. A fast gabble may make a dramatic, emotional point, but cannot convey intellectual content.

Practice in a few empty halls, with the help of a friend, will soon convince you of the need for this minimum length of pause. It will also help your awareness of your own optimum rate.

The use of a carefully considered pause before a word, **draws attention to that word and brings it into sharper focus.** It also adds **weight to the meaning** and **charge to the feeling** behind it. The best way to learn the power of the pause is to find out for yourself by introducing artificial pauses into otherwise normal conversation on informal occasions—at lunch-time, a sweet shop or a coffee bar.

This use of pause—the **exploitation of silence**—and the stillness that frequently accompanies it, is very personal. Many students will gabble incomprehensibly rather than allow themselves a single pause—as if the sound of the voice is a comfort and protection against the fears and anxieties of lack of confidence. (The same symptoms appear in movement. Many students will fiddle and fidget with fingers, clothes, cigarettes or the backs of chairs rather than suffer, *for them*, an ordeal of stillness.) The habit stems from nervousness and anxiety and can only be overcome through confidence. Trying out deliberate pauses of unusual and contrasting length as a conscious exercise can go a long way to convincing even the most apprehensive student that the pause actually works. Thinking of the pause as the power and presence of silence, rather than the mere absence of words, will more rapidly give command, mastery and understanding.

Before exposing yourself to comment from fellow students or actors, try using more pause in social, informal or domestic conversations. In these situations you will not have peers listening for your every word, breath and inflection. You will discover that the use of pauses of varied length, will not bore your listeners, but will help retain their interest. It is only another way of exploiting the sensitivity of the ear to change and reinforcing the impact of sensible sounds by contrasting silences.

When you have gained confidence by exploiting pauses in informal situations—perhaps with a friend who is also experimenting—you will feel more prepared to introduce them into the class or rehearsal situation.

Climax

There is a final contributory factor to the creation of effective rhythm—climax. Accent dealt with the internal pattern of sounds in words, and emphasis dealt with that pattern in phrases and sentences. Climax generally needs the span of a paragraph—to keep the same yardstick. By strict dictionary definition, climax means a **series of ascending steps** as in a ladder, but general usage gives it the particular meaning of the **last of such steps**—the final or the ultimate. Climax can be achieved by using an **ascending scale of pitch**, an **increase in volume** or an **accelerated rate of delivery**. Pitch, volume or rate can be separately stepped up to create climax, but it is more usual to find all three working in harness.

There are two basic methods: the first is to make the **rate of change uniform** until the steps can be no further extended—the physical resources of speaker and listener automatically delineating the limits; the second is to **increase the rate of change itself**.

The combinations and permutations of pitch, volume and rate, each or all with constant or accelerating rates of change, are endless. Increase your awareness of the mechanics of climax by isolating the elements and concentrating on them separately. It will not be easy. There is an automatic tendency for pitch to rise as volume or speed of delivery increases, and vice versa. The exercises at the end of the chapter will enable you to improve control over these elements separately and together.

(Most people, individually or in groups, have little difficulty in accelerating to a climatic point. There are few, however, who are able to control deceleration with as much exactitude. Practise by tapping on a table with your finger. Concentrate exclusively on the rate of declimax, ignoring any variation in volume.)

Vowel Elongation

The elements of rhythm—time-beat, pause and climax—have been outlined. Before moving on to a different aspect—tune—it is appropriate to consider the **special elongation of vowels**. Just as there are many speakers who, in their natural delivery, make full use of pause by drawing out the silences, so there are those who gain special effects by **dwelling unexpectedly on certain vowel sounds**. There can be few who are unaware of the following example: 'DAAAAAAAAHRling; I just LOOOOOOOOOved your thing.' This particular style is ostentatious and the type of speaker easily recognized, but the example highlights the possibilities of a less forced application. The method is an extension of the principle discussed under *Emphasis* above, but the lengths to which it can be properly taken justify special mention. Consider the following examples:

'Now here is a **real** example.'
'You must **try** to remember.'
'That's **far** enough'—and closely associated with this example,
'**Fair** enough' and '**All** right'.

The elongation of the vowel sound is a matter of personal taste. Some speakers dwell on them hardly more than the examples given under 'Emphasis'. Others pull them out to more than a second's duration. Try for yourself—in private at first and later on socio-domestic occasions. You will discover their purpose more fully through kinetic experience—the actual feel of the words in your mouth and the response of the rest of your body—than through any mental experiment or exercise.

Tune

Many of us are quite unaware of the tunes of speech we use in everyday life. I vividly remember working as a bus conductor and noticing the different ways passengers asked for their tickets. There were those who would use a **sharply falling inflection** when saying 'Threepenny, please'. The pitch would drop markedly from the opening syllable to the closing one, making the request sound like an order, even though the word 'please' was used. There were those who never used the word 'please', but because their voices had a **rising inflection** on the one word 'Threepenny' it was less of an order and more of a request—certainly more friendly. The study of the use of tune in the English language could occupy a lifetime. Even the most apparently monotonous speakers use a rich and complex systems of tunes. The analysis of these can be fascinating, if by no means easy. Fortunately, there are two main divisions of tune which help clarify an otherwise complex sound picture.

Falling Inflection

If the overall pattern of the change of pitch of the voice has a **falling inflection** it suggests **certainty and finality**. It suggests this in the context of the sentence or phrase—it also suggests it in the context of the relationship between speaker and listener. With its air of finality, a closing falling inflection is no encouragement to a listener to respond. Amiable discussion and free-ranging conversation with someone who constantly uses a falling inflection is almost impossible.

Rising Inflection

A regularly repeated tune will of course be boring. If the tune consists of a falling inflection the speaker will also appear to be rude and unfriendly. This is because we use an overall **rising inflection** when asking a question. A question implies an answer and an answer requires participation from the listener. The use of the rising inflection when asking questions colours its use in general conversation—even when not used to ask a question. It still leaves the impression there is a place for the listener to participate actively. The rising inflection does not always suggest there should be a direct response from the listener but it does create the possibility.

Natural Pitch and Inflection

A constant repetition of tune—the pattern of the pitch—is a boring embarrassment to everyone. It is not suggested you should make a conscious effort to include unnecessary rising inflections in your everyday speech. An awareness of the pitch of your voice—checked with a friend against a piano or a guitar at your normal speaking level—together with an ear for the way you are using it, will be a good first step in training. Nothing is more irritating to a listener or does more disservice to a speaker than the adoption of unnecessary and artificial tunes. This applies equally to acting, public speaking, private and social conversation.

You should begin your exercises and training from your natural pitch and your natural inflections. Gain complete awareness of them and grow slowly from them, increasing your range slowly but regularly. Your voice and speech habits are an integral part of your personality. It has taken you many years to achieve them. Do not try to change them overnight, nor to adopt features that are totally alien to you. The patterns you use are a result of the physical characteristics of your voice and speech organs, your present social and cultural background and the combined forces of family, school and friends in your early life. Your speech is you and you are your speech. Think carefully before making any major changes. Let **awareness and flexibility** be your aims rather than any set pattern no matter how 'ideal'.

Variations of Pitch and Inflection

Tune is created by varying the pitch of the voice and inflecting the variations. There are two major differences in the use of tune in speaking and singing. In singing the pitch changes in **steps according to a musical scale** and there is **little internal inflection in individual syllables**. In speaking, the pitch changes not by marked and definite steps, but **on a sliding scale**—in a gradual slope—and **internal inefiction in individual syllables is constantly used.**

Currently, the blurred edges between art forms have created a style that is neither speech nor song and can be used by actors and singers. Most of this work is still experimental. The broad divisions laid down here will apply for some time. For those interested in this no man's land of vocal experiment the work of the Freehold and the Traverse Theatre Company will often demonstrate its characteristics and is worth careful attention in any case. The compositions of Lucian Berio and the song style of Kathy Berberian are excellent examples of the common ground on the music side.

When a singer approaches a text there is a **tune clearly noted by the composer.** An actor has no such notation to instruct or guide him. He creates the tunes to be used and since the pitch can be anywhere on the gradual slope of his natural range, the choice is wide. An awareness of your natural pitch and style of inflection is the first requirement in increasing range and improving flexibility. Such an awareness will also help **prevent unnecessary excesses in** the early stages of training. In the interpretation of a text there are two important technical aspects. The first is the **level of pitch** selected as normal for the character. The second is the **quantity and range of inflection**—the inner variation—within that pitch. More is said later about how you might arrive at these decisions.

It is *artistically* important they should be sufficient and necessary to communicate your intention. It is important to you *personally* they should be well within your range at the time. **You must be sure you can sustain the pitch and inflections without mental or physical strain.** No matter how valid a particular manner of speech may be for the character, if you strain your voice in executing the style, you should reject it. If you have to concentrate hard to sustain the pitch and pattern your mental energy will be siphoned off and the overall effectiveness of your performance will be reduced. The nearer to your normal pitch and inflection you make your choice, the easier it will be for you to sustain.

Most people naturally change their pitch according to their emotional state. It is a very personal matter and there is no absolute law, but one or two pitch changes occur regularly enough to be noteworthy. In anger or intensity, pitch rises and in sympathy and sadness it falls. Part of the reason is to be found in physical causes. The body images appropriate and/or necessary to the expression or communication of anger are tense and animated. Tension naturally affects the speech organs and the pitch automatically rises. In sympathy or sadness there is a quieter, more relaxed kinetic state and the pitch consequently drops.

A careful study of the way people use pitch and tune in normal conversation will highlight these general principles. A similar study of singers in action—whether pop or grand opera—will afford excellent examples to train the ear, and demonstrate some of the principles regarding pitch. They should also provide amusing possibilities for personal exercises.

Accent and Dialect

Tune plays an important part in the creation of local accent and dialect. Not long ago there was a vogue of plays set in the West Country; more recently there has been a swing to the North.

It is difficult to make out a case for the necessity of assumed local accents or dialect—whether or not the script suggests them. **The more local accent is essentially necessary to the performance of a play the less is the play likely to have basic merit.** There are few good plays where the exactitudes of particular accent or dialect are essential. It is not important for Macbeth to have a Scottish accent nor is it necessary that Shakespeare's plays should be performed with the pronunciation and oratory for which they were created. The characters created by Tennessee Williams and Sean O'Casey have a life and significance of their own. In performance they carry the ring of truth and the stamp of drama without reference to local accent or place of origin.

The specifics of place and time are seldom so crucial that accent is needed to make the dramatic point. Most worthwhile plays transcend the trivia of local accent and dialect. There are few that explore or exploit its inner significance.

However, if you decide it is necessary to use an accent, whether from a part of Great Britain, another English-speaking country or a non-English-speaking country, the best method is to take your examples from source. Try to meet the people who naturally use the accent you wish to adopt. Listening to their total approach—vowel and rhythm patterns—is the best possible training. Failing this, there are many tape-recordings and records available. It may be possible for you to approach friends, colleagues or theatre enthusiasts in the appropriate area and have a recording specially made for you. **Whichever way you choose you should prepare yourself for hours of listening.** In this way you will stand the greatest chance of mastering the ethos of the accent and so avoid the snare of picking up an apparently symptomatic tune or vowel formation and allowing it to grow out of context.

Once the decision to use a local accent has been taken, it should be pursued with diligence and concentration. There is nothing worse than a local accent inaccurately rendered.

At one time theatres and drama schools adamantly insisted that all actors should speak 'Standard English' or 'Received Pronunciation'. Fortunately this narrow-minded view has been replaced by a more sensible insistence on a **voice that has strength and quality** and **speech that has flexibility.** No longer will an actor be refused a job or a student a diploma merely because he retains in his normal speech some of the sounds and patterns of his home environment.

Although social flexibility is increasing it is not yet easy to touch upon local accents when training students. There is still a backlog of value judgments regarding one accent being more acceptable than another—all thoughts of intelligibility apart—that make it wise to proceed cautiously. Films and television, however, have done a lot to relax the way in which people can begin to think about their own accent and dialect.

Using Tape-recorders and Friends

The voice is such a vivid reflection of the inner spirit that few of us can be totally objective about our voices. We approach our own speech habits with great sensitivity. It is this personal sensitivity that makes the training of voice and speech so different from, say, teaching typing or knitting. Failures in the latter do not build up tensions and inhibitions with such speed and intensity as can voice and speech work. The possession of a tape-recorder and the comments of a valued friend can help considerably in easing these problems.

Unless you can turn to a tape-recorder—preferably with the help of a friend—you will never gain a proper impression of the sound of your own voice as it is heard by other people. They hear the sound of your voice through **vibrations in the air.** You hear it through **vibrations in your head.** The difference between the two is so marked that many people reject the evidence of a tape-recorder when they first hear a playback of their own voices. Intellectually they may accept it as the sound of their voice but the unexpected nature of the sound makes it difficult to accept emotionally or psychologically.

The presence of a wise friend can vouch for the efficiency of any tape-recorder, and can help convince you how near the sound of your voice the playback actually is.

A friend can also help in another way. There are few occasions in the theatre when you will use your voice without being seen. What you do with your body while speaking not only affects the general reception a listener will give, it also directly affects what he hears and understands. A tape-recorder will reproduce the sounds—a perceptive friend will tell you something of the full impact of those sounds as a result of what he saw. There is a strong case to be made for 'hearing' with the eyes. What you see with your eyes will affect, not only your sense of hearing and the sounds the ears pick up, but also the meaning you perceive from those sounds. You have only to consider how you listen to someone whom, at first glance, you found physically unattractive to understand the nature of the forces at work. On many occasions the impact of your body image will be no more than marginal; it will, however, always be present. (Do not confuse this with movement and gesture. They inform on their own account. The issue here is concerned with the singular fact that your body image will, through the eyes of your audience, affect what they hear and how they receive it.) A tape-recorder, a reliable friend and a mirror will enable you to experiment with many of the exercises at the end of the chapter.

Importance of Relaxation and Enjoyment

In concluding these technical aspects of the training of voice and speech the importance of a relaxed approach cannot be over-stressed. Relaxation allows the voice and speech organs to work without strain and, therefore, effectively. Without relaxation, efforts to increase volume will lead to shouting and a reduction in the quality of the voice. A relaxed approach will also help you progress and develop from your natural style and resources without assuming or imposing affectations. Progress will come easily and without tension. You will develop the resources you have without straining to add unnatural qualities.

Above all, make sure you enjoy listening to the sound of the human voice. It is the most complex and flexible musical instrument you will ever possess. Listen to it in action. Listen to your own—not with the indulgent pride of possession—but with the sincere intention of affording your listeners the greatest possible courtesy and consideration. In this way you will improve your own techniques, your own enjoyment and that of your listeners at one and the same time.

Approaching a Text: Some Practical Examples

So far, this chapter has dealt with the technical aspects of voice and speech. Moreover, it has dealt with them as separate components. It is now time to consider how they combine and how that combination should be used to approach a text. It was suggested earlier that there is ample scope for wide choice in the way an actor uses his voice and speech organs. The choice is wide no matter the text, but every play contains within it stylistic elements which reduce the limits of choice. More will be said of stylistic elements in Chapters Ten to Thirteen. They are raised here since it is essential that any practising or exercising of voice and speech should be undertaken in the context of a total situation. Repetition of mechanical exercises unrelated to full experience may encourage a feeling that they have a life of their own. What is merely a means may become an end in itself.

There are many ways for an actor to approach the text. They are fully explored later. At this stage it is essential to bear in mind the style and content of the words as they are written—without reference to elements of character development and appreciation, movement patterns within the production, costume, make-up, etc.

All these are important in the growth of the play, the actor's attitude to his character; and the way the character speaks. What a character actually does in the course of the action will affect the voice and speech pattern the actor uses for the role as will what other characters say about him and to him. At this stage the main consideration is the training of the actor's voice and speech. Crucial to this is what he gains from the playwright's words as they jump from the page.

All texts give some indication of the way the words might be spoken. The better the text, the more it states its own needs and disciplines in unmistakable terms. Consider the following extracts and read them silently. Don't concentrate on intellectual meaning at first. Let the words flow through your mind as quickly as possible. Rather than inject your thoughts and feelings into the words, let the words work on you. Read through the passages silently and a sufficient number of times for their natural dynamic to come easily to you.

WAITING FOR GODOT
Samuel Beckett

LUCKY: Given the existence as uttered forth in the public
works of Puncher and Wattmann of a personal
God quaquaquaqua with white beard
quaquaquaqua outside time without extension
Who from the heights of divine apathia divine
athambia divine aphasia loves us dearly with some
exceptions for reasons unknown but time will tell

THE SPORT OF MY MAD MOTHER
Ann Jellicoe

PATTY: Take a section the size of a curler.
CALDARO, DODO AND FAK: Take a section the size of a curler.
PATTY: Thoroughly saturate with the lotion.
CALDARO, DODO AND FAK: Thoroughly saturate with the lotion.
PATTY: Fold an end paper over and under.
CALDARO, DODO AND FAK: Fold an end paper over and under.
PATTY: Wind it firmly to the root of the hair.
CALDARO, DODO AND FAK: Wind it firmly to the root of the hair.
CALDARO, DODO, PATTY AND FAK:
Take a section the size of a curler.
Thoroughly saturate with the lotion
Fold an end paper over and under
Wind it firmly to the root of the hair.
CALDARO: Again!
CALDARO, DODO, PATTY AND FAK:
Take a section the size of a curler
Thoroughly saturate with the lotion
Fold an end paper over and under.
Wind it firmly to the root of the hair.
Take a section.
Saturate.
Fold a paper.
Wind it firm.

THE SILVER TASSIE

Sean O'Casey

FIRST SOLDIER: Cold and wet and tir'd.
SECOND SOLDIER: Wet and tir'd and cold.
THIRD SOLDIER: Tir'd and cold and wet.
FOURTH SOLDIER: Twelve blasted hours of ammunition transport fatigue.
FIRST SOLDIER: Twelve weary hours.
SECOND SOLDIER: And wasting hours.
THIRD SOLDIER: And hot and heavy hours.
FIRST SOLDIER: Toiling and thinking to build the wall of force that blocks the way from here to home.
SECOND SOLDIER: Lifting shells.
THIRD SOLDIER: Carrying shells.
FOURTH SOLDIER: Piling shells.
FIRST SOLDIER: In the falling, pissing rine and whistling wind.
SECOND SOLDIER: The whistling wind and falling, drenching rain.
THIRD SOLDIER: The God-dam rain and blasted whistling wind.
FIRST SOLDIER: And the shirkers sife at home coil'd up at ease.
SECOND SOLDIER: Shells for us and pianos for them.
THIRD SOLDIER: Fur coats for them and winding-sheets for us.
FOURTH SOLDIER: Warm.
SECOND SOLDIER: And dry.
FIRST SOLDIER: An' 'appy.

(A slight pause)

BARNEY: An' they call it re-cu-per-at-ing!

THE TEMPEST

William Shakespeare

CALIBAN: All the infections that the Sun sucks up
From bogs, fens, flats, on Prosper fall, and make him
By inch-meal a disease: his spirits hear me,
And yet I needs must curse. But they'll nor pinch,
Fright me with urchin-shows, pitch me i'th' mire,
Nor lead me like a firebrand, in the dark
Out of my way, unless he bid 'em; but
For every trifle, are they set upon me,
Sometime like apes, that mow and chatter at me,
And after bite me: then like hedgehogs, which
Lie tumbling in my barefoot way, and mount
Their pricks at my footfall: sometime am I
All wound with adders, who with cloven tongues
Do hiss me into madness, Lo, now, lo!

BLITHE SPIRIT
Noël Coward

ELVIRA: Nobody but a monumental bore would have thought of having a honeymoon at Budleigh Salterton.

CHARLES: What's the matter with Budleigh Salterton?

ELVIRA: I was an eager young bride, Charles—I wanted glamour and music and romance. All I got was potted palms, seven hours a day on a damp golf course, and a three-piece orchestra playing 'Merrie England'.

CHARLES: It's a pity you didn't tell me so at the time.

ELVIRA: I did, but you wouldn't listen. That's why I went out on the moors that day with Captain Bracegirdle. I was desperate.

CHARLES: You swore to me that you'd gone over to see your aunt in Exmouth!

ELVIRA: It was the moors.

CHARLES: With Captain Bracegirdle?

ELVIRA: With Captain Bracegirdle.

CHARLES (*furiously*): I might have known it! What a fool I was—what a blind fool! Did he make love to you?

ELVIRA (*sucking her finger and regarding it thoughtfully*): Of course.

CHARLES: Oh, Elvira!

ELVIRA: Only very discreetly—he was in the cavalry, you know.

When you have done this and are well in sympathy with the words, whisper them to yourself a number of times. Then speak them aloud in whatever way they seem to you to come alive best. When you feel you have thoroughly mastered the peculiar style of each passage, try to impose that style on one of the others. You will discover incongruities and apparent impossibilities. You will also come across perhaps unexpected similarities and echoes. If you have succeeded in restraining yourself from intellectualizing and interpreting the extracts and they have **grown into a life of their own**, you will have experienced an essential quality any text offers. You will have discovered **how much of the work is already done for the actor by the writer**—when the job is done well. Suggestions of pitch, pace, volume and all their variations are **built into the words**. Provided the actor has a sensitive ear and a quick eye the words spring from the page and speak themselves. The words 'possess' the actor's mouth without conscious effort on his part.

There is a story of Samuel Beckett who, after a four-hour session with a director who was making little progress with play or players, could contain himself no longer. The director asked for his advice. Before making a symbolic exit from the rehearsal, Beckett replied: 'For Christ's sake—just say the bloody words.'

When the playwright has done his job well the hard initial grind is taken out of the actor's task. He is left with the challenge of progressing from a well-founded beginning position. He does not have to cast around in the hope that he might find one of his own. His efforts can be channelled into the art and craft of interpreting and communicating—not researching. An actor's job is to act. The easier the playwright makes it for him to get to that stage of the work the more the actor is likely to succeed.

EXERCISES
The exercises that follow are graded from simple experiments with separate components to complex explorations of texts. You are recommended to use the exercises regularly—preferably daily. Vary your choice and your approach but make sure you cover as many aspects as you reasonably can.

A wide range of exercises for voice and speech will be found in *The Art of Speaking Made Simple*. They can be used to advantage in conjunction with those below.

Rhythm
A. *With a Metronome*
If you do not have a metronome available, use a clock or a watch. Choose a beat within your present ability range—you will only become frustrated if you begin the exercises too fast. If you are using a wrist-watch—and the additional concentration required can only be beneficial—you may find it difficult at first to work with every beat. Begin by using one in four—then one in two and finally every beat.

Accompany the beat with the sounds described below—at first using each sound separately and later mixing them in any way you find interesting. Keep the work varied and complex so that you are constantly extending yourself but **begin slowly and increase your speed gradually.**

1. Finger clicking.
2. Toe tapping.
3. Hand clapping.
4. Heel clicking.
5. Exploding voiceless plosives. T P K
6. Exploding voiced plosives. D B G
7. 'Clacking' in the back of the mouth. Seal the blade of the tongue to the roof of the mouth. Create a vacuum by lowering the blade strongly. Finally explode the vacuum.
8. 'Bottle-cork-popping' with the tip of the tongue. Place the tip of the tongue ready in position to explode a 'T'. Curl the tip of the tongue up and back. Throw the tip forward at the same time opening the mouth as if to hurl a huge stone in an arc. Make the movement of the tongue tip as **strong as possible.** Use no voice and test the strength of the action by the loudness of the popping.
9. Tap with a finger-nail on table-top.
10. Tap with more than one finger-nail so that the sounds are regular but not simultaneous.
11. Words of one syllable.
12. Words of more than one syllable.
13. Short phrases.
14. Longer phrases.
15. 'Train noises'.
    (*a*) Click.
    (*b*) Clack.
    (*c*) Click-clack.
    (*d*) Clickety-clack.
    (*e*) Click-clackety.
    (*f*) Clickety-clackety.
    (*g*) Sh—Sh—Sh (Voiceless and sounded on incoming and outgoing breaths).

(*h*). Ff—Ff—Ff (Voiceless and sounded on incoming and outgoing breaths.)
(*i*). Himenanoosh.

When you are thoroughly accustomed to working on the beat, repeat the exercises using the *off beat* (the *silences* between the beats) but keep your work absolutely regular.

Repeat the exercises working **across** the beat. Work with the beat at first to establish, then:

   i. Speed up, leaving the beat behind, and then slow down to meet it again.
   ii. Slow down, letting the beat leave you behind, then speed up to catch it again.

B. *Without a Metronome*

Repeat the exercises in 'A' at speeds you find difficult, but still maintaining regularity.

Repeat working up to and down from climaxes of volume.

Repeat working up to and down from climaxes of speed. (You may find it helpful to use the following aids: a jumping bean allowed to rise from the horizontal to the vertical; a coin spun on a smooth surface; a glass marble, golf or other compressed ball bounced on a smooth surface. Use each of their rhythmic sounds or movements.)

Limbering

1. Put vowels and consonants together in patterns that appeal to you. (For example: **Mood, Mode, Maud,** or **Stish, Stush, Stesh, Stash.**) Make them into recurring sound patterns: first, with **little** internal vowel inflection—later, with **maximum** inflections. (For example: Give **Mood** 4 beats; **Mode** and **Maud** 1 beat *or* **Mood** and **Mode** 1 and **Maud** 6 beats).

(*a*) Repeat with different speeds. Finally as fast as possible.

(*b*) Sing and speak them up and down the scale.

(*c*) Sing and speak them to musical tunes you know well: top of the pops, nursery rhymes, TV advertising jingles, the classics and improvised tunes. Concentrate more on changes of pitch from vowel to vowel than on internal changes within the vowel. Be fully conscious of the artificiality of the tunes you use.

2. Pull faces with the aid of a mirror—concentrate on lips, tongue, cheeks and jaw.

3. Blow 'raspberries' in as many different ways as you can. Pay particular attention to the placing of the escaping air and the muscles you are using. Vary the tension in the muscles from minimum to maximum—but always make the noise.

4. Trill the tongue tip. Vary from minimum to maximum the tension in the muscles; the position of the jaw; the speed of the trilling; the volume of the sound; the position of the lips. Use with and without voice.

5. Similarly, make the lips vibrate and 'trill' by blowing air between them (like a horse). Use one or more fingers to help if needed. Vary as in the previous exercise.

6. With the aid of a mirror alternatively smile and pout. Ensure your lips are fully extended in each position. Make the changes slowly at first and later speed up as fast as you can. Vary the exercise by covering the teeth with the lips or baring them.

7. Whisper words, phrases and sentences. Try the exercises by yourself at first. Whisper:

(*a*) so that you alone can hear.
(*b*) across a table-top.
(*c*) to fill a small room.
(*d*) to fill a large room.
(*e*) to fill a hall or large stage.
(*f*) in the open air—with the above variations.

Work with a friend. Use the same pattern to develop strength and volume. Use real words and also make up your own. Insist on clarity. Listen carefully. You may find it helps to repeat your partner's whispers to check accuracy.

8. Use the following words and phrases. By varying the way you say them, give them as many different meanings as you can:

YES NO ME YOU I DO NOT KNOW PLEASE
THANK YOU I WILL I WON'T YOU WILL YOU WON'T
NEVER
HELLO GOOD-BYE SORRY I'M SORRY YOU'RE SORRY
SATURDAY TWO PINTS PLEASE I FEEL SO HAPPY
(Choose similar phrases of your own. Try them with a friend.)

Extend the range of variations by including chanting and plainsong. Create satirical styles by over inflecting and let them be the basis for a speaking voice. Use that voice to read aloud from a newspaper.

9. Experiment and practise daily with tongue twisters.
MIXED BISCUITS YELLOW LORRY/LEATHER—RED LORRY/
LEATHER
SIX THISTLES PROPER COPPER COFFEE POT CUP OF COCOA,
etc.

10. Repeat the following as quickly as possible without losing the sense: 'Jones, where Smith had had 'had had', had had 'had'; 'had had' had had the examiners' approval'.

Using a Tape-recorder

You will benefit considerably if you are able to use a tape-recorder in all the previous exercises—as a simple check on your work. The following exercises exploit the use of a tape-recorder and should offer some pleasant light relief.

1. *Backwards speech.* In its written form the backwards version of the word 'tap' is 'pat'. The change is quite a mild one. In its vocal form the change becomes extreme and complex.

The following exercise will require you to listen with great care and to use voice and speech organs in a new way. It can be difficult, frustrating and fascinating.

Choose a monosyllable that begins with a plosive—do, too, pea, car. Record your voice saying the word a number of times with as little variation as possible. (This saves you winding back again and again.) Reverse the tape and listen to the sound as it is played backwards. Practise the sound you hear. When you feel you have gone some way to mastering it, record it a number of times. Reverse the tape again and listen.

Be patient and do not try to go on to more complex sounds until you have become reasonably expert with the 'simple' ones.

2. *Half and double speeds.* Record your voice speaking one or two simple phrases and sentences. Play these over again and again at half or double speed until you are confident you have a clear memory image of the speed and pitch. Record your voice again. This time adopt the pitch and speed appropriate and then play it back at double or half-speed to counteract your variations and listen for your 'normal' voice. The more accurately you have rendered your recorded version, the less will you be able to detect any abnormality.

If you are going to speak at double speed you will need to record at double speed for 'normal' speech at normal playback.

3. *Disguises.* Make recordings in an assumed voice. Try to disguise your voice completely and check the result by playing back the recording to friends without telling them.

Attempt the impersonation of a radio or television news-reader's voice. Record it and check the quality of your impersonation against further broadcasts or recordings—or with your friends as above.

4. *Dialogue.* Hold conversation in which the characters—two or three—are all played by you. Use a text or improvise. Check with friends.

5. *Faults.* Use the tape-recorder to help you satirize your own speech idiosyncracies. Alternate emphasizing them with eradicating them. This will help you gain control over them. If you feel you have no idiosyncracy—check with friends or a teacher of voice and speech!

Special Speech and Voices

Using the full range of variables to create speech and voice, try the following as stimuli:

1. Create a voice and speech pattern for a character from a particular body position that catches your eye in a shop or the street. Use the body position to help you create appropriate speech.

Choose a painting; a photograph; a piece of sculpture; a piece of clothing—a hat, a shoe, a tie, etc.; a vegetable. Let a voice quality and a speech pattern emerge from the single object you have chosen.

2. Give voice qualities and speech patterns to everyday objects. Let them come alive and hold conversations. You play all the parts.

For example: chairs; tables; objects; toys; animals; chocolates. Use one of each variety from a selection of liquorice allsorts—let them each have a special voice and talk with one another.

3. Create your own languages. Let them vary from gentle adaptations of English to complete mumbo-jumbo-doodling with every kind of vocalization. Create a real character to go with each one.

4. Experiment with different types of 'computer' talk. Create simple and complex models and let them talk to one another.

Texts for Practice

The following extracts have been chosen because they contain that special, inner dynamic mentioned earlier in the chapter. Work by yourself at first and later with a friend. Make sure you are fully aware of the flow and movement of the words as you bring them into lively speech. Use all your resources and experiment with different interpretations. Discover the overall style and the details that help communicate the inner urgency and the external meaning. Tell yourself you have a listener who is constantly saying 'I know what he is saying. What does he mean?'

The first extract is given with some detailed suggestions. Use all or none at your discretion. They are not intended to be definitive, or comprehensive—merely starters.

LUTHER

John Osborne

TETZEL: Are you wondering who I am, or what I am? Is there anyone here among you, any small child, any cripple, or any sick idiot who hasn't heard of me, and doesn't know why I am here? No? Well, speak up then if there is? What, no one? Do you all know me then? Do you all know who I am? If it's true, it's very good, and just as it should be. Just as it should be, and no more than that! However, however—just in case—just in case, mind, there is one blind, maimed midget among you today who can't hear, I will open his ears and wash them out with sacred soap for him!

In the introduction to the scene the author says of TETZEL: 'He is splendidly equipped to be an ecclesiastical huckster, with alive, silver hair, the powerfully calculating voice, range and technique of a trained orator, the terrible, riveting charm of a dedicated professional able to winkle coppers out of the pockets of the poor and desperate.'

You will benefit most from the exercises if you **try them out loud straight away**. Wait until you have experienced the 'body feel' of the words before coming to a conclusion about any one style.

Pause and Speed

1. Speak the first two sentences as fast as you can, making no break between any of the words, or the sentences. Pause for a long time before the first 'No' and even longer before the second. Pause before continuing—for as long as you feel comfortable—and then speak slowly.

2. (*a*) Start at an average speed and accelerate until you are at peak speed for 'Do you all know who I am?' then decelerate to 'sacred soap for him!' Keep the progress to, and retreat from, the climax symmetrical.

(*b*) Reverse the procedure.

3. Take the following pauses as marked and note any differences in impact they help you achieve:

(*a*) 'Are you wondering . . . who I am, . . . or what I am? Is there . . . anyone here among you, . . . any . . . small child . . . any . . . cripple, . . . or any . . . sick . . . idiot . . . who hasn't heard of me, and . . . doesn't know . . . why I am here?'

(*b*) 'Are you wondering who I am, or . . . what I am? Is there anyone here among you, any small child, any cripple, or any . . . sick idiot who hasn't . . . heard of me and doesn't know . . . why I am here?'

(*c*) 'Are you wondering who . . . I am, or what . . . I am? Is there anyone . . . here among you . . . any small child, any cripple, or any sick idiot who hasn't heard of . . . me?'

Pitch

Repeat the exercises in 1, 2 and 3 above substituting variation in pitch for variation in speed.

Volume

Repeat the exercises substituting variations in volume.

Practise the passages with the **variations kept separate**—do not be trapped by allowing an increase in volume to affect your pitch or speed.

When you are satisfied you can control the separate elements as you wish, combine them in any way you like. Keep to the suggestions given for practice in the first instance, then vary at your own discretion.

Stress and Pronunciation

Take the words 'any small child' from the second sentence and without leaning heavily on the vowels, emphasize one more than the others: '**any** small child'—'any **small** child'—'any small **child**'.

Note the difference it makes in the context of the sentence as a whole.

Take the same words and vary them as follows: 'any **smaaaaaaall** child'— 'any small **cheeeeeild**'.

A later sentence: 'However, **hoooooooowever**—just in case' or 'Hoooooooo-owever, however—**juuuuuuuuuuuuust** in case—just in case, mind'. Again: 'just in case, mind, there is one **bliiiiiiiind** maimed, midget'. Try these examples out of context for practice and then try them in the full speech to assess their efficacy.

Follow a similar procedure with all the extracts. They will not all offer such a wide range of oratory—but they all contain their own special challenges and opportunities. Try them all—and leave them for a while as soon as they cease to be enjoyable.

LUTHER
John Osborne

TETZEL: Are you wondering who I am, or what I am? Is there anyone here among you, any small child, any cripple, or any sick idiot who hasn't heard of me, and doesn't know why I am here? No? No? Well speak up then if there is? What, no one? Do you all know me then? Do you all know who I am? If it's true it's very good, and just as it should be. However, however— just in case—just in case, mind, there is one blind, maimed midget among you today who can't hear, I will open his ears and wash them out with sacred soap for him! And, as for the rest of you. I know I can rely on you all to listen patiently while I instruct him. Is that right? Can I go on? I'm asking you, is that right, can I go on? I say 'can I go on'?

(Pause)

Thank you. And what is there to tell this blind, maimed midget who's down there somewhere among you? No, don't look round for him, you'll only scare him and then he'll lose his one great chance, and it's not likely to come again, or if it does come, maybe it'll be too late. Well, what's the good news on this bright day? What's the information you want? It's this! Who is this friar with his red cross? Who sent him, and what's he here for? Don't try to work it out for yourself because I'm going to tell you now, this very minute. I am John Tetzel, Dominican, inquisitor, sub-commissioner to the Archbishop of Mainz, and what I bring you is indulgences. Indulgences made by the red blood of Jesus Christ, and the red cross you see standing up here behind me is the standard of those who carry them. Look at it! Go on, look at it! What else do you see hanging from the red cross? Well, what do they look like? Why, it's the arms of his holiness, because why? Because it's him who sent me here. Yes, my friend, the Pope himself has sent me with indulgences for you! Fine, you say, but what are indulgences? And what are they to me? What are indulgences? They're only the most precious and noble of God's gifts to me, that's all they are! Before God, I tell you I wouldn't swap my privilege at this moment with that of St Peter in Heaven because I've already saved more souls with my indulgences than he could ever have done with all his sermons. You think that's bragging, do you? Well, listen a little more carefully, my friend, because this concerns you! Just look at it this way. For every mortal sin you commit, the Church says that after confession and contrition, you've got to do penance—either in this life or in purgatory—for seven years. Seven years! Right? Are you with me? Good. Now then, how many mortal sins are committed by you—by you—in a single day? Just think for one moment: in one single day of your life. Do you know the answer? Oh, not so much as one a day. Very well then, how many in a month? How many in six months? How many in a year? And how many in a whole lifetime? Yes, you needn't shuffle your feet—it doesn't bear thinking about, does it? You couldn't even add up all those years without a merchant's clerk to do it for you! Try and add up all the years of torment piling up! What about it? And isn't there anything you can do about this terrible situation you're in? Do you really want to know? Yes! There is something, and that something I have here with me now up here, letters, letters of indulgence. Hold up the letters so that every one can see them. Is there anyone so small he can't see? Look at them, all properly sealed, an indulgence in every envelope, and one of them can be yours to-day, now, before it's too late! Come on, come up as close as you like, you won't squash me so easily. Take a good look. There isn't any one sin so big that one of these letters can't remit it. I challenge any one here, any member of this audience, to present me a sin, anything, any kind of a sin, I don't care what it is, that I can't settle for him with one of these precious little envelopes. Why, if any one had ever offered violence to the blessed Virgin Mary, Mother of God, if he'd only pay up—as long as he paid up all he could— he'd find himself forgiven. You think I'm exaggerating? You do, do you? Well, I'm authorized to go even further than that. Not only am I empowered to give you these letters of pardon for the sins you've already committed. I can give you pardon for those sins you haven't even committed (*pause . . . then slowly*) but, which, however you intend to commit! But, you ask—and it's a fair question—but, you ask, why is our Holy Lord prepared to distribute such a rich grace to me? The answer, my friends, is all too simple. It's so that we can restore the ruined church of St Peter and St Paul in Rome! So that it won't have its equal anywhere in the world. This great church contains the bodies not only of the holy apostles Peter and Paul, but of a hundred thousand martyrs and no less than forty-six popes! To say nothing of the relics like St Veronica's handkerchief, the burning bush of Moses and the very rope with which Judas Iscariot hanged himself! But, alas, this fine old building is threatened with destruction and all these things with it, if a sufficient restoration fund isn't raised soon. (*With passionate irony*) . . . Will anyone dare to say that the cause is not a good one? (*Pause*) . . . Very well, and won't you, for as little as one quarter of a florin, my friend, buy yourself one of these letters, so that in the hour of death, the gate through which sinners enter the world of torment shall be closed against you, and the gate leading to the joy of paradise be flung open for you? And, remember this, these letters aren't just for the living but for the dead too. There can't be one amongst you who hasn't at least one dear one who has departed—and to who knows what? Why, these letters are for them too. It isn't even necessary to repent. So don't hold back, come forward, think of your dear ones, think of yourselves! For twelve groats, or whatever it is we think you can afford, you can rescue your father from agony and yourself from certain disaster. And if you only have the coat on your back to call your own, then strip it off, strip it off now so that you too can obtain grace. For remember: As soon as your money rattles in the box and the cash bell rings, the soul flies out of purgatory and sings! So, come on then. Get your money out! What is it then, have your wits flown away with your faith? Listen then, soon, I shall take down the cross, shut the gates of heaven, and put out the brightness of this sun of grace that shines on you here today.

(*He flings a large coin into the open strong box, where it rattles furiously.*)
The Lord our God reigns no longer. He has resigned all power to the Pope. In the name of the Father, and of the Son and of the Holy Ghost. Amen.
(*The sound of coins clattering like rain into a great coffer as the light fades.*)

THE IMPORTANCE OF BEING EARNEST
Oscar Wilde

LADY BRACKNELL: Well, I must say, Algernon, that I think it is high time that Mr Bunbury made up his mind whether he was going to live or to die. This shilly-shallying with the question is absurd. Nor do I in any way approve of the modern sympathy with invalids. I consider it morbid. Illness of any kind is hardly a thing to be encouraged in others. Health is the primary duty of life. I am always telling that to your poor uncle, but he never seems to take much notice . . . as far as any improvement in his ailment goes. I should be much obliged if you would ask Mr Bunbury, from me, to be kind enough not to have a relapse on Saturday, for I rely on you to arrange my music for me. It is my last reception, and one wants something that will encourage conversation, particularly at the end of the season when every one has practically said whatever they had to say, which, in most cases, was probably not much.

A PHOENIX TOO FREQUENT
Christopher Fry

(*An underground tomb, in darkness except for the very low light of an oil-lamp. Above ground the starlight shows a line of trees on which hang the bodies of several men. It also penetrates a gate and falls on to the first of the steps which descend into the darkness of the tomb.* DOTO *talks to herself in the dark.*)

DOTO: Nothing but the harmless day gone into black
  Is all the dark is. And so what's my trouble?
  Demons is so much wind. Are so much wind.
  I've plenty to fill my thoughts. All that I ask
  Is don't keep turning men over in my mind,
  Venerable Aphrodite. I've had my last one
  And thank you, I thank thee. He smelt of sour grass
  And was likeable. He collected ebony quoits.
              (*An owl hoots near at hand.*)
  O Zeus! O some god or other, where is the oil?
  Fire's from Prometheus. I thank thee. If I
  Mean to die I'd better see what I'm doing.

(*She fills the lamp with oil. The flame burns up brightly and shows* DYNAMENE,
beautiful and young, leaning asleep beside a bier.)
  Honestly, I would rather have to sleep
  With a bald bee-keeper who was wearing his boots
  Than spend more days fasting and thirsting and crying
  In a tomb. I shouldn't have said that. Pretend
  I didn't hear myself. But life and death
  Is cat and dog in this double-bed of a world.
  My master, my poor master, was a man
  Whose nose was as straight as a little buttress,
  And now he has taken it into Elysium
  Where it won't be noticed among all the other straightness.
              (*The owl cries again and wakens* DYNAMENE.)
  Oh, them owls. Those owls. It's woken her.

SERJEANT MUSGRAVE'S DANCE
John Arden

MUSGRAVE (*at the top of his passion*): By God, I hope I am! D'ye hear me, d'ye
  hear me, d'ye hear me—I'm the Queen of England's man, and I'm wearing
  her coat and I know her Book backwards. I'm Black Jack Musgrave, me,
  the hardest serjeant of the line—I work my life to bugle and drum, for
  eighteen years I fought for one flag only, salute it in the morning, can you
  haul it down at dark? The Last Post of a living life? Look—I'll show it to
  you all. And I'll dance for you beneath it—hoist up the flag, boy—up, up,
  up!
(ATTERCLIFFE *has nipped up the ladder, holding the rope. He loops the rope over
the cross-bar of the lamp-bracket, drops to the plinth again, flings open the lid of
the big box, and hauls on the rope.*)
(HURST *beats frantically on his drum. The rope is attached to the contents of the
box, and these are jerked up to the cross-bar and reveal themselves as an artic-
ulated skeleton dressed in a soldier's tunic and trousers, the rope noosed round
the neck. The People draw back in horror.* MUSGRAVE *begins to dance, waving
his rifle, his face contorted with demoniac fury.*)

MUSGRAVE (*as he dances, sings, with mounting emphasis*):
  Up he goes and no one knows
  How to bring him downwards

Dead man's feet
Over the street
Riding the roofs
And crying down your chimneys
Up he goes and no one knows
Who it was that rose him
But white and red
He waves his head
He sits on your back
And you'll never never lose him
Up he goes and no one knows
How to bring him downwards.

(*He breaks off at the climax of the song, and stands panting. The drum stops.*)

THE WOMEN AT THE TOMB
Michel de Ghelderode

Prefatory Note:
The manuscript of this play, written in 1928, bore the reference, 'A Play for Marionettes'. The author has deleted this indication so that the work is not thought reserved for wooden actors only—although there are certain expressions that belong to them in their own right, such as strange gestures as portrayed by the Flemish Primitives.

(*The house is empty. The door is open on to the street.*)

THE MIDWIFE: Let's go in here, woman. It's a house that's been abandoned, like so many this fatal day. The angry crowds are trampling women underfoot.

THE LAYER-OUT: This is a Christian's house, I'll bet. The Christians have dug holes in the countryside to hide in. Some are skulking in trees. What madness! The Son of God is dead, but his madness goes on. The ideas have been amputated, but the stumps are still alive. Are you the midwife? Yes, you are. Show your face. Good evening to you, woman, who help children out of the belly and wash them!

THE MIDWIFE: There's my face. You help old children to die and wash them. A lot need to die for you to be satisfied.

THE LAYER-OUT: True enough. For you, a lot of women need to swell up under the laughter of the moon.

THE MIDWIFE: Yes. Tonight I shall go from door to door. Women who were big will have been afraid. The mountain has cried out and the world has fallen into the depths of a vault. We've seen the moon making strange faces. The bellies of all these women will burst like a bomb, and, tell me, what fruits am I going to bring forth from them?

THE LAYER-OUT: I declare my night'll be as good as yours. The old dead have got up on their rotten legs. They'll have to be put back again—if they're found. In all decency they ought to be laid out afresh. Without counting the living in Jerusalem who will have dropped down dead with fright. Shut the door. To us, who are afraid of nothing, since we know where men come from and where they go to, to us, misfortune will bring forth good fortune, and this black Friday will be a golden Friday . . . (*Pause*) Woman, was Christ also born of a woman, in agony?

THE MIDWIFE: I don't know. Did he die as others die?
THE LAYER-OUT: I don't know. Who laid him out? The people in his band?
THE MIDWIFE: Nobody knows. Did you notice that all the women were out of
their wits?
THE LAYER-OUT: It's like that every time there are executions, when they see
the wounds. A lot of women'll be making love tonight.
THE MIDWIFE: Huh!... They were saying that when the graves opened, women
threw themselves at the revived corpses and hugged them. You'll see they'll
give birth to purple children.
THE LAYER-OUT: We're living in strange times. It's a huge piece of witchcraft.
THE MIDWIFE: Quiet! Someone's stopped in front of the house.

THE KNACK
Ann Jellicoe

TOM: What do you think of our . . .
NANCY: What?
TOM: Our piano: Do you like it? Our piano?
NANCY: What piano?
TOM: This piano.
NANCY: Piano?
TOM: Yes.
NANCY: That's not a piano.
TOM: Yes it is, it's a piano.
NANCY: It's a bed.
TOM: It's a piano, honest, listen: ping!
NANCY: It's a bed.
TOM: It's a piano, isn't it, Colin?
COLIN: Eh?
TOM: This is a piano.
COLIN: Piano?
TOM: Piano.
COLIN: Oh yes, a piano, Ping.
NANCY: It's a bed.
TOM (*using the edge of the bed as keyboard*): Ping (*high*) ping (*low*). Ping (*run-
ning his finger right down: glissando*) p-i-i-i-i-i-ng.
COLIN (*middle*): Ping.
NANCY: It's a bed.
TOM: Bechstein.
NANCY: Bechstein.
TOM (*high*) ping. (*medium high*) ping. (*medium low*) ping. (*low*) ping.
NANCY: It's a bed.
TOM (*1st 3 bars 'Blue Danube' starting low*): Ping ping ping ping ping.
NANCY: It's a bed.
COLIN: Rosewood.
TOM (*4th and 5th bars B.D.*):
ping ping
ping ping.
NANCY: It's a bed.

TOM (*6th, 7th and 8th bars B.D.*):
ping ping ping ping ping
ping ping.
COLIN (*taking over 9th bar*): ping ping.
TOM AND COLIN (*together playing chords in unison 10th–16th bars*):
ping ping ping ping ping
ping ping
ping ping
ping ping ping ping ping
ping ping.
NANCY (*tentative, taking over*): ping ping.
TOM AND COLIN (*gently encouraging* NANCY *who joins in*):
(17th, 18th and 19th bars B.C.)
ping ping ping ping ping
ping ping
ping ping
(*All three letting go with great rich chords*)
ping ping ping ping ping
ping ping
ping ping
ping ping ping ping ping
ping ping ping ping
ping ping ping ping
NANCY: ping
COLIN: ping
NANCY: ping
COLIN: ping
NANCY: ping
COLIN: plong
NANCY: plong
COLIN: plong plong
NANCY: ping plong
COLIN: plong
NANCY: ping
COLIN: ping
NANCY: plong
      (*Pause*)
COLIN: plong
      (*Pause*)
NANCY: plong
      (*Pause*)
COLIN: plong
TOLEN: Why be so childish about a bed?

Author's Note: All the above could be rearranged or improvised to suit different actors and different productions provided the sequence of events is clear:
(1) TOM and COLIN charm NANCY into entering into the game.
(2) TOM retires leaving COLIN and NANCY getting on rather well, a growing relationship which TOLEN interrupts.

ENDGAME
Samuel Beckett

(*Centre, in an armchair on castors, covered with an old sheet,* HAMM.
Motionless by the door, his eyes fixed on HAMM, CLOV. *Very red face.*
Brief tableau.
CLOV *goes and stands under window left. Stiff, staggering walk. He looks up at
window left. He turns and looks at window right. He goes and stands under window right. He looks up at window right. He turns and looks at window left. He
goes out, comes back immediately with a small step-ladder, carries it over and
sets it down under window left, gets up on it, draws back curtain. He gets down,
takes six steps (for example) towards window right, goes back for ladder, carries
it over and sets it down under window right, gets up on it, draws back curtain. He
gets down, takes three steps towards window left, goes back for ladder, carries
it over and sets it down under window left, gets up on it, looks out of window.
Brief laugh. He gets down, takes one step towards window right, goes back for
ladder, carries it over and sets it down under window right, gets up on it, looks
out of window. Brief laugh. He gets down, goes with ladder towards ashbins,
halts, turns, carries back ladder and sets it down under window right, goes to
ashbins, removes sheet covering them, folds it over his arm. He raises one lid,
stoops and looks into bin. Brief laugh. He closes lid. Same with other bin. He
goes to* HAMM, *removes sheet covering him, folds it over his arm. In a dressing-
gown, a stiff toque on his head, a large bloodstained handkerchief over his face,
a whistle hanging from his neck, a rug over his knees, thick socks on his feet,*
HAMM *seems to be asleep.* CLOV *looks him over. Brief laugh. He goes to door,
halts, turns towards auditorium.*)

CLOV (*fixed gaze, tonelessly*): Finished, it's finished, nearly finished, it must be
nearly finished. (*Pause*) Grain upon grain, one by one, and one day, suddenly, there's a heap, a little heap, the impossible heap. (*Pause*) I can't be
punished any more. (*Pause*) I'll go now to my kitchen, ten feet by ten feet
by ten feet, and wait for him to whistle me. (*Pause*) Nice dimensions, nice
proportions, I'll lean on the table, and look at the wall, and wait for him to
whistle me.

(*He remains a moment motionless, then goes out. He comes back immediately,
goes to window right, takes up the ladder and carries it out. Pause.* HAMM *stirs.
He yawns under the handkerchief. He removes the handkerchief from his face.
Very red face. Black glasses.*)

HAMM: Me—(*he yawns*)—to play. (*He holds the handkerchief spread out before
him*) Old stancher! (*He takes off his glasses, wipes his eyes, his face, the
glasses, puts them on again, folds the handkerchief and puts it neatly in the
breast-pocket of his dressing-gown. He clears his throat, joins the tips of his
fingers.*) Can there be misery—(*he yawns*)—loftier than mine? No doubt.
Formerly. But now? (*Pause*) My father? (*Pause*) My mother? (*Pause*) My
. . . dog? (*Pause*) Oh I am willing to believe they suffer as much as such
creatures can suffer. But does that mean their sufferings equal mine? No
doubt. (*Pause*) No, all is a—(*he yawns*)—absolute (*proudly*) the bigger a
man is the fuller he is. (*Pause. Gloomily*) And the emptier. (*He sniffs*) CLOV!
(*Pause*) No, alone. (*Pause*) What dreams! Those forests! (*Pause*) Enough,
it's time it ended, in the refuge too. (*Pause*) And yet I hesitate, I hesitate to
. . . to end. Yes, there it is, it's time it ended and yet I hesitate to—(*he

yawns)—to end. (*Yawns*). God I'm tired, I'd be better off in bed. (*He whistles. Enter* CLOV *immediately. He halts beside the chair.*) You pollute the air! (*Pause*) Get me ready, I'm going to bed.

CLOV: I've just got you up.

HAMM: And what of it?

CLOV: I can't be getting you up and putting you to bed every five minutes, I have things to do.

(*Pause*)

HAMM: Did you ever see my eyes?

CLOV: No.

HAMM: Did you never have the curiosity, while I was sleeping, to take off my glasses and look at my eyes?

CLOV: Pulling back the lids? (*Pause*) No.

HAMM: One of these days I'll show them to you. (*Pause*) It seems they've gone all white. (*Pause*) What time is it?

CLOV: The same as usual.

HAMM (*gesture towards window right*): Have you looked?

CLOV: Yes.

HAMM: Well?

CLOV: Zero.

HAMM: It'd need to rain.

CLOV: It won't rain.

(*Pause*)

HAMM: Apart from that, how do you feel?

CLOV: I don't complain.

HAMM: You feel normal?

CLOV (*irritably*): I tell you I don't complain!

HAMM: I feel a little queer. (*Pause*) Clov!

CLOV: Yes.

HAMM: Have you not had enough?

CLOV: Yes! (*Pause*) Of what?

HAMM: Of this . . . this . . . thing.

CLOV: I always had. (*Pause*) Not you?

HAMM (*gloomily*): Then there's no reason for it to change.

CLOV: It may end. (*Pause*) All life long the same questions, the same answers.

HAMM: Get me ready. (CLOV *does not move*) Go and get the sheet. (CLOV *does not move*) Clov!

CLOV: Yes.

HAMM: I'll give you nothing more to eat.

CLOV: Then we'll die.

HAMM: I'll give you just enough to keep you from dying. You'll be hungry all the time.

CLOV: Then we shan't die. (*Pause*) I'll go and get the sheet.

(*He goes towards the door.*)

HAMM: No! (CLOV *halts*) I'll give you one biscuit per day. (*Pause*) One and a half. (*Pause*) Why do you stay with me?

CLOV: Why do you keep me?

HAMM: There's no one else.

CLOV: There's nowhere else.

(*Pause*)

HAMM: You're leaving me all the same.
CLOV: I'm trying.
HAMM: You don't love me.
CLOV: No.
HAMM: You loved me once.
CLOV: Once!
HAMM: I've made you suffer too much. (*Pause*) Haven't I?
CLOV: It's not that.
HAMM (*shocked*): I haven't made you suffer too much?
CLOV: Yes!
HAMM (*relieved*): Ah you gave me a fright! (*Pause. Coldly*) Forgive me. (*Pause. Louder*) I said, Forgive me.
CLOV: I heard you. (*Pause*) Have you bled?
HAMM: Less. (*Pause*) Is it not time for my pain-killer?
CLOV: No.

(*Pause*)

HAMM: How are your eyes?
CLOV: Bad.
HAMM: How are your legs?
CLOV: Bad.
HAMM: But you can move.
CLOV: Yes.
HAMM (*violently*): Then move! (CLOV *goes to back wall, leans against it with his forehead and hands*) Where are you?
CLOV: Here.
HAMM: Come back! (CLOV *returns to his place beside the chair*) Where are you?
CLOV: Here.
HAMM: Why don't you kill me?
CLOV: I don't know the combination of the larder.

THE DUMB WAITER
Harold Pinter

BEN: Kaw!

(*He picks up the paper.*)

What about this? Listen to this!

(*He refers to the paper.*)

A man of eighty-seven wanted to cross the road. But there was a lot of traffic, see? He couldn't see how he was going to squeeze through. So he crawled under a lorry.
GUS: He what?
BEN: He crawled under a lorry. A stationary lorry.
GUS: No?
BEN: The lorry started and ran over him.
GUS: Go on!
BEN: That's what it says here.
GUS: Get away.
BEN: It's enough to make you want to puke, isn't it?
GUS: Who advised him to do a thing like that?
BEN: A man of eighty-seven crawling under a lorry!

GUS: It's unbelievable.

BEN: It's down here in black and white.

GUS: Incredible.

(*Silence.* GUS *shakes his head and exits.* BEN *lies back and reads. The lavatory chain is pulled once off left, but the lavatory does not flush.* BEN *whistles at an item in the paper.* GUS *re-enters.*)

GUS: I want to ask you something.

BEN: What are you doing out there?

GUS: Well, I was just . . .

BEN: What about the tea?

GUS: I'm just going to make it.

BEN: Well, go on, make it.

GUS: Yes, I will. (*He sits in a chair. Ruminatively*) He's laid on some very nice crockery this time, I'll say that. It's sort of striped. There's a white stripe.

(BEN *reads*)

It's very nice. I'll say that.

(BEN *turns the page*)

You know, sort of round the cup. Round the rim. All the rest of it's black, you see. Then the saucer's black, except for right in the middle, where the cup goes, where it's white.

(BEN *reads*)

Then the plates are the same, you see. Only they've got a black stripe—the plates—right across the middle. Yes, I'm quite taken with the crockery.

BEN (*still reading*): What do you want plates for? You're not going to eat.

GUS: I've brought a few biscuits.

BEN: Well, you'd better eat them quick.

GUS: I always bring a few biscuits. Or a pie. You know I can't drink tea without anything to eat.

BEN: Well, make the tea then, will you? Time's getting on.

(GUS *brings out the flattened cigarette packet and examines it.*)

GUS: You got any cigarettes? I think I've run out.

(*He throws the packet high up and leans forward to catch it.*)

I hope it won't be a long job, this one.

(*Aiming carefully, he flips the packet under his bed*)

Oh, I wanted to ask you something.

BEN (*slamming his paper down*): Kaw!

GUS: What's that?

BEN: A child of eight killed a cat!

GUS: Get away.

BEN: It's a fact. What about that, eh? A child of eight killing a cat!

GUS: How did he do it?

BEN: It was a girl.

GUS: How did she do it?

BEN: She . . .

(*He picks up the paper and studies it.*)

It doesn't say.

GUS: Why not?

BEN: Wait a minute. It just says—Her brother, aged eleven, viewed the incident from the toolshed.

GUS: Go on!

BEN: That's bloody ridiculous.

(*Pause*)

GUS: I bet he did it.

BEN: Who?

GUS: The brother.

BEN: I think you're right.

(*Pause*)

(*Slamming down the paper*) What about that, eh? A kid of eleven killing a cat and blaming it on his little sister of eight! It's enough to . . .

(*He breaks off in disgust and seizes the paper.*)

'WOMAN—ANGEL OF . . .?'
Derek Bowskill

BATHSHEBA: I was a woman.
A woman taken.
A woman taken in adultery.

No, don't smile. Don't snigger.
I know to-day, and in this place
It's difficult not to be taken in adultery.
It's difficult not to be taken.
Difficult not to take.
In fact, adultery as a concept
(*There's clever*)
Seems not to exist.
But for me it did.
And I was taken in it.
You may ask me why.
(Yes. Go on. Ask me why)

Well.
You see.
It was like this.
Those two men over there—
Boxers; wrestlers; film stars; heroes; champions;
Were engaged, as they say, in mortal combat.
Being a woman, though not even there,
I knew they were fighting over me.
No. That's not quite right, is it?
Doesn't fit the image.
They were struggling for my favours.
No. Still not quite right.
Ah! Got it.
Antagonist and Protagonist laboured for possession.
Neither of them said it.
In fact, it is more than likely that neither of them knew it.
Both thought they were defending a righteous cause.
Fighting on the side of Justice.
Battling for Peace.

David was splendidly clever, splendidly clever.
And Goliath was—just—huge.
I Bathsheba,
Who wasn't even there,
Knew their urgent, inner need,
Saw the image in their mind
And sensed my obligation
To the man.

When such a man
First
Dreams your image
Then
Sees you naked
Then
Calls you up
Calls you
Calls.
What can you do.
But answer.
Be taken, as I was,
In adultery.

Everyone objected at the time.
Especially thingy,
The Hittite,
. . . My husband.
Also all the priests; the army; friends at court; relatives; wives; mistresses;
call girls; mothers; virgins—the lot.
As well as every single do-gooder; righteous hypocrite; scandal-monger,
bitch and moralising bastard in the area.
But I soon put a stop to it all.
I made, for me, a very rare public appearance, and explained the whole area
of my vision, their dreams, and everything.
They listened and understood.
David even brought the army.
They understood.
And that helped everyone.
Before that I was a woman
Taken in adultery.
Now it's much nicer.
Now I am
Just
Bathsheba.

SALOME: He saw me first.
He looked at me. He looked at me.
Well I wasn't having that.
He said, more or less,
'Come and be saved.'
Well I wasn't having that either.
He called me a lost of nasty names

Said ever such rude things
Said I was a tart
Accused me of immoral conduct:
And me a vestal virgin.
Well I wasn't having that.

But most of all
He looked at me.
I said to him once
'Whatcha looking at me for?
What have I done?'
And he wouldn't even answer.
Just looked.

I knew what he was thinking.
Knew what he was after all the time.
He'd just stand there.
His eyes boring straight into you
Undressing you.
If I hadn't known what he was after
I would have sworn he was trying to see into my head.
See what I was thinking.
Well, I wasn't having that.
So I said to our Mum
—and she'd seen him at it—
'Let's give him a lesson'.
And we did.
Mum and me knew how to get round Dad.
Well I did anyway
'Cos he wasn't my real Dad
And he fancied me.
He was well past it
But wouldn't give up trying
Anyway, you could see it from
That look in his eye.
That look.
Yeah—well where was I.

Ah. Round about that time I had a part-time job at the temple.
I used to dance a bit. You know.
The official hand-out said
'The function of the temple dancer, is to crystallise in poetic movement the
ecstasies of the devotees and to precipitate in them the wish to celebrate, with
an appropriate vestal, the final rites of spiritual and religious communion
through the expressed reflection of divine physical union.'
Well that's what it was—wasn't it?
So—
I did my dancing bit
Till the old man didn't know whether he was
Coming or going.

I was just about ready to pop the question
When Mum blows her top
and says she wants his
Head on a plate
No. Serious.
That's what she said
'Head on a bloody plate.'
Bloody plate indeed.
I gave up . . .
She was stoned;
And the old man was slobbering
The priests had had enough
And the guards went berserk.

The next thing I knew,
There it was.
'Head on a bloody plate.'
An' him still looking.
Even then he saw me first
Looked at me.
Looked at me.
And then the strangest thing of all
It seemed like everyone had gone
Except me
And him
And him still looking.
Now don't get me wrong.
I'm not hysterical
I've been around
Bit of a flirt
One of the boys
I know what's what.
And I know what happened
Couldn't have happened.
And I know it did.
He looked at me.
He looked at me.
And I had a hole in my head.
He looked at me
Till I kissed him
Till I kissed him.
Suddenly it didn't matter any more.
It was all over.
There had been just one more execution
That was all.
But
He looked at me
Till I kissed him.
Till I kissed him.
Well. I wasn't having that.

CHAPTER NINE

BODY AND MOVEMENT

'What Shall I Do With My Hands?'

'What shall I do with my hands?' or 'Where shall I put my feet?' are thoughts that occupy many actors—experienced and inexperienced alike. Sometimes the anxiety they cause is so deep that the thoughts and questions are put into words. They are not easy for the director to answer.

It is easy to be cynically critical of those actors who feel the kind of inadequacy that leads to these questions. It is much more difficult to help them. Their apparently simple questions are often disguises for real cries of help. This chapter will not show you what to do with your hands nor will it tell you where to put your feet. It will, however, make some suggestions that should eliminate the need to ask the questions. **Bodily movement is the basis of all that has gone before—breathing, speaking, imagining, concentrating.** None of these can occur without the sufficient and necessary body movement that on the one hand sustains life and on the other creates the activities themselves. The movement concerned may be almost imperceptible to the naked eye but while there is life there is movement supporting it.

Rhythm

In the previous chapter rhythm was described as 'that flow and movement, or the appearance of flow and movement, sufficient and necessary to give a natural impression of life and vitality'. Whether the body is in motion or at rest it should have its essential peculiar rhythm. Without rhythm the body will appear when in motion to consist of disparate parts. There will be no underlying unity to the diversity of action and the movements will draw attention to themselves. Without rhythm the body will appear when not in motion to be completely without potential. It will contain no suggestion of latent energy or dynamic at rest—it will appear to be exhausted or dead. In either case the lack of rhythm will attract attention and suggest a weakness of one kind or another.

It is this lack of rhythm that so firmly stamps the dying animal or a human corpse. In the one, the movements often contain an element of panic or hysteria and in the other, what otherwise might be a living body at rest is seen to be merely still.

Balance

For the body to have rhythm whether in motion or at rest it must also have balance. If you watch one of your friends trying to stand on one leg, with eyes closed and a book on his head, you will soon see the spasmodic movements that indicate a lack of balance. Travelling in a tube train or descending the stairs of a double-decker bus while it is travelling will demonstrate the body's natural response to any sense of imbalance.

The ordinary act of walking shows clearly how the body organizes its parts to ensure a good balance encourages proper rhythm. Walking naturally, you will counteract any imbalance created when moving your left leg forward by automatically moving your right arm forward. This natural opposition works in the same way as a pair of scales. To retain a state of balance, any movement needs to be countered by one which is equal and opposite. Try walking with your right leg and right arm moving forward together. You will notice the way the body tends to resist. It moves, turns and sways to compensate for the lack of balance otherwise created.

A proper combination of rhythm and balance in the body clearly shows that it has a capacity for sustaining the condition—be it in motion or at rest. It shows the capability of change and a readiness to respond. There is an ever-present statement of energy and a promise of continuity about good body movement. Its qualities are essentially plastic and mobile. There is nothing rigid, spasmodic or mechanical. These qualities all combine in the ideal for which a good actor is constantly searching—**economy of action and grace of execution.**

Beginnings—Middles—Ends

As the previous chapter pointed out, rhythm is not the same as time-beat. Calculated steps, measures, pauses and beats have a large part to play in the creation of rhythm and they are susceptible of analysis. Whatever the nature of the movement or gesture, or the quality of rhythm it possesses, it is possible to break it down into phrases which have important and identifiable stages—simple though they may be; beginning—middle—end. You must choose for yourself a suitably calibrated measure. It will help to consider the following sequence:

A Practical Example

Typing a letter. It is possible to claim that full rhythm ought to take note of the original motivating moment behind the action. Since it would be difficult—some philosophers claiming it impossible—to diagnose such a moment with any certainty, the following examples are contained within limits appropriate to stage work.

Phrase 1: Enter the room—move to the desk—sit down—prepare typewriter and paper—type letter—tidy up—stand—move to the door—leave the room.
Phrase 2: Only those actions at the desk.
Phrase 3: The actual typing of the letter.
Phrase 4: The typing of a sentence.
Phrase 5: The typing of a word.
Phrase 6: The typing of an individual letter.

With all these phrases there is a natural beginning, middle and end. A proper measure will be able to accommodate all the examples since any particular phrase may need to be played with a special rhythm to gain a special effect. For example, the whole scene may need to be rushed. It may need to be played as a long, drawn out laborious process all the way through. It may be necessary to play the scene very fast except for the actual typing of the letter. The build-up to the letter may be slow and the actual execution of the letter fast. The variations will depend upon the need of the scene.

Prime Phrases of Movement

Since the build-up of any large-scale phrase of rhythm depends upon the smaller constituent phrases it is necessary to find a measure for the smallest significant phrase. Phrase 6 is relevant in this circumstance and is defined here as a **prime movement** (or **prime phrase of movement**) since it can be broken down no further in terms of meaningful gesture for communication. **It is the way these prime phrases of movement are put together that creates rhythm.**

There are many methods of striking the keys of a typewriter but they have in common the *approximation* of a finger to a key; the *application* of pressure and the *release* of pressure. In the context of Phrase 6 these may be looked upon as the beginning, middle and end of the phrase. Every action can be broken down into similar units but the prime phrase is not always as clearly divided into distinct parts as with this particular example. Consider striking a match; combing the hair; tying a shoelace; and sitting down or standing up. These are all examples where the beginnings, middles and ends have lines of demarcation which are blurred even to the most perceptive observer of movement.

It is most important for an actor to be aware of the prime movement phrases of every action he makes—and its division into the three main subunits. A good rhythm will be created when the time-span for the prime phrase has been properly chosen and the **relationship between the end of one phrase and the beginning of the next is right.** It has been claimed that the Post-Office Tower could be brought to the ground by shooting at it peas from a peashooter—if the rhythm were right.

In the theatre, the signs of incorrect rhythm are easily detected. If the end of a prime phrase is not immediately taken up by the beginning of another the audience will become bored and lethargic, if on the other hand the beginning of a prime phrase overlaps the end of the preceding one the audience will become tense and restless.

This question of rhythm and timing affects an audience mainly through two of its senses—sight and hearing. Chapter Ten deals with the subject from the point of the text and its speaking. The point to be made here is that in any audience there will be roughly fifty-fifty division between those who are audiles and those who are visiles. Audiles are more receptive to what they hear and visiles to what they see. At any one time it is essential to have a proper relationship between spoken word and body movement. This is essential not only in the overall pattern of sensibility and motivation but also in the inner pattern of prime phrases.

Awareness—Economy and Grace

Very few people spend much time consciously organizing their rhythm of movement or speech. They rely on their natural patterns and use them unconsciously. In the organized microcosm of the stage an actor must be keenly aware of the rhythm he is using and its effect upon his audience. It will not however be necessary for him to analyse in complete detail every single movement he makes throughout the performance. A careful and probing analysis of crucial moments will enable him to create the general rhythm within which he will work. (This particularly applies to study of the text—see Chapter Ten). He will then more readily achieve that economy of action and grace of execution which is the stamp of a good actor.

Good posture, correct breathing and the proper exercise of muscular tensions and relaxation are essential if an actor is to achieve economy. A body that will perform reliably, flexibly and apparently without effort is essential if he is to achieve grace. Economy and grace will never be realized without **control and flexibility.** They are important in everyday life—to an actor they are crucial.

The Need to Look

In Chapter Eight it was made clear that one of the greatest aids to effective speech was sensitive hearing and accurate listening. In a similar way an actor's eyes help him gain a deep understanding of the part the body plays in expression and communication. There is much to be gained merely by **looking for and seeing** the way people use their bodies—hands, feet, spine, shoulders; sitting, standing, walking, running or lying down. **Being aware of** looking, touching and being touched are as essential to good movement training as hearing and listening were to speech.

Look around you in shops and restaurants and see how people use their bodies to communicate. Some have a wide range of movement, gesture and facial expression. Some have a very narrow one. Some use a lot of movement and some use hardly any. While you are noticing the way people use their hands and faces to help them relate, remember the real test for any movement or gesture is **what happens as a result of it.** Take special note of the responses the person speaking gains as a result of his movement and gesture. Notice how useful and appropriate the movement is; how much is wasted; how many opportunities are seized and how many lost. In particular watch out for those displacement activities that are used in times of stress or minor emotional discomfort—fiddling with a cigarette, a tea-cup, clothing or hair. Notice how often the hands are used to bolster up a flagging confidence—not to help the speaker make a point but to create a world of security for himself.

Body Image

The body speaks its own language long before it is close enough for anyone to see the details mentioned in the last paragraph. Think of the impression you receive from a first sight of a man on a bike—a woman in a passing train— the driver of a car well in front. Many relationships are formed and sometimes continued as a result of that first body image—the general impression received from the way a person walks, stands or sits. The tilt to the head; the angle of the shoulders; the way the elbows are held in or out; the line of the knees when walking—all these create powerful statements. Statements which inform with an impact greatly exceeding the sum of their parts. Just as in rhythm there appears to be an indefinable something which defies final analysis so is there with body image. **The total impression transcends a mere addition of the components.**

Body Feel

Not only does body image have an impact for onlookers, it also affects the individual himself. The experience may be defined as 'body feel'.

No matter what the activity, each individual has appropriate body positions for it. Positions in which he feels good. Positions which help the role being played or the activity being performed by providing the individual concerned with a measure of support and a feeling of satisfaction. Some people are so inflexible in their attitudes to their body images that they can only read or concentrate, listen or knit if they arrange their body in certain, particular ways. The chosen position will of course be closely related to what is physically comfortable for the task in hand—but affecting it deeply will be the **emotional overtone of the suitability of the feel to the person concerned**. In some it is not highly developed, but with others it is more important than clothing. In the wrong position—something as slight as the height of a seat from the ground being half an inch out—they will feel as uncomfortable as if they were undressed or dressed in embarrassing clothing.

Body image and body feel are important in all areas of personal experience expression and communication. They are more important than would appear possible in a society which does little to educate them. To realize their efficiency and impact you have only to consider how, on first sight of an old friend, memories will flood the mind at the stimulus of no more than the way you see him hold his hand—or, in the distance, the way one arm swings a fraction more than the other.

Consider the difference in relationships between two people, one of whom is standing and the other sitting; or one is standing tall and straight and the other small and bent; or one who actively gestures and one who is quite passive. Without a word being spoken the basis of relating and communicating is deeply effected. When the positions change the body image and body feel change with them. So will the basis of relating and communicating.

It is typically British not to be aware of body image and body feel in spite of their importance in personal relationships and interpersonal communications. Touching people is still suspect in Britain even in an age of slightly relaxed conventions. 'Do not touch' is not only a warning notice for dangerous machinery—it is also a way of life. For human animals spending the first nine months of their life in the closest touch with another human being, this offers a real challenge.

Self-awareness or Self-consciousness?

There is for some a tendency to believe that awareness of body image and body feel leads automatically to inhibited self-consciousness. It is not a serious risk. It is one that must be taken unless you are content to take the greater risk of failing to communicate real intent, thoughts and feelings.

For example, walking through a doorway. There are many ways of walking through and equally as many positions of arrival once through it. Inside the room there may be friends—a particular friend—an interviewing board—your superior at work in a critical frame of mind—a nervous child. Whatever the situation, the body image you present and the body feel you experience will directly affect the relationships created for at least a number of minutes— possibly much much longer. The body image itself may have appeared for a matter of seconds at the most, perhaps not even as long as a single second. Since body image and body feel can make such a significant impact with such force it seems logical to improve ones awareness of it. For an actor in training the logic is indisputable and attractive.

'Everyone Loves to Dance'

The typically British attitude to body awareness casts its grey cloud over body movement itself. It is still not the done thing to express feelings freely by movement or dance—in spite of the fact that, inside, everyone loves to dance. Movement and dance were probably the first forms of man's expression. They were certainly the first forms of artistic expression—the theatre of movement, dance and rituals.

I remember being taken into the hall of a primary school and being asked to look at a 'movement' class. One small girl was not responding to the sounds of drum and cymbal as the teacher thought proper: 'She can't; never will, that one. Nothing I can do will get her to move properly.'

What interested me about this judgment was that, only fifteen minutes earlier, the girl had been filled with all the enthusiasm of showing her birthday presents to her teacher in the classroom. At that time she had been alive and bubbling with significant movement. She had wanted to tell the teacher about her birthday doll. To express her excitement she had been twisting the hem of her dress in what I can only describe as a finger dance of pure joy. Unfortunately the teacher had not seen it that way and had told the girl to 'Keep still' and 'Stand still' so many times that in the end the child gave up and retreated to her place.

Her finger dance to her birthday doll was meaningful and necessary. Its implications were unnoticed by the teacher. The movement class in no way related to the child's condition. It was hardly surprising that the child was hesitant and anxious in expressing her feelings in 'dance'.

Personal Style

The urge to dance—even the wish—is in all of us. There are few in whom it is encouraged and fostered. There are even fewer who are offered the best kind of encouragement—the development of their own personal style of movement and dance. Most children who show any ability in dance or enjoyment of movement are too often rushed off to the fond embrace of a dance teacher who will probably insist, far too early, on the rigid instruction of ballet techniques.

A personal style of movement and dance gives a secure platform of confidence from which an individual can jump with safety into exploration, innovation and a search for flexibility. The introduction of techniques too soon will not only cramp style but may well kill all enthusiasm and enjoyment.

In the sense that any series of conscious movements expressing a state of thought or feeling is dance, an actor needs to be a dancer. He may not need a classical style and he may not wish for the services of a choreographer, but his movement will grow into dance. At the extreme, in the same way as some plays need actors' voices to grow from speech into song and there exists a no-man's-land between singing and speaking, so do others require actors' movements to grow into dance, and there is an equal no-man's-land between dancing and moving. Whenever the joys and fear of the human condition are expressed in movement a symbolic quality tends to emerge. As result of this, dance grows.

Each of the extracts at the end of the last chapter had a marked style in the use of words—some more ritualistic than others. From *The Silver Tassie* to *Blithe Spirit*; from *Sergeant Musgrave's Dance* to *The Dumb Waiter* the words demand their peculiar style and rhythm—not only in the way they are uttered but also in the body images that accompany and support them. This chapter sets out to help you on a journey of discovery of the many ways and means you will need if your body is to meet the demands of such texts.

The Body—the Working Machine

This is not a handbook of anatomy and physiology and what follows will no more than outline the main facts. If you wish to gain a thorough knowledge of the subject it will be better to consult appropriate specialist literature. From the point of view of an actor's work it will be best to study those handbooks on the subject drawn up specifically for painters and sculptors. They will highlight the facts with the kind of insight that an actor needs.

The human body is made up of five main types of 'stuff'. They are generally called tissues and are divided as follows:

1. **Epithelial tissue.**
2. **Connective tissue**—including cartilage and bone.
3. **Muscular tissue.**
4. **Nervous tissue.**
5. **Blood.**

Epithelial tissue. All the cells which form a covering inside and outside the body and its cavities come into this category—the skin, the mucous membranes of the mouth and nose, the inner services of the bladder and bowel, etc. All are examples of epithelial tissue.

Connective tissue. This forms the body framework and supportive/connective material which give the body its shape. It can be subdivided as follows:

(*a*) *Fibrous tissue.* When together in any quantity this looks like pearly plastic fibres. It is very strong with only little elasticity. It has these functions:
to bind the bones together at the joints—*ligaments*;
to connect the muscles to the bones—*tendons*;
to cover and protect other organs and tissues—*membranes*.

(*b*) *Adipose tissue.* This is far better known as fat. It has these functions:
to retain body heat;
to protect underlying parts;
to provide a reserve of nourishment.

(*c*) *Cartilage or gristle.* Its main function is that of a shock-absorber or preventor. It is used also to prevent damage where two bones meet at a joint, by creating smooth surfaces which permit the necessary gliding action.

(*d*) *Osseous tissue.* This is better known as bone. It has these functions:
to provide the basic skeletal framework for the body;
to offer protection for vital organs;
to provide securing points so that the muscular system can operate.

Muscular tissue. There are three kinds of muscular tissue:
(*a*) *Voluntary muscle.*
(*b*) *Involuntary muscle.*
(*c*) *The heart muscle—cardiac.*

(*a*) The voluntary muscles are those you are most frequently aware of. They are the ones used for walking, standing, lifting, throwing, etc. Since they are under your **direct control** they are called **voluntary**. They make up the ordinary red meat of the body and consist of cells which can be shortened or elongated at will.

(*b*) The involuntary muscles work by themselves and you have no control over them. For example, those in the stomach, continue their work in the digestive process and you have no means of consciously controlling them.

(*c*) The heart muscle cannot be influenced by you taking thought to do so—but if you run to catch a bus the heart will respond by providing the necessary blood circulation.

In a similar way the vocal muscles cannot be brought into action unless you actually use them to vocalize.

Nervous tissue. This consists of cells which generate and receive impulses and fibres which pass the impulses on. The speed at which their processes work is unbelievably fast.

There is the **central nervous system** which exchanges all incoming and outgoing messages, the sensory nerves receive incoming intelligence and the motor nerves send out instructions for action—if and when necessary. It also provides the body with its memory bank.

The nerves themselves convey the messages to be exchanged. They operate to and from between the spinal chord and the brain.

In addition there is the **autonomic nervous system** (*it runs itself*) controlling the rate of activity for the organs of food digestion and blood circulation, etc.

Blood. The blood consists of lymph—a clear fluid—holding in suspension the red and white corpuscles. It circulates the body, distributing nourishment and collecting waste. All the tissues of the body are built to take up lymph in the same way as a sponge takes up water. This is the way they are fed.

Another area of considerable importance to everyone, but of *special significance to actors, dancers and athletes* is that of **the joints**.

Joints occur when two or more bones meet. They may be freely movable as in hip and shoulder; partly movable as in the spine or not at all movable as in the skull.

There are **four kinds of movable joints**:

1. *Ball and socket*—as in the hip joint. Movement is allowed in any direction
2. *Hinge*—as in the knee or elbow. Movement is allowed in only one plane—backwards and forwards, just like a hinge.
3. *Gliding*—as in the small bones in the wrist and ankle. Movement is restricted to one surface moving over another in a limited range. It is enabling rather than executive.
4. *Pivot*—as between radius and ulna—the two bones of the forearm where one bone rotates on the other.

None of the foregoing is intended to be more than an introduction to the basic mechanics of the body. Do not treat it as anything different. If you wish for more detail you should refer to specialist literature.

As an aid to the exercises that come at the end of the chapter, as well as the previous paragraphs, you may wish to make use of a chart of the bones and tissues of the body—a muscle map. These are easily available at bookshops. If there is any area of doubt in your mind about any approach to physical work or the exercises that come later, take expert advice. Nothing suggested in this book should cause more than minor aches lasting longer than two days. Should you have any signs or symptoms different from these, take expert advice.

Before moving on to the exercises themselves there are a few areas of movement work for the stage that justify special mention. Wearing period costume and representing a character much older than yourself are two examples of situations that often cause problems. Two more are stage fights and stage embraces. In a world where the two most popular sports seem to be kissing and killing it is surprising they are surrounded by as much mystery and inhibition as they frequently are.

Period Movement

Any period movement grows out of a way of life. An important and specific contributory factor at work, within that general way of life, is clothing. Not only does clothing or the lack of it at any period reflect the nature and the times of the way of life it also provides garments suited to the activities of the period. It is, therefore, important to see the clothing of any period as a reflection of its way of life.

Clothing does more than merely reflect the state of mind and the condition of living. It goes a long way towards creating them. **It also dictates a style of movement.** The garments—and perhaps more importantly the under-garments —of any period encourage certain patterns of movement and discourage, if not totally prevent, others.

Consider the classic case of medieval movement from a woman's point of view. The 'shoulders-back-and-down-semi-pregnant droop' style of walking was literally forced upon any woman who dressed in the fashion of the times. The collection of heavy clothing was suspended mainly from the shoulders and much of it fell behind the back. The only possible style of walking that could be sustained without difficulty and over-fatigue was the one outlined above.

Consider another classic case—Henry VIII as known in his bloomer-type trousers. It was not entirely from choice or because he was fat that he did not hold his legs together. The amount of material in the trousers and their cut made it impossible for the legs to be approximated.

There are many specialist books on the subject of period clothes and period movement. You may find them useful as reference sources. Turn first to historical paintings and sculptures then to the clothes themselves. If you are taking part in an historical play, give yourself plenty of time to become acquainted with the cut and style of the clothes. Get used to the feel of them as you actually wear them. Get hold of genuine replicas of the garments—especially under-garments—and give yourself plenty of practice in wearing them. If you cannot get accurate replicas, practice with proper substitutes. Once you have experienced the sensation of the Elizabethan woman's corset with its vertical rod of bone from sternum to pubis you will never sit with an incorrect angle to your spine. The well-known straight back may have been partly motivated by vanity or aesthetics—it was also a necessity for simple survival.

A combination of studying paintings and sculptures of the period with regular practice in wearing the clothes will help you approach the purpose and feel of the particular period movement. Once you have the body feel, the right image will slowly grow and you will begin to achieve mastery over the clothes and the range of movements possible and proper. When you have this mastery you will be able to use it in presenting your role. It is important to remember that historical accuracy is of little purpose on its own account. **It is what you are able to achieve in dramatic terms by using the clothes and the movement that is paramount.** In any case, there is still sufficient room for debate regarding most historical periods to permit any pundit to find an error in what you have done—if he be so inclined.

When you have absorbed the purpose and feel of the clothes and the closely related movement you will be able to vary your movements within appropriate limits to gain the effects you want. Much of the right atmosphere can be created, and much detail suggested, once you are able to work the correct outlines, shapes and rhythms.

Whatever claims may be made for historical accuracy, the designer will need to balance them against the claims for interpreting the play. He will also be influenced by the particular fashion of his own times. There is no objective eye which will accept a definitive design pattern for a certain period. Each audience sees what it sees only after the actual object has been filtered through the consciousness of the observer. Every designer must take this into consideration. This question of design relative to the period being represented and the period in which it is being presented will come up again in more detail in Chapter Nineteen.

The same principles apply to the design and execution of period dance. If it occupies a lengthy or central part in your play it will be best for you to use the services of a specialist teacher of dance—preferably one who has some experience of working for the theatre. Whether you approach a specialist or not, remember it is the basic feel and flow you need to get right. You will then have a vehicle capable of carrying the dramatic meaning you wish to communicate. No amount of verisimilitude will create dramatic tension or meaning by itself. The dance must be a river of movement that will carry the boat of your intent. It must do so without the tide running out or the water swamping the boat.

'Ageing'

There is an interesting near-dichotomy that applies to both acting and living; no matter how old the body may be it is still the person—the character— within it that is most important; no matter how much of a character the person may be, he is still held within the prison of his body. It is something of a sombre note to strike at this point but one of the most secure pieces of knowledge we have is that our bodies are decaying every moment of our lives. Ronald Duncan makes this point extremely well in his play *The Gift*—we are dying as we live and breathe, and so are all the things we use and know and wear.

If you are to play a character whose age is much removed from your own, your first research should take you to looking at people in that age bracket. Look at their general body image and watch carefully the detail of their movement.

Although there is no archetype for old age, there are one or two features which generally accompany the process of ageing. The main characteristics are **loss of flexibility, agility, speed and effortless exactitude.** Rising from a chair is no longer one simple action but a series of complicated actions; a whole arm may have to be brought into action where before a finger flick would have been used; the whole body may have to be turned to let the eyes come to rest on a particular object.

This last example serves well. Before the process of ageing has begun to have any real impact, only the head will be turned to look behind. The movement will be quick and easy and the head will turn effortlessly with the neck. With the onset of age, more and more of the body may have to be turned—

shoulders, waist and hips—and the action will no longer be speedy and effortless. Finally, it may even be necessary to shuffle on the feet to look behind—the body no longer of being capable of making the turning movements.

If your performance is to carry the stamp of truth, the character you create must be **gripped by his body feel** and his **body image must reflect his inner spirit**. Whatever specific actions and movements you choose as starters or whatever grow out of your preparation, they must hang together as a whole. They must each in their own way reflect the inner spirit of the character. The physical facets may be diverse. If your character is to work they will be different physical manifestations of **one total persona, radiating from a central core**. Each will lead to the centre and each will stem from it. They will be different modes of expression of the condition of one person, not disparate reflections of the states of many. They may be drawn from many sources but you must unify them in the character of the role you are creating. If you can find no ready purpose or justification for any specific mannerism or movement pattern you have tried (no matter with how much apparent success), it is probably best to dispense with it and start from another position. At any one stage in your preparation or rehearsal period you may be left with only one significant movement or gesture pattern. Don't worry. It is probably the most telling of them all and from it a total vocabulary may grow.

Fighting

With only two people concerned in a stage fight it is the intensity and truth of their actions which will communicate their symbolized battle of wills. When there are more people involved—as in a battle scene—it becomes of greater importance to have the exact moves, strokes, victories and defeats accurately and exactly plotted. The need for overall organization grows as the number of combatants increases.

The final choice of weapons can frequently be made in consultation with the actors concerned. There are few plays where the exact shape and nature of the instrument is crucial. Since this is so, it is best to give the actors plenty of time to find out for themselves which weapons offer the greatest opportunities to continue and progress their acting. There is a very real danger that the enjoyment and absorption of the fight itself will reduce the intensity of the acting. A good director will be able to make use of this and, in a sense, the fight itself can become the actual drama. If this is to be the case it must be conscious and willed and not happen by chance with the actors being unaware of it.

A large proportion of the body's everyday vocabulary is suitable to use in a fight sequence. There is no need to think you must undertake weeks of highly specialized training. Athletics and gymnastic classes will certainly help—they will be of help to an actor in any case—and boxing and wrestling techniques can be put to good service. They are not, however, essential.

Whatever kind of fight you are to be concerned with, you should start from your own movement vocabulary and let variations grow from it, rather than try to learn complex and sometimes difficult techniques which you may not be able to absorb well enough in the time available for you to use them as **tools of acting** in your performance. In stage fights, a little done well—absorbed into your performance and executed with intensity and honesty—will be dramatically most effective.

Let any noises that emerge in rehearsal from the interaction of weapons be carefully noted and repeated. Noise from clashing weapons—provided it is not obviously pseudo or inappropriate—can be even more effective than the sight of the weapons themselves. From time to time it can be used as a substitute for actual fighting action. The same is not true of vocal sound. Shouts, screams and cries; squeals and groans are only properly effective if the action and the characters performing it justify them. If they do not appear to grow fully from the violence of the physical action or if the tension under-pinning the fight scene is not sufficiently charged, any vocalization will appear to be ham. The effect will be to reduce the impact of the scene, not to increase it. (In any scene the style and the volume of the voice and speech must match the style and quantity of the movement. Neither will be effective unless the characters portrayed see themselves with those voices and those body images. A character can burst into song, lyrical poetry or dance if he sees himself in a poetic situation. When he does, the moment will be sufficiently charged for him to express himself validly in that way. If the rest of the characters—his stage audience—see him in that way also he will communicate validly the experience exactly as he expresses it. If the other characters do not see him in that light, the theatre audience will have been signalled and what he communicates will amuse them. Both situations will have been fully justified and the audience will be responding as cast and director would wish. If these conditions are not met the audience will be uncomfortable. They may laugh. They will be laughing, however, not in sympathy with the character or at his ridiculous position, but at an actor playing a role in an unsatisfactory way.) **Violent vocalization is no substitute for dynamic action or inner tension.** It can symbolize their presence but never disguise their absence.

Embracing

Just as with fights, plenty of time should be allowed for the cast to fence (or flirt) with the weapons of the sex war. In addition there will be the challenge of human chemistry at work in a more, or less, subtle style than in a fight scene. Time must be allowed for the novelty to work off. Even in these enlightened days, not every actor and actress can immediately absorb the experience of a new partner to embrace. There is also the need to explore the various forms of expression that the experience will need.

Earlier it was suggested that the actor should try out in private the different forms of personal expression that he dredges from his inner self. Here the dredging must be done from within a pair—working in close harness. Indeed, in many stage embraces, it is more to the point to suggest that the pair is a single double-bodied animal. Either view requires them to have plenty of time to work together. There may still be some minor shyness or embarrassment to be overcome. If it is more than minor, the director must give serious thought to immediate recasting.

At one time, not far back in the present century, the modes of expression of affection between the sexes that were generally accepted or acceptable on stage were: hand holding; starry looking eye to eye contact; cheek to cheek kissing; mouth to cheek kissing and mouth to mouth kissing. The latter would always rivet the audience one way or another. It was the extreme form of acceptable stage embracing. This situation no longer obtains. Nor does the expectation that the kissing will have to stop at hetereosexual exchanges. The whole gamut of body to body embracing is now open to proper exploitation. This relaxation of convention is a boon to the actor, since it enables him to use gestures of affection—erotic or non-erotic—without involving his mouth whenever passion is required. When mouth to mouth kissing was the ultimate it meant a lack of opportunity to speak at the most telling moment. Now that embargo has gone. The vocabulary of affection is wider than it has been for a long time in the history of the theatre.

If the full vocabulary of embracing is used to explore and elaborate the expression of experience between the two concerned, it should automatically prevent the classic error of stage kissing—the approximation of lips and perhaps a shoulder or two, with pelvises separated by well over twelve inches. This almost always springs from, not bad technique, but simple sexual shyness. In the past the touching of the hips/pelvic area has been a matter for delicacy or embarrassment. A proper exploration of all the methods of embracing open to the couple concerned should ensure they do not fall into the trap.

Busy fondling is no substitute for purposeful affection or intense passion. A stage embrace usually signifies the presence of feelings, that in language, would justify a poetic/lyrical style. The rule for poetic expression applies to movement and gesture also: **the minimum number of actions carrying the maximum degree of charge**.

EXERCISES

The following exercises are divided into two main sections. The first sets up a comprehensive pattern of personal and group limbering. It should be undertaken regularly and you should be careful not to try to progress too quickly. A little and often is a golden rule. Fifteen to twenty minutes, preferably twice a day, is a good average. There should be no sense of strain and if you proceed slowly and carefully you will experience only those aches which naturally arise when you use muscles that have not been exercised for some time. Any such aches should pass within two days. **If, in spite of working slowly and regularly, you get serious aches, or they do not disappear with gentle re-exercise, TAKE EXPERT ADVICE.**

The best way to avoid serious discomfort is to **limber regularly** and to **proceed slowly**. Previously under-exercised muscles will naturally make their presence felt. Careful perseverance will ensure you gain maximum benefit with minimum inconvenience. Treat the limbering exercises as you would the routine for running and servicing a car. They are intended to help you prepare your vehicle for the road. They are not driving lessons—neither are they races or rallies. Those functions are covered by the second section. In that section there are exercises to help you broaden the vocabulary of your expressive movement. There is ample scope for experimentation and exploration and you will find you can try most of them straightaway—by yourself, with a friend or in a group. Make sure you keep a proper balance between the limbering and the expressive work. Always limber first and never rush into intense physical exertion without a proper period to warm up. If you do you run the risk of seriously damaging your muscles. Careful limbering will do this warming up for you —this is one of its functions—and at the same time help you achieve the flexibility you need. **WORK REGULARLY, SLOWLY AND WITHOUT STRAIN.**

Limbering

Pre-limber warm-up

1. **Cat.** Lie down and relax on the floor. Check for total relaxation. Slowly and in a quite relaxed manner curl into the position naturally adopted by a cat when asleep. Slowly stretch as a cat does until every part of your body is fully extended. Then slowly extend each part of the body separately as a cat does. Slowly move into the all fours position and arch your back. Gradually uncurl until you are standing upright. Slowly reach up with the arms until they are stretched to their fullest above the head.

2. Circle the head slowly to the left—no more than twelve times. Circle to the right similarly. Make sure the muscles are being stretched a little. Avoid unnecessary strain and tension. Stop at once if you feel dizzy.

3. Circle the left shoulder backwards slowly. Feel the muscles being eased and stretched. Repeat with the right shoulder. Repeat circling forwards—shoulders separately. Repeat with shoulders together.

4. Circle the left elbow in a clockwise direction. Support the upper arm with the right hand: (*a*) in the vertical plane; (*b*) in the horizontal plane. Repeat with the right elbow. Repeat in an anticlockwise position.

5. Circle the left wrist in a clockwise direction. Repeat with the right wrist. Repeat in an anticlockwise direction. Repeat with wrists together.

6. Circle the fingers separately and together—clockwise and anticlockwise. (You will find it difficult to move one finger without moving the others. An aid to concentration is not to look at the fingers while they are being circled. It does not matter if the other fingers move, but looking at them may cause a distraction. Make sure the muscles are just being stretched as in the previous exercises.)

7. Place your hands in front of you with arms outstretched at shoulder level —palms facing outwards. Slowly stretch arms to full sideways position. The hands should move to a position slightly behind the shoulders. Return to front position. Stretch to a vertical position with the upper arm just brushing the ears. Repeat.

8. Bend slowly forward from the waist. Make sure the pelvis does not move. Bend to one side and then the other. Bend backwards. Each time bend slowly and make sure the pelvis does not move. Repeat the exercise until you begin to feel free enough to circle the torso through the preceding positions—clockwise and anticlockwise. You may find it helpful to keep your hands on your waist to check any movement of the pelvis.

9. Keep your pelvis absolutely still. Move your rib cage with a sliding motion from side to side.

10. Bend forward from the top of the thighs, keeping the back straight. Keep bending slowly until you feel the muscles in the thighs being stretched. Once you have gained increased flexibility, repeat the circular movement from the previous exercise—clockwise and anticlockwise.

11(*a*) Get a good balance on one leg and swing the other like a pendulum. Repeat not more than twelve times. Repeat with the other leg.

(*b*) Stretch one leg to the side—up and out as far as possible, keeping the knee facing upwards. Stretch with little kicks. Do not overstrain. Repeat with the other leg.

12. Holding the thigh with both hands to give proper support, circle the knee. The exercise is similar to 4(*b*). Repeat with other leg—clockwise and anticlockwise.

13. Sit on the floor with one leg bent at the knee. Rest the other leg on the knee. Circle the ankle of the free leg. Clockwise and anticlockwise. Repeat with the other leg.

14. Sit on the floor with legs straight out in front and together. Stretch feet together so that soles are parallel to the floor, then point them to the ceiling. Repeat not more than six times.

N.B. These exercises are part of a prelimber warm-up process. **They are not intended to be undertaken strenuously.** Each movement should stretch the muscles slightly—increasing in range only slowly. Take care to avoid strain. Over enthusiasm can be hurtful and harmful. The sequence should take no more than fifteen minutes.

A Fuller Limber

When you have finished your prelimber you may use any of the exercises in the list and extend them to suit your particular needs. During these occasions you can properly aim at fuller extension and greater effort.

You will find the following exercises useful to include in the work that follows your prelimber.

1. *Standing:* (*a*) With your right hand hold on to a chair for support. Kick your left leg as follows: three times to the front—three times to the side (making sure that knees are facing upwards)—three times to the rear. Do not move your torso. Repeat the exercise for the other leg.

(*b*) Still holding on to a chair, place your feet in second position—about twelve inches apart and at quarter to three (or as near as possible without strain) and slowly bend your knees. Make sure your knees stay immediately above your toes. Check they do not come forward. Keep your back straight and your shoulders relaxed. Bend slowly and return slowly to a standing position. Repeat three times. (The second position, as outlined above, is an excellent exercise for balance if used without the aid of a supporting chair. It is probably wisest to use it as a balance exercise *with the help of a friend*).

(*c*) Supporting yourself still—holding with the right hand—grasp hold of the instep of your left foot with your left hand. The palm of your hand should be facing the instep. Bend the supporting leg and slowly straighten both. Do not lose the grasp of the hand on the instep. Repeat three times. Repeat with the other leg.

2. *Sitting:* (*a*) Make sure you have plenty of space and are not sitting on easily movable or ruckable rugs or carpets. Keep your back straight, your shoulders relaxed and your legs extended together and closed. By extending your legs one at a time, shuffle your way along the floor. Make sure you extend the leg as far as possible. Travel as far as possible on one stroke. It is essential that you keep your shoulders still and relaxed.

(*b*) Extend your legs together in front of you. Grasp the outside of the feet with your hands. Pull and bend forward until your chest touches your knees. Pull and 'bounce' to obtain maximum effect. The knees must not be bent.

(*c*) Open your legs as far as possible and keep them straight. Raise your arms straight above your head with the upper arm brushing the ear. Keeping the back as straight as possible bend forward:

(i) over one leg.
(ii) over the other.
(iii) to the front.

Repeat.

(*d*) When you have achieved good flexibility with the last exercise circle from the hips so that on the forward journey the arms skim the legs and on the backward journey the back skims the floor. Repeat clockwise and anticlockwise. (Do not attempt this exercise until you are able to undertake the previous ones easily. It is an advanced exercise and should not be used until sufficient strength has been built up.)

(*e*) Sit with your legs extended and together to the front. Hold your arms out to the sides horizontally with the palms facing down. Slowly rock yourself from side to side. Increase the range each time until the palms touch the floor. Use a gentle push to keep the rocking going. Develop an even rhythm and flow. You may be helped to do this by singing a chorus from 'Daisy Daisy'. Make sure you have proper breath control and good voice and speech production. (In fact many of the exercises from Chapter Eight can be incorporated into movement work.)

(*f*) From a sitting position lie down on one side and cushion your face on the palm of your hand. Raise your uppermost leg as far as possible to the ceiling. Move it as slowly as possible and return it to the starting position in the same way. Repeat three times. Turn over and repeat with the other leg.

3. *Supine*: (*a*) Raise one leg very slowly until it is at right-angles to the body. Equally slowly lower it to the floor. It is important to keep both legs absolutely straight and extended. The toes should be pointed. Repeat with the other leg. Repeat with both legs.

You should aim at doing the exercises as slowly as possible. Try to extend the time you take whenever you do the exercise.

(*b*) Raise one leg until it is at right-angles to the body. Stretch it across the body until it touches the floor on the far side. Keep the legs straight and the toes pointed. Work as slowly as you can. Repeat with the other leg.

(*c*) Raise the knees until the soles of the feet are flat on the floor. Slowly raise the pelvis as far as possible without moving feet or shoulders—in particular they should not leave the floor.

4. *Prone*: (*a*) Raise your hands, palms downwards, under your shoulders. The legs are extended and together. Keeping the body from the waist downwards in touch with the floor, push with the arms until they are fully extended. Repeat three times. (*N.B. This is not a simple press-up.*)

(*b*) Repeat the exercise as closely as you can with the arms held out straight in front with the upper arm brushing the ear.

(*c*) Place your arms by your sides. Repeat the exercise but keep the torso in touch with the floor and raise the legs. Keep them straight and close together.

(*d*) Place your arms straight as in (*b*) and combine exercises (*b*) and (*c*). The body will now be bow-shaped. Rock gently backwards and forwards.

(*e*) Bend the knees and reach backwards with the arms to grasp the front of the ankles/feet with the hands. The body will now be even more bow-shaped. Rock gently backwards and forwards.

N.B. Take plenty of time between the exercises. Do not rush. Do not overstrain. Relax as necessary between any of the exercises.

Movement Exercises

1. Look at people in the street, in shops, on buses; watch them in newsreels; on film and television; watch actors at work in films, on television and on the stage.

(*a*) Look carefully at the **total body images** they present.
(*b*) Watch for the **special rhythms and patterns of movement** they use.
(*c*) Isolate the details of their movements—hands, feet, legs, elbows, heads. Concentrate exclusively on the way they use these particular parts of their body for two or three minutes at a time.

2. Look at paintings and sculptures in the same way as in the previous exercise. Study artists' sketches and anatomical handbooks provided for painters and sculptors. Study paintings, sketches and sculpture from other periods and other cultures.
3. Look at paintings, sculpture, household objects, sweets, toys, etc. Bring them alive:

(*a*) By reflecting their shapes and angles in a technical way.
(*b*) Repeat the exercise giving the movement strong emotional overtones.
(*c*) Repeat the exercise creating characters and personalities from the body positions.

4. Create different body shapes and positions for everyday sounds. For example—dripping tap, electric and non-electric vacuum-cleaner, telephone and door bells, striking a match, footsteps, bacon frying.
5. Repeat the exercises in 4 using the sounds of your own voice—naturally and with special variations; your friends' voices, voices you hear on the telephone, gramophone records and tape-recordings.
6. Bring to life the body shapes and positions from Exercises 4 and 5.

(*a*) Move them technically.
(*b*) Repeat with strong emotional overtones.
(*c*) Repeat with character and personality.

7. Create patterns of movement for different machines. For example: fast electric dynamos and slow steam hammers, tape-recorders, car engines, typewriters, clocks, etc. Also create imaginary machines. Use different parts of the body in isolation at first for the exercise. When you have experimented with different parts of the body, begin to build them up into a total unit. Try the exercise by yourself and later with a friend or in a group. The exercise works particularly well with small groups. Do the exercises first in silence and later add the sounds that would normally accompany such machines. For a more advanced exercise accompany fast machine movements with slow sounds and quiet machine movements with loud sounds. Then vary the combinations as appropriate.
8. *Clothes.* Choose a range different from your normal clothing—hats, gloves, scarves, ties, sweaters, trousers and jackets (later sew up the pockets of the jackets and trousers).

(a) Choose an individual garment and study it carefully by touching and looking at it. Then create a body position to reflect its shape, texture and 'character'.

(b) Create the movements of a person who might wear such a garment.

(c) Wear and use the garment. Later wear and use it with other garments from your collection.

(d) Wear clothes that are the wrong size for you—either too small or too large. Pay particular attention to your movement when you are wearing boots or shoes that are the wrong size.

9. Experiment and explore different patterns of walking, standing and sitting. Make sure that they contrast markedly with your own natural patterns.

10. Repeat the rhythm exercises from Chapter Eight.

(a) Use different parts of the body in isolation—wrist, elbow, head, toes, etc.

(b) Repeat putting individual parts together.

(c) Use the whole body.

11. Sit in the same chair in as many different ways as possible. Sit in different chairs: (a) the same way; (b) in different ways.

12. You will need a friend to help with this exercise. Get him to sit in any way that is comfortable. Sit in exactly the same position as he is.

(a) Side by side.

(b) Face to face.

(c) Through a mirror.

13. Choose a simple everyday action like going up and down stairs; sitting in a car; lighting a cigarette; drinking coffee; etc. Notice carefully your natural pattern and then take every opportunity to vary and change your movement pattern.

14. *Music.* When listening to the radio, television, records or tape-recordings, conduct the music.

(a) Use different parts of the body separately—in different combinations. Finally conduct with the whole body.

(b) Use the music as a stimulus for expressive dance. Dance with different parts of the body separately at first and then with different combinations.

(c) Use a tape-recorder or record-player which allows you to change the speed. Play back at half and double speed for conducting and dancing.

15. Listen for special sound patterns that interest you. Use words, phrases and sentences in contrasting ways and use these as a basis for movement work. Use some of the voice and speech exercises from Chapter Eight—take them to extreme vocalization and interpret them in movement.

Create your own chants and sound patterns. Dance with separate parts of the body as you sing.

16. Use formal dances—the tango, the waltz, etc.—to express different emotional overtones. Dance in anger, in fear, in joy, in anxiety. Use recorded music and also create your own. Repeat the exercise with a friend. Later, extend it into a dance for a small group.

17. Choose an everyday action—washing up, pouring tea, dusting the furniture, going shopping, etc.—and go through the movements: (*a*) in slow-motion; (*b*) in double quick time. Repeat the exercise with a friend and in small groups.

18. Choose a particular gesture or movement pattern that you have noticed someone using.

(*a*) Exaggerate it.
(*b*) Repeat it with different parts of the body.
(*c*) Let other parts of the body echo and support it.
(*d*) Let it permeate the whole body.
(*e*) Let the whole body exaggerate the movement to the final extreme.

19. Take a series of movements and gestures from any of the previous exercises.

(*a*) Repeat them naked in front of a mirror. (It is a help to use more than one mirror if you can arrange to do so.) Watch the different parts of the body, carefully noticing action and interaction.
(*b*) Repeat the exercise wearing only one item of clothing. Notice how this affects your attitude to the exercise as well as your execution of them.

20. Repeat the exercise in the above but use the item of clothing to assist, support and clarify your movement expression.
Repeat using different items of clothing separately and together.
Repeat a pattern of movement in the front of the mirror.

(*a*) Start fully clothed and remove garments one at a time. Notice the difference in impact as more clothes are shed.
(*b*) Repeat the exercise from being naked to fully clothed.

21. Float, swim or just *mess about* in the sea, a river, a swimming or bathing pool. Echo the movements of the water. Use the support of the water to help you create new movement patterns.

22. Climb rocks, chairs, step-ladders, etc. Play out scenes—with or without vocal sounds—by yourself. Notice carefully any unusual body positions you create while climbing and experiment with them to express emotional overtones.

23. *Fights*: (*a*) *Falling*. Repeat the following sequence making it express different feelings and intentions.

1. Stand upright in a relaxed position.
2. Slowly begin to relax and sway backwards or from side to side.
3. Begin to give at the knees and recover a little.
4. Give more at the knees and finally turn slowly as you touch the floor.
5. Roll over as slowly as you can when you reach the floor. You should come into contact with the floor with feet and legs first, then the rest of the body and finally the head. Use your hands and arms as little as possible to support you on your way down. You should aim at performing the fall **without using hands or arms**. Repeat the exercises slowly at first. Speed up as you become more expert.
(*b*) Use whatever gymnastic exercises you are familiar with to express different intensions and emotions.

(*c*) Practise shadow-boxing.

(*d*) Practise 'pretend' boxing and wrestling with a friend. Also arm-to-arm and wrist-to-wrist strength, fighting on a table-top.

   (i) Normal speed.

   (ii) Double quick time.

   (iii) Slow motion.

(*e*) Imagine you are being struck all over the body by slashing sabres; pointed knives, bullets. Be strangled or have your arm twisted. Repeat with noises and without. Repeat in slow motion and double speed. Use different-sized pieces of wood from toothpicks to six-feet lengths of 2″ × 2″ timber as weapons. Create different fight sequences from Lilliputians to Little Johns. Use with sounds and without. Repeat with a friend and in small groups. Use household objects as if they were newly invented weapons. Mime every kind of fighting with no substitute for the weapons. Repeat with a partner and in small groups.

24. Almost any ball game will help you study and improve your movement vocabulary.

With friends, use different-sized balls—bouncing, throwing and catching them. Repeat the exercises without a ball. With a friend and in small groups play the ball games in mime. Repeat at half and double speed.

Note carefully:

1. The exercises are intended to suggest ways of approaching training. They are not definitive or comprehensive.

2. Many of the exercises from Chapters Four, Five and Six will be useful for movement training.

3. Never undertake strenuous movement work or exercises without proper warming up and limbering.

4. It is sensible to begin and end every movement session with a short period of relaxation (see Chapter Seven).

CHAPTER TEN

WORKING ON A TEXT—I

Whose Text?

Before a working script gets into an actor's hands it will have gone through many processes. On many occasions it will no longer be the text the author originally created. It may have been revised—sometimes changed radically—as a result of early performances. It may have been amended as a result of pressure from publishers or theatre managements. It may contain a wealth of detailed instructions regarding settings, lighting and complicated stage directions.

Acting Editions

In the last case it will be sold as an acting edition and there are actors and directors who will treat the business it describes as if it were definitive. Some will slavishly follow the recipes and some will turn to them when their own powers of invention fail. In any case it is not easy to be entirely unaffected by the italicized instructions. Some of them *may* have been included by the author and be of deep significance to him. It is more likely they will have been taken straight from a West End production and set down in full. The production may or may not have been a good one. The cast may or may not have spent time, thought and rehearsal in getting deep below the surface of the author's work and sincerely offering their best intentions and efforts to communicate what he had in mind. What they achieved—no matter how they did so—was for **their performances to their audiences.** It was not a blueprint for repetition—it can hardly be called recreation—by others. The very facts of time, place, facilities, conditions and above all the cast being different, ought to speak for themselves and prohibit such replicas. They do not, and acting editions thrive. Not that this is a bad thing entirely—it is the use to which they are put that may preclude the author's purpose from being understood by the cast and thus his meaning withheld from the audience. It is the author's work a company should seek to bring alive, not a repeat performance of the presentations of others. Acting editions may be of interest—even of help and guidance (unlikely as this may be)—but they can only be a hindrance to a company wishing to get into touch with the meaning and message of the author. Bringing an author's work from printed dialogue to vibrant actuality is a task already complex and challenging. The left-overs of other companies' efforts make it more so.

Writing, Reading and Production

The arts of play-writing, play-reading and play production have only little in common, and it is useful to know something of the other two, no matter which particular area is being studied.

Writing a Play

All writers go through similar processes. The order, balance, timing and importance they give to the separate parts differ markedly. The processes themselves remain fairly constant. There is the initial thought or feeling that triggers the whole process. It may be only the germ of an idea, situation, character or story. It may be a riveting opening scene, a tragic climax or a slow anticlimatic conclusion. For some writers it is the awareness of the need to write and for others it is a story line complete with beginning, middle and end.

After the initial motivation there is a period of incubation. This may be conscious thought or a quite unconscious, but regular, returning to the theme. The writer may not know he *has been* thinking about the play until *after* thinking about it. The period may be one of experimentation with ideas and situations, or deep exploration of characters, their lives and motives. It may be a period of search and research into another era of history or another culture. It may appear to be a dormant and unfruitful time that is marked by the frustration of inactivity, or it may be an agonizing period of chasing elusive solutions. For some writers this is a long period, lasting many months—even years. For others it is a comparatively short period—marked by an explosion of mental and emotional activity.

Some writers find the incubatory period spills into and becomes part of the process of realization. They may spend a few days actually working on the opening of the play, say, and may achieve total success with that part. While this has been happening another part of the play may have been smouldering at the back of the mind, waiting to burst into flame in the front.

In the actual writing there are many differentials between authors' methods. Some will start at the beginning and, just like Alice, carry on until they reach the end. (Some begin without having an end in mind. They know the play to be finished only when they have stopped writing.) Some authors create a climactic scene and work outwards—building up to it and away from it. Some follow the progress of individual characters through a scene or through the whole play—building up other characters and incidents as they occur *en passant*. Some plot and plan and scheme and build unit by unit—constantly reshaping and replacing. Some write slowly and with great care while others dash away thousands of words red hot with no attention to detail.

Most writers make opportunities for revision. Some like to do it straightaway while others prefer to distance themselves by at least a period of months. A few writers never revise. They ensure their work grows slowly and do not progress to a following unit until they are quite sure of what they have already done. Some writers hold extreme views about their work—once it is completed—carrying their attitudes so far that they have no wish to see it again.

An understanding of something of the rhythm of the playwright's task will help in approaching a text and bringing it alive.

The Resident Playwright

In Shakespeare's day it was not unusual for a writer to be a permanent member of a theatre company. He would work in close co-operation with the company—probably being an actor himself—knowing exactly what conditions of casting and performance he was writing for. Happily there is a return to the idea of the resident dramatist at the present time. Public money—national and local—is aiding in a small way community theatres to work more closely with writers. Universities, colleges and even the profession itself are creating the right environment to foster the idea. Although it is slow, the movement is growing and the next two decades suggest a promise of meaningful collaboration. The off-Broadway, off-Shaftesbury Avenue companies have given the lead on a number of occasions and as a result many writers new to the theatre have emerged. Here is the comment of an old hand. It is taken from the preface to his play *Sam the Highest Jumper of Them All.*

SAM THE HIGHEST JUMPER OF THEM ALL

William Saroyan

'From Paris in February of 1960 I wrote to Joan Littlewood to say that I had enjoyed seeing Brendan Behan's play *The Hostage* in London. The manager of the Theatre Royal, Gerald Raffles, replied and invited me to direct one of my own plays at the Theatre Royal. I sent him three published plays and two ideas I had for new plays. He chose one of the three plays, *Jim Dandy*, but a few days later he wondered if I might be able to make a play in the theatre out of one of the ideas. I said I could, although the procedure would make great demands on the players. On March 1st I arrived in London and went to work, meeting players and writing the play. A rough draft was finished in nine or ten days. Two benefit performances were given early in April, and on the 6th the play opened to the press and general public. The house was packed and the response of the audience gave me the impression that they liked it. The reviews, however, informed me that the play was meaningless and amateurish.'

Reading a Play

The reader also has a **creative** process. If the play is to work for a reader, he must be equipped with something of the thought and feeling processes of a director. He must be able to realize within himself the three-dimensional animal the writer had in mind. He must be able to manage the external and internal rhythms of the play at one and the same time. Reading a play is not a linear process nor is it the comparatively simple task of picturing in the mind's eye and ear, action and words as they are described. The playwright puts into words an **inner energy and purpose** that three-dimensional performance by an actor will bring to life **by acting**. It is a lively, sensitive overall view that qualifies a director to perform his job. A reader of plays must have this quality—unless he is to approach the play as a special kind of novel.

You will experience something of the difficulty of the reader's task if you turn down the sound the next time you watch a television play. You will gain even more if you turn down the vision while still listening to the sound. It is possible to make considerable errors of judgment in either case. The special techniques of the radio play prevent listeners from making the same kind of errors. A radio play is a half-way house between a play-reading and its presentation as an act of theatre.

Producing a Play

Creating the physical performance of a play is often compared with the building of a house and the author's text with the blueprint plans. This can be misleading in two particulars: it suggests the activity brings together otherwise unrelated materials, ideas and skills; it also suggests that the blueprint programmes materials, fabric, texture, assembly, construction, relationships and interrelationships. It suggests the presence of a set of inviolable rules and regulations covering strategy and tactics alike. Although it posits the presence of individuals in a team, it does not require of them anything but the strict observance of the rules. There are surveyors and labourers; skilled technicians and site foremen and they have their parts to play. No part requests inspired personal contribution. Rather, it tolerates it within the erection of a monument, the overall design and intricate detail of which are pre-ordained. This does not seem the essential quality behind the creation of an act of theatre.

Consider instead the growth of an oak tree. It requires an acorn as its peculiar programme carrier. If the author is seen as the creator of the acorn the the director can be seen as gardener or horticulturalist. If the acorn is to grow properly, it requires fertile soil, sunlight and rain. It needs to be fed and tended and, from time to time, protected from over-exposure to the elements and over-running by weeds. The young tree will put down roots and put up limbs and branches. It will grow *all of a piece* and its growth will sympathetically reflect the forces at work on it. Root, branch, limb and leaf will all play their part until, in the fulness of time, it will blossom and become a tree *qua* tree. It grows as a whole and, while it will always be an oak tree, the *kind* of oak tree will depend upon the contributory elements enabling its growth.

The idea could be pursued into a conceit of ridiculous proportions—it is relevant to note that it is just as difficult to analyse a 'good' oak tree as it is a 'good' play.

Whichever comparison you choose—house or tree—the reader of a play is left with blueprint or acorn and none of the devices, techniques, elements or materials that are needed to grow either of them to full completion. He must provide all the resources from his inner self and this is no easy task. To make it more difficult he must do it in isolation. There will be no audience with which to create and share responses. There will be no sense of occasion; no group to offer protection to the self; no ritual and no celebration. He will have to provide, substitute and compensate for it all, if he is to attempt to recreate the essential act of theatre.

A Director's Approach

In one sense the director of a play is in an easier position than a reader. The challenges to his imagination are the same, but he does not have to recreate the event—merely to see that its potential exists within the text he is reading. He needs to see the organism he is studying possesses the germ of life. He doesn't need to spread in front of his mind a recreation of its possible maturity. That would deny the validity of the essential growth factor. He needs to be able to recognize the life-force within the organism for *what it is* and determine whether or not he has the right environment, elements, tools and techniques to bring it to a rich growth and flowering. Having recognized a potential that attracts him, the rest of his process is to tend all the elements with care and skill. The operation from beginning to end being rather like a gardener starting with a seed catalogue and finally producing prize blooms.

An Actor's Approach

The actor's creative process is by comparison a complex one. There are many factors that he must consider. There are the special and different needs of: the author—the director—the other actors—the audience—himself. His approach to the text is crucial since he can have no opportunity to contact either author or audience. (Audiences are still remarkable for their passivity. The range of their responses is strictly limited, most of the time, to what kindness and manners allow.) The director and the rest of the cast are involved within the situation and not available for objective comment. He is, therefore, entirely alone on his encounter with the text. It is a direct confrontation between the needs of the author as expressed in the text and those of the actor as he reads it.

What is a Character?

From all this he must abstract what is proper to pursue. He must be able to recognize his own strengths and weaknesses when placed side by side with the text. He must see his own points of identification with the text and his points of departure. Above all he must be able to adjudicate between what the author actually says and what he really means—between what the character in the play says and what he means. It is often said the art of theatre lies in the creation of conflict. The conflict between what a character says and what he means gives rise to much of the strength and purpose in many good plays. The conflict goes further.

The ingredients that go to the creation of a character are these:

1. What the character says when alone:
   (*a*) to himself; (*b*) to the audience.
2. What he says to the other characters:
   (*a*) individually: (i) about themselves; (ii) about others. (*b*) in groups.
3. How he responds to other characters:
   (*a*) individually; (*b*) in groups.
4. What he *does* compared with what he *says*:
   (*a*) immediately; (*b*) during the course of the play.
5. What the other characters:
   (*a*) say to him; (*b*) say about him; (*c*) do to him.

The Place of Stage Directions

Much of this can be gained from the actual dialogue and/or the stage directions. Some authors write at great length to describe what the characters do, look like, dress, eat, speak, etc. Bernard Shaw is an excellent example of a playwright who writes almost more in stage directions than in dialogue. Read just one of his plays and decide for yourself how sufficient and necessary are the comments he makes. You might also read his notes at the end of *Pygmalion* and decide what their function is.

Tennessee Williams

In *Camino Real* Tennessee Williams—always an author to consider the total theatre effect of his scripts—spells out in detail the following:

CAMINO REAL
Tennessee Williams

Block Thirteen

In the blackout the STREETCLEANERS *place a barrel in the centre and then hide in the Pit.*

KILROY, *who enters from the right, is followed by a spotlight. He sees the barrel and the menacing* STREETCLEANERS *and then runs to the closed door of the Siete Mares and rings the bell. No one answers. He backs up so he can see the balcony and calls.*

KILROY: Mr. Gutman! Just gimme a cot in the lobby. I'll do odd jobs in the morning. I'll be the Patsy again. I'll light my nose sixty times a minute. I'll take prat-falls and assume the position for anybody that drops a dime on the street. . . . Have a heart! Have just a LITTLE heart. Please!

(There is no response from GUTMAN's *balcony.* JACQUES *enters. He pounds his cane once on the pavement.)*

JACQUES: Gutman! Open the door! —GUTMAN! GUTMAN!

*(*EVA, *a beautiful woman, apparently nude, appears on the balcony.)*

GUTMAN *(from inside)*: Eva darling, you're exposing yourself!

> *(He appears on the balcony with a portmanteau.)*

JACQUES: What are you doing with my portmanteau?

GUTMAN: Haven't you come for your luggage?

JACQUES: Certainly not! I haven't checked out of here!

GUTMAN: Very few do . . . but residences are frequently terminated.

JACQUES: Open the door!

GUTMAN: Open the letter with the remittance check in it!

JACQUES: In the morning!

GUTMAN: Tonight!

JACQUES: Upstairs in my room!

GUTMAN: Downstairs at the entrance!

JACQUES: I won't be intimidated!

GUTMAN *(raising the portmanteau over his head)*: What?!

JACQUES: Wait!—

> *(He takes the letter out of his pocket.)*
Give me some light.

> *(*KILROY *strikes a match and holds it over* JACQUES' *shoulder.)*
Thank you. What does it say?

GUTMAN:—Remittances?

KILROY *(reading the letter over* JACQUES' *shoulder)*:—discontinued . . .

> *(*GUTMAN *raises the portmanteau again.)*

JACQUES: Careful, I have—

(The portmanteau lands with a crash. The BUM *comes to the window at the crash* A. RATT *comes out to his doorway at the same time.)*

—fragile—mementoes . . .

(He crosses slowly down to the portmanteau and kneels as . . . GUTMAN *laughs and slams the balcony door.* JACQUES *turns to* KILROY. *He smiles at the young adventurer.)*

—'And so at last it has come, the distinguished thing!'

> *(A.* RATT *speaks as* JACQUES *touches the portmanteau.)*

A. RATT: Hey, Dad—Vacancy here! A bed at the 'Ritz Men Only'. A little white ship to sail the dangerous night in.

JACQUES: Single or double?

A. RATT: There's only singles in this pad.

JACQUES (*to* KILROY): Match you for it.

KILROY: What the hell, we're buddies, we can sleep spoons! If we can't sleep we'll push the wash stand against the door and sing old popular songs till the crack of dawn! . . . 'Heart of my heart, I love that melody!' . . . You bet your life I do.

(JACQUES *takes out a pocket handkerchief and starts to grasp the portmanteau handle.*)

In the introduction to the play the author states his purpose as follows:

'But I repeat that symbols, when used respectfully, are the purest language of plays. Sometimes it would take page after tedious page of exposition to put across an idea that can be said with an object or a gesture on the lighted stage.

To take one case in point: the battered portmanteau of Jacques Casanova is hurled from the balcony of a luxury hotel when his remittance cheque fails to come through. While the portmanteau is still in the air, he shouts: 'Careful, I have—'—and when it has crashed to the street he continues—'fragile—mementoes . . .'. I suppose that is a symbol, at least it is an object used to express as directly and vividly as possible certain things which could be said in pages of dull talk.'

Other Authors

At the other end of the spectrum are the texts of Shakespeare. They are well provided with exits, entrances, alarums, flourishes and excursions. Apart from those 'necessaries' there is nothing but the odd bear.

In her play *The Knack*, Ann Jellicoe can write the following: '*Author's Note*: All the above* could be **re-arranged or improvised to suit different actors and different productions** provided the sequence of events is clear:

(1) TOM and COLIN charm NANCY into entering the game.
(2) TOM retires leaving COLIN and NANCY getting on rather well, a growing relationship which TOLEN interrupts.'

The range open to an author is obviously wide. It seems difficult to know where to place the following series of instructions taken at random from a single page of a play which shall be nameless:

There are two characters only: 'A' and 'B'—the dialogue is indicated by dots.

A—(*rising*) . . . . . . (*picking up his books*) . . . . . (*he moves up into the bay*) (*He rises, collecting his books, etc.*) (*To below the steps*) . . . . (*looking out of the window*) . . . . (*stepping through the garden door*) . . . . . . (*B is spreading the tablecloth*)

B—(*calling*) . . . . .

A—(*returning*) . . . . .

B—. . . . .

A—. . . . .

B—(*goes out L. A puts things, including his books, down on the table*)

A—. . . . .

B—(*enters L. Goes to rostrum up C.*) . . . . .

* See page 104.

A—(*picks up salad bowl from table. Replaces it and picks up his books again*)
A—(*Goes up R*) . . . . .
B—. . . . . (*Glancing upward*) . . . . . (*B moves to the other end of the table*)
A—. . . . .
B—. . . . .
A—(*A crosses L*) . . . . .
B—(*B goes down L*) . . . . .
A—(*coming down crossing*) . . . . .
B—(*goes out L*) . . . . .
A—(*Returns to the table. Picks up his things, including his books from the table*)
B—(*enters L*) . . . . .
A—(*crosses and sits*) . . . . .
B—(*crosses and sits*) . . . . .
A—(*stands*) . . . . .

To support this set of detailed instructions there are just over one hundred words of dialogue—fewer than the directions. The conversation is about trivia and 'A' is asked once to move his books from the table—a piece of dialogue which adequately speaks for itself. It can hardly be claimed that the 'stage directions' are dynamic, important or even relevant. The reader is given no reason for the constant moving about. The scene loses nothing if the two characters sit still for the whole dialogue. Even the moving of the books is unnecessary, although the request does support 'A's' untidiness which is established early in the play. **As they stand, the directions do nothing but confuse the inexperienced reader or actor who will not feel entirely at ease in rejecting what he may well believe to be the author's intentions.** If the actor is experienced enough to detect the hand of the West End shorthand writer, they will merely irritate.

This is not to suggest there is no place in the text for indications regarding stage business. Those instructions are the concern of the author and the more sensitive and experienced he is, the more the business he purposefully includes in the text will rise to the stature of symbolism.

Symbolism

Symbolism in the theatre has become a byword for the boringly sombre. Piled behind it is the force of the whole Symbolist Theatre Movement. This usually means the less good plays of Yeats and Maeterlinck—unfortunate since symbolism has much to offer that is in no way boring or sombre. It is an economic method of triggering responses—a kind of three-dimensional short-hand between author and audience. **A symbol is an object, or series of objects, which when used or referred to immediately summons an organized pattern of emotional and intellectual responses.** The object or series of objects must, without strain, be capable of carrying the meaning required. Just as the use of a poetic or highly theatrical manner of delivery is 'ham' unless the character sees himself in a poetic or theatrical situation, so a symbol becomes a gimmick if it cannot carry the appropriate charge. (There is a potential irony available to authors in the exploitation of this **undercharging** of character or situation. It is fertile material for comedy. This is **intentional use by the author** and not a **mistake of actor or director.**) This is not to suggest that symbols can only be used to carry messages of great import—merely to reinforce the suggestion of the need for proportion between symbol and message. A pedal-car is a more suitable vehicle for a toddler than a jet fighter, and a hydrogen bomb more suited to the destruction of the universe than a toy pistol. The well-chosen symbol never appears to be consciously chosen. It seems natural and necessary. Here are some plays which make particular use of symbols. The first three are contained within the titles.

The Wild Duck—Ibsen
The Seagull—Chekhov
Lady Windermere's Fan—Wilde
Macbeth—Shakespeare—Blood and knives
Camino Real—Williams—The Refuse Collectors
The Fire Raisers—Frisch—Sirens
The Caretaker—Pinter—Sidcup and Papers
Waiting for Godot—Beckett—Godot and the Tree.

Examine the plays for yourself. Make a note of how many times the symbols are used or referred to. Decide whether they are well chosen and whether or not they carry out their function. Notice how the authors make their symbols work for them. Compare their methods. Make a list of the other symbols that appear in the plays.

Action and Business

Not all stage business achieves the status of symbolism. In the theatre of naturalism (perhaps better named behaviourism—but see Chapter Sixteen) it would be an *embarras de richesse* if this were to occur since the main plank in this style of theatre is acceptable, credible personal behaviour. A successful symbol is sufficient, necessary and peculiarly appropriate to the style, content and theme of the play.

The same requirements apply to stage business. It should stem from and provide a secure base for acceptable behaviour from credible characters living in recognizable conditions. If there is too little business the audience will be led to believe there is something unusual about the stage characters. If there is too much it will be impossible to separate the significant from the supportive. **Stage business should illuminate without exposing the light source and clothe the characters and their actions without disguising or camouflaging them.** In this sense all stage business should contain elements of the symbolic. The possibility of confusion arises only because the choice within a naturalistic play is very wide. The whole range of the trivia of living is available: reading newspapers, smoking cigarettes, mixing and drinking cocktails, making beds, laying tables and eating meals being but a few examples of the kind of business that litters many popular naturalistic plays. Almost any single piece of business could be replaced by almost any other—but **something** must be chosen since it is **not acceptable for characters to do nothing.**

The way 'action' and 'business' on the stage are separated in many texts is indicative of the central necessity of the first and the peripheral option of the second. Dramatic action speaks for itself. The text requires it—implicitly or explicitly—and no additional instruction is needed. Stage business does not, and cannot, stand self-justified in the same way. **Action is dramatically executive and business is supportive and explanatory.** The selection and presentation of stage business is therefore a delicate task requiring **wise and sensitive choice** in the initial phases and **ruthless pruning and refinining** in the second. An audience must be given the proper signals to help it assess what is significant and what is supportive—what is central, what is marginal and what is peripheral.

When you next watch or read a play containing business drawn from the trivia of living, ask yourself what is being gained, for example, by the washing up of crockery, or the lighting of a pipe. Make a short list of other activities that could, acceptably and credibly, be substituted. Decide whether any or all of them by virtue of *body image* or the *nature of the activity* make positive statements—emotional, social, political, etc.—without the addition, or in spite of, an individual actor's contribution. For example, what is the unique contribution of combing the hair? How much of its message or signal can be achieved by filing the nails, straightening a tie, touching up make-up, inspecting shirt-cuffs or looking in a mirror? Remember, the **function of stage business is to illuminate by selection not confuse by accumulation.**

Translations

Stage directions in published texts can frequently make the task of directors and actors more difficult. They can, as has been shown, stand between the author and his audience, dampening the impact of his work and even confusing his meaning. An even greater source of confusion to actors and audience alike can be the translation of a text. Consider the following examples from a play by the Czech brothers Josef and Karel Capek. In each case the first extract is from the 1950 edition of *International Modern Plays* No. 989 in Everyman's Library published by J. M. Dent & Sons Ltd. The second is from a 1923 edition by Humphrey Milford, published by Oxford University Press. Variation begins at the beginning.

A   THE LIFE OF THE INSECTS
Comedy in Three Acts with
Prelude and Epilogue
by
JOSEF AND KAREL CAPEK
Sole authorized translation from the Czech by
PAUL SELVER

B   And so *ad infinitum*
(*The Life of the Insects*)
An Entomological Review, in Three Acts
a Prologue and an Epilogue
by
THE BROTHERS CAPEK
The authorized translation from the
Czech by Paul Selver

FREELY ADAPTED FOR THE ENGLISH STAGE
BY NIGEL PLAYFAIR AND CLIFFORD BAX

'So, Naturalists observe, a flea
Has smaller fleas that on him prey;
And these have smaller still to bite 'em,
And so proceed *ad infinitum.*'
DEAN SWIFT.

A

PEDANT (*runs in with a net*): Ha, ha. Oh, oh, oh. What fine specimens. Apatura Iris. Apatura Clythia. The painted lady and the light-blue butterfly. Ha, ha, what magnificent creatures. Oh, just you wait, I'll have you. Ha, ha, they're off again. Ha, ha, cautiously, careful, hush, softly, softly, ah, ah, gently, gently—aha, oho, careful, careful, ath, oho, oho—

VAGRANT: Hi, what are you catching butterflies for? Good day to you, kind sir.

PEDANT: Softly, softly, careful. Don't move. They've settled on you. Butterflies. Nymphalidae. Careful, keep still. They settle on everything that smells. On mud, On offal. On garbage. Careful, they've settled on you. Oho, oho.

VAGRANT: Let them be. They're playing.

PEDANT: What, playing? Their play is only the overture to pairing. The male pursues the female, the bride slips away, lures him on, the pursuer tickles her with his feelers, sinks down, exhausted, the female flits off, a new, stronger, sturdier male will come, the female slips away, entices the lover after her, aha, aha. Do you catch my meaning? That's the way of nature. The eternal contest of love. The eternal mating. The eternal round of sex. Rush, softly.

VAGRANT: And what will you do with them when you catch them?

PEDANT: What will I do? Well, the butterfly must be identified, recorded, and assigned a place in my collection. But the pollen mustn't be rubbed off. The net should be of delicate texture. The butterfly should be carefully killed by crushing its breast. And then impaled on a pin. And fastened down with paper strips. And placed in the collection when it's properly dried. It should be protected against dust and moth. Put a small sponge of cyanide into the case.

VAGRANT: And what's all that for?

PEDANT: Love of nature. Man alive, you've no love of nature! Aha, there they are again. Ha, ha, careful, careful, softly. You won't escape me, ha, ha.

(Runs off.)

VAGRANT: Eternal mating, love's eternal contest,
'Tis even so; 'tis ever pairing time,
As said the pedant. Kindly pardon me
For being drunk. Why, I can see quite well.
Everything's twofold, everything's in pairs,
Here, there, and here again, and everywhere,
All things in pairs. Clouds, gnats, and trees,
All things embrace and fondle, dally, provoke, and pursue,
Birds in the tree-tops, I see you, I see you,
I see all. And you two, yonder in the shadow,
I see you linking your fingers, struggling hotly and softly,
Let none of you think I don't see you from here.
That's eternal mating. Kindly pardon me.
I'm drunk, but I'm a sport. (*Covers his eyes.*) I see nothing.
Do what you will. I'll shout before I uncover my eyes.

(Darkness.)

All things strive to pair. Only you, standing here in the darkness,
Alone, alone, alone you wander your crooked way,
Vainly, vainly, vainly would you lift your hands

In love's hide-and-seek. Enough. But ye shall take joy of each other,
Wherefore I applaud you, that's a goodly thing
And nature's wise order, as the pedant said.
—All things strive to pair. Now do I behold
The blissful garden of love bedecked with flowers.
　　　　　　　(*The back curtain rises.*)
Wherein young pairs, beauteous twin begins,
Butterflies swept along by the gust of love,
In rapturous flight, as though they were at play,
Unendingly they bear eternal matings
For all things strive to pair.
　　　　(*He uncovers his eyes. The scene is lit up.*)
　　　　　　　　　　　　　　　Where am I?

B

LEPIDOPTERIST: There they go, there they go! Fine specimens! APATURA IRIS—
APATURA CLYTHIA—light blue butterfles and the Painted Lady. Wait a
minute—I'll get you! That's just it—they won't wait, the silly creatures. Off
again. . . . Hullo—somebody here. They're settling on him. Now! Carefully.
Slowly. Tiptoe! One, two, three!

(*A butterfly settles on the tip of the* TRAMP'S *nose. The* LEPIDOPTERIST *makes a
dab with his net.*)

TRAMP: 'Ullo! What yer doin'? Ketchin' butterflies?
LEPIDOPTERIST: Don't move! Careful now! They're settling again. Funny
creatures—they'll settle on mud, on any sort of garbage, and now they're
settling on you.
TRAMP: Let 'em go. They're 'appy.
LEPIDOPTERIST: Idiot! I've lost them, confound you! There they go, there they
go!
TRAMP: It's a shime—it is, reely.

(*The* LEPIDOPTERIST *rushes out, R. The* TRAMP *stretches his arms, takes a pull
at the emptied bottle, yawns, staggers to his feet and drops down again.*)

(*Speaking to the audience*) All right—all right! Don't you worry. I 'aven't
'urt myself! I know what you think—you think I'm screwed—some of you!
Rotten observation—low visibility—that's what you're suffering from. You
didn't catch me staggering, did you? I fell like a tree—like a hero! I was
rehearsing, that's what I was doing—the fall of man! The fall of man!
There's a picture for yer! Ah, you little flowers—you didn't think I was
drunk, did you? You've too much respect for me! I'm a man, that's what I
am—a lord of creation! A great thing to be, I tell yer! 'Now then, pass along
there, my man!' That's what they say to me. It's wonderful! 'Clear up that
rubbish heap, my man, and I'll give you a tanner, my man.' It's a fine thing
to be a man. (*He succeeds in getting his balance.*)

　　　　　　　(*Enter the* LEPIDOPTERIST, *R.*)

LEPIDOPTERIST: Two,—splendid Nymphalidae!
TRAMP: No offence, mister, but why'jer catch them when they're all so 'appy
playing?

LEPIDOPTERIST: Playing, you call it. I'm afraid you haven't the scientific mind, my friend. It's the overture to the natural system by which Nature keeps up the balance of the population—that's what you call 'playing'. The male pursues the female; the female allures, avoids—selects—the eternal round of sex!

TRAMP: What will you do with them when you catch them?

LEPIDOPTERIST: What shall I do? Well, each insect must be identified, recorded and assigned a place in my collection. The butterfly must be carefully killed, and then carefully pinned, and properly dried, and care must be taken that the powder is not rubbed off. And it must be protected against dust and draught. A little cyanide of potassium.

TRAMP: And what's it all for?

LEPIDOPTERIST: Love of nature—if you loved nature as much as I did, my man—Careful—didn't I tell you—they're off again. Never mind, I'll get you, see if I don't.

(*Exit.*)

TRAMP: 'E's clever, that there bloke. And as for me,
P'raps I am screwed; but if I am, 'oo cares?
That ain't the only reason why I see
Everythink double, everythink in pairs.
Them little birds up there . . . I see you plain!
Tweety-weety-weet . . . Lord! 'ow they bill and coo,
As yer might say. Them butterflies again,
What sport they 'ave—ow prettily they woo!
Love's what they want. Some day they'll get it, p'raps:
Everythink does—or mostways everythink . . .
(S'pose you'd a girl who loved all kinds of chaps—
Wouldn't you damn yerself, and take to drink?)
Well, 'ere's the world, and though I'm down and out,
It's worth while learnin' what it's all about.

(CURTAIN)

CHAPTER ELEVEN

WORKING ON A TEXT—II

The Play as Literature

In addition to the obstacles of added stage directions and the risks of translation there is the attitude of mind with which an actor first approaches the text. The tradition that any good play is also good literature dies hard. The classroom study of play texts for academic examinations does nothing to redress the balance. Any actor who has escaped the inculcation of our literary heritage enough to be able to approach a text with an open mind is indeed lucky. There are few people who do not bring to a text at least a slight overtone of literary criticism.

This is not to suggest that a good play should be anti-literary (although such a school of thought is growing—supported by hastily snatched quotations from a much maligned and even more misunderstood Artaud) but merely that **the residual literary element contained in most good plays is no test of their quality as vehicles for the theatre.** Much of our trouble in coming to proper twentieth-century grips with Shakespeare is caused by the fact that he is our greatest poet as well as our greatest dramatist. We tend to be so overawed by the magnificence of his poetic skill that we find it difficult to let his plays speak for themselves. A rich literary residue can be a bonus in a play script. Since it is not quintessential to the nature of a play it can also hinder its proper appreciation.

A play—an act of theatre—stands midway between a novel and a poem on the one hand and song and dance on the other. Not only does it occupy a central position, it also combines elements of all four art forms. The following over-simplification will clarify the main platforms:

The novel is concerned to **explore the human condition,** frequently through descriptions of intricate personality traits, explorations of motives, examinations of emotional overtones as well as direct narrative and dialogue. We meet the novel in concrete, permanent form and there is a continuing opportunity for backward or forward reference. The author expects his work to be read in quiet solitude. He neither creates it nor presents it for performance.

The poem is more concerned with the **exposure of the human condition.** It may explore, examine and describe but mainly as a *means* of exposure—thereby confronting the reader with his own inner spirit. There is the same opportunity for continuing reference as with the novel. Most poets expect their work to be read under the same conditions as a novel. Some poets hope for performance—in their case mainly recitation—and a few write specifically for it.

The song **proclaims the human condition.** Its written notation enables an esoteric minority to claim to be able to create in their imagination a satisfactory performance of words and music. Some song contains such little dramatic element that this may be true. Some has such a high proportion— opera to Grand Opera—that the actuality of the ritual is needed for the form to work. (The wide range of song style, especially the oratorio where the performer should obliterate self and be only vessel or vehicle, and the availability of good recordings blurs the edges of definition with regard to this area.) The author/composer creates for performance and only part of the material is concrete and permanent.

The dance **celebrates the human condition**. It is so frequently accompanied (if not inspired) by music that this is now traditional. The novel may deal with intellectual subtleties and the poem with sophisticated emotional expressions. Song may touch on both areas in a simpler way. Dance is most successful with man's elemental animality. Emotions and instincts—the basic chemistry of personal interaction—are the best concerns of dance. Dance is created exclusively for performance and while it can be recorded on film and tape the loss of the here-and-now element of the spontaneous recreation of the ritual as the performance progresses is crucial. (Notations to record dance are in existence, but their complexity removes them from relevance here.) Even the most lyrical solo dance loses when seen on film.

Paintings, sculpture, films and television are examples of art forms where the spectator has less of a co-operative part to play. The ingredients are not under his control in the way a novel or a poem is, nor is he called on to participate in any way that might affect the presentation. The activity is more of a stimulus to the individual than an invitation to co-operate or communicate.

A play sets out to bring together all the elements outlined above. **It explores, exposes, proclaims and celebrates the human condition.** It uses elements of film, television, painting and sculpture in its form of presentation. An author writes with all these objectives in mind as well as the knowledge that he will be interpreted by actors, actresses, directors, choreographers, composers, designers, lighting and sound consultants, costume specialists, etc., etc., *et al*. **In the final resort he must inform all these people—and his audience—through the medium of his script.** Diligent and meticulous he may be—informed and inspired as well—he knows that it is the dialogue he has created, **the actual words to be uttered**, not the additional detail, that will gain or lose his platform.

Viewed in this way, an author's text is like an iceberg—the ice itself being the words and their grammar, accidence, syntax and whatever definitive information they may carry. The visible tip of the iceberg is the rhythm and style of the writing—the unseen, underwater portion being the inner meaning of the play.

Rhythm and Style—Two Approaches

The text may be approached through quiet study or vocal execution. The first method will aim at analysing to the final irreducible to allow an accurate version to emerge in its own time. The second aims at exposing through direct experience and body feel. Both methods have their supporters and both can be defended. A third method puts them together, using direct experience as a stimulus and analytic study as a check. This method has the merit of bringing actor and author into full confrontation as soon as possible. It aims to help the actor get into touch with the guts of the play without hindrance. It also requires him to check his interpretation against conscious analysis—whether he started from inner intuition or kinetic experience, or a combination of both.

The sooner an actor can get into touch with an author's rhythm and style, the sooner will he be able to perceive the totality of the intent—**the combined forces of external style and internal meaning.** If an actor is to communicate the inner meaning of the play he needs to know how to get it out and across. The author made it accessible to understanding through his command of rhythm and style. Consider the following extracts:

Practical Examples

(Before you analyse them or think about their style and rhythm in a conscious way **READ EACH EXTRACT STRAIGHT THROUGH ALOUD.** Don't worry if this means making an occasional error. It is more important for you to get the **experience of the movement of the words** than it is to reproduce the detail with complete exactitude. You should, of course, aim at combining flow and accuracy. On the first approach to, and appraisal of, a script it is important that you gain as full an understanding of the overall rhythm as possible. It is difficult, if not impossible, to gain such an understanding by later study if the initial steps have been slow or even halting in the cause of exactitude. There is plenty of time for any inaccuracy to be corrected once the proper rhythm and style have emerged. **Give the words chance to work on you. Let them make their impact. READ THEM THROUGH ALOUD)**

JULIUS CAESAR

William Shakespeare

FLAVIUS: Hence ! Home, you idle creatures, get you home!
Is this a holiday? What, know you not,
Being mechanical, you ought not walk
Upon a laboring day without the sign
Of your profession? Speak, what trade art thou?
CARPENTER: Why, sir, a carpenter.
MARULLUS: Where is thy leather apron and thy rule?
What dost thou with thy best apparel on?
You, sir, what trade are you?
COBBLER: Truly, sir, in respect of a fine workman, I am but, as you would say, a cobbler.
MARULLUS: But what trade are thou? Answer me directly.
COBBLER: A trade, sir, that, I hope, I may use with a safe conscience, which is indeed, sir, a mender of bad soles.
FLAVIUS: What trade, thou knave? Though naughty knave, what trade?
COBBLER: Nay, I beseech you, sir, be not out with me: yet, if you be out, sir, I can mend you.
MARULLUS: What mean'st thou by that? Mend me, thou saucy fellow?
COBBLER: Why, sir, cobble you.
FLAVIUS: Thou art a cobbler, art thou?
COBBLER: Truly sir, all that I live by is with the awl: I meddle with no tradesman's matters, nor women's matters; but withal, I am indeed, sir, a surgeon to old shoes: when they are in great danger, I recover them. As proper men as ever trod upon neat's leather have gone upon my handiwork.

FLAVIUS: But wherefore art not in thy shop today?
  Why dost thou lead these men about the streets?
COBBLER: Truly, sir, to wear out their shoes, to get myself into more work.
  But indeed, sir, we make holiday to see Caesar and to rejoice in his triumph.
MARULLUS: Wherefore rejoice? What conquest brings he home?
  What tributaries follow him to Rome,
  To grace in captive bonds his chariot wheels?
  You blocks, you stones, you worse than senseless things!
  O you hard hearts, you cruel men of Rome,
  Knew you not Pompey? Many a time and oft
  Have you climbed up to walls and battlements,
  To tow'rs and windows, yea, to chimney tops,
  Your infants in your arms, and there have sat
  The livelong day, with patient expectation,
  To see great Pompey pass the streets of Rome.
  And when you saw his chariot but appear,
  Have you not made an universal shout,
  That Tiber trembled underneath her banks
  To hear the replication of your sounds
  Made in her concave shores?
  And do you now put on your best attire?
  And do you now cull out a holiday?
  And do you now strew flowers in his way
  That comes in triumph over Pompey's blood?
  Be gone!
  Run to your houses, fall upon your knees,
  Pray to the gods to intermit the plague
  That needs must light on this ingratitude.
FLAVIUS: Go, go, good countrymen, and, for this fault,
  Assemble all the poor men of your sort;
  Draw them to Tiber banks and weep your tears
  Into the channel, till the lowest stream
  Do kiss the most exalted shores of all.
                    (*Exeunt all the Commoners.*)
  See, whe'r their basest mettle be not moved;
  They vanish tongue-tied in their guiltiness.
  Go you down that way towards the Capitol;
  This way will I. Disrobe the images,
  If you do find them decked with ceremonies.
MARULLUS: May we do so?
  You know it is the feast of Lupercal.
FLAVIUS: It is no matter; let no images
  Be hung with Caesar's trophies. I'll about
  And drive away the vulgar from the streets;
  So do you too, where you perceive them thick.
  These growing feathers plucked from Caesar's wing
  Will make him fly an ordinary pitch,
  Who else would soar above the view of men
  And keep us all in servile fearfulness.
                    (*Exeunt.*)

BLITHE SPIRIT
Noël Coward

CHARLES: Well, to begin with, I haven't forgotten Elvira. I remember her very distinctly indeed. I remember how fascinating she was, and how maddening. I remember how badly she played all games and how cross she got when she didn't win. I remember her gay charm when she had achieved her own way over something and her extreme acidity when she didn't. I remember her physical attractiveness, which was tremendous, and her spiritual integrity, which was nil.

RUTH: You can't remember something that was nil.

CHARLES: I remember how morally untidy she was.

RUTH: Was she more physically attractive than I am?

CHARLES: That was a very tiresome question, dear, and fully deserves the wrong answer.

RUTH: You really are very sweet.

CHARLES: Thank you.

RUTH: And a little naïve, too.

CHARLES: Why?

RUTH: Because you imagine that I mind about Elvira being more physically attractive than I am.

CHARLES: I should have thought any woman would mind—if it were true. Or perhaps I'm old-fashioned in my view of female psychology.

RUTH: Not exactly old-fashioned, darling, just a bit didactic.

CHARLES: How do you mean?

RUTH: It's didactic to attribute to one type the defects of another type. For instance, because you know perfectly well that Elvira would mind terribly if you found another woman more attractive physically than she was, it doesn't necessarily follow that I should. Elvira was a more physical person than I. I'm certain of that. It's all a question of degree.

CHARLES (*smiling*): I love you, my love.

RUTH: I know you do; but not the wildest stretch of imagination could describe it as the first fine careless rapture.

CHARLES: Would you like it to be?

RUTH: Good God, no!

CHARLES: Wasn't that a shade too vehement?

RUTH: We're neither of us adolescent, Charles; we've neither of us led exactly prim lives, have we? And we've both been married before. Careless rapture at this stage would be incongruous and embarrassing.

CHARLES: I hope I haven't been in any way a disappointment, dear.

RUTH: Don't be so idiotic.

CHARLES: After all, your first husband was a great deal older than you, wasn't he? I shouldn't like you to think that you'd missed out all along the line.

RUTH: There are moments, Charles, when you go too far.

CHARLES: Sorry, darling.

RUTH: As far as waspish female psychology goes, there's a rather strong vein of it in you.

CHARLES: I've heard that said about Julius Caesar.

RUTH: Julius Caesar is neither here nor there.

CHARLES: He may be for all we know. We'll ask Madame Arcati.

RUTH (*rises and crosses to L.*): You're awfully irritating when you're determined to be witty at all costs, almost supercilious.

CHARLES: That's exactly what Elvira used to say.

RUTH: I'm not at all surprised. I never imagined, physically triumphant as she was, that she was entirely lacking in perception.

(CHARLES *rises and goes to the R. of* RUTH)

CHARLES: Darling Ruth!

RUTH: There you go again!

CHARLES (*kissing her lightly*): As I think I mentioned before, I love you, my love.

RUTH. Poor Elvira!

CHARLES: Didn't that light, comradely kiss mollify you at all?

RUTH: You're very annoying, you know you are. When I said 'Poor Elvira' it came from the heart. You must have bewildered her so horribly.

CHARLES: Don't I ever bewilder you at all?

RUTH: Never for an instant. I know every trick.

CHARLES: Well, all I can say is that we'd better get a divorce immediately.

RUTH: Put my glass down, there's a darling.

CHARLES (*taking it*): She certainly had a great talent for living. It was a pity that she died so young.

RUTH: Poor Elvira!

CHARLES (*crossing to and putting the glasses on the drinks table*): That remark is getting monotonous.

RUTH (*moving upstage a pace*): Poor Charles, then.

CHARLES: That's better.

RUTH: And later on, poor Ruth, I expect.

CHARLES (*coming to above the C. table*): You have no faith, Ruth. I really do think you should try to have a little faith.

RUTH (*moving to the L. arm of the armchair*): I shall strain every nerve.

CHARLES: Life without faith is an arid business.

RUTH: How beautifully you put things, dear.

CHARLES: I aim to please.

RUTH: If I died, I wonder how long it would be before you married again?

CHARLES: You won't die. You're not the dying sort.

RUTH: Neither was Elvira.

CHARLES: Oh yes, she was, now that I look back on it. She had a certain ethereal, not-quite-of-this-world quality. Nobody could call you, even remotely, ethereal.

ROMEO AND JULIET
William Shakespeare

ROMEO: If I profane with my unworthiest hand
    This holy shrine, the gentle sin is this.
  My lips, two blushing pilgrims, ready stand
    To smooth that rough touch with a tender kiss.

JULIET: Good pilgrim, you do wrong your hand too much,
    Which mannerly devotion shows in this.
  For saints have hands that pilgrims' hands do touch,
    And palm to palm is holy palmers' kiss.

ROMEO: Have not saints lips, and holy palmers too?
JULIET: Ay, pilgrim, lips that they must use in prayer.
ROMEO: O, then, dear saint, let lips do what hands do!
    They pray: grant thou, lest faith turn to despair.
JULIET: Saints do not move, though grant for prayers' sake.
ROMEO: Then move not while my prayer's effect I take.
    He kisses her
    Thus from my lips, by thine my sin is purged.
JULIET: Then have my lips the sin that they have took.
ROMEO: Sin from my lips? O trespass sweetly urged!
    Give me my sin again.
    He kisses her.

ROMEO AND JULIET

William Shakespeare

ROMEO: But soft! What light through yonder window breaks?
    It is the East, and Juliet is the sun!
    Arise, fair sun, and kill the envious moon,
    Who is already sick and pale with grief
    That thou her maid art far more fair than she.
    Be not her maid, since she is envious.
    Her vestal livery is but sick and green,
    And none but fools do wear it. Cast it off.
    It is my lady. O, it is my love!
    O that she knew she were!
    She speaks. Yet she says nothing. What of that?
    Her eye discourses. I will answer it.
    I am too bold. 'Tis not to me she speaks.
    Two of the fairest stars in all the heaven,
    Having some business, do entreat her eyes
    To twinkle in their spheres till they return.
    What if her eyes were there, they in her head?
    The brightness of her cheek would shame those stars
    As daylight doth a lamp. Her eyes in heaven
    Would through the airy region stream so bright
    That birds would sing and think it were not night.
    See how she leans her cheek upon her hands!
    O that I were a glove upon that hand,
    That I might touch that cheek!
JULIET: Ay me!
ROMEO: She speaks.
    O, speak again, bright angel!—for thou art
    As glorious to this night, being o'er my head,
    As is a winged messenger of heaven
    Unto the white-upturned wondering eyes
    Or mortals that fall back to gaze on him
    When he bestrides the lazy, puffing clouds
    And sails upon the bosom of the air.

JULIET: O Romeo, Romeo!—wherefore art thou Romeo?
Deny thy father and refuse thy name.
Or, if thou wilt not, be but sworn my love,
And I'll no longer be a Capulet.

ROMEO (*aside*):
Shall I hear more, or shall I speak at this?

JULIET: 'Tis but thy name that is my enemy.
Thou art thyself, though not a Montague.
What's Montague? It is nor hand nor foot
Nor arm nor face nor any other part
Belonging to a man. O, be some other name!
What's in a name? That which we call a rose
By any other word would smell as sweet
So Romeo would, were he not Romeo called,
Retain that dear perfection which he owes
Without that title. Romeo, doff thy name;
And for thy name, which is no part of thee,
Take all myself.

ROMEO: I take thee at thy word.
Call me but love, and I'll be new baptized.
Henceforth I never will be Romeo.

JULIET: What man art thou that, thus bescreened in night,
So stumblest on my counsel?

ROMEO: By a name
I know not how to tell thee who I am.
My name, dear saint, is hateful to myself,
Because it is an enemy to thee.
Had I it written, I would tear the word.

JULIET: My Ears have yet not drunk a hundred words
Of thy tongue's uttering, yet I know the sound.
Art thou not Romeo, and a Montague?

ROMEO: Neither, fair maid, if either thee dislike.

JULIET: How camest thou hither, tell me, and wherefore?
The orchard walls are high and hard to climb,
And the place death, considering who thou art,
If any of my kinsmen find thee here.

ROMEO: With love's light wings did I o'erperch these walls.
For stony limits cannot hold love out,
And what love can do, that dares love attempt.
Therefore thy kinsmen are no stop to me.

JULIET: If they do see thee, they will murder thee.

ROMEO: Alack, there lies more peril in thine eye
Than twenty of their swords! Look thou but sweet,
And I am proof against their enmity.

JULIET: I would not for the world they saw thee here.

ROMEO: I have night's cloak to hide me from their eyes.
And but thou love me, let me find me here.
My life were better ended by their hate
Than death prorogued, wanting of thy love.

JULIET: By whose direction foundest thou out this place?

ROMEO: By love, that first did prompt me to inquire.
   He lent me counsel, and I lent him eyes.
   I am no pilot; yet, wert thou as far
   As that vast shore washed with the farthest sea,
   I should adventure for such merchandise.

Having read them through aloud, go back over the passages and pay special attention to the way they are presented—the length of lines, sentences, phrases and paragraphs as indicated by the text itself.

Notice the use of capital letters, commas, colons and full-stops, etc. Look for the way the author uses vowels and consonants—long, short, plosive, etc.—to create a dynamic pattern.

Beginnings—Middles—Ends

Just as in the 'Typing a letter' example of movement on the stage it was possible to consider sequences that had a unity within themselves and then proceed to break them down until left with **prime phrases** only, so is the same treatment possible with the script. The author makes a number of phrases or divisions clearly important in his choice of acts and scenes. The same **beginning—middle—end** measure still applies. (With many plays this first division is over-simplified by the author neatly providing one act for each—no doubt influenced partly by the traditional organization of refreshments. Leonard Pronko, in his splendid study of the experimental theatre in France, *Avant-garde*, quotes Beckett's reference to his play *Waiting for Godot* as follows: 'One act would have been too little and three acts would have been too much'.)

The plays from which the extracts are taken are divided as follows:

Julius Caesar:
ACT I—3 scenes; ACT II—4 scenes; ACT III—3 scenes; ACT IV—3 scenes; ACT V—5 scenes. A total of 18 scenes.

Blithe Spirit:
ACT I—2 scenes; ACT II—3 scenes; ACT III—2 scenes. A total of 7 scenes.

Romeo and Juliet:
ACT I—5 scenes; ACT II—6 scenes; ACT III—5 scenes; ACT IV—5 scenes; ACT V—3 scenes. A total of 24 scenes.

The number of acts and scenes that an author uses affects the overall rhythm of the piece. Each act and each scene can be divided into beginning—middle—end until, as with the movement sequence, prime units are exposed.

Prime Units

At one end of the spectrum the three-act play automatically presents the major subdivision. There is one act for each part. At the other end of the spectrum a division into words, or even syllables, could be claimed to be the logical reduction. Since the concern is with a **prime unit that carries a rational message** the best measure is that of phrases. This is no hard and fast rule, as will be shown, and dependent upon the author's style there is considerable movement between the two main units—the single word and the complete sentence.

Detailed Examples

The extract from *Julius Caesar* is a complete and self-contained scene. It falls readily into four major parts: 1. lines 1–27; 2. lines 28–52; 3. lines 53–57; 4. lines 58–72. Each has a clearly identifiable beginning and end. The middles are not so readily noticeable, but, for the present purpose, this is not a disadvantage.

A close examination of lines 1–27 reveals the rhythm to have a **long stroke**. The following division seems the nearest to prime phrases, without going into the non-rational and non-communicative:

1. Hence! Home, you idle creatures, get you home!
(In this, as in other examples, performance may further subdivide. This will be more in the nature of tactics of stress and emphasis than strategy of dynamic rhythm and style.)
2. Is this a holiday?
3. What, know you not, being mechanical, you ought not walk upon a labouring day without the sign of your profession?
4. Speak, what trade art thou?
5. Why, sir, a carpenter.

It is possible that an actor or director, wishing to make some specific point, could justifiably pluck out 'you idle creatures' and 'being mechanical'. This would be running against the general pattern of rhythm and would have special motivation. The words themselves hang together in the greater rhythm rather and do not call out for a phrase of their own.

It is worth noting that there is nothing accidental about the way the words achieve this strength of stroke and length of rhythmic phrase. Take the simple example of the carpenter's first words 'Why, sir, a carpenter'. There is no great overtone of meaning or mood that he is required to express at the time. The information in his reply is straightforward and factual. With hardly any change in mood or meaning he could easily have said any of the following:

'Carpenter'; 'A Carpenter'; 'Sir, a carpenter'; 'Why, a carpenter.'
The choice of the full phrase requires a longer rhythmic stroke. This tends to suggest a dignity that informs the whole play. This long rhythmic stroke, together with the sparing use of metaphor, gives the play its sobriety and clarity (which, however, some have seen as sombre and bald).

Consider the first two speeches of the cobbler. While it is possible to break them into small prime units by the use of pause—between *fine* and *workman* for example—this goes against the natural urge and urgency of the words to **hang together as a dynamic unit**. The force of the words themselves is towards cohesion.

Consider the two sentences of Marullus beginning (line 34) 'Many a time and oft . . .' and (line 40) 'And when you saw his chariot but appear. . . .' The first is difficult to deliver except with one overall sweep. The second is almost impossible.

A long stride or stroke is not exclusive to Shakespeare—nor to verse or poetic drama. Indeed, many plays written in verse form—whether classic or free—achieve a markedly different rhythm.

Consider the second extract. The vehicle is straightforward, credible conversation selected by an author who has an ear for sophistication and a taste for making his points through the superficial. There is nothing of the grandeur of Rome or the tragedy of Verona, but the sweep of the rhythm would be appropriate to either.

The extract is not self-contained but the individual speeches of Charles and Ruth are. The prime units that immediately suggest themselves are these separate speeches. The places for variation or special consideration occur between the speeches—not during them. This is substantiated by the short exchanges as well as the longer speeches. Examples of the latter are:

CHARLES: Well, to begin with, I haven't forgotten Elvira. I remember her very distinctly indeed. I remember how fascinating she was, and how maddening. I remember how badly she played all games and how cross she got when she didn't win. I remember her gay charm when she had achieved her own way over something and her extreme acidity when she didn't. I remember her physical attractiveness, which was tremendous, and her spiritual integrity, which was nil.

Assessing the speech superficially, reading it silently for 'meaning', may give the impression that the opportunities for abstracting prime units and using pause for impact between them, abound in the six sentences. The following seems possible and attractive:

Well
to begin with
I haven't
forgotten Elvira
I remember her
very
distinctly
indeed
how fascinating
she was
and
how
maddening.

Such a subdivision of the lines may appear to help create dramatic meaning and character. It is only when the words are felt and tasted in the mouth that their inner movement makes it clear that such a **small measure of rhythm or stroke causes discomfort and the words themselves move against it**. Another example is:

RUTH: It's didactic to attribute to one type the defects of another type. For instance, because you know perfectly well that Elvira would mind terribly if you found another woman more physically attractive than she was, it doesn't necessarily follow that I should. Elvira was a more physical person than I. I'm certain of that. It's all a question of degree.

The first two sentences are much longer than the last three. But even with the shortest there is still the feeling that the movement should continue in a smooth, uninterrupted manner. There is nothing in the flow of rest of the speech to encourage a long pause before 'It's all a question of degree'. Intellectually, there is every reason to justify pause for final thought before summing up; for impact; for Charles to interrupt if he wishes. But the feel of the preceding flow makes it almost impossible not to continue straight to the end.

The following exchange consists of shorter sentences:

RUTH: You can't remember something that was nil.

CHARLES: I remember how morally untidy she was.

RUTH: Was she more physically attractive than I am?

CHARLES: That was a very tiresome question, dear, and fully deserves the wrong answer.

RUTH: You really are very sweet.

CHARLES: Thank you.

RUTH: And a little naïve, too.

CHARLES: Why?

RUTH: Because you imagine that I mind about Elvira being more physically attractive than I am.

Even with these shorter statements and questions, there is still the demand from the words themselves to be delivered with a **rhythm of long reach**. The last three sentences of Ruth's are broken by two interjections from Charles. It is possible, and in fact important, to discover the proper rhythm and timing for Charles to use for the Thank you and Why?, but there is no justification for treating them as final and prime phrases. To do so would be to detract from the main flow of the piece which, at that time, is in Ruth's hands. The initiative for prime phrases of rhythm stays with her.

The passage beginning: CHARLES: 'It was a pity she died so young' to CHARLES: 'You have no faith, Ruth', exhibits similar characteristics, with the responsibility for the creation of the rhythm being shared between the two.

The opening sentence in this last sequence is a good example of the choice that an actor must make from time to time when the decision regarding the prime phrase could be argued. The full speech from Charles is: 'She certainly had a great talent for living. It was a pity she died so young.' Each sentence could be claimed to have its own, essential rhythm of beginning—middle—end. Equally can it be claimed that the proper phrasing would cover both. This would mean, for the first choice, that 'living' would be an end and 'It' a beginning. Whether the choice is made as a result of the kinetic experience of saying the words, or as an intellectual matter of interpretation, the product in terms of delivery/meaning is the same. The first choice separates the apparent thought-processes behind the two sentences and the second unites them. Apparent thought-processes behind the text are dealt with later in the chapter and kinetic experience rather than intellectual interpretation is the present concern. The way an individual actor approaches the text when first speaking it—his breath control; vocal and speech agility; his natural pattern and rhythm of speech—will all affect his choice of the shorter or longer rhythm.

Consider the following lines from the third extract. They come from a self-contained scene which has something in common with the second. They are both duologue scenes between lovers and both contain their own brand of conceit.

ROMEO: If I profane with my unworthiest hand
    This holy shrine, the gentle sin is this.
    My lips, two blushing pilgrims, ready stand
    To smooth that rough touch with a tender kiss.

From an intellectual or commonsense point of view the two sentences each make perfectly good sense if spoken as prime phrases. In the mouth, experienced physically, they strongly resist such an interpretation. The same urge runs through the whole scene. It is also to be found in the fourth extract. The following well-known quotation is symptomatic of a text, which by its unique dynamic, demands prime phrases as short as single words:

JULIET: O Romeo, Romeo!—wherefore art thou Romeo?
Deny thy father and refuse thy name.
Or, if thou wilt not, be but sworn my love,
And I'll no longer be a Capulet.

Perhaps contrary to expectation, the longer prime phrases and rhythmic sweeps are used in the lighter vehicle—the 'improbable farce'—while the shorter achieve their impact in the 'two hour's traffic of our stage'.

Shape

The following three extracts share a similar construction. In each, there is **preparatory dialogue** leading to an **explosion of dramatic expression**. Each uses a **short prime phrase** and on many occasions there is a **strong suggestion that the rhythm is halting**.

THE CHERRY ORCHARD
Anton Chekhov

LIUBOV ANDRYEEVNA: It's you, Yermolai Aleksyeevich? Why have you been so long? Where is Leonid?
LOPAHIN: Leonid Andryeevich returned with me, he's coming along.
LIUBOV ANDRYEEVNA (*agitated*): Well, what happened? Was there an auction? Speak, tell me!
LOPAHIN (*embarrassed, fearing to betray his joy*): The auction was over by four o'clock. . . . We missed our train and had to wait until half-past nine. (*With a deep sigh.*) Ugh! My head's going round . . .

(*Enter* GAYEV: *he carries some parcels in his right hand and wipes away his tears with his left.*)

LIUBOV ANDRYEEVNA: Lionia, what happened? Well, Lionia? (*Impatiently, with tears.*) Tell me quickly, for God's sake! . . .
GAYEV (*does not reply, but waves his hand at her. To* FEERS, *weeping*): Here, take this . . . it's some anchovies and Kerch herrings. . . . I've had nothing to eat all day. . . . What I've been through!

(*Through the open door leading to the billiard-room comes the sound of billiard balls in play and* YASHA'S *voice saying:* 'Seven and eighteen'. GAYEV'S *expression changes and he stops crying.*)

I'm dreadfully tired. Come, Feers, I want to change. (*Goes out through the ballroom,* FEERS *following.*)
PISHCHIK: What happened at the auction? Come, do tell us!
LIUBOV ANDRYEEVNA: Has the cherry orchard been sold?
LOPAHIN: It has.
LIUBOV ANDRYEEVNA: Who bought it?
LOPAHIN: I did.

(*A pause.*)

(LIUBOV ANDRYEEVNA *is overcome; only the fact that she is standing beside a table and a chair prevents her from falling.* VARIA *takes a bundle of keys off her belt, throws them on the floor in the middle of the drawing-room and walks out.*)
Yes, I bought it. Wait a moment, ladies and gentlemen, do, please. I don't feel quite clear in my head, I hardly know how to talk . . . (*Laughs.*) When we got to the auction, Deriganov was there already. Of course, Leonid Andryeevich only had fifteen thousand roubles, and Deriganov at once bid thirty over and above the mortgage. I could see how things were going, so I muscled in and offered forty. He bid forty-five, I bid fifty-five; he kept on adding five thousand each time and I added ten thousand each time. Well, it finished at last—I bid ninety thousand over and above the mortgage, and I got the property. Yes, the cherry orchard's mine now! Mine! (*Laughs.*) My God! the cherry orchard's mine! Come on, tell me I'm drunk, tell me I'm out of my mind, say I've imagined all this . . . (*Stamps his foot.*) Don't laugh at me! If only my father and grandfather could rise from their graves and see everything that's happened . . . how their Yermolai, their much-beaten, half-literate Yermolai, the lad that used to run about with bare feet in the winter . . . how he's bought this estate, the most beautiful place on God's earth! Yes, I've bought the very estate where my father and grand-father were serfs, where they weren't even admitted to the kitchen! I must be asleep, I must be dreaming, I only think it's true . . . it's all just my imagi-nation, my imagination's been wandering . . . (*Picks up the keys, smiling tenderly.*) She threw these down because she wanted to show she's not mis-tress here any more. (*Jingles the keys.*) Well, never mind. (*The band is heard tuning up.*) Hi! you musicians, come on now, play something, I want some music! Now then, all of you, just you wait and see Yermolai Lopahin take an axe to the cherry orchard, just you see the trees come crashing down! We're going to build a whole lot of new villas, and our children and great-grandchildren are going to see a new living world growing up here. . . . Come on there, let's have some music!
(*The band plays.* LIUBOV ANDRYEEVNA *has sunk into a chair and is crying bitterly.*)
(*Reproachfully.*) Why didn't you listen to me before, why didn't you? My poor, dear lady, you can't undo it now. (*With great emotion.*) Oh, if only we could be done with all this, if only we could alter this distorted unhappy life somehow!
PISHCHIK (*taking his arm, in a subdued voice*): She's crying. Come into the ball-room, leave her alone. . . . Come along. . . . (*Takes his arm and leads him away to the ballroom.*)
LOPAHIN: Never mind! Come on, band, play up, play up! Everything must be just as I wish it now. (*Ironically.*) Here comes the new landowner, here comes the owner of the cherry orchard! (*He pushes a small table accidentally and nearly knocks over some candle-sticks.*) Never mind, I can pay for every-thing! (*Goes out with* PISHCHIK.)
(*No one remains in the ballroom or drawing-room save* LIUBOV ANDRYEEVNA, *who sits hunched up in a chair, crying bitterly. The band continues playing quietly.* ANIA *and* TROFIMOV *enter quickly;* ANIA *goes up to her mother and kneels beside her,* TROFIMOV *remains standing by the entrance to the ballroom.*)
ANIA. Mamma! . . . Mamma, you're crying? Dear, kind, sweet Mamma, my darling precious, how I love you! God bless you, Mamma! The cherry orchard's sold, it's quite true, there isn't any cherry orchard any more, it's

true ... but don't cry, Mamma, you still have your life ahead of you, you still have your dear, innocent heart. You must come away with me, darling, we must get away from here! We'll plant a new orchard, even more splendid than this one—and when you see it, you'll understand everything, your heart will be filled with happiness, like the sun in the evening; and then you'll smile again, Mamma! Come with me, darling, do come! ...

THE MAIDS
Jean Genet

CLAIRE (*complainingly, Madame's voice*): You're talking far too much, my child. Far too much. Shut the window. (SOLANGE *shuts the window*.) Draw the curtains. Very good, Claire!

SOLANGE: It's late. Everyone's in bed. ... We're playing an idiotic game.

CLAIRE (*she signals with her hand for silence*): Claire, pour me a cup of tea.

SOLANGE: But ...

CLAIRE: I said a cup of tea.

SOLANGE: We're dead-tired. We've got to stop. (*She sits down in an armchair*.)

CLAIRE: Ah, by no means! Poor servant girl, you think you'll get out of it as easily as that? It would be too simple to conspire with the wind, to make the night one's accomplice. Solange, you will contain me within you. Now pay close attention.

SOLANGE: Claire ...

CLAIRE: Do as I tell you. I'm going to help you. I've decided to take the lead. Your role is to keep me from backing out, nothing more.

SOLANGE: What more do you want? We're at the end ...

CLAIRE: We're at the very beginning.

SOLANGE: They'll be coming ...

CLAIRE: Forget about them. We're alone in the world. Nothing exists but the altar where one of the two maids is about to immolate herself—

SOLANGE: But—

CLAIRE: Be still. It will be your task, yours alone, to keep us both alive. You must be very strong. In prison no one will know that I'm with you, secretly. On the sly.

SOLANGE: I'll never be able ...

CLAIRE: Please, stand up straight. Up straight, Solange! Claire! Darling, stand straight now. Up straight. Pull yourself together.

SOLANGE: You're overwhelming me.

CLAIRE: A staff! A standard! Claire, up straight! I call upon you to represent me!

SOLANGE: I've been working too hard. I'm exhausted.

CLAIRE: To represent me in the world. (*She tries to lift her sister and keep her on her feet*.) My darling, stand up straight.

SOLANGE: Please, I beg of you.

CLAIRE (*domineeringly*): I beg of you, stand up straight. Solemnly, Claire! Pretty does it, pretty does it! Up Claire! Up on your paws! (*She holds her by the wrists and lifts her from her chair*.) Up on your paws! Now then! Up! Up!

SOLANGE: You don't realize the danger—

CLAIRE: But, Solange, you're immortal! Repeat after me—

SOLANGE: Talk. But not so loud.

CLAIRE (*mechanically*): Madame must have her tea.

SOLANGE (*firmly*): No, I won't.

CLAIRE (*holding her by the wrists*): You bitch! Repeat. Madame must have her tea.

SOLANGE: I've just been through such a lot. . . .

CLAIRE (*more firmly*): Madame will have her tea . . .

SOLANGE: Madame will have her tea . . .

CLAIRE: Because she must sleep . . .

SOLANGE: Because she must sleep . . .

CLAIRE: And I must stay awake.

SOLANGE: And I must stay awake.

CLAIRE (*she lies down on Madame's bed*): Don't interrupt again. I repeat. Are you listening? Are you obeying? (SOLANGE *nods 'yes'*.) I repeat: My tea!

SOLANGE (*hesitating*): But . . .

CLAIRE: I say: my tea.

SOLANGE: But, Madame.

CLAIRE: Good. Continue.

SOLANGE: But, Madame, it's cold.

CLAIRE: I'll drink it anyway. Let me have it. (SOLANGE *brings the tray*.) And you've poured it into the best, the finest tea set. (*She takes the cup and drinks, while* SOLANGE, *facing the audience, delivers the end of her speech*.)

SOLANGE: The orchestra is playing brilliantly. The attendant is raising the red velvet curtain. He bows. Madame is descending the stairs. Her furs brush against the green plants. Madame steps into the car. Monsieur is whispering sweet nothings in her ear. She would like to smile, but she is dead. She rings the bell. The porter yawns. He opens the door. Madame goes up the stairs. She enters her flat—but, Madame is dead. Her two maids are alive: they've just risen up, free, from Madame's icy form. All the maids were present at her side—not they themselves, but rather the hellish agony of their names. And all that remains of them to float about Madame's airy corpse is the delicate perfume of the holy maidens which they were in secret. We are beautiful, joyous, drunk, and free!

A STREETCAR NAMED DESIRE
Tennessee Williams

STANLEY: If I didn't know that you was my wife's sister I'd get ideas about you!

BLANCHE: Such as what?

STANLEY: Don't play so dumb. You know what!—Where's the papers?

BLANCHE: Papers?

STANLEY: Papers! That stuff people write on!

BLANCHE: Oh, papers, papers! Ha-ha! The first anniversary gift, all kinds of papers!

STANLEY: I'm talking of legal papers. Connected with the plantation.

BLANCHE: There were some papers.

STANLEY: You mean they're no longer existing?

BLANCHE: They probably are, somewhere.

STANLEY: But not in the trunk.

BLANCHE: Everything that I own is in that trunk.

STANLEY: Then why don't we have a look for them. (*He crosses to the trunk, shoves it roughly open, and begins to open compartments.*)

BLANCHE: What in the name of heaven are you thinking of! What's in the back of that little boy's mind of yours? That I am absconding with something, attempting some kind of treachery on my sister?—Let me do that! It will be faster and simpler . . . (*She crosses to the trunk and takes out a box.*) I keep my papers mostly in this tin box. (*She opens it.*)

STANLEY: What's them underneath? (*He indicates another sheaf of paper.*)

BLANCHE: These are love-letters, yellowing with antiquity, all from one boy. (*He snatches them up. She speaks fiercely.*) Give those back to me!

STANLEY: I'll have a look at them first!

BLANCHE: The touch of your hands insults them!

STANLEY: Don't pull that stuff.

(*He rips off the ribbon and starts to examine them.* BLANCHE *snatches them from him, and they cascade to the floor.*)

BLANCHE: Now that you've touched them I'll burn them!

STANLEY: (*staring, baffled*): What in hell are they?

BLANCHE (*on the floor gathering them up*): Poems a dead boy wrote. I hurt him the way that you would like to hurt me, but you can't. I'm not young and vulnerable any more. But my young husband was and I—never mind about that! Just give them back to me!

STANLEY: What do you mean by saying you'll have to burn them?

BLANCHE: I'm sorry, I must have lost my head for a moment. Everyone has something he won't let others touch because of their—intimate nature . . . (*She now seems faint with exhaustion and sits down with the strong box and puts on a pair of glasses and goes methodically through a large stack of papers.*) Ambler & Ambler. Hmmmmmm . . . Crabtree . . . More Ambler & Ambler.

STANLEY: What is Ambler & Ambler?

BLANCHE: A firm that made loans on the place.

STANLEY: Then it was lost on a mortgage?

BLANCHE (*touching her forehead*): That must've been what happened.

STANLEY: I don't want no ifs, ands, or buts! What's all the rest of them papers? (*She hands him the entire box. He carries it to the table and starts to examine the papers.*)

BLANCHE: (*picking up a large envelope containing more papers*): There are thousands of papers, stretching back over hundreds of years, affecting Belle Reve as, piece by piece, our improvident grandfathers and father and uncles and brothers exchanged the land for their epic fornications—to put it plainly! (*She removes her glasses with an exhausted laugh.*) Till finally all that was left—and Stella can verify that!—was the house itself and about twenty acres of ground, including a graveyard, to which now all but Stella and I have retreated. (*She pours the contents of the envelope on the table.*) Here all of them are, all papers! I hereby endow you with them! Take them, peruse them—commit them to memory, even! I think it's wonderfully fitting that Belle Reve should finally be this bunch of old papers in your big, capable hands! . . . I wonder if Stella's come back with the lemon-coke . . . (*She leans back and closes her eyes.*)

STANLEY: I have a lawyer acquaintance who will study these out.

BLANCHE: Present them to him with a box of aspirin tablets.

STANLEY (*becoming somewhat sheepish*): You see, under the Napoleonic code—a man has to take an interest in his wife's affairs—especially now that she's going to have a baby.

The shortness of stroke is put to quite different uses in each of the extracts. Questions and pauses are common and main factors governing the movement of the text.

Treat the extracts in the same way as the previous examples—**READ THEM ALOUD AND LET THEM CREATE THEIR OWN RHYTHM.** Later, study and analyse them in detail.

Internal Contrast

There are two interesting examples of the basic rhythm of the pieces being radically changed. The first comes from *The Maids*. In the context of the extract—but not the whole play—the three sentences:

'**Poor servant girl, you think you'll get out of it as easily as that? It would be too simple to conspire with the wind, to make the night one's accomplice. Solange you will contain me within you**' cut across the set pattern. The change is created almost entirely by the length of the sentences and their construction. A similar contrast occurs shortly after: '**Nothing exists but the altar where one of the two maids is about to immolate herself.**' In each case there is the additional factor of the inclusion of unexpected words—conspire, accomplice, contain, immolate.

The second example comes from *A Streetcar Named Desire* and is created by the growth of the intensity of the dramatic situation in which Blanche sees herself. It is heralded by the use of words that can only be intended to impress Stanley and reduce his status—absconding, treachery, yellowing with antiquity, vulnerable, improvident and epic fornications. The rhythm of the piece varies in its stroke but, apart from the purposeful contrast in Blanche's style, it is a short one. (A careful study of the text suggests that the classic performance of Marlon Brando with its prime phrases of monosyllabic structure—methodical or 'method' as it was advertised—is not entirely justified on internal grounds.)

When you come to study and analyse the texts in detail, notice how difficult it is to increase the reach of the rhythm of the three passages. **Manipulating a short-stroke text into a longer rhythm is a much more difficult task than breaking down an elongated stroke into short ones.** Working against the inner dynamic of the text is only worthwhile in so far as it illuminates the author's purpose and makes it easier to realize and deliver his intention.

Poetry or Verse?

The following four extracts are from poetic works, two of which are in recognizable verse format. The first is taken from *Riders to the Sea* by J. M. Synge. Before you read the full extract, SPEAK ALOUD the following short passages:

'There does be a power of young men floating round in the sea, and what way would they know if it was Michael they had, or another man like him, for when a man is nine days in the sea, and the wind blowing, it's hard set his own mother would be to say what man was in it.'

'Michael has a clean burial in the far north, by the grace of the Almighty God. Bartley will have a fine coffin out of the white boards, and a deep grave surely. What more can we want than that? No man at all can be living for ever, and we must be satisfied.'

The first passage is one long sentence with vibrant springing throughout. It is a perfect example of words that speak themselves, creating their own rhythm. Here is the complete extract:

RIDERS TO THE SEA
J. M. Synge

(*She pauses again with her hand stretched out towards the door. It opens softly and old women begin to come in, crossing themselves on the threshold, and kneeling down in front of the stage with red petticoats over their heads.*)

MAURYA (*half in a dream, to* CATHLEEN): Is it Patch, or Michael, or what is it at all?

CATHLEEN: Michael is after being found in the far north, and when he is found there how could he be here in this place?

MAURYA: There does be a power of young men floating round in the sea, and what way would they know if it was Michael they had, or another man like him, for when a man is nine days in the sea, and the wind blowing, it's hard set his own mother would be to say what man was in it.

CATHLEEN: It's Michael, God spare him, for they're after sending us a bit of his clothes from the far north.

(*She reaches out and hands* MAURYA *the clothes that belonged to* MICHAEL. MAURYA *stands up slowly and takes them in her hands.* NORA *looks out*).

NORA: They're carrying a thing among them, and there's water dripping out of it and leaving a track by the big stones.

CATHLEEN (*in a whisper to the women who have come in*): Is it Bartley it is?

ONE OF THE WOMEN: It is, surely, God rest his soul.

(*Two younger women come in and pull out the table. Then men carry in the body of* BARTLEY, *laid on a plank, with a bit of sail over it, and lay it on the table.*)

CATHLEEN (*to the women as they are doing so*): What way was he drowned?

ONE OF THE WOMEN: The grey pony knocked him over into the sea, and he was washed out where there is a great surf on the white rocks.

(MAURYA *has gone over and knelt down at the head of the table. The women are keening softly and swaying themselves with a slow movement.* CATHLEEN *and* NORA *kneel at the other end of the table. The men kneel near the door.*)

MAURYA (*raising her head and speaking as if she did not see the people around her*): They're all gone now, and there isn't anything more the sea can do to me. . . . I'll have no call now to be up crying and praying when the wind breaks from the south, and you can hear the surf is in the east, and the surf is in the west, making a great stir with the two noises, and they hitting one on the other. I'll have no call now to be going down and getting Holy Water in the dark nights after Samhain, and I won't care what way the sea is when the other women will be keening. (*To* NORA) Give me the Holy Water, Nora; there's a small sup still on the dresser. (NORA *gives it to her.*)

MAURYA (*drops* MICHAEL'S *clothes across* BARTLEY'S *feet, and sprinkles the Holy Water over him*): It isn't that I haven't prayed for you, Bartley, to the Almighty God. It isn't that I haven't said prayers in the dark night till you wouldn't know what I'd be saying; but it's a great rest I'll have now, and it's time, surely. It's a great rest I'll have now, and great sleeping in the long nights after Samhain, if it's only a bit of wet flour we do have to eat, and may be a fish that would be stinking.

(*She kneels down again, crossing herself, and saying prayers under her breath.*)

CATHLEEN (*to an old man*): Maybe yourself and Eamon would make a coffin when the sun rises. We have fine white boards herself bought, God help her, thinking Michael would be found, and I have a new cake you can eat while you'll be working.

THE OLD MAN (*looking at the boards*): Are there nails with them?

CATHLEEN: There are not, Colum; we didn't think of the nails.

ANOTHER MAN: It's a great wonder she wouldn't think of the nails, and all the coffins she's seen made already.

CATHLEEN: It's getting old she is, and broken.

(*MAURYA stands up again very slowly, and spreads out the pieces of* MICHAEL'S *clothes beside the body, sprinkling them with the last of the Holy Water.*)

NORA (*in a whisper to* CATHLEEN): She's quiet now and easy; but the day Michael was drowned you could hear her crying out from this to the spring well. It's fonder she was of Michael, and would anyone have thought that?

CATHLEEN (*slowly and clearly*): An old woman will be soon tired with anything she will do, and isn't it nine days herself is after crying and keening, and making great sorrow in the house?

MAURYA (*puts the empty cup mouth downwards on the table, and lays her hands together on* BARTLEY'S *feet*): They're all together this time, and the end is come. May the Almighty God have mercy on Bartley's soul, and on Michael's soul, and on the souls of Sheamus and Patch, and Stephen and Shawn (*bending her head*); and may He have mercy on my soul, Nora, and on the soul of every one is left living in the world

(*She pauses, and the keen rises a little more loudly from the women, then sinks away.*)

MAURYA (*continuing*): Michael has a clean burial in the far north by the grace of the Almighty God. Bartley will have a fine coffin out of the white boards, and a deep grave surely. What more can we want than that? No man at all can be living for ever, and we must be satisfied.

(*She kneels down again, and the curtain falls slowly.*)

Riders to the Sea is written in the prose-dialogue of ordinary conversation. There is no suggestion in the layout that the work is 'poetic', yet a definition of poetic as 'the fewest words carrying the maximum charge' clearly places the work in that category. The same principle applies to the next extract:

SERJEANT MUSGRAVE'S DANCE
John Arden

SCENE THREE: The churchyard.

(*Sunset.* HURST *enters and walks about, whistling nervously. The* SLOW COLLIER *enters and looks at him. They pass each other, giving each other good hard stares. The* SLOW COLLIER *is about to leave the stage when he turns round and calls.*)

SLOW COLLIER: Hey! Soldier!

HURST: Aye?

SLOW COLLIER: How many on you is there?

HURST: Four.

SLOW COLLIER: Four ... Four dead red rooks and be damned.

HURST: What? What's that?

SLOW COLLIER (*contemptuously*). Arrh ...

(*He slouches out.* HURST *makes to follow, but decides not to, and continues walking about.* MUSGRAVE *enters.*)

MUSGRAVE: Coldest town I ever was in. What did you see?

HURST: Hardly a thing. Street empty, windows shut, two old wives on a doorstep go indoors the minute I come. Three men on one corner, two men on another, dirty looks and no words from any on 'em. There's one man swears a curse at me just now. That's all.

MUSGRAVE: H'm ...
> (*He calls to offstage.*)
> Hello! We're over here!
> (ATTERCLIFFE *enters.*)
> What did you see?

ATTERCLIFFE: Hardly a thing. Street empty, doors locked, windows blind, shops cold and empty. A young lass calls her kids in from playing in the dirt—she sees me coming, so she calls 'em. There's someone throws a stone—

MUSGRAVE: A stone?

ATTERCLIFFE: Aye. I don't know who did it and it didn't hit me, but it was thrown.

HURST: It's a cold poor town, I'm telling you, serjeant.

MUSGRAVE: Coldest town I ever was in. And here's the fourth of us.
> (*Enter* SPARKY.)
> What did you see?

SPARKY: Hardly a thing. Street empty, no chimneys smoking, no horses, yesterday's horsedung frozen on the road. Three men at a corner-post, four men leaning on a wall. No words: but some chalked up on a closed door—they said: 'Soldiers go home'.

HURST: Go home?

SPARKY: That's it, boy: home. It's a place they think we have somewhere. And what did you see, serjeant?

MUSGRAVE: Nothing different from you. .... So, here is our town and here are we. All fit and appropriate.

HURST (*breaking out suddenly*): Appropriate? Serjeant, now we've come with you so far. And every day we're in great danger. We're on the run, in red uniforms, in a black-and-white coalfield; and it's cold; and the money's running out that you stole from the Company office; and we don't know who's heard of us or how much they've heard. Isn't it time you brought out clear just what you've got in mind?

MUSGRAVE (*ominously*): Aye? Is it? And any man else care to tell me what the time is?

ATTERCLIFFE (*reasonably*): Now serjeant, please, easy—we're all your men, and we agreed—

HURST: All right: if we are your men, we've rights.

MUSGRAVE (*savagely*): The only right you have is a rope around your throat and six foot to drop from. On the run? Stole money? I'm talking of a murdered officer, shot down in a street fight, shot down in one night's work. They put that to the rebels, but I know you were the man. We deserted, but you killed.

HURST: I'd a good reason . . .

MUSGRAVE: I know you had reason, else I'd not have left you alive to come with us. All I'm concerned about this minute is to tell you how you stand. And you stand in my power. But there's more to it than a bodily blackmail —isn't there?—because my power's the power of God, and that's what's brought me here and all three of you with me. You know my words and purposes—it's not just authority of the orderly room, it's not just three stripes, it's not just given to me by the reckoning of my mortal brain—well, where does it come from?

(*He flings this question fiercely at* HURST.)

HURST (*trying to avoid it*): All right, I'm not arguing—

MUSGRAVE: Where!

HURST (*frantically defensive*): I don't believe in God!

MUSGRAVE: You don't? Then what's this!

(*He jabs his thumb into* HURST'*s cheek and appears to scrape something off it.*)

HURST: Sweat.

MUSGRAVE: The coldest winter for I should think it's ten years, and the man sweats like a bird-bath!

HURST (*driven in a moral corner*): Well, why not, because—

MUSGRAVE (*relentless*): Go on—because?

HURST (*browbeaten into incoherence*): All right, because I'm afraid.

In *Riders to the Sea* the length of the prime phrasing is as obvious on the printed page as it is when spoken aloud. This does not apply to the extract above. Most sentences have a very broken format and some cannot even properly be referred to as sentences. The content of the extract suggests an abrupt approach—perhaps even staccato. But when the words are spoken aloud they expose a **powerful undercurrent with a long reach.** Consider the three similar reports of Hurst, Attercliffe and Sparky. **The conversational presentation of the dialogue disguises the strength of the poetic style.** Hurst's report could be presented in another way:

Hardly a thing
Street empty
Windows shut
Two old wives on a doorstep go indoors the minute I come
Three men on one corner
Two men on another
Dirty looks
And no words from any on 'em
There's one man swears a curse at me just now.
That's all.

In its published version, the layout of the words—complete with the bending of grammar—achieves a *balance* between **dialogue/conversation for a three-dimensional naturalistic character and the ritualistic prose as presented in the treated version above.** This is possibly what the author had in mind. In the introduction to the text the author says 'This is a realistic, but not a naturalistic play'. He also refers to it as a mixture of 'verse, prose and song'. The power of the writing is such that a first reading exposes all this with strength and clarity. (It may be clouded by heady discussions on the **meaning** of the play. Such activities are best left to audiences and critics. The text itself states its own needs. Much more than Shaw, has Arden succeeded in writing an actor-proof play.)

The next extract uses verse format. In spite of the long sentences and the light, delicate touch—almost a combination of *Blithe Spirit* and *Romeo and Juliet*—**the overall rhythm consists of short reach prime phrases**. This gives the text an interesting tension, since the author's wish seems to be for a smooth, flowing style with a long reach. As you read the extract, pay special attention to the two sentences: **'For me, the world is all with Charon, all, all . . .'** and **'What a mad blacksmith creation is . . .'.** It is almost impossible to treat either with a **long stroke without satirizing the author's style.**

A PHOENIX TOO FREQUENT
Christopher Fry

DYNAMENE: Now, if you wish, you may cry, Doto.
  But our tears are very different. For me
  The world is all with Charon all, all,
  Even the metal and plume of the rose garden,
  And the forest where the sea fumes overhead
  In vegetable tides, and particularly
  The entrance to the warm baths in Arcite Street,
  Where we first met;—all!—the sun itself
  Trails an evening hand in the sultry river
  Far away down by Acheron. I am lonely,
  Virilius. Where is the punctual eye
  And where is the cautious voice which made
  Balance-sheets sound like Homer and Homer sound
  Like balance-sheets? The precision of limbs, the amiable
  Laugh, the exact festivity? Gone from the world.
  You were the peroration of nature, Virilius.
  You explained everything to me, even the extremely
  Complicated gods. You wrote them down.
  In seventy columns. Dear curling calligraphy!
  Gone from the world, once and for all. And I taught you
  In your perceptive moments to appreciate me.
  You said I was harmonious, Virilius,
  Moulded and harmonious, little matronal
  Ox-eye, your package. And then I would walk
  Up and down largely, as it were making my own
  Sunlight. What a mad blacksmith creation is
  Who blows his furnaces until the stars fly upward
  And iron Time is hot and politicians glow
  And bulbs and roots sizzle into hyacinth
  And orchis, and the sand puts out the lion,
  Roaring yellow, and oceans bud with porpoises,
  Blenny, tunny and the almost unexisting

Blindfish; throats are cut, the masterpiece
Looms out of labour; nations and rebellions
Are spat out to hand on the wind—and all is gone
In one Virilius, wearing his office tunic,
Checking the pence column as he went.
Where's animation now? What is there that stays
To dance? The eye of the one-eyed world is out.
(*She weeps*).

In an entirely different style Eliot uses a similar format. The syllabic verse pattern, by no means exact with either author, is the same, as is the presentation of the work **on the page**. (Wole Soyinka in *The Lion and the Jewel* presents an interesting contrast.) Before you read through the next extracts, study the following passage. It is one sentence.

1. As published:

When you've dressed for a party
And are going downstairs, with everything about you
Arranged to support you in the role you have chosen,
Then sometimes, when you come to the bottom step
There is one step more than your feet expected
And you come down with a jolt.

2. Rearranged as prose:

When you've dressed for a party and are going downstairs, with everything about you arranged to support you in the role you have chosen, then sometimes, when you come to the bottom step there is one step more than your feet expected and you come down with a jolt.

Either presentation strongly suggests the author had in mind a rhythm of long reach prime phrases. When spoken, **there is a danger that it will sound jagged**—no matter how polished the delivery may be. **The relationship of vowels and consonants prevents the easy execution of what the author apparently had in mind.** This conflict is little more than marginal in the sentence quoted but it recurs throughout the play. The second extract below is a good example.

The first extract is happier in its effect, since the tensions created are used effectively to build up character, situation and atmosphere. The overall rhythm the author seems to be seeking, is constantly punctuated—if not indeed punctured—by the powerful inner style. It is difficult to conclude this was Eliot's conscious intention. It is as if *Sweeney Agonistes* were trapped within, making every attempt to break out.

THE COCKTAIL PARTY
T. S. Eliot

ACT ONE. SCENE I

(The drawing-room of the Chamberlaynes' London flat. Early evening. EDWARD CHAMBERLAYNE, JULIA SHUTTLETHWAITE, CELIE COPELSTONE, PETER QUILPE, ALEXANDER MACCOLGIE GIBBS, and an UNIDENTIFIED GUEST.)

ALEX
You've missed the point completely, Julia:
There were no tigers. That was the point.

JULIA

Then what were you doing, up in a tree:
You and the Maharaja?

ALEX

My dear Julia!
It's perfectly hopeless. You haven't been listening.

PETER

You'll have to tell us all over again, Alex.

ALEX

I never tell the same story twice.

JULIA

But I'm still waiting to know what happened.
I know it started as a story about tigers.

ALEX

I said there were no tigers.

CELIA

Oh do stop wrangling,
Both of you. It's your turn, Julia.
Do tell us that story you told the other day, about Lady Kootz and the
wedding cake.

PETER

And how the butler found her in the pantry, rinsing her mouth out with
champagne.
I like that story.

CELIA

I love that story.

ALEX

I'm never tired of hearing that story.

JULIA

Well, you all seem to know it.

CELIA

Do we all know it?
But we're never tired of hearing you tell it.
I don't believe everyone here knows it.
(*To the* UNIDENTIFIED GUEST)
You don't know it, do you?

UNIDENTIFIED GUEST

No, I've never heard it.

CELIA

Here's one new listener for you, Julia;
And I don't believe that Edward knows it.

EDWARD

I may have heard it, but I don't remember it.

CELIA

And Julia's the only person to tell it.
She's such a good mimic.

JULIA

Am I a good mimic.

PETER

You a are good mimic. You never miss anything.

ALEX

She never misses anything unless she wants to.

CELIA

Especially the Lithuanian accent.

JULIA

Lithuanian? Lady Klootz?

PETER

I thought she was Belgian.

ALEX

Her father belonged to a Baltic family—
One of the oldest Baltic families
With a branch in Sweden and one in Denmark.
There were several very lovely daughters:
I wonder what's become of them now.

JULIA

Lady Klootz was very lovely, once upon a time.
What a life she led! I used to say to her: 'Greta!
You have too much vitality.' But she enjoyed herself.
(*To the* UNIDENTIFIED GUEST)
Did you know Lady Klootz?

UNIDENTIFIED GUEST

No, I never met her.

CELIA

Go on with the story about the wedding cake.

JULIA

Well, but it really isn't my story.
I heard it first from Delia Verinder
Who was there when it happened.
(*To the* UNIDENTIFIED GUEST)
Do you know Delia Verinder?

UNIDENTIFIED GUEST

No, I don't know her.

JULIA

Well, one can't be too careful
Before one tells a story.

ALEX

Delia Verinder?
Was she the one who had three brothers?

JULIA

How many brothers? Two, I think.

ALEX

No, there were three, but you wouldn't know the third one:
They kept him rather quiet.

JULIA

Oh, you mean that one.

ALEX

He was feeble-minded.

JULIA

Oh, not feeble-minded:
He was only harmless.

ALEX
Well then, harmless.
JULIA
He was very clever at repairing clocks;
And he had a remarkable sense of hearing—
The only man I ever met who could hear the cry of bats.
PETER
Hear the cry of bats?

JULIA
He could hear the cry of bats.
CELIA
But how do you know he could hear the cry of bats?
JULIA
Because he said so. And I believed him.
CELIA
But if he was so . . . harmless, how could you believe him?
He might have imagined it.

JULIA
My darling Celia,
You needn't be so sceptical. I stayed there once
At their castle in the North. How he suffered!
They had to find an island for him
Where there were no bats.
ALEX
And is he still there?
Julia is really a mine of information.
CELIA
There isn't much that Julia doesn't know.
PETER
Go on with the story about the wedding cake.

THE COCKTAIL PARTY
T. S. Eliot

UNIDENTIFIED GUEST

Yes, it's unfinished;
And nobody likes to be left with a mystery.
But there's more to it than that. There's a loss of personality;
Or rather, you've lost touch with the person
You thought you were. You no longer feel quite human.
You're suddenly reduced to the status of an object—
A living object, but no longer a person.
It's always happening, because one is an object
As well as a person. But we forget about it
As quickly as we can. When you've dressed for a party
And are going downstairs, with everything about you
Arranged to support you in the role you have chosen,
Then sometimes, when you come to the bottom step
There is one step more than your feet expected

And you come down with a jolt. Just for a moment
You have the experience of being an object
At the mercy of a malevolent staircase.
Or, take a surgical operation.
In consultation with the doctor and the surgeon,
In going to bed in the nursing home,
In talking to the matron, you are still the subject,
The centre of reality. But, stretched on the table,
You are a piece of furniture in a repair shop
For those who surround you, the masked actors;
All there is of you is your body
And the 'you' is withdrawn. May I replenish?

A Challenge

The last extract in this section is presented without comment and as something of a challenge. Remember; the purpose of the exercise is to determine the **rhythm of the play from the author's text**—by execution or analysis.

THE BRIG

Kenneth H. Brown

SCENE TWO

(*The outside compound. The curtain opens with the prisoners formed in two equal ranks at attention facing the long side of the fence with their backs to the wall of the Brig. Outside the fence stands* LINTZ *with a shotgun cradled in his arms. It is about six o'clock in the morning and still quite dark. The outside door is open and* GRACE *stands in the doorway. The bright light inside pours into the darkness through the windows and the opened door, and beyond the door the cabinet containing the cigarettes and razors of the prisoners is clearly visible.*)

LINTZ: Did everyone have enough to eat this morning?

ALL PRISONERS: Yes, sir.

LINTZ: I didn't hear you, Two.

TWO: Yes, sir.

LINTZ: Your stomach all right, Two?

TWO: Yes, sir.

LINTZ: Front and centre, Two.

(TWO *runs from his position in the ranks and stands in front of the formation.*)
Give me twenty-five, Two.

(TWO *falls on his stomach and begins to do push-ups, but falls motionless after ten of them.*)
On your feet, Two. Start running around the edge of the compound.

(TWO *begins running and continues as the scene progresses.*)
Those who are not smoking fall out and form two ranks to your right. Move.

(FOUR, SIX, *and* TEN *break from various points in the ranks and form near the right end of the compound.* GRACE *goes inside and opens the cabinet.*)
Break, One.

(ONE *runs toward the door. As he snaps his cap and passes through the door, he collides with* TEPPERMAN *who appears there. He falls, gets up, and stands at attention in front of* TEPPERMAN.)

TEPPERMAN (*long, loud, and all suffering*): Woe. You touched me, you lousy insect. You actually came in contact with my clothing, infesting it with the disease of your stinking self. Now I will have to take a shower.

ONE (*terrified*): I'm sorry, sir.

TEPPERMAN (*punching the prisoner in the stomach*): Never tell me you're sorry, boy. Move.

(*The prisoner runs through the door and stands at attention in front of the cabinet where* GRACE *is standing.*)

ONE: Sir, Prisoner Number One, sir.

(GRACE *takes a pack of cigarettes from a box, taking one and throwing it at the prisoner. The prisoner catches it and remains at attention at the cabinet.*)

GRACE: Split.

(*The prisoner does an about-face and runs to the doorway, stopping and coming to attention.* TEPPERMAN *is standing there.*)

ONE: Sir, Prisoner Number One requests permission to cross the white line, sir.

TEPPERMAN: Cross.

(*The prisoner returns to his position in ranks. As he arrives,* THREE *automatically breaks from ranks and goes through the same process, getting one cigarette, and so on for the others remaining in the larger formation. As the ceremony ends, all are in possession of one cigarette.*)

LINTZ: Three, front and centre.

(THREE *breaks from the ranks and stands in front of the formation.* LINTZ *takes a lighter from his pocket, lights it, and places the lighter, burning, through the fence.* THREE *lights his cigarette from the outstretched hand of the guard, does an about-face, and returns to the ranks.*)

Parade rest.

(*The men assume a stiff at-ease position, smoking.* LINTZ *moves to the place where the three men are standing at attention.*)

Two, join the nonsmokers.

(TWO, *who has been running around in circles, joins the smaller group.*)

Non-smokers, at a half step, forward, march. To the rear, march. Squad, halt. Parade rest.

(*The smaller group responds to the commands, marching with small steps in the limited area and ending up in the same place, in the same position as those smoking.*)

TEPPERMAN: Smokers, put your cigarettes in your mouths. Smokers, attention.

(*The smoking group responds to the commands and is at attention with cigarettes dangling from their lips.* TEPPERMAN *walks through the ranks pausing occasionally, taking a cigarette from the mouth of one, then another of the prisoners and crushing it beneath his foot. As he does so, he informs the prisoner for the reason for it.*)

Talking at chow. . . . Slow getting up this morning. . . . Too much time in the head. . . . Sloppy rack. . . . Bare feet on the deck . . .

(TEPPERMAN *walks through the outside door and disappears within the Brig. The formation does not move.*)

LINTZ: Parade rest. Continue smoking. Nonsmokers, rejoin the formation.

(*The smaller formation rejoins the larger one, assuming at once a motionless position of parade rest. The only movements are the hands of the prisoners who are smoking, moving from their lips to their sides, taking and returning the cigarettes to and from their mouths.)*

Pull 'em out.

(The prisoners smoking pinch the flame from the front of their cigarettes, rub them lightly in their palms to ensure they are out, tear the paper from them, allowing the tobacco to fall to the ground, roll the paper in a ball, and drop it.)

When I give you the word, I want you to get inside and break down for a shakedown. Is that clear?

ALL PRISONERS: Yes, sir.

LINTZ: I can't hear you.

ALL PRISONERS: Yes, sir.

LINTZ: You better sound off.

ALL PRISONERS: Yes, sir.

LINTZ: Get inside.

(The prisoners break off to the left, front rank first, and begin to disappear through the outside door in single file. Soon the outside compound is empty. LINTZ unloads his shotgun, opens the large double gates enough to step through them, locks and checks them, steps through the outside door, and closes it behind him. A flourish of activity can be seen through the windows.)

Curtain

CHAPTER TWELVE

WORKING ON A TEXT—III

Inner Meaning—What is Said and What is Meant

Whatever research, analysis or realization is practised on the text, it is, in the final resort, a means to an end—**the discovery, exposure or excavation of the inner meaning of the author's work.** The words as they appear on the page, are the tools with which an actor reveals, not what the author says, but **what he means.** It is a sad commentary on the human condition that words, vehicles of such subtlety, sophistication and infinite variety, should be used not to expose thoughts and feelings, but to cover them up. The skill with which any politician parries the questions of an experienced interviewer symbolizes the situation. Questions and answers alike seem to conspire to cover rather than to expose—to disguise rather than illuminate.

A playwright, particularly in a naturalistic/realist/behavioristic play, uses this differential between what is said and what is meant to full advantage. What is meant can relate to what is said on a one-to-one basis. More frequently what is meant is **something more or something less** than what is said; sometimes it is used to over-expose and sometimes to under-expose; it can directly contradict or completely cover up.

Just as for rhythm, the same two choices of approaching the inner meaning of a text are available; **direct and experiential or indirect and analytical.** Once again, the two are not mutually exclusive, but it is wiser not to block the perceptive/creative process by too much or too early analysis. The practical and experiential does not so easily block the analytical—if it does so at all. Many would claim it to be the only proper preparation for it, and a playwright's script is written for active performance not silent reading. Clearly both approaches are essential, consciously or otherwise and the method suggested here is a free movement between analysis and execution, with the practical tasting of the experience coming first in time and in importance.

Examples and Comments

Consider these three extracts. As with the previous passages you are recommended to **READ THEM ALOUD in the first instance.**

A STREETCAR NAMED DESIRE
Tennessee Williams

BLANCHE (*softly*): Hello! The Little Boys' Room is busy right now.
MITCH: We've—been drinking beer.
BLANCHE: I hate beer.
MITCH: It's—a hot weather drink.
BLANCHE: Oh, I don't think so; it always makes me warmer. Have you got any cigs? (*She has slipped on the dark red satin wrapper.*)
MITCH: Sure.
BLANCHE: What kind are they?

176

MITCH: Luckies.

BLANCHE: Oh, good. What a pretty case. Silver?

MITCH: Yes, Yes; read the inscription.

BLANCHE: Oh, is there an inscription? I can't make it out. (*He strikes a match and moves closer.*) Oh! (*reading with feigned difficulty*)
>'And if God choose,
>I shall but love thee better—after death!'

Why, that's from my favourite sonnet by Mrs. Browning.

MITCH: You know it?

BLANCHE: Certainly I do!

MITCH: There's a story connected with that inscription.

BLANCHE: It sounds like a romance.

MITCH: A pretty sad one.

BLANCHE: Oh?

MITCH: The girl's dead now.

BLANCHE (*in a tone of deep sympathy*): Oh!

MITCH: She knew she was dying when she give me this. A very strange girl, very sweet—very!

BLANCHE: She must have been fond of you. Sick people have such deep, sincere attachments.

MITCH: That's right, they certainly do.

BLANCHE: Sorrow makes for sincerity, I think.

MITCH: It sure brings it out in people.

BLANCHE: The little there is belongs to people who have experienced some sorrow.

MITCH: I believe you are right about that.

BLANCHE: I'm positive that I am. Show me a person who hasn't known any sorrow and I'll show you a shuperficial—Listen to me! My tongue is a little thick! You boys are responsible for it. The show let out at eleven and we couldn't come home on account of the poker game so we had to go somewhere and drink. I'm not accustomed to having more than one drink. Two is the limit—and three! (*She laughs.*) Tonight I had three.

STANLEY: Mitch!

MITCH: Deal me out. I'm talking to Miss—

BLANCHE: DuBois.

MITCH: Miss DuBois?

BLANCHE: It's a French name. It means woods and Blanche means white, so the two together mean white woods. Like an orchard in spring! You can remember it by that.

MITCH: You're French?

BLANCHE: We are French by extraction. Our first American ancestors were French Huguenots.

MITCH: You are Stella's sister, are you not?

BLANCHE: Yes, Stella is my precious little sister. I call her little in spite of the fact she's somewhat older than I. Just slightly. Less than a year. Will you do something for me?

MITCH: Sure. What?

BLANCHE: I bought this adorable little coloured paper lantern at a Chinese shop on Bourbon. Put it over the light bulb! Will you, please?

MITCH: Be glad to.

BLANCHE: I can't stand a naked light bulb, any more than I can a rude remark or a vulgar action.

MITCH (*adjusting the lantern*): I guess we strike you as being a pretty rough bunch.

BLANCHE: I'm very adaptable—to circumstances.

MITCH: Well, that's a good thing to be. You are visiting Stanley and Stella?

BLANCHE: Stella hasn't been so well lately, and I came down to help her for a while. She's very run down.

MITCH: You're not—?

BLANCHE: Married? No, no. I'm an old maid schoolteacher!

MITCH: You may teach school but you're certainly not an old maid.

BLANCHE: Thank you, sir! I appreciate your gallantry!

MITCH: So you are in the teaching profession?

BLANCHE: Yes. Ah, yes . . .

MITCH: Grade school or high school or—

STANLEY (*bellowing*): Mitch!

MITCH: Coming!

BLANCHE: Gracious, what lung-power! . . . I teach high school. In Laurel.

MITCH: What do you teach? What subject?

BLANCHE: Guess!

MITCH: I bet you teach art of music? (BLANCHE *laughs delicately*.) Of course I could be wrong. You might teach arithmetic.

BLANCHE: Never arithmetic, sir; never arithmetic! (*with a laugh*) I don't even know my multiplication tables! No, I have the misfortune of being an English instructor. I attempt to instil a bunch of bobby-soxers and drug-store Romeos with reverence for Hawthorne and Whitman and Poe!

MITCH: I guess that some of them are more interested in other things.

BLANCHE: How very right you are! Their literary heritage is not what most of them treasure above all else! But they're sweet things! And in the spring, it's touching to notice them making their first discovery of love! As if nobody had ever known it before!

(*The bathroom door opens and* STELLA *comes out.* BLANCHE *continues talking to* MITCH.)

Oh! Have you finished? Wait—I'll turn on the radio.

(*She turns the knobs on the radio and it begins to play 'Wien, Wien, nur du allein'.* BLANCHE *waltzes to the music with romantic gestures.* MITCH *is delighted and moves in awkward imitation like a dancing bear.* STANLEY *stalks fiercely through the portières into the bedroom. He crosses to the small white radio and snatches it off the table. With a shouted oath, he tosses the instrument out of the window.*)

STILL LIFE

Noël Coward

SCENE II

(The scene is the same and the time is about the same. Nearly three months have passed since the preceding scene, and it is now July. MYRTLE is resplendent in a light overall. BERYL'S appearance is unaltered. The tables are all unoccupied.)

MYRTLE (*slightly relaxed in manner*): It's all very fine, I said, expecting me to do this, that and the other, but what do I get out of it? You can't expect me to be a cook-housekeeper and char rolled into one during the day, and a loving wife in the evening just because you feel like it. Oh, dear no. There are just as good fish in the sea, I said, as ever came out of it, and I packed my boxes then and there and left him.

BERYL: Didn't you ever go back?

MYRTLE: Never. I went to my sister's place at Folkestone for a bit, and then I went in with a friend of mine and we opened a tea-shop in Hythe.

BERYL: And what happened to him?

MYRTLE: Dead as a door-nail inside three years!

BERYL: Well, I never!

MYRTLE: So you see, every single thing she told me came true—first them clubs coming together, an unexpected journey, then the Queen of diamonds and the ten—that was my friend and the tea-shop business. Then the Ace of Spades three times running—

(STANLEY *enters.*)

STANLEY: Two rock and an apple.

MYRTLE: What for?

STANLEY: Party on the up platform.

MYRTLE: Why can't they come in here for them?

STANLEY: Ask me another. (*He winks at* BERYL.)

MYRTLE: Got something in your eye?

STANLEY: Nothing beyond a bit of a twinkle every now and again.

BERYL (*giggling*): Oh, you are awful!

MYRTLE: You learn to behave yourself, my lad. Here are your rock cakes. Beryl, stop sniggering and give me an apple off the stand.

(BERYL *complies.*)

Not off the front, silly, haven't you got any sense? Here—(*She takes one from the back of the stand so as to leave the symmetry undisturbed.*)

STANLEY: This one's got a hole in it.

MYRTLE: Tell 'em to come and choose for themselves if they're particular—go on now.

STANLEY: All right—give us a chance.

MYRTLE: What people want to eat on the platform for I really don't know. Tell Mr. Godby not to forget his tea.

STANLEY: Righto!

(*He goes out as* ALEC *and* LAURA *come in.* LAURA *is wearing a summer dress,* ALEC *a grey flannel suit.*)

ALEC: Tea or lemonade?

LAURA: Tea, I think—it's more refreshing, really. (*She sits down at the table by the door.*)

(ALEC *goes to the counter.*)

ALEC: Two teas, please.

MYRTLE: Cakes or pastry?

ALEC (*to* LAURA): Cakes or pastry?

LAURA: No, thank you.

ALEC: Are those Bath buns fresh?

MYRTLE: Certainly they are—made this morning.

ALEC: Two, please.

(MYRTLE *puts two Bath buns on a plate, meanwhile* BERYL *has drawn two cups of tea.*)

MYRTLE: That'll be eightpence.

ALEC: All right. (*He pays her.*)

MYRTLE: Take the tea to the table, Beryl.

ALEC: I'll carry the buns.

(BERYL *brings the tea to the table.* ALEC *follows with the buns.*)

ALEC: You must eat one of these—fresh this morning.

LAURA: Very fattening.

ALEC: I don't hold with such foolishness.

(BERYL *returns to the counter.*)

MYRTLE: I'm going over my accounts. Let me know when Albert comes in.

BERYL: Yes, Mrs. Bagot.

(BERYL *settles down behind the counter with 'Peg's Paper'.*)

LAURA: They do look good, I must say.

ALEC: One of my earliest passions—I've never outgrown it.

LAURA: Do you like milk in your tea?

ALEC: Yes, don't you?

LAURA: Yes—fortunately.

ALEC: Station refreshments are generally a wee bit arbitrary, you know.

LAURA: I wasn't grumbling.

ALEC (*smiling*): Do you ever grumble—are you ever sullen and cross and bad-tempered?

LAURA: Of course I am—at least not sullen exactly—but I sometimes get into rages.

ALEC: I can't visualize you in a rage.

LAURA: Oh, I really don't see why you should.

ALEC: Oh, I don't know—there are signs, you know—one can usually tell—

LAURA: Long upper lips and jaw lines and eyes close together?

ALEC: You haven't any of those things.

LAURA: Do you feel guilty at all? I do.

ALEC (*smiling*): Guilty?

LAURA: You ought to more than me, really—you neglected your work this afternoon.

ALEC: I worked this morning—a little relaxation never did anyone any harm. Why should either of us feel guilty?

LAURA: I don't know—a sort of instinct—as though we were letting something happen that oughtn't to happen.

ALEC: How awfully nice you are!

LAURA: When I was a child in Cornwall—we lived in Cornwall, you know—May, that's my sister, and I used to climb out of our bedroom window on summer nights and go down to the cove and bathe. It was dreadfully cold but we felt very adventurous. I'd never have dared do it by myself, but sharing the danger made it all right—that's how I feel now, really.

ALEC: Have a bun—it's awfully bad for you.

LAURA: You're laughing at me!

ALEC: Yes, a little, but I'm laughing at myself, too.

LAURA: Why?

ALEC: For feeling a small pang when you said about being guilty.

LAURA: There you are, you see!

ALEC: We haven't done anything wrong.

LAURA: Of course we haven't.

ALEC: An accidental meeting—then another accidental meeting—then a little lunch—then the movies—what could be more ordinary? More natural?

LAURA: We're adults, after all.

ALEC: I never see myself as an adult, do you?

LAURA (*firmly*): Yes, I do. I'm a respectable married woman with a husband and a home and three children.

ALEC: But there must be a part of you, deep down inside, that doesn't feel like that at all—some little spirit that still wants to climb out of the window— that still longs to splash about a bit in the dangerous sea.

LAURA: Perhaps we none of us ever grow up entirely.

ALEC: How awfully nice you are!

LAURA: You said that before.

ALEC: I thought perhaps you hadn't heard.

LAURA: I heard all right.

ALEC (*gently*): I'm respectable, too, you know. I have a home and a wife and children and responsibilities—I also have a lot of work to do and a lot of ideals all mixed up with it.

LAURA: What's she like?

ALEC: Madeleine?

LAURA: Yes.

ALEC: Small, dark, rather delicate—

LAURA: How funny! I should have thought she'd be fair.

ALEC: And your husband? What's he like?

LAURA: Medium height, brown hair, kindly, unemotional and not delicate at all.

ALEC: You said that proudly.

LAURA: Did I? (*She looks down.*)

ALEC: What's the matter?

LAURA: The matter? What could be the matter?

ALEC: You suddenly went away.

LAURA (*brightly*): I thought perhaps we were being rather silly.

ALEC: Why?

LAURA: Oh, I don't know—we are such complete strangers, really.

ALEC: It's one thing to close a window, but quite another to slam it down on my fingers.

LAURA: I'm sorry.

ALEC: Please come back again.

LAURA: Is tea bad for one? Worse than coffee, I mean?

ALEC: If this is a professional interview, my fee is a guinea.

LAURA (*laughing*): It's nearly time for your train.

ALEC: I hate to think of it, chugging along, interrupting our tea party.

LAURA: I really am sorry now.

ALEC: What for?

LAURA: For being disagreeable.

ALEC: I don't think you could be disagreeable.

LAURA: You said something just now about your work and ideals being mixed up with it—what ideals?

ALEC: That's a long story.

LAURA: I suppose all doctors ought to have ideals, really—otherwise I should think the work would be unbearable.

ALEC: Surely you're not encouraging me to talk shop?

LAURA: Do you come here every Thursday?

ALEC: Yes. I come in from Churley, and spend a day in the hospital. Stephen Lynn graduated with me—he's the chief physician here. I take over from him once a week, it gives him a chance to go up to London and me a chance to observe and study the hospital patients.

LAURA: Is that a great advantage?

ALEC: Of course. You see I have a special pigeon.

LAURA: What is it?

ALEC: Preventive medicine.

LAURA: Oh, I see.

ALEC (*laughing*): I'm afraid you don't.

LAURA: I was trying to be intelligent.

ALEC: Most good doctors, especially when they're young, have private dreams —that's the best part of them, sometimes though, those get over-professionalized and strangulated and—am I boring you?

LAURA: No—I don't quite understand—but you're not boring me.

ALEC: What I mean is this—all good doctors must be primarily enthusiasts. They must have, like writers and painters and priests, a sense of vocation— deep-rooted, unsentimental desire to do good.

LAURA: Yes—I see that.

ALEC: Well, obviously one way of preventing disease is worth fifty ways of curing it—that's where my ideal comes in—preventive medicine isn't anything to do with medicine at all, really—it's concerned with conditions, living conditions and common-sense and hygiene. For instance, my speciality is pneumoconiosis.

LAURA: Oh, dear!

ALEC: Don't be alarmed, it's simpler than it sounds—it's nothing but a slow process of fibrosis of the lung due to the inhalation of particles of dust. In the hospital here there are splendid opportunities for observing cures and making notes, because of the coal mines.

LAURA: You suddenly look much younger.

ALEC (*brought up short*): Do I?

LAURA: Almost like a little boy.

ALEC: What made you say that?

LAURA (*staring at him*): I don't know—yes I do.

ALEC (*gently*): Tell me.

LAURA (*with panic in her voice*): Oh, no—I couldn't really. You were saying about the coal mines—

ALEC (*looking into her eyes*): Yes—the inhalation of coal dust—that's one specific form of the disease—it's called anthracosis.

LAURA (*hyponotized*): What are the others?

ALEC: Chalicosis—that comes from metal dust—steel works, you know—

LAURA: Yes, of course. Steel works.

ALEC: And silicosis—stone dust—that's gold mines.

LAURA (*almost in a whisper*): I see.

(*There is the sound of a bell.*)

That's your train.

ALEC (*looking down*): Yes.

LAURA: You mustn't miss it.

ALEC: No.

LAURA (*again the panic in her voice*): What's the matter?

ALEC (*with an effort*): Nothing—nothing at all.

LAURA (*socially*): It's been so very nice—I've enjoyed my afternoon enormously.

ALEC: I'm so glad—so have I. I apologize for boring you with those long medical words—

LAURA: I feel dull and stupid, not to be able to understand more.

ALEC: Shall I see you again?

(*There is the sound of a train approaching.*)

LAURA: It's the other platform isn't it? You'll have to run. Don't worry about me—mine's due in a few minutes.

ALEC: Shall I see you again?

LAURA: Of course—perhaps you could come over to Ketchworth one Sunday. It's rather far, I know, but we should be delighted to see you.

ALEC (*intensely*): Please—please—

(*The train is heard drawing to a standstill.*)

LAURA: What is it?

ALEC: Next Thursday—the same time—

LAURA: No—I can't possibly—I—

ALEC: Please—I ask you most humbly—

LAURA: All right. (*He gets up.*)

LAURA: Run—

ALEC (*taking her hand*): Good-bye.

LAURA (*breathlessly*): I'll be there.

ALEC: Thank you, my dear.

(*He goes out at a run, colliding with* ALBERT GODBY, *who is on his way in.*)

ALBERT: 'Ere—'ere—take it easy now—take it easy—(*He goes over to the counter.*)

(LAURA *sits quite still staring in front of her as the lights fade.*)

A PHOENIX TOO FREQUENT
Christopher Fry

DYNAMENE: If I misjudged you
I apologize, I apologize. Will you please leave us?
You were wrong to come here. In a place of mourning
Light itself is a trespasser; nothing can have
The right of entrance except those natural symbols
Or mortality, the jabbing, funeral, sleek—
With-omen raven, the death-watch beetle which mocks
Time: particularly, I'm afraid, the spider
Weaving his home with swift self-generated
Threads of slaughter; and, of course, the worm.
I wish it could be otherwise. Oh dear,
They aren't easy to live with.

DOTO: Not even a *little* wine, madam?

DYNAMENE: Here, Doto?

DOTO: Well, on the steps, perhaps,
Except it's so draughty.
DYNAMENE: Doto! Here?
DOTO: No, madam;
I quite see.
DYNAMENE: I might be wise to strengthen myself
In order to fast again; it would make me abler
For grief. I will breathe a little of it, Doto.
DOTO: Thank god. Where's the bottle?
DYNAMENE: What an exquisite bowl.
TEGEUS: Now that it's peacetime we have pottery classes.
DYNAMENE: You made it yourself?
TEGEUS: Yes. Do you see the design?
The corded god, tied also by the rays.
Of the sun, and the astonished ship erupting
Into vines and vine-leaves, inverted pyramids
Of grapes, the uplifted hands of the men (the raiders),
And here the headlong sea, itself almost
Venturing into leaves and tendrils, and Proteus
With his beard braiding the wind, and this
Held by other hands is a drowned sailor—
DYNAMENE: Always, always.
DOTO: Hold the bowl steady, madam,
Pardon.
DYNAMENE: Doto, have you been drinking?
DOTO: Here, madam?
I coaxed some a little way towards my mouth, madam,
But I scarcely swallowed except because I had to. The hiccup
Is from no breakfast, madam, and not meant to be funny.
DYNAMENE: You may drink this too. Oh, how the inveterate body.
Even when cut from the heart, insists on leaf,
Puts out, with a separate meaningless will,
Fronds to intercept the thankless sun.
How it does, oh, how it does. And how it confuses
The nature of the mind.
TEGEUS: Yes, yes, the confusion;
That's something I understand better than anything.
DYNAMENE: When the thoughts would die, the instincts will set sail
For life. And when the thoughts are alert for life
The instincts will rage to be destroyed on the rocks.
To Virilius it was not so; his brain was an ironing-board
For all crumpled indecision: and I follow him,
The hawser of my world. You don't belong here,
You see; you don't belong here at all.
TEGEUS: If only
I did. If only you knew the effort it costs me
To mount those steps again into an untrustworthy,
Unpredictable, unenlightened night,
And turn my back on—on a state of affairs,
I can only call it a vision, a hope, a promise,

A—By that I mean loyalty, enduring passion,
Unrecking bravery and beauty all in one.
DOTO: He means you, or you and me; or me, madam.
TEGEUS: It only remains for me to thank you and to say
That whatever awaits me and for however long
I may be played by this poor musician, existence,
Your person and sacrifice will leave their trace
As clear upon me as the shape of the hills
Around my birthplace. Now I must leave you to your husband.
DOTO: Oh! You, madam.
DYNAMENE: I'll tell you what I will do.
I will drink with you to the memory of my husband,
Because I have been curt, because you are kind,
And because I'm extremely thirsty. And then we will say
Good-bye and part to go to our opposite corruptions,
The world and the grave.
TEGEUS: The climax to the vision.
DYNAMENE (*drinking*): My husband, and all he stood for.
TEGEUS: Stands for.
DYNAMENE: Stands for.
TEGEUS: Your husband.
DOTO: The master.
DYNAMENE: How good it is,
How it sings to the throat, purling with summer.
TEGEUS: It has a twin nature, winter and warmth in one,
Moon and meadow. Do you agree?
DYNAMENE: Perfectly;
A cold bell sounding in a golden month.
TEGEUS: Crystal in harvest.
DYNAMENE: Perhaps a nightingale
Sobbing among the pears.
TEGEUS: In an old autumnal midnight.
DOTO: Grapes.—Pardon. There's some more here.
TEGEUS: Plenty.
I drink to the memory of your husband.
DYNAMENE: My husband.
DOTO: The master.
DYNAMENE: He was careless in his choice of wines.
TEGEUS: And yet
Rendering to living its rightful poise is not
Unimportant.
DYNAMENE: A mystery's in the world.
Where a little liquid, with flavour, quality, and fume
Can be as no other, can hint and flute our senses
As though a music played in harvest hollows
And a movement was in the swathes of our memory.
Why should scent, why should flavour come
With such wings upon us? Parsley, for instance.
TEGEUS: Seaweed.
DYNAMENE: Lime trees.

DOTO: Horses.
TEGEUS: Fruit in the fire.
DYNAMENE: Do I know your name?
TEGEUS: Tegeus.
DYNAMENE: That's very thin for you,
  It hardly covers your bones. Something quite different,
  Altogether other. I shall think of it presently.
TEGEUS: Darker vowels, perhaps.
DYNAMENE: Yes, certainly darker vowels.
  And your consonants should have a slight angle,
  And a certain temperature. Do you know what I mean?
  It will come to me.
TEGEUS: Now your name—
DYNAMENE: It is nothing
  To any purpose. I'll be to you the She
  In the tomb. You have the air of a natural-historian
  As though you were accustomed to handling birds' eggs,
  Or tadpoles, or putting labels on moths. You see?
  The genius of dumb things, that they are nameless.
  Have I found the seat of the weevil in human brains?
  Our names. They make us broody; we sit and sit
  To hatch them into reputation and dignity.
  And then they set upon us and become despair,
  Guilt and remorse. We go where they lead. We dance
  Attendance on something wished upon us by the wife
  Of our mother's physician. But insects meet and part
  And put the woods about them, fill the dusk
  And freckle the light and go and come without
  A name among them, without the wish of a name
  And very pleasant too. Did I interrupt you?
TEGEUS: I forget. We'll have no names then.
DYNAMENE: I should like
  You to have a name, I don't know why; a small one
  To fill out the conversation.
TEGEUS: I should like
  You to have a name too, if only for something
  To remember. Have you still some wine in your bowl?
DYNAMENE: Not altogether.
TEGEUS: We haven't come to the end
  By several inches. Did I splash you?
DYNAMENE: It doesn't matter.
  Well, here's to my husband's name.
TEGEUS: Your husband's name.
DOTO: The master.
DYNAMENE: It was kind of you to come.
TEGEUS: It was more than coming. I followed my future here,
  As we all do if we're sufficiently inattentive
  And don't vex ourselves with questions; or do I mean
  Attentive? If so, attentive to what? Do I sound
  Incoherent?

DYNAMENE: You're wrong. There isn't a future here,
  Not here, not for you.
TEGEUS: Your name's Dynamene.
DYNAMENE: Who—Have I been utterly irreverent? Are you—
  Who made you say that ? Forgive me the question,
  But are you dark or light? I mean which shade
  Of the supernatural? Or if neither, what prompted you?
TEGEUS: Dynamene—
DYNAMENE: No, but I'm sure you're the friend of nature,
  It must be so, I think I see little Phoebuses
  Rising and setting in your eyes.
DOTO: They're not little Phoebuses,
  They're hoodwinks, madam. Your name is on your brooch.
  No little Phoebuses tonight.
DYANEMENE: That's twice
  You've played me a trick. Oh, I know practical jokes
  Are common on Olympus, but haven't we at all
  Developed since the gods were born? Are gods
  And men both to remain immortal adolescents?
  How tiresome it all is.
TEGEUS: It was you, each time,
  Who said I was supernatural. When did I say so?
  You're making me into whatever you imagine
  And then you blame me because I can't live up to it.
DYNAMENE: I shall call you Chromis. It has a breadlike sound.
  I think of you as a crisp loaf.
TEGEUS: And now
  You'll insult me because I'm not sliceable.
DYNAMENE: I think drinking is harmful to our tempers.
TEGEUS: If I seem to be frowning, that is only because
  I'm looking directly into your light: I must look
  Angrily, or shut my eyes.
DYNAMENE: Shut them.—Oh,
  You have eyelashes! A new perspective of you.
  Is that how you look when you sleep?
TEGEUS: My jaw drops down.
DYNAMENE: Show me how.
TEGEUS: Like this.
DYNAMENE: It makes an irresistible
  Moron of you. Will you waken now?
  It's morning; I see a thin dust of daylight
  Blowing on to the steps.
TEGEUS: Already? Dynamene,
  You're tricked again. This time by the moon.
DYNAMENE: Oh well,
  Moon's daylight, then. Doto is asleep.
TEGEUS: Doto
  Is asleep . . .
DYNAMENE: Chromis, what made you walk about
  In the night? What, I wonder, made you not stay

Sleeping wherever you slept? Was it the friction
Of the world on your mind? Those two are difficult
To make agree. Chromis—now try to learn
To answer your name. I won't say Tegeus.
TEGEUS: And I
Won't say Dynamene.
DYNAMENE: Not?
TEGEUS: It makes you real.
Forgive me, a terrible thing has happened. Shall I
Say it and perhaps destroy myself for you?
Forgive me first, or, more than that, forgive
Nature who winds her furtive stream all through
Our reason. Do you forgive me?
DYNAMENE: I'll forgive
Anything, if it's the only way I can know
What you have to tell me.
TEGEUS: I felt us to be alone;
    Here in a grave, separate from any life,
    I and the only one of beauty, the only
    Persuasive key to all my senses,
    In spite of my having lain day after day
    And pored upon the sepals, corolla, stamen, and bracts
    Of the yellow bog-iris. Then my body ventured
    A step towards interrupting your perfection of purpose
    And my own renewed faith in human nature.
    Would you have believed that possible?
DYNAMENE: I have never
    Been greatly moved by the yellow bog-iris. Alas,
    It's as I said. This place is for none but the spider,
    Raven and worms, not for the living man.
TEGEUS: It has been a place of blessing to me. It will always
    Play in me, a fountain of confidence
    When the world is arid. But I know it is true.
    I have to leave it, and though it withers my soul
    I must let you make your journey.
DYNAMENE: No.
TEGEUS: Not true?
DYNAMENE: We can talk of something quite different.
TEGEUS: Yes, we can!
    Oh yes, we will! Is it your opinion
    That no one believes who hasn't learned to doubt?
    Or, another thing, if we persuade ourselves
    To one particular Persuasion, become Sophist,
    Stoic, Platonist, anything whatever,
    Would you say that there must be areas of soul
    Lying unproductive therefore, or dishonoured
    Or blind?
DYNAMENE: No, I don't know.
TEGEUS: No. It's impossible
    To tell. Dynamene, if only I had

Two cakes of pearl-barley and hydromel
I could see you to Hades, leave you with your husband
And come back to the world.
DYNAMENE: Ambition, I suppose,
Is an appetite particular to man.
What is your definition?
TEGEUS: To desire to find
A reason for living.
DYNAMENE: But then, suppose it leads,
As often, one way or another, it does, to death.
TEGEUS: Then that may be life's reason. Oh, but how
Could I bear to return, Dynamene? The earth's
Daylight would be my grave if I had left you
In that unearthly night.
DYNAMENE: O Chromis—
TEGEUS: Tell me,
What is your opinion of Progress? Does it, for example,
Exist? Is there ever progression without retrogression?
Therefore is it not true that mankind
Can more justly be said increasingly to Gress?
As the material improves, the craftsmanship deteriorates
And honour and virtue remain the same. I love you,
Dynamene.
DYNAMENE: Would you consider we go round and round?
TEGEUS: We concertina, I think; taking each time
A larger breath, so that the farther we go out
The farther we have to go in.
DYNAMENE: There'll come a time
When it will be unbearable to continue.
TEGEUS: Unbearable.
DYNAMENE: Perhaps we had better have something
To eat. The wine has made your eyes so quick
I am breathless beside them. It is
Your eyes, I think; or your intelligence
Holding my intelligence up above you
Between its hands. Or the cut of your uniform.
TEGEUS: Here's a new roll with honey. In the gods' names
Let's sober ourselves.
DYNAMENE: As soon as possible.
TEGEUS: Have you
Any notion of algebra?
DYNAMENE: We'll discuss you, Chromis.
We will discuss you, till you're nothing but words.

Submerged in Behaviour?

All three passages carry overtones and undertones of sexual advances. All
can be played acceptably with the words **saying no more than appears on the
surface.** They exemplify the difficulty of interpreting a naturalistic text. If the
words failed to stand on a surface interpretation, it would be clear something
was missing. In the passages above there is **no obvious absence that indicates a**

lack of rational sense—from a behaviouristic point of view. From the dramatic view, however, there is little point to the scenes unless something more than the surface dialogue is intended. The discovery of that something more is the task that faces actor and director.

There is the additional challenge of deciding whether or not the characters are aware of what lies below the surface of their words. In everyday life there are some people who consciously use language to flatter, attack or deceive. They know what they are saying and they know what they mean. They are keenly aware of their fencing, skirting or playing with words. There are others who have no idea how much of what they say is completely at odds with what they mean, or how much an apparently simple comment about the weather indicates the presence of powerful emotions. The actor must decide how much more or how much less is said than is meant and how aware of the differential and the mechanics the characters are.

In the first example it is likely that Mitch is much less aware than Blanche. Less aware of the process in himself—what he says and what he means have more of a one-to-one relationship—and probably unaware of it, and even the possibility of it, in Blanche. Blanche is no doubt totally aware of all her nuances; fully conscious of her delicate tact and sympathetic consideration (it is unlikely that Blanche could formulate the thought that she practises deceit—with or without attached conceits) and hypersensitive to Mitch's reactions.

In the second, the underlying meaning is made explicit in the last few seconds of the scene. The scene is given in full so that the slow development towards the final clarification can be seen at work. The author deliberately gives Alec the passage about diseases to create an extreme case of the inner meaning being disassociated from what is said. Even in terms of character build up there is nothing particularly relevant about a doctor having a mild enthusiasm for his vocation and a special interest in one aspect of it. It can be argued that the level of deception in *Still Life* is low and Laura and Alec are caught up and absorbed like children—quite unaware of the forces surrounding them. It can be equally argued they are fully aware of what is happening and are both playing the same deceptive waiting game, counting on the fact that if neither of them is actually explicit, their situation is 'safe' in every way.

The approach Blanche makes to Mitch, and Alec makes to Laura are both open to interpretation. Because the style is behaviouristic, any conclusion will depend upon additional decisions about the characters concerned. Since these are affected, and must be, by the inner meaning of their lines, the process is similar to a snake eating its tail. It is not easy to know when sincere thought unearths the author's hidden intention and when agile invention is piling up unjustified innovative motives.

The third example shows the author exposing the mechanics of the hidden meaning. The scene is a covered and partly covered courtship. At the end of the passage the characters are consciously playing with the technique. Since the fencing is fully justified by character and situation there is an excellent opportunity for comic interpretation. Even though the author has exposed the method and both characters are aware of what is happening and why, there is still a decision to be made regarding the light in which they see themselves. They can be fully absorbed and carried away by romantic intensity. Alternatively, one or both can treat the situation in a light-hearted manner. It is a perfect example of the 'he knows she knows he knows'—'he knows she knows but doesn't know she knows he knows', etc., etc. !!!

Half-submerged?

The following extract is similar, in so far as there are elements that are exposed, half-exposed and unexposed. What is made explicit, in the extract as well as throughout the play, is the battle for supremacy in personal relationships. In the extract, Inez is trying to gain the *affection* of Estelle and *reduce the status* of Garcin. Some of the approaches are exposed and some are hidden. At times the text overstates what is meant and at others it covers it completely. The sequence from Estelle's first mention of a glass to her line 'Are you really . . . attracted by me?' shows this in action.

IN CAMERA

Jean-Paul Sartre

INEZ: Look here! What's the point of playacting, trying to throw dust in each other's eyes? We're all tarred with the same brush.

ESTELLE (*indignantly*): How dare you!

INEZ: Yes, we are criminals—murderers—all three of us. We're in hell, my pets, they never make mistakes, and people aren't damned for nothing.

ESTELLE: Stop! For heaven's sake . . .

INEZ: In hell! Damned souls—that's us, all three!

ESTELLE: Keep quiet! I forbid you to use such disgusting words.

INEZ: A damned soul—that's you, my little plaster saint. And ditto our friend there, the noble pacifist. We've had our hour of pleasure, haven't we? There have been people who burnt their lives out for our sakes—and we chuckled over it. So now we have to pay the reckoning.

GARCIN (*raising his fist*): Will you keep your mouth shut, damn it.

INEX (*confronting him fearlessly, but with a look of vast surprise*): Well, well! (*A pause.*) Ah, I understand now. I know why they've put us three together.

GARCIN: I advise you to . . . to think twice before you say any more.

INEZ: Wait! You'll see how simple it is. Childishly simple. Obviously there aren't any physical torments—you agree, don't you? And yet we're in hell. And no one else will come here. We'll stay in this room together, the three of us, for ever and ever. . . . In short, there's someone absent here, the official torturer.

GARCIN (*sotto voce*): I'd noticed that.

INEZ: It's obvious what they're after—an economy of man-power . . . or devil-power, if you prefer. The same idea as in the cafeteria where customers serve themselves.

ESTELLE: What ever do you mean?

INEZ: I mean that each of us will act as torturer of the two others.

(*There is a short silence, while they digest this information.*)

GARCIN (*gently*): No, I shall never be your torturer. I wish neither of you any harm, and I've no concern with you. None at all. So the solution's easy enough; each of us stays put in his or her corner, and takes no notice of the others. You here, you here, and I there. Like soldiers at our posts. Also, we mustn't speak. Not one word. That won't be difficult; each of us has plenty of material for self-communings. I think I could stay ten thousand years with only my thoughts for company.

ESTELLE: Have I got to keep silent, too?

GARCIN: Yes. And that way we . . . we'll work out our salvation. Looking into ourselves, never raising our heads. Agreed?

INEZ: Agreed.

ESTELLE (*after some hesitation*): I agree.

GARCIN: Then . . . Good-bye.

(*He goes to his sofa, and buries his head in his hands. There is a long silence; then* INEZ *begins singing to herself.*)

INEZ: (*singing*):

> What a crowd in Whitefriars Lane!
> They've set trestles in a row,
> With a scaffold and the knife,
> And a pail of bran below.
> Come, good folks, to Whitefriars Lane,
> Come to see the merry show!
>
> The headsman rose at crack of dawn,
> He'd a long day's work in hand,
> Chopping heads off generals,
> Priests and peers and admirals,
> All the highest in the land.
> What a crowd in Whitefriars Lane!
>
> See them standing in a line,
> Ladies all dressed up so fine.
> But their heads have got to go,
> Heads and hats roll down below.
> Come, good folks, to Whitefriars Lane,
> Come to see the merry show!

(*Meanwhile* ESTELLE *has been plying her powder-puff and lipstick. She looks round for a mirror, fumbles in her bag, then turns towards* GARCIN.)

ESTELLE: Excuse me, have you a glass? (GARCIN *does not answer.*) Any sort of glass, a pocket-mirror will do. (GARCIN *remains silent.*) Even if you won't speak to me, you might lend me a glass.

(*His head still buried in his hands,* GARCIN *ignores her.*)

INEZ (*eagerly*): Don't worry! I've a glass in my bag. (*She opens her bag. Angrily.*) It's gone! They must have taken it from me at the entrance.

ESTELLE: How tiresome!

(*A short silence.* ESTELLE *shuts her eyes and sways, as if about to faint.* INEZ *runs forward and holds her up.*)

INEZ: What's the matter?

ESTELLE (*opens her eyes and smiles*): I feel so queer. (*She pats herself.*) Don't you ever get taken that way? When I can't see myself I begin to wonder if I really and truly exist. I pat myself just to make sure, but it doesn't help much.

INEZ: You're lucky. I'm always conscious of myself—in my mind. Painfully conscious.

ESTELLE: Ah yes, in your mind. But everything that goes on in one's head is so vague, isn't it? It makes one want to sleep. (*She is silent for a while.*) I've six big mirrors in my bedroom. There they are. I can see them. But they don't see me. They're reflecting the carpet, the settee, the window . . . but how empty it is, a glass in which I'm absent. When I talked to people I always made sure there was one near by in which I could see myself. I watched myself talking. And somehow it kept me alert, seeing myself as the others saw me. . . . Oh dear! My lipstick! I'm sure I've put it on all crooked. No, I can't do without a looking-glass for ever and ever, I simply can't.

INEZ: Suppose I try to be your glass? Come and pay me a visit, dear. Here's a place for you on my sofa.

ESTELLE: But—(*Points to* GARCIN.)

INEZ: Oh, he doesn't count.

ESTELLE: But we're going to . . . to hurt each other. You said it yourself.

INEZ: Do I look as if I wanted to hurt you?

ESTELLE: One never can tell.

INEZ: Much more likely you'll hurt me. Still, what does it matter? If I've got to suffer, it may as well be at your hands, your pretty hands. Sit down. Come closer. Closer. Look into my eyes. What do you see?

ESTELLE: Oh, I'm there! But so tiny I can't see myself properly.

INEZ: But I can. Every inch of you. Now ask me questions. I'll be as candid as any looking-glass.

(ESTELLE *seems rather embarrassed and turns to* GARCIN, *as if appealing to him for help.*)

ESTELLE: Please, Mr. Garcin. Sure our chatter isn't boring you?

(GARCIN *makes no reply.*)

INEZ: Don't worry about him. As I said, he doesn't count. We're by ourselves. . . . Ask away.

ESTELLE: Are my lips all right?

INEZ: Show! No, they're a bit smudgy.

ESTELLE: I thought as much. Luckily (*throws a quick glance at* GARCIN) no one's seen me. I'll try again.

INEZ: That's better. No. Follow the line of your lips. Wait! I'll guide your hand. There. That's quite good.

ESTELLE: As good as when I came in?

INEZ: Far better. Crueller. You mouth looks quite diabolical that way.

ESTELLE: Good gracious! And you say you like it! How maddening, not being able to see for myself! You're quite sure, Miss Serrano, that it's all right now?

INEZ: Won't you call me Inez?

ESTELLE: Are you sure it looks all right?

INEZ: You're lovely, Estelle

ESTELLE: But how can I rely upon your taste? Is it the same as my taste? Oh, how sickening it all is, enough to drive one crazy!

INEZ: I have your taste, my dear, because I like you so much. Look at me. No, straight. Now smile. I'm not so ugly, either. Aren't I nicer than your glass?

ESTELLE: Oh, I don't know. You scare me rather. My reflection in the glass never did that; of course I knew it so well. Like something I had tamed. . . I'm going to smile, and my smile will sink down into your pupils, and heaven knows what it will become.

INEZ: And why shouldn't you 'tame' me? (*The women gaze at each other,* ESTELLE *with a sort of fearful fascination.*) Listen! I want you to call me 'Inez'. We must be great friends.

ESTELLE: I don't make friends with women very easily.

INEZ: Not with postal clerks, you mean? Hullo, what's that—that nasty red spot at the bottom of your cheek? A pimple?

ESTELLE: A pimple? Oh, how simply foul! Where?

INEZ: There . . . You know the way they catch larks—with a mirror? I'm your lark-mirror, my dear, and you can't escape me. . . . There isn't any pimple, not a trace of one. So what about it? Suppose the mirror started telling lies? Or suppose I covered my eyes—as he is doing—and refused to look at you, all that loveliness of yours would be wasted on the desert air. No, don't be afraid, I can't help looking at you, I shan't turn my eyes away. And I'll be nice to you, ever so nice. Only you must be nice to me, too.

(*A short silence.*)

ESTELLE: Are you really . . . attracted by me?

INEZ: Very much indeed.

(*Another short silence.*)

ESTELLE (*indicating* GARCIN *by a slight movement of her head*): But I wish he'd notice me, too.

INEZ: Of course! Because he's a man! (*to* GARCIN.) You've won. (GARCIN *says nothing.*) But look at her, damn it! (*Still no reply from* GARCIN.) Don't pretend. You haven't missed a word of what we've said.

GARCIN: Quite so; not a word. I stuck my fingers in my ears, but your voices thudded in my brain. Silly chatter. Now will you leave me in peace, you two? I'm not interested in you.

INEZ: Not in me, perhaps—but how about this child? Aren't you interested in her? Oh, I saw through your game; you got on your high horse just to impress her.

GARCIN: I asked you to leave me in peace. There's someone talking about me in the newspaper office and I want to listen. And, if it'll make you any happier, let me tell you that I've no use for the 'child', as you call her.

ESTELLE: Thanks.

GARCIN: Oh, I didn't mean it rudely.

ESTELLE: You cad!

(*They confront each other in silence for some moments.*)

GARCIN: So that's that. (*Pause.*) You know I begged you not to speak.

ESTELLE: It's her fault; she started. I didn't ask anything of her and she came and offered me her . . . her glass.

INEZ: So you say. But all the time you were making up to him, trying every trick to catch his attention.

ESTELLE: Well, why shouldn't I!

GARCIN: You're crazy, both of you. Don't you see where this is leading us? For pity sake, keep your mouth shut. (*Pause.*) Now let's all sit down again quite quietly; we'll look at the floor and each must try to forget the others are there.

(*A longish silence.* GARCIN *sits down. The women return hesitantly to their places. Suddenly* INEZ *swings round on him.*)

The Submerged Exploited?

In *The Caretaker* the author uses dialogue which is basically naturalistic, credible and taken from everyday life. The work is of particular interest because the author has taken as his theme the inner meaning of language. It is built on the foundation that **what is said is never meant and what is meant is never said.** Everything is understated and almost every word means something different from its normal use. It is a complex exercise in construction. It is an even more complex exercise in perception and understanding. It is possible to claim the author has discovered a symbolic, poetic ritual for the times. It is also possible to claim he has invented a highly esoteric code of non-meaningful utterance to mystify, mislead and defy understanding. In the following passage there is **residual element of credible meaning** in the text. Most of it may be compared with a descant, or solo improvised, *freak out*, where melody, beat and supporting harmonies are missing.

THE CARETAKER
Harold Pinter

ACT TWO

(*A few seconds later.*)
(MICK *is seated*, DAVIES *on the floor, half-seated, crouched. Silence.*)
MICK: Well?
DAVIES: Nothing, nothing. Nothing.
(*A drip sounds in the bucket overhead. They look up.* MICK *looks back to* DAVIES.)
MICK: What's your name?
DAVIES: I don't know you. I don't know who you are.
(*Pause.*)
MICK: Eh?
DAVIES: Jenkins.
MICK: Jenkins?
DAVIES: Yes.
MICK: Jen . . . kins.
(*Pause.*)
You sleep here last night?
DAVIES: Yes.
MICK: Sleep well?
DAVIES: Yes.
MICK: I'm awfully glad. It's awfully nice to meet you.
(*Pause.*)
What did you say your name was?
DAVIES: Jenkins.
MICK: I beg your pardon?
DAVIES: Jenkins.
(*Pause.*)
MICK: Jen . . . kins.
(*A drip sounds in the bucket.* DAVIES *looks up.*)
You remind me of my uncle's brother. He was always on the move, that man. Never without his passport. Had an eye for the girls. Very much your

build. Bit of an athlete. Long-jump specialist. He had a habit of demonstrating different run-ups in the drawing-room round about Christmas time.
Had a penchant for nuts. That's what it was. Nothing else but a penchant.
Couldn't eat enough of them. Peanuts, walnuts, brazil nuts, monkey nuts,
wouldn't touch a piece of fruit cake. Had a marvellous stop-watch. Picked
it up in Hong Kong. The day after they chucked him out of the Salvation
Army. Used to go in number four for Beckenham Reserves. That was before
he got his Gold Medal. Had a funny habit of carrying his fiddle on his back.
Like a papoose. I think there was a bit of the Red Indian in him. To be
honest, I've never made out how he came to be my uncle's brother. I've
often thought that maybe it was the other way round. I mean that my uncle
was his brother and he was my uncle. But I never called him uncle. As a
matter of fact I called him Sid. My mother called him Sid too. It was a funny
business. Your spitting image he was. Married a Chinaman and went to
Jamaica.

(Pause.)

I hope you slept well last night.

DAVIES: Listen! I don't know who you are!

MICK: What bed you sleep in?

DAVIES: Now look here—

MICK: Eh?

DAVIES: That one.

MICK: Not the other one?

DAVIES: No.

MICK: Choosy.

(Pause.)

How do you like my room?

DAVIES: Your room?

MICK: Yes.

DAVIES: This ain't your room. I don't know who you are. I ain't never seen you
before.

MICK: You know, believe it or not, you've got a funny kind of resemblance to
a bloke I once knew in Shoreditch. Actually he lived in Aldgate. I was stay-
ing with a cousin in Camden Town. This chap, he used to have a pitch in
Finsbury Park, just by the bus depot. When I got to know him I found out
he was brought up in Putney. That didn't make any difference to me. I know
quite a few people who were born in Putney. Even if they weren't born in
Putney they were born in Fulham. The only trouble was, he wasn't born in
Putney, he was only brought up in Putney. It turned out he was born in the
Caledonian Road, just before you get to the Nag's Head. His old mum was
still living at the Angel. All the buses passed right by the door. She could
get a 38, 581, 30 or 38A, take her down the Essex Road to Dalston Junction
in next to no time. Well, of course, if she got the 30 he'd take her up Upper
Street way, round by Highbury Corner and down to St. Paul's Church, but
she'd get to Dalston Junction just the same in the end. I used to leave my
bike in her garden on my way to work. Yes, it was a curious affair. Dead
spit of you he was. Bit bigger round the nose but there was nothing in it.

(Pause.)

Did you sleep here last night?

DAVIES: Yes.

MICK: Sleep well?

DAVIES: Yes!

MICK: Did you have to get up in the night?

DAVIES: No!

(*Pause.*)

MICK: What's your name?

DAVIES (*shifting, about to rise*): Now look here!

MICK: What?

DAVIES: Jenkins!

MICK: Jen . . . kins.

(DAVIES *makes a sudden movement to rise. A violent bellow from* MICK *sends him back.*)

(*A shout.*) Sleep here last night?

DAVIES: Yes . . .

MICK (*continuing at a great pace*): How'd you sleep?

DAVIES: I slept—

MICK: Sleep well?

DAVIES: Now look—

MICK: What bed?

DAVIES: That—

MICK: Not the other?

DAVIES: NO!

MICK: Choosy.

(*Pause.*)

(*Quietly.*) Choosy.

(*Pause.*)

(*Again amiable.*) What sort of sleep did you have in that bed?

DAVIES (*banging on the floor*): All right!

MICK: You weren't uncomfortable?

DAVIES (*groaning*): All right!

(MICK *stands, and moves to him.*)

MICK: You a foreigner?

DAVIES: No.

MICK: Born and bred in the British Isles?

DAVIES: I was!

MICK: What did they teach you?

(*Pause.*)

How did you like my bed?

(*Pause.*)

That's my bed. You want to mind you don't catch a draught.

DAVIES: From the bed?

MICK: No, now, up your arse.

(DAVIES *stares warily at* MICK, *who turns.* DAVIES *scrambles to the clothes horse and seizes his trousers.* MICK *turns swiftly and grabs them.* DAVIES *lunges for them.* MICK *holds out a hand, warningly.*)

You intending to settle down here?

DAVIES: Give me my trousers then.

MICK: You settling down for a long stay?

DAVIES: Give me my bloody trousers!

MICK: Why, where you going?

DAVIES: Give me and I'm going, I'm going to Sidcup!

(MICK *flicks the trousers in* DAVIES' *face several times.* DAVIES *retreats. Pause.*)

MICK: You know, you remind me of a bloke I bumped into once, just the other side of the Guildford by-pass—

DAVIES: I was brought here!

(*Pause.*)

MICK: Pardon?

DAVIES: I was brought here! I was brought here!

MICK: Brought here? Who brought you here?

DAVIES: Man who lives here . . . he . . .

(*Pause.*)

MICK: Fibber.

DAVIES: I was brought here, last night . . . met him in a caff . . . I was working . . . I got the bullet . . . I was working there . . . bloke saved me from a punch up, brought me here, brought me right here.

(*Pause.*)

MICK: I'm afraid you're a born fibber, en't you? You're speaking to the owner. This is my room. You're standing in my house.

DAVIES: It's his . . . he seen me all right . . . he . . .

MICK (*pointing to* DAVIES' *bed*): That's my bed.

DAVIES: What about that, then?

MICK: That's my mother's bed.

DAVIES: Well she wasn't in it last night!

MICK (*moving to him*): Now don't get perky, son, don't get perky. Keep your hands off my old mum.

DAVIES: I ain't . . . I haven't . . .

MICK: Don't get out of your depth, friend, don't start taking liberties with my old mother, let's have a bit of respect.

DAVIES: I got respect, you won't find anyone with more respect.

MICK: Well, stop telling me all these fibs.

DAVIES: Now listen to me, I never seen you before, have I?

MICK: Never seen my mother before either, I suppose?

(*Pause.*)

I think I'm coming to the conclusion that you're an old rogue. You're nothing but an old scoundrel.

DAVIES: Now wait—

MICK: Listen, son. Listen, sonny. You stink.

DAVIES: You ain't got no right to—

MICK: You're stinking the place out. You're an old robber, there's no getting away from it. You're an old skate. You don't belong in a nice place like this. You're an old barbarian. Honest. You got no business wandering about in an unfurnished flat. I could charge seven quid a week for this if I wanted to. Get a taker tomorrow. Three hundred and fifty a year exclusive. No argument. I mean, if that sort of money's in your range don't be afraid to say so. Here you are. Furniture and fittings, I'll take four hundred or the nearest offer. Rateable value ninety quid for the annum. You can reckon water, heating and lighting at close on fifty. That'll cost you eight hundred and ninety if you're all that keen. Say the word and I'll have my solicitors draft you out a contract. Otherwise I've got the van outside, I can run you to the police station in five minutes, have you in for trespassing, loitering with intent, daylight robbery, filching, thieving and stinking the place out. What do you say? Unless you're really keen on a straightforward purchase. Of course, I'll get my brother to decorate it up for you first. I've got a brother who's a number one decorator. He'll decorate it up for you. If you want more space, there's four more rooms along the landing ready to go. Bathroom, living-room, bedroom and nursery. You can have this as your study. This brother I mentioned, he's just about to start on the other rooms. Yes, just about to start. So what do you say? Eight hundred odd for this room or three thousand down for the whole upper storey. On the other hand, if you prefer to approach it in the long-term way I know an insurance firm in West Ham'll be pleased to handle the deal for you. No strings attached, open the above board, untarnished record; twenty per cent interest, fifty per cent deposit; down payments, back payments, family allowances, bonus schemes, remission of term for good behaviour, six months lease, yearly examination of the relevant archives, tea laid on, disposal of shares, benefit extension, compensation on cessation, comprehensive indemnity against riot, civil commotion, labour disturbances, storm, tempest, thunderbolt, larceny or cattle all subject to a daily check and double check. Of course we'd need a signed declaration from your personal medical attendant as assurance that you possess the requisite fitness to carry the can, won't we? Who do you bank with?

(*Pause.*)

Who do you bank with?

(*The door opens.* ASTON *comes in.* MICK *turns and drops the trousers.* DAVIES *picks them up and puts them on.* ASTON, *after a glance at the other two, goes to his bed, places a bag which he is carrying on it, sits down and resumes fixing the toaster.* DAVIES *retreats to his corner.* MICK *sits in the chair. Silence. A drip sounds in the bucket.*)

Meaning Camouflaged?

If the previous extract exploited the use of dialogue to the frontiers of meaningful conversation, it did so within a convention of naturalism for the characters concerned. At all times they were presented as behaving and speaking normally. The next two extracts take a further step away from meaningful conversation, ordinary people and average social situations. Time, place, character and language are subject only to the laws of a severely ritualistic act of theatre. **The inner meaning is the only meaning.** The external text is only significant as a vehicle to inform the audience of experiences to which dictionary references and definitions are mainly irrelevant and quite often misleading. The second passage shows this principle in its extreme form. It is an interesting challenge to decide exactly where to start to discover the author's precise intention.

THE SPORT OF MY MAD MOTHER
Ann Jellicoe

(*Enter* GRETA *dressed as the others. She mingles with them unnoticed.*)

CONE: Please to remember
ALL: Please to remember
                     Please to remember the fifth of November
                     Please to remember the fifth of November
                         gunpowder, treason and plot.
                     (*All six are strung out across the stage.*)

DODO (*her hat falling off*): There are six . . . there are six . . . (DODO *runs left*)

PATTY (*frightened*): Fak!

FAK: Eh?

                     (FAK *and* PATTY *go right.*)

DODO: Caldaro . . . Caldaro . . . Caldaro . .

CALDARO: All right, honey.

(CALDARO *goes to* DODO. *The others reform so that their identity is confused.*)

CONE: Caldaro.

CALDARO: Yes?

FAK: Where you from, Caldaro?

CALDARO: The U.S.

PATTY: What part of the U.S.

CALDARO: Illinois.

CONE: What town in Illinois?

CALDARO: Rockford.

GRETA (*speaking with an Australian accent*): Your family comes from—?

CALDARO: Uh?

PATTY: Your family.

CALDARO: Italy—Naples.

FAK: Pampinato comes from Naples.

CALDARO: I'm sorry I don't know him.

CONE: How d'you get your cigarettes?

CALDARO: From a friend.

CONE: Who? . . . What's his name?

PATTY: Afraid?

CONE: Afraid to get mixed up?

CALDARO: This is stupid. Stupid! For heaven's sake, Cone, take off that silly mask.

FAK: You're trying to put us off.

PATTY: You're afraid to tell us.

CONE: Is there any harm in telling us?

CALDARO: There's no harm.

PATTY: Then why not tell us?

CALDARO: This is a stupid situation.

CONE: Is this a stupid situation?

FAK: You know Petticoat Lane.

CALDARO: What else?

FAK: Nice district Aldgate.

CALDARO: I wouldn't know.

FAK: Petticoat Lane is in Aldgate.
CALDARO: Why don't you go play Guy Fawkes?
CONE: Who gets your cigarettes?
CALDARO: Conrad Scaeffer.
PATTY: Any other friends?
CALDARO: Plenty: Clive West, Mary Allen, Zachary Hope, Alma—
CONE: Why not give the real names?
CALDARO: Eh?
CONE: The people you really know.
FAK: The people you really go around with.
CALDARO: This is idiotic! Fantastic!
FAK: Gringo!
GRETA: Pivesky!
FAK: Turps!
CONE: Pampinato!
CALDARO: I don't know them.
PATTY: What reason have you to know them?
FAK: Why should you know them?
CONE: Did we say you did?

(CALDARO *tries to get at* GRETA.)

CALDARO: You—

(GRETA *slips away and* CALDARO *finds* CONE.)

CONE: Who's Scaeffer?
CALDARO: What?
PATTY: Who's Scaeffer?
GRETA: Scaeffer!
CALDARO: Did—
PATTY: Journalist?
FAK: What paper?
GRETA: Mother born?
CALDARO: What?
PATTY: Mother born.
CALDARO: Detroit.
CONE: Sure she was born in Detroit?
CALDARO: Yes, yes! Detroit!
FAK: Who's Scaeffer?
CALDARO: A journalist—no—I—
PATTY: What do you do?
GRETA: Write?
CALDARO: Yes—sometimes—
FAK: Letters?
PATTY: To friends?
CALDARO: Yes.
GRETA: Name them.
CALDARO: What?
FAK: Don't ask questions.
CONE: Afraid?
CALDARO: Afraid?
FAK: Afraid of trouble?
CONE: Your mother was born in Pittsburgh.

CALDARO: No.
PATTY: Yes yes yes.
FAK: Yes.
GRETA: Yes.
CALDARO: No—in—
CONE: Cleveland.
CALDARO: No.
PATTY: Yes.
FAK: Yes.
GRETA: Yes.
CONE: Who's Scaeffer.
CALDARO: Journalist.
PATTY: What paper.
CALDARO: I—I—
PATTY: Showgirl—Mary Allen?
CALDARO: No—a—
GRETA: What?
CALDARO: Stenographer.
PATTY: Who for?
CALDARO: Men in shoes—in a shoe company—
CONE: Name?
CALDARO: How should I know? I don't—
FAK: Pampinato.
CALDARO: What?
CONE: Know that name?
CALDARO: I—I heard it.
CONE: So you heard it!
GRETA: Your mother was born in—?
CALDARO: Sure—I mean Detroit.
GRETA: Sure?
CALDARO: Sure I'm sure.
CONE: Absolutely sure?
CALDARO: Why not! Why not!
PATTY: Brothers!
CALDARO: Brothers.
FAK: Brothers.
CONE: Brothers.
CALDARO: Brothers, brothers my mother was born in . . .
CONE: Pampinato!
CALDARO: Yes?
CONE: You seen him.
CALDARO: I—
PATTY: Your friends—
FAK: They'll get you into trouble.
PATTY: Catch you out. Catch! Catch!
CALDARO: No.
GRETA: Who's Mary Pivesky?
CONE: You know her.
PATTY: Gringo.
CALDARO: Who? Who?

FAK: Don't know him?
CALDARO: Not said—
CONE: The shoemaker—
CALDARO: What?
PATTY: You deny—
CALDARO: Shoe? Shoe?
PATTY: —Said you—
FAK: —Get it out—
PATTY: Say you—
CALDARO: No shoe—
PATTY: Said—
FAK: Get—
CONE: Get—
GRETA: Mother born Pittsburgh.
CALDARO: Mamma!
CONE: Lepstein.
FAK: You know him.
CONE: He's a friend of yours.
PATTY: Say Turps.
CONE: Know him.
FAK: Shoemaker.
PATTY: Liar.
FAK: Who's—who's—
CONE: Who's Zachary Hope?
PATTY: You won't tell us.
FAK: You're afraid.
CONE: You're afraid.
FAK: What you afraid of?
PATTY: Afraid.
CONE: Afraid to tell.
FAK: Tell us!
PATTY: Tell!
CONE: Stop! . . . Notice something?
FAK: No-one's talking.
CONE: You're right . . . no-one's talking. . . . Why you not talking, Caldaro?
. . . You know . . . he thinks we're stupid.
FAK: Stupid?
CONE: Look at his face! Look at his face! We make him sick: 'Take off that
silly mask, Cone, you make me sick.'
FAK: Make him talk!
PATTY: Talk!
CONE: Where's Dodo? Where's the little bitch? Come here! Come here!
Cotcha! All right, Dodo: tell Caldaro to talk. Tell your friend to speak.
DODO: Speak.
CONE: Louder, Dodo, louder.
DODO: Speak. Speak.
(DODO escapes and exits.)
CONE (*screaming*): Answer, Answer. Answer.
FAK: Sock!
PATTY: Smash!

CONE: Why don't you answer?

CALDARO: Because I won't submit to this degradation.

FAK: Eh?

CONE: Degradation!

PATTY: Yawooerl!

CONE: Degradation! Yoweooh! Yoweeoh!

PATTY: Yawooerl! Yawooerl! Ugh! Ugh!

FAK: Whaow! Aherooigh! Aherooigh!

(*Screaming with anger*, PATTY, CONE *and* FAK *fall upon* CALDARO. FAK *picks up the gun and raises it to club* CALDARO.)

THE SPORT OF MY MAD MOTHER
Ann Jellicoe

PATTY: Listening for Greta? Looking for Greta, eh? Why's she not here, eh? Changed! She's different! And it's going to get worse. Worse. Bah! Mummy's boy Master Coney! Doesn't love him any more! She! She! She's losing interest and especially is Master Coney!

(CONE *turns on her.*)

... I ... I ...

FAK (*inarticulate, trying to distract* CONE): Ah.

CONE: Eh?

FAK: ... Dolly.

CONE: Dolly?

FAK: Dolly!

CONE: Dolly!

FAK: Dolly!

(CONE *turns to* PATTY *again.* FAK *goes to her other side and by his desperation draws* CONE'S *attention beyond her.*)

FAK: Dolly! Dolly!

CONE: Dolly?

FAK: Dolly!

CONE: Dolly!

FAK: Dolly

CONE: Dolly

FAK: Dolly.

(CONE *and* FAK *have hypnotized each other.* PATTY *tries to get away and in so doing draws them on to her.*)

FAK (*at* PATTY): Dolly

CONE (*at* PATTY): Dolly.

FAK: Dolly

CONE: Dolly

FAK: Dolly.

PATTY: Shoo.

FAK: Shoo.

PATTY: Shoo.

CONE: Shoo.

FAK: Shoo. Shoo.

PATTY: Shoo. Shoo.

CONE: Shoo. Shoo.

(PATTY *screams.*)

PATTY (*to audience, as if drowning*): Help! Help me! Help!
CALDARO: Stop . . . (*He walks into their midst*) . . . What goes on here?
PATTY: Eh?
FAK: Them . . . One of them.
CONE: He's alone . . . (*walking up to* CALDARO) Nice isn't he?
PATTY (*they begin to amble round* CALDARO): Nice—
FAK: Cecil Gee—
CONE: Careful not to crush—
PATTY: Pardon.
FAK: Excuse me.
CONE: He don't look very well—
FAK: Bit daft ain't he?
PATTY: Hi Mister!
FAK: Can you hear?
CALDARO (*amazed*): Hey.
PATTY: He's loose.
FAK: He's loony.
CONE: Quack! Quack!
PATTY: Potty!
FAK: Look!
CALDARO: What!
CONE: Mm . . . pooch!
FAK: Boo!
CALDARO: Animals—
CONE: Boo! Boo!
CALDARO:—Like stampeding—
PATTY: Bim! Bam!
CONE: Bang! Bang!
FAK (*bringing out his gun*): Yak! Yak! Yak! Yak!
PATTY: Boo, boo boo boo!
CONE: Yak! Yak!
CALDARO: Control. Control.
FAK: Yak yak yak yak!
PATTY: Tcha! Tcha! Tcha!
FAK: Yay yak yak yak!
PATTY: Tcha tcha tcha tcha!
CALDARO (*making a great effort to collect himself and dominate them*): What
   are you trying to do?
(CONE *behind* CALDARO *gives him a sharp blow at the base of the skull—unseen
by the others.*)
CALDARO: Ah!
(CALDARO *collapses forward against* FAK *who is sent staggering away firing his
gun wildly.* CALDARO *falls and is still.*)
FAK: One o' them! One o' them! One o' them!

Direct or Indirect?

In *Hamlet*—poetic theatre involving direct audience address—the author
has no problem in balancing inner meaning with external language. The two
become one. Not only is what is said what is meant—**what is said goes on to
explain and amplify what is meant.** Consider the following two examples of the

exploration of thought and feeling regarding possible suicide. The convention of the first allows the author to speak directly to his subject. The second requires a circuitous route if the experience is to be explored and not merely allowed to occur. In spite of the distancing effect of more than three and a half centuries, there can be no doubt of the first author's intent whereas the second is so burdened with the trappings of naturalism that any ultimate statement he may have intended regarding Hester's thoughts, feelings and actions requires real excavation. It is a matter for debate whether the gas-fire and Hester's performance with it add or detract from the imaginative communication of experience.

HAMLET, PRINCE OF DENMARK

William Shakespeare

HAMLET: To be, or not to be, that is the question:
Whether 'tis nobler in the mind to suffer
The slings and arrows of outrageous Fortune,
Or to take arms against a sea of troubles,
And by opposing end them: to die to sleep;
No more; and by a sleep, to say we end
The heart-ache, and the thousand natural shocks
That flesh is heir to? 'tis a consummation
Devoutly to be wish'd. To die to sleep,
To sleep, perchance to dream; ay, there's the rub,
For in that sleep of death, what dreams may come,
When we have shuffled off this mortal coil,
Must give us pause. There's the respect
That makes calamity of so long life:
For who would bear the whips and scorns of time,
The oppressor's wrong, the proud man's contumely,
The pangs of dispiz'd love, the Law's delay,
The insolence of office, and the spurns
That patient merit of the unworthy takes,
When he himself might his quietus make,
With a bare bodkin? who would fardels bear,
To grunt and sweat under a weary life,
But that the dread of something after death,
The undiscovered country, from whose bourn
No traveller returns, puzzles the will,
And makes us rather bear those ills we have,
Than fly to others that we know not of.
Thus conscience does make cowards of us all,
And thus the native hue of resolution
Is sicklied o'er, with the pale cast of thought,
And enterprises of great pith and moment,
With this regard their currents turn awry,
And lose the name of action.

THE DEEP BLUE SEA
Terence Rattigan

(PHILIP *nods and goes.* HESTER *closes the door after him. After a second of utter stillness she moves quietly to the window, and gently closes it. Then she goes to her bag and searches for a coin. Not finding what she is looking for she turns quickly to the table on to which* FREDDIE *had thrown the shilling. She picks it up and walks to the gas meter, inserts the coin, and we hear it drop. She turns to the front door and locks it. Then she places a rug carefully on the floor against the door. Turning, she picks up the empty bottle of aspirin, looks at it, and puts it down. Then she pulls from her pocket the sleeping pills given her by* MILLER, *takes a glass from the table, goes into the kitchen, and reappears, having filled it with water. Her breath is now coming in short gasps, as if she has been undergoing some strong physical exertion, althouth her movements until now have not been hurried. There is a knock on the door, arresting her in the action of putting the pills into her mouth.*)

(*Impatiently.*) Yes? Who is it?

MILLER (*off*): Miller.

HESTER: What do you want? I'm just going to bed.

MILLER (*off*): I want to see you.

HESTER: Won't it keep to the morning?

MILLER (*off*): No.

(HESTER *impatiently goes to the door, pulls the rug up, and throws it on to the sofa where it falls to the floor. She unlocks the door and lets* MILLER *in.*)

(*Indicating key.*) Determined not to be disturbed?

HESTER: I usually lock my door at night.

MILLER: It's lucky you didn't last night.

HESTER: (*indicating the glass of water*): I was just going to take your pills.

MILLER: So I see.

HESTER: Do you think they're strong enough, Doctor. Could you let me have another two or three in case they don't work?

(MILLER, *without replying, picks up the rug from the floor and puts it on the sofa. Then, watched by* HESTER, *he strolls to the gas-fire and with a casual flick of his foot, kicks on the tap. We hear the hiss of escaping gas. He kicks it off.*)

I said could you let me have—

MILLER: I heard you. The answer is no.

HESTER: Why not?

MILLER: I've been involved enough with the police. I don't want to be accused now of giving drugs to a suicidal patient. (*He holds out his hand.*)

HESTER: Aren't you letting your imagination run away with you, Doctor?

MILLER: No. I want those pills back, please.

HESTER: Why?

MILLER: If you put a rug down in front of a door it's wiser to do it when the lights are out.

HESTER (*hysterically*): Why are you spying on me? Why can't you leave me alone?

MILLER: I'm not trying to decide for you whether you live or die. That choice is yours and you have quite enough courage to make it for yourself—

HESTER: (*with a despairing cry*): Courage!

MILLER: Oh yes. It takes courage to condemn yourself to death. Most suicides die to escape. You're dying because you feel unworthy to live. Isn't that true?

HESTER (*wildly*): How do I know what's true? I only know that after tonight I won't be able to face life any more.

MILLER: What is there so hard about facing life? Most people seem to be able to manage it.

HESTER: How can anyone live without hope?

MILLER: Quite easily. To live without hope can mean to live without despair.

HESTER: Those are just words.

MILLER: Words can help you if your mind can only grasp them. (*He twists her roughly round to face him. Harshly.*) Your Freddie has left you. He's never going to come back again. Never in the world. Never.

    (*At each word she wilts as if at a physical blow.*)

HESTER (*wildly*): I know. I know. That's what I can't face.

MILLER (*with a brutal force*): Yes, you can. That word 'never'. Face that and you can face life. It's your only chance.

HESTER: What is there beyond hope?

MILLER: Life. You must believe that. It's true—I know.

    (HESTER'S *storm of tears is subsiding. She raises her head to look at him.*)

HESTER (*at length*): You can still find some purpose in living.

MILLER: What purpose?

HESTER: You have your work at the hospital.

MILLER: For me the only purpose in life is to live it. My work at the hospital is a help to me in that. That is all. If you looked perhaps you might also find some help for yourself.

HESTER: What help?

MILLER: Haven't you got your work too? (*He makes a gesture towards the paintings.*)

HESTER: Oh that. (*Wearily*). There's no escape for me through that.

MILLER: Not through that, or that. (*With a wide gesture he indicates the later paintings.*) But perhaps through that. (*He points to the early painting.*) I'm not an art expert, but I believe there was talent here. Just a spark, that's all, which with a little feeding might have become a little flame. Not a great fire, which could have illumined the world—oh no—I'm not saying that. But the world is a dark enough place for even a little flicker to be welcome. (*He hands her a glass of water, which she drinks. Then he turns back to the picture.*) I'd like to buy that.

(HESTER *gazes at the picture listlessly for a moment. Then she gets up wearily, goes to the picture, and hands it to him. He smiles.*) How much?

HESTER: It's a gift.

(MILLER *shakes his head, still smiling. He pulls out his wallet and removes two pound notes.* HESTER *shakes her head.* MILLER *puts the notes on the table.*)

MILLER: Look. I'm going to put these notes down here. It's what I can afford to give you—not what I think the picture's worth. If you're determined not to sell it, slip the notes into an envelope and address them to me. I shall understand, and be sorry. Good night.

HESTER: Good night, Doctor.

MILLER *(turning)*: Not Doctor, please.

(*Pause.*)

HESTER: Good night, my friend.

MILLER: I could wish that you meant that.

HESTER *(quietly)*: What makes you so sure that I don't mean it?

MILLER *(also quietly)*: I hope that I may be given a proof that you do—by tomorrow morning.

HESTER: Are you asking me to make my choice in order to help you?

MILLER *(smiling)*: Surely I have a right to feel sad if I lose a newfound friend— especially one whom I so much like and respect.

HESTER *(bitterly)*: Respect?

MILLER: Yes, respect.

HESTER: Please, don't be too kind to me.

(*He approaches her quickly and takes her shoulders.*)

MILLER: Listen to me. To see yourself as the world sees you may be very brave, but it can also be very foolish. Why should you accept the world's view of you as a weak-willed neurotic—better dead than alive? What right have they to judge? To judge you they must have the capacity to feel as you feel. And who has? One in a thousand. You alone know how you have felt. And you alone know how unequal the battle has always been that your will has had to fight.

HESTER: 'I tried to be good and failed.' Isn't that the excuse that all criminals make?

MILLER: When they make it justly, it's a just excuse.

HESTER: Does it let them escape the sentence?

MILLER: Yes, if the judge is fair—and not blind with hatred for the criminal— as you are for yourself.

HESTER: If you could find me one extenuating circumstance—one single reason why I should respect myself—even a little.

An Attempted Marriage?

Approaching the release of the inner meaning of the text through poetic format occupied Eliot in a different way from Shakespeare. The following extract shows that in order to bring external text and final meaning into a one-to-one relationship the author puts his characters self-consciously through hoops to achieve a platform from which Reilly can feel free to discard some of the incumbrances of acceptable, naturalistic conversation. **Not only does Reilly quote poetry; he asks permission to do so.** Eliot must have considered it necessary to include this as a **sort of apology** for Reilly addressing his stage audience as if they were the theatre audience. Perhaps it might have been better done by direct audience address since the author's intention to expose significant meaning does not entirely succeed. The following lines show there is still more that is meant than is said:

REILLY: 'That shows some insight on your part, Mrs. Chamberlayne;
But such experience can only be hinted at
In myths and images.' . . . to . . .

LAVINIA: 'Oh, Edward, I knew! I knew what you were thinking!
Doesn't it help you, that I feel guilty too?'

The author seems to be pulled apart by the two forces—**natural characters communicating through ordinary conversation and the needs of informing his** audience through direct poetic utterance—needs which appear to accompany his theme and narrative. Identifying which of these has ascendancy at any one moment is a rewarding experience in highlighting the tensions between external and internal rhythms and meanings.

THE COCKTAIL PARTY
T. S. Eliot

REILLY

You state the position correctly, Julia.
Do you mind if I quote poetry, Mrs. Chamberlayne?

LAVINIA

Oh no, I should love to hear you speaking poetry . . .

JULIA

She has made a point, Henry.

LAVINIA

. . . if it answers my question.

REILLY

Ere Babylon was dust
The magus Zoroaster, my dead child,
Met his own image walking in the garden.
That apparition, sole of men, he saw.
For know there are two worlds of life and death:
One that which thou beholdest; but the other
Is underneath the grave, where do inhabit
The shadows of all forms that think and live
Till death unite them and they part no more!
When I first met Miss Coplestone, in this room,
I saw the image, standing behind her chair,
Of a Celia Coplestone whose face showed the astonishment
Of the first five minutes after a violent death.
If this strains your credulity, Mrs. Chamberlayne,
I ask you only to entertain the suggestion
That a sudden intuition, in certain minds,
May tend to express itself at once in a picture.
That happens to me, sometimes. So it was obvious
That here was a woman under sentence of death.
That was her destiny. The only question
Then was, what sort of death? I could not know;
Because it was for her to choose the way of life
To lead to death, and, without knowing the end
Yet choose the form of death. We know the death she chose.
I did not know that she would die in this way;
She did not know. So all that I could do
Was to direct her in the way of preparation.
That way, which she accepted, led to this death.
And if that is not a happy death, what death is happy?

EDWARD

Do you mean that having chosen this form of death
She did not suffer as ordinary people suffer?

REILLY

Not at all what I mean. Rather the contrary.
I'd say that she suffered all that we should suffer
In fear and pain and loathing—all these together—
And reluctance of the body to become a thing.
I'd say she suffered more, because more conscious
Than the rest of us. She paid the highest price
In suffering. That is part of the design.

LAVINIA

Perhaps she had been through greater agony beforehand.
I mean—I know nothing of her last two years.

REILLY

That shows some insight on your part, Mrs. Chamberlayne;
But such experience can only be hinted at
In myths and images. To speak about it
We talk of darkness, labyrinths, Minotaur terrors.
But the world does not take the place of this one.
Do you imagine that the Saint in the desert
With spiritual evil always at his shoulder
Suffered any less from hunger, damp, exposure,
Bowel trouble, and the fear of lions,
Cold of the night and heat of the day, than we should?

EDWARD

But if this was right—if this was right for Celia—
There must be something else that is terribly wrong,
And the rest of us are some how involved in the wrong.
I should only speak for myself. I'm sure that *I* am.

REILLY

Let me free your mind from one impediment:
You must try to detach yourself from what you still feel
As your responsibility.

EDWARD

                              I cannot help the feeling
That, in some way, my responsibility
Is greater than that of a band of half-crazed savages.

LAVINIA

Oh, Edward, I knew! I knew what you were thinking!
Doesn't it help you, that I feel guilty too?

REILLY

If we all were judged according to the consequences
Of all our words and deeds, beyond the intention
And beyond our limited understanding
Of ourselves and others, we should all be condemned.
Mrs. Chamberlayne, I often have to make a decision
Which may mean restoration or ruin to a patient—
And sometimes I have made the wrong decision.
As for Miss Coplestone, because you think her death was waste
You blame yourselves, and because you blame yourselves
You think her life was wasted. It was triumphant.
But I am no more responsible for the triumph—

And just as responsible for her death as you are.

LAVINIA

Yet I know I shall go on blaming myself
For being so unkind to her . . . so spiteful.
I shall go on seeing her at the moment
When she said good-bye to us, two years ago.

EDWARD

Your responsibility is nothing to mine, Lavinia.

LAVINIA

I'm not sure about that. If I had understood you
Then I might not have misunderstood Celia.

REILLY

You will have to live with these memories and make them
Into something new. Only by acceptance
Of the past will you alter its meaning.

JULIA

Henry, I think it is time that I said something:
Everyone makes a choice, of one kind or another,
And then must take the consequences. Celia chose
A way of which the consequence was Kinkanja.
Peter chose a way that leads him to Boltwell:
And he's got to go there . . .

PETER

I see what you mean.
I wish I didn't have to. But the car will be waiting,
And the experts—I'd almost forgotten them.
I realise that I can't get out of it—
And what else can I do?

ALEX

It is your film.
And I know that Bela expects great things of it.

PETER

So now I'll be going.

EDWARD

Shall we see you again, Peter,
Before you leave England?

LAVINIA

Do try to come to see us.
You know, I think it would do us all good—
You and me and Edward . . . to talk about Celia.

PETER

Thanks very much. But not this time—
I simply shan't be able to.

EDWARD

But on your next visit?

PETER

The next time I come to England, I promise you.
I really do want to see you both, very much.
Good-bye, Julia. Good-bye, Alex. Good-bye, Sir Henry.

(*Exit.*)

JULIA

. . . And now the consequence of the Chamberlayne's choice
Is a cocktail party. They must be ready for it.
Their guests may be arriving at any moment.

REILLY

Julia, you are right. It is also right
That the Chamberlaynes should now be giving a party.

LAVINIA

And I have been thinking, for these last five minutes,
How I could face my guests. I wish it was over.
I mean . . . I was glad you came . . . I am glad Alex told us . . .
And Peter had to know . . .

EDWARD

Now I think I understand . . .

LAVINIA

Then I hope you will explain it to me!

EDWARD

Oh, it isn't much
That I understand yet! But Sir Henry has been saying,
I think, that every moment is a fresh beginning;
And Julia, that life is only keeping on;
And somehow, the two ideas seem to fit together.

LAVINIA

But all the same . . . I don't want to see these people.

REILLY

It is your appointed burden. And as for the party,
I am sure it will be a success.

JULIA

And I think, Henry,
That we should leave before the party begins.
They will get on better without us. You too, Alex.

LAVINIA

We don't want you to go!

ALEX

We have another engagement.

REILLY

And on this occasion I shall not be unexpected.

JULIA

Now, Henry. Now, Alex. We're going to the Gunnings.
(*Exeunt* JULIA, REILLY *and* ALEX.)

LAVINIA

Edward, how am I looking?

EDWARD

Very well.
I might almost say, your best. But you always look your best.

LAVINIA

Oh, Edward, that spoils it. No woman can believe
That she always looks her best. You're rather transparent,
You know, when you're trying to cheer me up.
To say I always look my best can only mean the worst.

EDWARD
I never shall learn how to pay a compliment.

LAVINIA
What you should have done was to admire my dress.

EDWARD
But I've already told you how much I like it.

LAVINIA
But so much has happened since then. And besides,
One sometimes like to hear the same compliment twice.

EDWARD
And now for the party.

LAVINIA
Now for the party.

EDWARD
It will soon be over.

LAVINIA
I wish it would begin.

EDWARD
There's the doorbell.

LAVINIA
Oh, I'm glad. It's begun.

(CURTAIN)

The Contrast Exploited

In the following extract, the conflict between what is said and what is meant is **brought to the surface and the characters manipulate the concept throughout the play.** In *The Maids* the conflict is a **constant undercurrent.** In *The Caretaker* it is part of the **fibre of the play.** In *A Phoenix Too Frequent*, it appears and **takes a selfconscious bow** from time to time. In *The Fire Raisers* it is, at one and the same time, **the theme of the play and a symbol of the theme.** From time to time it is fully exposed in the nature of bluff, counter-bluff and double-bluff. It is an excellent example of an author layering his hidden meanings with skilful use of camouflage and yet providing a sufficiency of subtle signposts that there is never any danger of a layer being overlooked or confused.

THE FIRE RAISERS
Max Frisch

SCHMITZ: 'Goosey, Goosey Gander—'

(*He sings at the top of his voice.*)

'Goosey, Goosey Gander, where shall I wander?'
EISENRING: That's enough.
SCHMITZ: 'Where shall I wander? Upstairs and downstairs—'.
EISENRING: He's drunk.
SCHMITZ: 'And in my lady's chamber—pot.'
EISENRING: Don't listen, madam.
BIEDERMANN: Chamber-pot, that's funny.
ALL THE MEN: 'Goosey, Goosey Gander—'

(*They make a part song of it, singing sometimes very loud, sometimes very softly, alternating it in every possible way, with laughter and noisy bonhomie. There is a pause, but then it is* BIEDERMANN *who leads the jollity, till they are all exhausted.*)

BIEDERMANN: Well then—cheers!
    (*They raise their glasses, and sirens are heard in the distance.*)
    What was that?
EISENRING: Sirens.
BIEDERMANN: Joking apart!—
BABETTE: Fire raisers! Fire raisers!
BIEDERMANN: Don't yell.

(BABETTE *tears open the window and the sirens come closer, howling to chill the marrow, and race past.*)

BIEDERMANN: At least it's not here.
BABETTE: Where can it be?
EISENRING: Where the south wind is blowing from.
BIEDERMANN: At lease it's not here . . .
EISENRING: We generally do it like that. We get the fire engine off into some
    poor district on the outskirts, and later, when the balloon really goes up,
    they find the way back blocked.
BIEDERMANN: No, gentlemen, joking apart—
SCHMITZ: But that's how we do it, joking apart.
BIEDERMANN: Stop this nonsense, please. Moderation in everything. Can't you
    see my wife's as white as a sheet?
BABETTE: What about you?
BIEDERMANN: And anyway, sirens are sirens, I can't laugh about that, gentle-
    men. Somewhere everything has come to a stop, somewhere the house is on
    fire, otherwise our fire engine wouldn't be going out.
                    (EISENRING *looks at his watch.*)
EISENRING: We must go.
BIEDERMANN: Now?
EISENRING: I'm afraid so.
SCHMITZ: 'Upstairs and downstairs . . .'
                    (*Sirens wail again.*)
BIEDERMANN: Make some coffee, Babette!
                    (BABETTE *goes out.*)
BIEDERMANN: And you, Anna, what are you standing there gaping for?
                    (ANNA *goes out.*)
    Between ourselves, gentlemen, enough is enough. My wife has a weak heart.
    Let's have no more joking about arson.
SCHMITZ: We're not joking, Herr Biedermann.
EISENRING: We're fire raisers.
BIEDERMANN: Gentlemen, quite seriously now—
SCHMITZ: Quite seriously.
EISENRING: Quite seriously.
SCHMITZ: Why don't you believe us?
EISENRING: Your house, Herr Biedermann, is very favourably situated, you
    must admit that: five ignition points like this round the gas-holders, which
    are unfortunately guarded, and a good south wind blowing—
BIEDERMANN: It isn't true.

SCHMITZ: Herr Biedermann, if you think we're fire raisers, why not say so straight out?

(BIEDERMANN *looks like a whipped dog.*)

BIEDERMANN: I don't think you're fire raisers, gentlemen, it isn't true, you're being unfair to me, I don't think you're—fire raisers . . .

EISENRING: Cross your heart!

BIEDERMANN: No! No, no! No.

SCHMITZ: Then what do you think we are?

BIEDERMANN: My—friends . . .

They slap him on the back and leave him standing.)

Where are you going now?

EISENRING: It's time.

BIEDERMANN: I swear it, gentlemen, by God!

EISENRING: By God?

BIEDERMANN: Yes!

(*He slowly raises his right hand.*)

SCHMITZ: Willie doesn't believe in God any more than you do, Herr Biedermann—you can swear till you're blue in the face.

(*They walk on towards the door.*)

BIEDERMANN: What can I do to make you believe me?

(*He stands between them and the door.*)

EISENRING: Give us matches.

BEIDERMANN: Do what?!

EISENRING: We've none left.

BIEDERMANN: You want me to—

EISENRING: Yes. If you don't think we're fire raisers.

BIEDERMANN: Matches?

SCHMITZ: As a sign of trust, he means.

(BIEDERMANN *puts his hand in his pocket.*)

EISENRING: He hesitates. You see? He hesitates.

BIEDERMANN: Quiet!—but not in front of my wife . . .

(BABETTE *comes back.*)

BABETTE: The coffee will be here in a minute.

(*Pause.*)

Do you have to go?

BIEDERMANN: Yes, my friends—it's a pity, but there it is—the main thing is that you have come to feel—I don't want to make a song and dance about it, my friends, but why don't we address each other by our first names?

BABETTE: H'm.

BIEDERMANN: Let's drink to our friendship!

(*He takes a bottle and the corkscrew.*)

EISENRING: Tell your good husband not to open another bottle on that account. It's not worth it now.

(BIERDERMANN *uncorks the bottle.*)

BIERDERMANN: Nothing is too much, my friends, nothing is too much, and if there's anything you want—anything at all . . .

(*He hurriedly fills the glasses and hands them round.*)

My friends, let's drink!

(*They clink glasses.*)

Gottlieb—

(*He kisses* SCHMITZ *on the cheek*.)
SCHMITZ: Joe—
BIEDERMANN: Gottlieb.
(*He kisses* EISENRING *on the cheek*.)
EISENRING: Willie.
(*They stand and drink*.)
All the same, Gottlieb, we have to go now.
SCHMITZ: Unfortunately.
EISENRING: Madam—
(*Sirens wail*.)
BABETTE: It was a delightful evening.
(*Alarm bells ring*.)
EISENRING: Just one more thing, Gottlieb—
BIEDERMANN: What is it?
EISENRING: You know.
BIEDERMANN: If there's anything you want—
EISENRING: The matches.
(ANNA *has come in with the coffee*.)
BABETTE: What on earth's the matter?
ANNA: Out at the back—the sky, Frau Biedermann, from the kitchen window
—the sky is on fire . . .
(*The light has turned very red as* SCHMITZ *and* EISENRING *bow and leave.* BIEDER-
MANN *stands pale and rigid*.)
BIEDERMANN: Thank goodness it isn't here. Thank goodness it isn't here. . . .
Thank goodness—
(*Enter the* DOCTOR OF PHILOSOPHY.)
BIEDERMANN: What do you want?
PH.D.: I can remain silent no longer.
(*He takes a document from his breast pocket and reads*.)
'The undersigned, himself profoundly shocked by the events now taking
place which even from our standpoint, it seems to me, can only be character-
ized as criminal, makes the following declaration to the public:—'
(*Many sirens wail. He reads out a lengthy text of which not a word is intelligible,
dogs bark, alarm bells ring, there are shouts and sirens in the distance, the crack-
ling of fire nearby; then he comes up to* BIEDERMANN *and hands him the docu-
ment*.)
I dissociate myself.
BIEDERMANN: What of it?
PH.D.: I have said what I have to say.
(*He takes off his glasses and folds them up*.)
BIEDERMANN: Herr Doktor—
(*The* PH.D. *leaves*.)
Herr Doktor, what am I supposed to do with this?
(*The* PH.D. *steps over the footlights and sits down in the stalls*.)
BABETTE: Gottlieb—
BIEDERMANN: He's gone.
BABETTE: What was it you gave them? Did I see right?—Were they matches?
BIEDERMANN: Why not?
BABETTE: Matches?

BIEDERMANN: If they were really fire raisers, do you think they wouldn't have matches? . . . Babette, Babette, my dear little Babette!

(*The grandfather clock strikes, the light turns red and as the stage darkens there are heard: alarm bells, the barking of dogs, sirens, the crash of falling timber, hooting, the crackling of fire and cries, until the* CHORUS *moves front stage.*)

*   *   *

CHORUS: There is much that is senseless and nothing
  More so than this story:
  Which once it had started
  Killed many, ah, but not all
  And changed nothing.
    First explosion.
CHORUS LEADER: That was a gas-holder.
    Second explosion.
CHORUS: What all have foreseen
  From the outset,
  And yet in the end it takes place,
  Is idiocy,
  The fire it's too late to extinguish
  Called Fate.
    Third explosion.
    Another gas-holder.
    A series of terrible explosions follows.
CHORUS: Woe! Woe! Woe!
    (*Light in the auditorium.*)

Improvisatory Techniques

Improvisation and free rehearsal techniques will be of great help in exposing rhythm and meanings. (Many authors put their characters into situations they do not intend to use in the main work, just to try them out as three-dimensional organisms. Some do not discover this until after a particular scene has been written and some set out with a deliberate intention).

Improvisatory techniques will help the cast get more deeply into the physical action of the play. This is of special importance when the play has a setting or style which requires an unusual movement pattern. For example, *The Brig; The Quare Fellow; Ring Round the Moon.* Very few actors have the direct experience of the rigours of prison movement or dancing their way through life. Such physical interpretation will naturally affect the way the lines can be spoken and, on that account alone, improvisatory techniques will be helpful.

Experiment

They will also enable the cast to practise the variations that come to light after an initial acquaintance with the text. Different rhythms can be tried out and layers of inner meaning exposed. Characters can be placed in situations that do not occur in the script. The inner meanings of scenes can be acted out using improvised dialogue—ignoring entirely, if wished, the original words of the text. Situations only reported on stage can be tried out and appropriate language invented. The possibilities of a free approach to rehearsals are endless and can be fruitful.

Function

There is little danger in these, and other, improvisatory techniques, if it is remembered at all times that **the function of any such exercise is to illuminate the text.** In the first instance this illumination may be for the benefit of the actor **but he must be able to pass it on to the audience.** It will be of no service to actor or audience if he gains such insight to the play that he proceeds to per-form it **through symbols he has validly created in improvisations or rehearsals— but symbols that only he understands.** For example, in *A Streetcar Named Desire*, the actress playing Blanche might discover her way to the character's inner life through constantly biting her nails. This may well be a valid symbol, a means to expression or a displacement activity, and may help the creative process of the actress. There will come a time when she must consider what it will communicate to an audience. It may be valid experience for Blanche and actress alike. It may also express a universe of inner significance. **What actress and director must decide is how much of it will mean the same to an audience.** It is possible for it to add nothing to the play; it is also possible for it to mis-lead. The acid test for any thought, feeling or action created through a free rehearsal technique is not what it does for the actor, the rest of the cast or even the character—**but what it communicates to an audience.**

Learning Lines

The learning of lines is a subject frequently surrounded by heated contro-versy. There are many schools of thought about *how* it should be done and at *what time* in the preparation of a performance. The many varying opinions provide little common ground but one or two facts, provided by psychologists, are of assistance. The following notes are offered as guide-lines only, since, within the general pattern, everyone will have an individual best method.

The deeper the concentration and absorption the more intense will be the experience, and the faster the speed of learning.

Three twenty-minute sessions a day are more effective than one single hour. A 'little and often' is more economical than cramming.

It is more effective to learn in large units than in small ones. You will dis-cover for yourself whether this means ten pages, five pages, one page or half a page. The larger the unit you can deal with the better you will learn. Under no circumstances try to learn a sentence at a time. It is much more effective to concentrate on related, meaningful units. A suggested minimum is half a page of standard text. Tackle the material through from beginning to end each time.

Once you have begun to memorize the material, speak it aloud, and take a cue, prompt or reminder as soon as possible. Straining to remember will only inhibit. The fact that speaking aloud considerably helps reinforce memory is a more than happy accident for an actor.

The most influential factor in the learning process is that of motivation. The more you can approach the task of learning lines with a wish to do so, the more speedy, efficient and enjoyable will the task be.

Some actors like to learn their lines as they rehearse and learn their moves. Others like to learn their moves first. Some like to learn their lines only when they know how they are going to say them. All these views are out of keeping with the general approach to acting and production set out in this book. It would be a strange tennis or golf player who decided to learn the moves and strokes before learning how to hold a racquet or club. An actor's relationship with his lines is similar to a tennis player's with his racquet. **Complete identification and immediate availability of lines are essential before an actor can explore his role with the rest of the cast.** It is possible for moves, gestures and mouthings to be practised while lines are still unlearned. Generally speaking, these are a waste of time—if not an inhibiting process—and in any case have no connection with acting—which is the main purpose of any rehearsal. To act, you must be able to make free and flexible responses to the rest of the cast in the changing situations of the play. Searching and stumbling for words, or worse, reading from the text, will allow no such liberation of mind or body.

Some actors claim they do not learn lines until the rehearsals are well under way—or almost complete—because they will 'learn them the wrong way and will never be able to unlearn them'. Such a view suggests a complete misunderstanding of the total recall that an actor needs over his lines. If the lines can only be repeated in one particular manner it is because **they have been only half-learned** and the manner of delivery is being used as a support for their recall. A special inflection (or indeed a *move* or *gesture*) is being used to aid what is in fact **faulty recall**. Full and efficient memorizing carries with it no necessary aid or encumbrance. *Psychology Made Simple* carries a full chapter on 'Remembering'. The subject is treated comprehensively.

CHAPTER THIRTEEN

WORKING ON A TEXT—IV

Practical Approaches to the Text

The following extracts are given for additional practice in analysis and execution.

READ THEM ALOUD FIRST.

Study each of them for the basic qualities of rhythm and style.
Let character creation emerge through the kinetic experience of saying the words.
Study each of them for inner and external meanings.
Let character creation emerge from this analysis.
Differentiate between supportive and dynamic dialogue and business.
Improvise sequences with similar styles.
Improvise sequences with similar inner meanings.
Use the characters and situations as stimuli for improvised scenes.
Play out the scenes using your own words.
Write scenes which are replicas of those you admire.
Write scenes which are similar to those you admire.
Compare and contrast the styles of the extracts. If possible do this by making tape-recordings. Play back your recordings and read the text as you listen.

READ THE EXTRACTS ALOUD.

SALOME
Oscar Wilde

(SCENE—*A great terrace in the Palace of Herod, set above the banqueting-hall. Some soldiers are leaning over the balcony. To the right there is a gigantic staircase, to the left, at the back, an old cistern surrounded by a wall of green bronze. Moonlight.*)

THE YOUNG SYRIAN: How beautiful is the Princess Salome to-night!

THE PAGE OF HERODIAS: Look at the moon! How strange the moon seems! She is like a woman rising from a tomb. She is like a dead woman. You would fancy she was looking for dead things.

THE YOUNG SYRIAN: She has a strange look. She is like a little princess who wears a yellow veil, and whose feet are of silver. She is like a princess who has little white doves for feet. You would fancy she was dancing.

THE PAGE OF HERODIAS: She is a like a woman who is dead. She moves very slowly.

(*Noise in the banqueting-hall.*)

FIRST SOLDIER: What an uproar! Who are those wild beasts howling?

SECOND SOLDIER: The Jews. They are always like that. They are disputing about their religion.

FIRST SOLDIER: Why do they dispute about their religion?

SECOND SOLDIER: I cannot tell. They are always doing it. The Pharisees, for instance, say that there are angels, and the Sadduces declare that angels do not exist.

FIRST SOLDIER: I think it is ridiculous to dispute about such things.

THE YOUNG SYRIAN: How beautiful is the Princess Salome to-night!

THE PAGE OF HERODIAS: You are always looking at her. You look at her too much. It is dangerous to look at people in such fashion. Something terrible may happen.

THE YOUNG SYRIAN: She is very beautiful to-night.

FIRST SOLDIER: The Tetrarch has a sombre look.

SECOND SOLDIER: Yes; he has a sombre look.

FIRST SOLDIER: He is looking at something.

SECOND SOLDIER: He is looking at someone.

FIRST SOLDIER: At whom is he looking?

SECOND SOLDIER: I cannot tell.

THE YOUNG SYRIAN: How pale the Princess is! Never have I seen here so pale. She is like the shadow of a white rose in a mirror of silver.

THE PAGE OF HERODIAS: You must not look at her. You look too much at her.

FIRST SOLDIER: Herodias has filled the cup of the Tetrarch.

THE CAPPADOCIAN: Is that the Queen Herodias, she who wears a black mitre sewn with pearls, and whose hair is powdered with blue dust?

FIRST SOLDIER: Yes; that is Herodias, the Tetrarch's wife.

SECOND SOLDIER: The Tetrarch is very fond of wine. He has wine of three sorts. One which is brought from the Island of Samothrace, and is purple like the cloak of Caesar.

THE CAPPADOCIAN: I have never seen Caesar.

SECOND SOLDIER: Another that comes from a town called Cyprus, and is yellow like gold.

THE CAPPADOCIAN: I love gold.

SECOND SOLDIER: And the third is a wine of Sicily. That wine is red like blood.

THE NUBIAN: The gods of my country are very fond of blood. Twice in the year we sacrifice to them young men and maidens; fifty young men and a hundred maidens. But it seems we never give them quite enough, for they are very harsh to us.

THE CAPPADOCIAN: In my country there are no gods left. The Romans have driven them out. There are some who say that they have hidden themselves in the mountains, but I do not believe it. Three nights I have been on the mountains seeking them everywhere. I did not find them. And at last I called them by their names, and they did not come. I think they are dead.

FIRST SOLDIER: The Jews worship a god that you cannot see.

THE CAPPADOCIAN: I cannot understand that.

FIRST SOLDIER: In fact, they only believe in things that you cannot see.

THE CAPPADOCIAN: That seems to me altogether ridiculous.

THE VOICE OF JOKANAAN: After me shall come another mightier than I. I am not worthy so much as to unloose the latchet of his shoes. When he cometh, the solitary places shall be glad. They shall blossom like the lily. The eyes of the blind shall see the day, and ears of the deaf shall be opened. The newborn child shall put his hand upon the dragon's lair, he shall lead the lions by their manes.

SECOND SOLDIER: Make him be silent. He is always saying ridiculous things.

FIRST SOLDIER: No, no. He is a holy man. He is very gentle, too. Every day, when I give him to eat he thanks me.

THE CAPPADOCIAN: Who is he?

FIRST SOLDIER: A prophet.

THE CAPPADOCIAN: What is his name?

FIRST SOLDIER: Jokanaan.

THE CAPPADOCIAN: Whence comes he?

FIRST SOLDIER: From the desert, where he fed on locusts and wild honey. He was clothed in camel's hair, and round his loins he had a leather belt. He was very terrible to look upon. A great multitude used to follow him. He even had disciples.

THE CAPPADOCIAN: What is he talking of?

FIRST SOLDIER: We can never tell. Sometimes he says terrible things, but it is impossible to understand what he says.

THE CAPPADOCIAN: May one see him?

FIRST SOLDIER: No. The Tetrarch has forbidden it.

THE YOUNG SYRIAN: The Princess has hidden her face behind her fan! Her little white hands are fluttering like doves that fly to their dove-cots. They are like white butterflies. They are just like white butterflies.

THE PAGE OF HERODIAS: What is that to you? Why do you look at her? You must not look at her. . . . Something terrible may happen.

THE CAPPADOCIAN (*pointing to the cistern*): What a strange prison.

SECOND SOLDIER: It is an old cistern.

THE CAPPADOCIAN: An old cistern! It must be very unhealthy.

SECOND SOLDIER: Oh no! For instance, the Tetrarch's brother, his older brother, the first husband of Herodias the Queen, was imprisoned there for twelve years. It did not kill him. At the end of the twelve years he had to be strangled.

THE CAPPADOCIAN: Strangled? Who dared to do that?

SECOND SOLDIER (*pointing to the Executioner, a huge Negro*): That man yonder, Naaman.

THE CAPPADOCIAN: He was not afraid?

SECOND SOLDIER: Oh no! The Tetrarch sent him the ring.

THE CAPPADOCIAN: What ring?

SECOND SOLDIER: The death-ring. So he was not afraid.

THE CAPPADOCIAN: Yet it is a terrible thing to strangle a king.

FIRST SOLDIER: Why? Kings have but one neck, like other folk.

THE CAPPADOCIAN: I think it terrible.

THE YOUNG SYRIAN: The Princess rises! She is leaving the table! She looks very troubled. Ah, she is coming this way. Yes, she is coming toward us. How pale she is! Never have I seen her so pale.

THE PAGE OF HERODIAS: Do not look at her. I pray you not to look at her.

THE YOUNG SYRIAN: She is like a dove that has strayed. . . . She is like a narcissus trembling in the wind. . . . She is like a silver flower.

(*Enter Salome.*)

WAITING FOR GODOT
Samuel Beckett

(ESTRAGON, *sitting on a low mound, is trying to take off his boot. He pulls at it with both hands, panting. He stops, exhausted, rests, begins again. As before. Enter* VLADIMIR.)

ESTRAGON: (*giving up again*): Nothing to be done.

VLADIMIR (*advancing with short, stiff strides, legs wide apart*): I'm beginning to come round to that opinion. All my life I've tried to put it from me, saying, Vladimir, be reasonable, you haven't yet tried everything. And I resumed the struggle. (*He broods, musing on the struggle. To* ESTRAGON.) So there you are again.

ESTRAGON: Am I?

VLADIMIR: I'm glad to see you back. I thought you were gone for ever.

ESTRAGON: Me too.

VLADIMIR: Together again at last! We'll have to celebrate this. But how? (*He reflects.*) Get up till I embrace you.

ESTRAGON (*irritably*): Not now, not now.

VLADIMIR (*hurt, coldly*): May one enquire where his Highness spent the night?

ESTRAGON: In a ditch.

VLADIMIR (*admiringly*): A ditch! Where?

ESTRAGON (*without gesture*): Over there.

VLADIMIR: And they didn't beat you?

ESTRAGON: Beat me? Certainly they beat me.

VLADIMIR: The same lot as usual?

ESTRAGON: The same? I don't know.

VLADIMIR: When I think of it . . . all these years . . . but for me . . . where would you be . . . ? (*Decisively.*) You'd be nothing more than a little heap of bones at the present minute, no doubt about it.

ESTRAGON: And what of it?

VLADIMIR: It's too much for one man. (*Pause. Cheerfully.*) On the other hand what's the good of losing heart now, that's what I say. We should have thought of it when the world was young, in the nineties.

ESTRAGON: Ah, stop blathering and help me off with this bloody thing.

VLADIMIR: Hand in hand from the top of the Eiffel Tower, among the first. We were respectable in those days. Now it's too late. They wouldn't even let us up. (ESTRAGON *tears at his boot.*) What are you doing?

ESTRAGON: Taking off my boot. Did that never happen to you?

VLADIMIR: Boots must be taken off every day, I'm tired telling you that. Why don't you listen to me?

ESTRAGON (*feebly*): Help me!

VLADIMIR: It hurts?

ESTRAGON: Hurts! He wants to know if it hurts!

VLADIMIR (*angrily*): No one ever suffers but you. I don't count. I'd like to hear what you'd say if you had what I have.

ESTRAGON: It hurts?

VLADIMIR: Hurts! He wants to know if it hurts! (*Stooping.*) Never neglect the little things of life.

ESTRAGON: What do you expect, you always wait till the last moment.

VLADIMIR (*musingly*): The last moment . . . (*he meditates*). Hope deferred maketh the something sick, who said that?

ESTRAGON: Why don't you help me?

VLADIMIR: Sometimes I feel it coming all the same. Then I go all queer. (*He takes off his hat, peers inside it feels about inside it, shakes it, puts it on again.*) How shall I say? Relieved and at the same time . . . (*he searches for the word*) . . . appalled. (*With emphasis*) AP-PALLED. (*He takes off his hat again, peers inside it.* Funny. (*He knocks on the crown as if to dislodge a foreign body, peers into it again, puts it on again.*) Nothing to be done.

(ESTRAGON *with a supreme effort succeeds in pulling off his boot. He looks inside it, feels about inside it, turns it upside down, shakes it, looks on the ground to see if anything has fallen out, finds nothing, feels inside it again, staring sightlessly before him.*)

Well?

ESTRAGON: Nothing.

VLADIMIR: Show.

ESTRAGON: There's nothing to show.

VLADIMIR: Try and put it on again.

ESTRAGON (*having examined his foot*): I'll air it for a bit.

VLADIMIR: There's a man all over for you, blaming on his boots the faults of his feet. (*He takes off his hat again, looks inside it, feels about inside it, knocks on the crown, blows into it, puts it on again.*) This is getting alarming. (*Silence.* VLADIMIR *deep in thought,* ESTRAGON *pulling at his toes.*) One of the thieves was saved. (*Pause.*) It's a reasonable percentage. (*Pause.*) Gogo.

ESTRAGON: What?

VLADIMIR: Suppose we repented.

ESTRAGON: Repented what?

VLADIMIR: Oh . . . (*He reflects.*) We wouldn't have to go into the details.

ESTRAGON: Our being born?

(VLADIMIR *breaks into a hearty laugh which he immediately suppresses, his hand pressed to his stomach, his face contorted.*)

VLADIMIR: One daren't even laugh any more.

ESTRAGON: Dreadful privation.

VLADIMIR: Merely smile. (*He smiles suddenly from ear to ear, keeps smiling, ceases as suddenly.*) It's not the same thing. Nothing to be done. (*Pause.*) Gogo.

ESTRAGON (*irritably*): What is it?

VLADIMIR: Did you ever read the Bible?

ESTRAGON: The Bible . . . (*He reflects.*) I must have taken a look at it.

VLADIMIR: Do you remember the Gospels?

ESTRAGON: I remember the maps of the Holy Land. Coloured they were. Very pretty. The Dead Sea was pale blue. The very look of it made me thirsty. There's where we'll go, I used to say, there's where we'll go for our honeymoon. We'll swim. We'll be happy.

VLADIMIR: You should have been a poet.

ESTRAGON: I was. (*Gesture towards his rags.*) Isn't that obvious. (*Silence.*)

VLADIMIR: Where was I . . . How's your foot?

ESTRAGON: Swelling visibly.

VLADIMIR: Ah yes, the two thieves. Do you remember the story?

ESTRAGON: No.

VLADIMIR: Shall I tell it to you?

ESTRAGON: No.

VLADIMIR: It'll pass the time. (*Pause.*) It was two thieves, crucified at the same time as our Saviour. One—

ESTRAGON: Our what?

VLADIMIR: Our Saviour. Two thieves. One is supposed to have been saved and the other . . . (*he searches for the contrary of saved*) . . . damned.

ESTRAGON: Saved from what?

VLADIMIR: Hell.

ESTRAGON: I'm going. (*He does not move.*)

VLADIMIR: And yet . . . (*pause*) . . . how is it—this is not boring you I hope— how is it that of the four evangelists only one speaks of a thief being saved? The four of them were there—or thereabouts, and only one speaks of a thief being saved. (*Pause.*) Come on, Gogo, return the ball, can't you, once in a way?

ESTRAGON (*with exaggerated enthusiasm*): I find this really most extraordinarily interesting.

VLADIMIR: One out of four. Of the other three two don't mention any thieves at all and the third says that both of them abused him.

ESTRAGON: Who?

VLADIMIR: What?

ESTRAGON: What's all this about? (*Pause.*) Abused who?

VLADIMIR: The Saviour.

ESTRAGON: Why?

VLADIMIR: Because He wouldn't save them.

ESTRAGON: From hell?

VLADIMIR: Imbecile! From death.

ESTRAGON: I thought you said from hell.

VLADIMIR: From death, from death.

ESTRAGON: Well, what about it?

VLADIMIR: Then the two of them must have been damned.

ESTRAGON: And why not?

VLADIMIR: But the other Apostle says that one was saved.

ESTRAGON: Well? They don't agree, and that's all there is to it.

VLADIMIR: But all four were there. And only one speaks of a thief being saved. Why believe him rather than the others?

ESTRAGON: Who believes him?

VLADIMIR: Everybody. It's the only version they know.

ESTRAGON: People are bloody ignorant apes.

(*He rises painfully, goes limping to extreme left, halts, gazes into distance off with his hand screening his eyes, turns, goes to extreme right, gazes into the distance.* VLADIMIR *watches him, then goes and picks up the boot, peers into it, drops it hastily.*)

VLADIMIR: Pah! (*He spits.*)

(ESTRAGON *moves to centre, halts with his back to auditorium.*)

ESTRAGON: Charming spot. (*He turns, advances to front, halts facing auditorium.*) Inspiring prospects. (*He turns to* VLADIMIR.) Let's go.

VLADIMIR: We can't.

ESTRAGON: Why not?

VLADIMIR: We're waiting for Godot.

ESTRAGON: Ah! (*Pause.*) You're sure it was here?
VLADIMIR: What?
ESTRAGON: That we were to wait.
VLADIMIR: He said by the tree. (*They look at the tree.*) Do you see any others?
ESTRAGON: What is it?
VLADIMIR: I don't know. A willow.
ESTRAGON: Where are the leaves?
VLADIMIR: It must be dead.
ESTRAGON: No more weeping.
VLADIMIR: Or perhaps it's not the season.
ESTRAGON: Looks to me more like a bush.
VLADIMIR: A shrub.
ESTRAGON: A bush.
VLADIMIR: A—. What are you insinuating? That we've come to the wrong place?
ESTRAGON: He should be here.
VLADIMIR: We'll come back tomorrow.
ESTRAGON: And then the day after tomorrow.
VLADIMIR: Possibly.
ESTRAGON: And so on.
VLADIMIR: The point is—
ESTRAGON: Until he comes.
VLADIMIR: You're merciless.
ESTRAGON: We came here yesterday.
VLADIMIR: Ah no, there you're mistaken.
ESTRAGON: What did we do yesterday?
VLADIMIR: What did we do yesterday?
ESTRAGON: Yes.
VLADIMIR: Why . . . (*angrily*). Nothing is certain when you're about.
ESTRAGON: In my opinion we were here.
VLADIMIR (*looking round*): You recognize the place?
ESTRAGON: I didn't say that.
VLADIMIR: Well?
ESTRAGON: That makes no difference.
VLADIMIR: All the same . . . that tree . . . (*turning towards the auditorium*) . . . that bog.
ESTRAGON: You're sure it was this evening?
VLADIMIR: What?
ESTRAGON: That we were to wait.
VLADIMIR: He said Saturday. (*Pause.*) I think.
ESTRAGON: You think.
VLADIMIR: I must have made a note of it.

(*He fumbles in his pockets, bursting with miscellaneous rubbish.*)

ESTRAGON (*very insidious*): But what Saturday? And is it Saturday? Is it not rather Sunday? (*Pause.*) Or Monday? (*Pause.*) Or Friday?
VLADIMIR (*looking wildly about him, as though the date was inscribed in the landscape*): It's not possible!
ESTRAGON: Or Thursday?
VLADIMIR: What'll we do?

ESTRAGON: If he came yesterday and we weren't here you may be sure he won't come again today.

VLADIMIR: But you say we were here yesterday.

ESTRAGON: I may be mistaken. (*Pause.*) Let's stop talking for a minute, do you mind?

THE QUARE FELLOW
Brendan Behan

(*The prisoners march, the gate clangs behind them; the tramp of their feet is heard as they mark time inside.*)

WARDER REGAN (*voice from the prison wing*): Right, B. Wing, bang out your doors. B.1, get in off your steps and bang out your doors, into your cells and bang out your doors. Get locked up. BANG THEM DOORS! GET INSIDE AND BANG OUT THEM DOORS!

(*The last door bangs lonely on its own and then there is silence.*)

VOICE FROM BELOW (*singing*):

> The wind was rising,
> And the day declining
> As I lay pining in my prison cell
> And that old triangle
> Went jingle jangle

(*The triangle is beaten, the gate of the prison wing opens and the* CHIEF *and* WARDER DONELLY *come down the steps and approach the grave.*)

> Along the banks of the Royal Canal.

CHIEF (*resplendent in silver braid*): Who's that singing?

WARDER DONELLY: I think it's one of the prisoners in the chokey, sir.

CHIEF: Where?

WARDER DONELLY: In the punishment cells, sir.

CHIEF: That's more like it. Well, tell him to cut it out.

SONG:
> In the female prison
> There are seventy women . . .

WARDER DONELLY (*goes down to the area and leans and shouts*): Hey, you down there, cut it out, or I'll give you jingle jangle.

(*The song stops.* WARDER DONELLY *walks back.*)

CHIEF: Is the quare fellow finished his tea?

WARDER DONELLY: He is. He is just ready to come out for exercise, now. The wings are all clear. They're locked up having their tea. He'll be along any minute.

CHIEF: He's coming out here?

WARDER DONELLY: Yes, sir.

CHIEF (*exasperated*): Do you want him to see his grave, bloody well half dug? Run in quick and tell those bloody idiots to take him out the side door, and exercise him over the far side of the stokehold, and tell them to keep him well into the wall where he'll be out of sight of the cell windows. Hurry and don't let him hear you. Let on it's something about another duty. Warders! You'd get better in Woolworths.

(*He goes to the area and shouts down.*)

Hey, you down there. You in the cell under the steps. You do be singing there to keep yourself company? You needn't be afraid, it's only the Chief.

How long you doing down there? Seven days No. 1 and twenty-one days No. 2. God bless us and love us, you must have done something desperate. I may be able to do something for you, though God knows you needn't count on it, I don't own the place. You what? With who? Ah sure, I often have a bit of a tiff with the same man myself. We'll see what we can do for you. It's a long time to be stuck down there, no matter who you had the tiff with.

(Enter WARDER DONELLY.*)*

CHIEF: Well?

WARDEN DONELLY: It's all right, they've brought him out the other way.

(They look out beyond the stage.)

CHIEF: Looks as if they're arguing the toss about something.

WARDER DONELLY: Football.

CHIEF: Begod, look at them stopping while the quare fellow hammers his point home.

WARDER DONELLY: I was down in the condemned cell while he was getting his tea. I asked him if it was all right. He said it was, and 'Aren't the evenings getting a grand stretch?' he says.

CHIEF: Look at him now, putting his nose to the air.

WARDER DONELLY: He's a grand evening for his last.

CHIEF: I took the name of the fellow giving the concert in the punishment cells. In the morning when we get this over, see he's shifted to Hell's gates over the far side. He can serenade the stokehold wall for a change if he's light enough to make out his music.

*(*WARDER DONELLY *copies the name and number.)*

CHIEF: I have to attend to every mortal thing in this place. None of you seem to want to do a hand's turn, bar draw your money—you're quick enough at that. Well, come on, let's get down to business.

*(*WARDER DONELLY *goes and uncovers the grave.)*

CHIEF *(looking off)*. Just a minute. It's all right. They've taken him round the back of the stokehold. *(Looking at the grave.)* Not so bad, another couple of feet out of the bottom and we're elected. Regan should be down with the working party any minute, as soon as the quare fellow's finished his exercise.

WARDER DONELLY: There, he's away in now, sir. See him looking at the sky?

CHIEF: You'd think he was trying to kiss it good-bye. Well, that's the last he'll see of it.

WARDER DONELLY: No chance of a reprieve, sir?

CHIEF: Not a chance. Healey never mentioned fixing up a line with the Post Office. If there'd been any chance of developments he'd have asked us to put a man on all night. All he said was 'The Governor will get the last word before the night's out.' That means only one thing. Go ahead.

*(*WARDERS REGAN *and* CRIMMIN *come out with* PRISONERS A, B, C, D.*)*

WARDER REGAN: Working party all correct, sir. Come on, get those boards off. Bottom out a couple more feet and leave the clay at the top, nice and neat.

CHIEF: Oh, Mr. Regan.

WARDER REGAN: Take over, Mr. Crimmin.

CHIEF: Mr. Regan. All I was going to say was—why don't you take yourself a bit of a rest while these fellows are at work on the grave. It's a long old pull till eight tomorrow morning.

WARDER REGAN: Thank you, sir.

CHIEF: Don't mention it. I'll see you before you go down to the cell. Get yourself a bit of a smoke, in the hospital. Don't forget now.
(HE *and* WARDER DONELLY *go back in.*)
WARDER REGAN: Mr. Crimmin. The Chief, a decent man, he's after giving us his kind permission to go into hospital and have a sit down and a smoke for ourselves when these fellows have the work started. He knew we'd go in anyway, so he saw the chance of being floochalach, at no expense to the management. Here (*takes out a packet of cigarettes, and takes some from it*), here's a few fags for the lads.
CRIMMIN: I'll give them some of mine too.
WARDER REGAN: Don't do anything of the sort. One each is enough, you can slip them a couple when they're going to be locked up, if you like, but if these fellows had two fags each, they'd not work at all but spend the time out here blowing smoke rings in the evening air like lords. I'll slip in now, you come in after me. Tell them not to have them in their mouths if the Chief or the Governor comes out.
(*He goes up the steps to the hospital.*)
CRIMMIN (*calls* PRISONER C): Hey!
PRISONER C (*comes to him*): Seadh a Thomais?
CRIMMIN (*gives him cigarettes and matches*): Seo, cupla toitin. Taim f hein is an screw eile ag did inteach chiung an oispeasdal, noimest Roinn amach no toitini siud, is glacfaidh sign gal, M. thagann an Governor nor Chief, no an Principal, no blodh in bhur mbeil agaib iad. A'tuigeann tu?
PRISONER C: Tuigim, a Thomais, go raidh maith agat.
CRIMMIN (*officially*): Right, now get back to work.
PRISONER C: Yes, sir.
(CRIMMIN *goes up the hospital steps.*)
PRISONER C: He gave me some cigarettes.
(PRISONER D *has gone straight to the grave,* PRISONER B *is near it.*)
PRISONER A: May I never dig a grave for less! You two get on and do a bit of digging while we have a quiet burn, then we'll take over.
PRISONER C: He said to watch out for the Chief and them.
PRISONER B: Pass down a light to your man. He says he'd enjoy it better down there, where he can't be seen! Decent of him and Regan wasn't it?
PRISONER A: They'd have you dead from decency. That same Regan was like a savage in the bag shop today, you couldn't get a word to the fellow next to you.
PRISONER C: I never saw him like that before.
PRISONER B: He's always the same at a time like this, hanging seems to get on his nerves.
PRISONER A: Why should he worry, he won't feel it.
PRISONER B: He's on the last watch. Twelve till eight.
PRISONER A: Till death do us part.
PRISONER C: The quare fellow asked for him, didn't he?
PRISONER A: They all do.
PRISONER C: He asked to have Mr. Crimmin too.
PRISONER A: It'll break that young screw up, and him only a wet day in the place.
PRISONER B: Funny the way they all ask for Regan. Perhaps they think he'll bring good luck, him being good living.

PRISONER A: Good living! Whoever heard of a good living screw? Did you never hear of the screw, married the prostitute?

PRISONER B: No, what happened to him?

PRISONER A: He dragged her down to his own level.

PRISONER B: He told me once that if I kept off the beer I need never come back here. I asked him what about himself, and he told me he was terrible hardened to it and would I pray for him.

PRISONER C: When I was over in the Juvenile she used to talk like that to us. He said that the Blessed Virgin knew us better than the police or the judges—or ourselves even. We might think we were terrible sinners but she knew we were good boys only a bit wild . . .

PRISONER A: Bloody mad he is.

PRISONER C: And that we were doing penance here for the men who took us up, especially the judges, they being mostly rich old men with great opportunity for vice.

(PRISONER D *appears from the grave.*)

PRISONER A: The dead arose and appeared to many.

(PRISONER A *goes and rearranges the work which* PRISONER D *has upset*)

PRISONER B: What's brought you out of your fox hole?

PRISONER D: I thought it more discreet to remain in concealment while I smoked but I could not stop down there listening to talk like that, as a rate-payer, I couldn't stand for it, especially those libellous remarks about the judiciary.

(*He looks accusingly at the boy.*)

PRISONER C: I was only repeating what Mr. Regan said, sir.

PRISONER D: He could be taken up for it. According to that man, there should be no such thing as law and order. We could all be murdered in our beds, the innocent prey of every ruffian that took it into his head to appropriate our goods, our lives even. Property must have security! What do you think society would come to without police and judges and suitable punishments? Chaos! In my opinion hanging's too good for 'em.

PRISONER C: Oh, Mr. Regan doesn't believe in capital punishment, sir.

PRISONER D: My God, the man's an atheist! He should be dismissed from the public service. I shall take it up with the Minister when I get out of here. I went to school with his cousin.

PRISONER A: Who the hell does he think he is, a bloody high court judge?

PRISONER D: Chaos!

PRISONER B: He's in for embezzlement, there were two suicides and a bye-election over him.

PRISONER D: There are still a few of us who care about the state of the country, you know. My family's national tradition goes back to the Land War. Grandfather did four weeks for incitement to mutiny—and we've never looked back since. One of my young nephews, as a matter of fact, has just gone over to Sandhurst.

PRISONER B: Isn't that where you done your four years?

PRISONER A: No, that was Parkhurst.

PRISONER C (*to others*): A college educated man in here, funny, isn't it?

PRISONER D: I shall certainly bring all my influence to bear to settle this Regan fellow.

PRISONER C: You must be a very important man, sir.

PRISONER D: I am one of the Cashel Carrolls, my boy, related on my mother's side to the Killens of Killcock.

PRISONER B: Used to wash for our family.

PRISONER C: Go Bfoiridh. Dia rainn.

PRISONER D: Irish speaking?

PRISONER C: Yes, sir.

PRISONER D: Then it might interest you to know that I took my gold medal in Irish.

PRISONER C: Does that mean he speaks Irish?

PRISONER D: Of course.

PRISONER C: Oh, sir. Ta Caoliumn go leor agamsa. O'n gobliabh an amach, sir.

PRISONER B: That's fixed you.

PRISONER D: Quite. Tuighin thu.

PRISONER B: The young lad's from Kerry, from an island where they don't speak much else.

PRISONER D: Kerry? Well of course you speak with a different dialect to the one I was taught.

PRISONER B: The young screw Crimmin's from the same place. He sneaks up to the landing sometimes when the other screws aren't watching and there they are for hours talking through the spy hole, all in Irish.

PRISONER D: Most irregular.

PRISONER B: There's not much harm in it.

PRISONER D: How can there be proper discipline between warder and prisoner with that kind of familiarity?

PRISONER C: He does only be giving me the news from home and who's gone to America or England; he's not long up here and neither am I . . . the two of us do each be as lonely as the other.

PRISONER B: The lad here sings an old song betimes. It's very nice. It makes the night less lonely, each man alone and say maybe in the old cell. The quare fellow heard him singing and after he was sentenced to death he sent over word he'd be listening every night around midnight for him.

PRISONER A: You'd better make a big effort tonight, kid, for his last concert.

PRISONER C: Ah, God help him! Sure, you'd pity him all the same. It must be awful to die at the end of a swinging rope and a black hood over his poor face.

PRISONER A: Begod, he's not being topped for nothing—to cut his own brother up and butcher him like a pig.

PRISONER D: I must heartily agree with you sir, a barbarian if ever there was one.

PRISONER C: Maybe he did those things, but God help him this minute and he knowing this night his last on earth. Waiting over there he is, to be shaken out of his sleep and rushed to the rope.

PRISONER A: What sleep will he take? They won't have to set the alarm clock for a quarter to eight, you can bet your life on that.

PRISONER C: May he find peace on the other side.

PRISONER A: Or his brother waiting to have a word with him about being quartered in such an unmannerly fashion.

PRISONER C: None of us can know for certain.

PRISONER D: It was proved in a court of law that this man had experience as a pork butcher and put his expert knowledge to use by killing his brother with an axe and dismembering the body, the better to dispose of it.

PRISONER C: Go bfoiridh. Dia rainn.

PRISONER A: I wouldn't put much to the court of law part of it, but I heard about it myself from a fellow in from his part of the country. He said he had the brother strung up in an outhouse like a pig.

PRISONER D: Actually he was bleeding him into a farmhouse vessel according to the evidence. He should be hung three or four times over.

PRISONER A: Seeing your uncle was at school with the President's granny, perhaps he could fix it up for you.

PRISONER C: I don't believe he is a bad man. When I was on remand he used to walk around with me at exercise every day and he was sad when I told him about my brother, who died in the Yank's army, and my father, who was buried alive at the demolition of Manchester. . . . He was great company for me who knew no one, only jackeens would be making game of me, and I'm sorry for him.

PRISONER A: Sure, it's a terrible pity about you and him. Maybe the jackeens should spread out the red carpet for you and every other bog barbarian that comes into the place.

(*He moves away irritably.*)

Let's get a bit more off this bloody hole.

THE LIFE OF THE INSECTS
Josef and Karel Capek

ACT II—THE MARAUDERS

(*The scene represents a sandy hillock, with a scanty growth of grass, the size of a tree trunk. On the left side the lair of the Ichneumon Fly, on the right side the deserted cavity of a cricket. The* VAGRANT *lies asleep in the proscenium. A* CHRYSALIS *is fastened to a blade of grass. The* CHRYSALIS *is attacked by a gang of rapacious insects. From the left a small* BEETLE *runs in and unfastens it from the blade of grass. From the right a second one runs out, chases the first one off, and tries to snatch the* CHRYSALIS *away. From the prompt-box a third leaps forth, chases the second one away, and drags the* CHRYSALIS *off.*)

CHRYSALIS: I . . . I . . . I . . .

(*The third* BEETLE *plunges headlong into the prompt-box. From the left the first* BEETLE, *and from the right the second, run in and wrangle about the* CHRYSALIS. *The third darts out of the box and chases them both away, whereupon it takes the* CHRYSALIS *itself.*)

The whole earth is bursting, I am being born.

VAGRANT (*raising his head*): What's that?

(THIRD BEETLE *rushes into the box.*)

CHRYSALIS: Something great is at hand.

VAGRANT: That's good. (*Lays his head down. Pause.*)

MAN'S VOICE (*behind the scenes*): What are you up to?

WOMAN'S VOICE: Me?

FIRST VOICE: Yes you.

SECOND VOICE: Me?

FIRST VOICE: Yes, you.

SECOND VOICE: Me?

FIRST VOICE: Yes, you. Clumsy slattern.

SECOND VOICE: You wretch.

FIRST VOICE: Fathead!

SECOND VOICE: Dolt!

FIRST VOICE: Slut! Frump!

SECOND VOICE: Mud-pusher!

FIRST VOICE: Take care. Look out.

SECOND VOICE: Slowly.

FIRST VOICE: L-l-ook out.

(*A large ball of manure rolls on the stage, pushed by a pair of beetles.*)

MALE BEETLE: Nothing's happened to it?

FEMALE BEETLE: Oh dear I do hope not, I'm all of a tremble.

MALE BEETLE: Ha, ha, that's our capital. Our nest-egg. Our stock-in-trade. Our all.

FEMALE BEETLE: Oh, what a lovely little pile, what a treasure, what a beautiful little ball, what a precious little fortune.

MALE BEETLE: It's our only joy. To think how we've saved and scraped, toiled and moiled, denied ourselves, gone without this, stinted ourselves that—

FEMALE BEETLE: And worked our legs off and drudged and plodded to get it together and—

MALE BEETLE: And seen it grow and added to it, bit by bit. Oh, what a boon it is.

FEMALE BEETLE: Our very own.

MALE BEETLE: Our life.

FEMALE BEETLE: All our own work

MALE BEETLE: Just sniff at it, old girl. Oh, how lovely. Just feel the weight of it. And it's ours.

FEMALE BEETLE: What a godsend.

MALE BEETLE: What a blessing.

CHRYSALIS: The fetters of the world are rended,
Now another life is blended.
I am being born.

(*The* VAGRANT *raises his head.*)

FEMALE BEETLE: Husband!

MALE BEETLE: What is it?

FEMALE BEETLE: Ha, ha, ha, ha.

MALE BEETLE: Ha, ha, Ha, ha. Wife!

FEMALE BEETLE: What is it?

MALE BEETLE: Ha, ha, ha, it's fine to own something. Your property! The dream of your life! The fruit of your labours!

FEMALE BEETLE: Ha, ha, ha.

MALE BEETLE: I'm going off my head with joy. I'm ... I'm ... I'm ... going off my head with sheer worry. Upon my soul, I'm going off my head.

FEMALE BEETLE: Why?

MALE BEETLE: With worry. Now we've got our little pile. I've been so much looking forward to it, and now we've got it, we'll have to make another one. Nothing but work, work, work.

FEMALE BEETLE: Why another one?

MALE BEETLE: You stupid creature, so that we can have two, of course.

FEMALE BEETLE: Ah, two. Quite right.

MALE BEETLE: Ah, just fancy, two of them. At least two. Let's say even three. You know, every one who's made one pile has to make another.

FEMALE BEETLE: So that he can have two.

MALE BEETLE: Or even three.

FEMALE BEETLE: Husband!

MALE BEETLE: Well, what is it?

FEMALE BEETLE: I'm scared. Suppose someone was to steal it from us.

MALE BEETLE: What?

FEMALE BEETLE: Our little pile. Our joy, Our all.

MALE BEETLE: Our p-pile? My goodness, don't frighten me.

FEMALE BEETLE: We . . . we . . . we can't roll it about with us, till we've made another one.

MALE BEETLE: I tell you what, we'll invest it. In-vest it. We'll store it up. We'll bury it nicely. Wait a bit, in some hole, in some cranny. Out of harm's way, you know. It must be put aside.

FEMALE BEETLE: I only hope nobody'll find it.

MALE BEETLE: Eh? Not likely. What, steal it from us? Our little pile. Our treasure. Our little round nest-egg.

FEMALE BEETLE: Our precious little store. Our life. Our whole concern.

MALE BEETLE: Wait, stay here and watch—watch it. Keep an eye on it.
(Runs off.)

FEMALE BEETLE: Where are you off to now?

MALE BEETLE: To look for a hole . . . a little hole . . . a deep hole . . . to bury it in. Our precious gold . . . out of harm's way. *(Exit)* Be care . . . ful.

FEMALE BEETLE: Husband, husband, come here. . . . Wait a bit. . . . There's. . . . Husband. . . . He can't hear me. And I've found such a nice hole. Husband. He's gone. And I've found such a beautiful little hole. What a stupid he is. The booby. The fool. If only I could just have a look at it. No, I mustn't leave you, little pile. If I could . . . only . . . peep. Little pile, dear little pile, wait a moment, I'll be back at once. I'll only have just a peep, and I'll be back again. *(Runs to the back and turns round.)* Little pile, you'll be good and wait for me, won't you? I'll be back at once, little pile—
(Enters the lair of the Ichneumon Fly.)

CHRYSALIS: Oh, to be born, to be born. The new world.
(VAGRANT stands up.)

STRANGE BEETLE *(runs in from the wings, where he has been lurking)*: They've gone. Now's my chance.
(Rolls the pile away.)

VAGRANT: Here, don't knock me over.

STRANGE BEETLE: Out of the way, citizen.

VAGRANT: What's that you're rolling along?

STRANGE BEETLE: Ha, ha, ha. That's my pile. Capital. Gold.

VAGRANT *(flinching)*: That gold of yours smells.

STRANGE BEETLE: Gold don't smell. Roll along, pile, off you go. Bestir yourself. Come on. Possession's nine points of the law. Ha, ha, ha, my boy.

VAGRANT: What's that?

STRANGE BEETLE: Ah, it's nice to own something. *(Rolls the pile to the left.)* My treasure. You lovely nest-egg. My jewel. My all. What a thing to possess. A little fortune to invest. To bury carefully. L-l-look out.
(Exit.)

VAGRANT: To possess? Why not. Everyone likes something of his own.

FEMALE BEETLE (*returns*): Oh dear, oh dear. Someone's living there. A little chrysalis. We can't put you there, pile. Where is the pile? Oh, where has my pile gone to? Where is our dear little pile?

VAGRANT: Why, just this minute—

FEMALE BEETLE: You villain, give it here. Hand it back.

VAGRANT: Just this minute some gentleman rolled it over there.

FEMALE BEETLE: What gentleman? Who?

VAGRANT: A pot-bellied fellow, a fat, round man—

FEMALE BEETLE: My husband.

VAGRANT: A surly chap with crooked feet, a vulgar, conceited person—

FEMALE BEETLE: That's my husband.

VAGRANT: And he said it was nice to own something and to bury something.

FEMALE BEETLE: That's him. He must have found another hole. (*Calls out.*) Husband, wait a bit. Husband. Darling. Where is the stupid creature?

VAGRANT: That's where he rolled it to.

FEMALE BEETLE: The booby. Couldn't he have called me? (*Rushes to the left.*) Husband, wait a bit. The pile. (*Exit.*) The p-p-pile.

THREE SISTERS
Anton Chekhov
ACT ONE

(*A drawing-room in the Prozorovs' house; it is separated from a large ballroom at the back by a row of columns. It is midday; there is cheerful sunshine outside. In the ballroom the table is being laid for lunch.* OLGA, *wearing the regulation dark-blue dress of a secondary school mistress, is correcting her pupils' work, standing or walking about as she does so.* MASHA, *in a black dress, is sitting reading a book, her hat on her lap.* IRENA, *in white, stands lost in thought.*)

OLGA: It's exactly a year ago that Father died, isn't it? This very day, the fifth of May—your Saint's day, Irena. I remember it was very cold and it was snowing. I felt then as if I should never survive his death; and you had fainted and were lying quite still, as if you were dead. And now—a year's gone by, and we talk about it so easily. You're wearing white, and your face is positively radiant . . .

(*A clock strikes twelve.*)

The clock struck twelve then, too. (*A pause.*) I remember when Father was being taken to the cemetery there was a military band, and a salute with rifle fire. That was because he was a general, in command of a brigade. And yet there weren't many people at the funeral. Of course, it was raining hard, raining and snowing.

IRENA: Need we bring up all these memories?

(*Baron* TOOZENBACH, CHEBUTYKIN *and* SOLIONY *appear behind the columns by the table in the ballroom.*)

OLGA: It's so warm to-day that we can keep the windows wide open, and yet there aren't any leaves showing on the birch trees. Father was made a brigadier eleven years ago, and then he left Moscow and took us with him. I remember so well how everything in Moscow was in blossom by now, everything was soaked in sunlight and warmth. Eleven years have gone by, yet I remember everything about it, as if we'd only left yesterday. Oh,

Heavens! When I woke up this morning and saw this flood of sunshine, all this spring sunshine, I felt so moved and so happy! I felt such a longing to get back home to Moscow!

CHEBUTYKIN (*to* TOOZENBACH): The devil you have!

TOOZENBACH: It's nonsense, I agree.

MASHA (*absorbed in her book, whistles a tune under her breath.*)

OLGA: Masha, do stop whistling! How can you? (*A pause.*) I suppose I must get this continual headache because I have to go to school every day and go on teaching right into the evening. I seem to have the thoughts of someone quite old. Honestly, I've been feeling as if my strength and youth were running out of me drop by drop, day after day. Day after day, all these four years that I've been working at the school. . . . I just have one longing and it seems to grow stronger and stronger . . .

IRENA: If only we could go back to Moscow! Sell the house, finish with our life here, and go back to Moscow.

OLGA: Yes, Moscow! As soon as we possibly can.

(CHEBUTYKIN *and* TOOZENBACH *laugh.*)

IRENA: I suppose Andrey will soon get a professorship. He isn't likely to go on living here. The only problem is our poor Masha.

MASHA (*whistles a tune under her breath*).

IRENA: Everything will settle itself, with God's help. (*Looks through the window.*) What lovely weather it is to-day! Really, I don't know why there's such joy in my heart. I remembered this morning that it was my Saint's day, and suddenly I felt so happy, and I thought of the time when we were children, and Mother was still alive. And then such wonderful thoughts came to me, such wonderful stirring thoughts!

OLGA: You're so lovely to-day, you really do look most attractive. Masha looks pretty to-day, too. Andrey could be good-looking, but he's grown so stout. It doesn't suit him. As for me, I've just aged and grown a lot thinner. I suppose it's through getting so irritated with the girls at school. But today I'm at home, I'm free, and my headache's gone, and I feel much younger than I did yesterday. I'm only twenty-eight, after all. I suppose everything that God wills must be right and good, but I can't help thinking sometimes that if I'd got married and stayed at home, it would have been a better thing for me. (*Pause.*) I would have been very fond of my husband.

TOOZENBACH (*to* SOLIONY): Really, you talk such a lot of nonsense, I'm tired of listening to you. (*Comes into the drawing-room.*) I forgot to tell you: Vershinin, our new battery commander, is going to call on you to-day. (*Sits down by the piano.*)

OLGA: I'm very glad to hear it.

IRENA: Is he old?

TOOZENBACH: No, not particularly. Forty, forty-five at the most. (*Plays quietly.*) He seems a nice fellow. Certainly not a fool. His only weakness is that he talks too much.

IRENA: Is he interesting?

TOOZENBACH: He's all right, only he's got a wife, a mother-in-law and two little girls. What's more, she's his second wife. He calls on everybody and tells them that he's got a wife and two little girls. He'll tell you about it, too, I'm sure of that. His wife seems to be a bit soft in the head. She wears a long plait like a girl, she is always philosophizing and talking in high-flown language, and then she often tries to commit suicide, apparently just to annoy her husband. I would have run away from a wife like that years ago, but he puts up with it, and just grumbles about it.

SOLIONY (*enters the drawing-room with* CHEBUTYKIN): Now I can only lift sixty pounds with one hand, but with two I can lift two hundred pounds, or even two hundred and forty. So I conclude from that that two men are not just twice as strong as one, but three times as strong, if not more.

CHEBUTYKIN (*reads the paper as he comes in*): Here's a recipe for falling hair . . . two ounces of naphthaline, half-a-bottle of methylated spirit . . . dissolve and apply once a day . . . (*Writes it down in a notebook.*) Must make a note of it. (*To* SOLIONY.) Well, as I was trying to explain to you, you cork the bottle and pass a glass tube through the cork. Then you take a pinch of ordinary powdered alum, and . . .

IRENA: Ivan Romanych, dear Ivan Romanych!

CHEBUTYKIN: What is it, my child, what is it?

IRENA: Tell me, why is it I'm so happy to-day? Just as if I were sailing along in a boat with big white sails, and above me the wide, blue sky, and in the sky great white birds floating around?

CHEBUTYKIN (*kisses both her hands, tenderly*): My little white bird!

IRENA: You know, when I woke up this morning, and after I'd got up and washed, I suddenly felt as if everything in the world had become clear to me, and I knew the way I ought to live. I know it all now, my dear Ivan Romanych. Man must work by the sweat of his brow whatever his class, and that should make up the whole meaning and purpose of his life and happiness and contentment. Oh, how good it must be to be a workman, getting up with the sun and breaking stones by the roadside—or a shepherd—or a schoolmaster teaching the children—or an engine-driver on the railway. Good Heavens! It's better to be a mere ox or horse, and work, than the sort of young woman who wakes up at twelve, and drinks her coffee in bed, and then takes two hours dressing. . . . How dreadful! You know how you long for a cool drink in hot weather? Well, that's the way I long for work. And if I don't get up early from now on and really work, you can refuse to be friends with me any more, Ivan Romanych.

CHEBUTYKIN (*tenderly*): So I will, so I will . . .

OLGA: Father taught us to get up at seven o'clock and so Irena always wakes up at seven—but then she stays in bed till at least nine, thinking about something or other. And with such a serious expression on her face, too! (*Laughs.*)

IRENA: You think it's strange when I look serious because you always think of me as a little girl. I'm twenty, you know!

TOOZENBACH: All this longing for work. . . . Heavens! how well I can understand it! I've never done a stroke of work in my life. I was born in Petersburg, an unfriendly, idle city—born into a family where work and worries were simply unknown. I remember a valet pulling off my boots for me when I came home from cadet school. . . . I grumbled at the way he did it, and my mother looked on in admiration. She was quite surprised when other people looked at me in any other way. I was so carefully protected from work! But I doubt whether they succeeded in protecting me for good and all—yes, I doubt it very much! The time's come: there's a terrific thundercloud advancing upon us, a mighty storm is coming to freshen us up! Yes, it's coming all right, it's quite near already, and it's going to blow away all this idleness and indifference, and prejudice against work, this rot of boredom that our society is suffering from. I'm going to work, and in twenty-five or thirty years' time every man and woman will be working. Every one of us!

CHEBUTYKIN: I'm not going to work.

TOOZENBACH: You don't count.

SOLIONY: In twenty-five years' time you won't be alive, thank goodness. In a couple of years you'll die from a stroke—or I'll lose my temper with you and put a bullet in your head, my good fellow. (*Takes a scent bottle from his pocket and sprinkles the scent over his chest and hands.*)

CHEBUTYKIN (*laughs*): It's quite true that I never have done any work. Not a stroke since I left the university. I haven't even read a book, only newspapers. (*Takes another newspaper out of his pocket.*) For instance, here . . . I know from the paper that there was a person called Dobroliubov, but what he wrote about I've not the faintest idea . . . God alone knows . . .

    (*Someone knocks on the floor from downstairs.*)

There! They're calling me to come down: there's someone come to see me. I'll be back in a moment . . . (*Goes out hurriedly, stroking his beard.*)

IRENA: He's up to one of his little games.

TOOZENBACH: Yes. He looked very solemn as he left. He's obviously going to give you a present.

IRENA: I do dislike that sort of thing . . .

OLGA: Yes, isn't it dreadful? He's always doing something silly.

MASHA: 'A green oak grows by a curving shore, And around that oak hangs a golden chain' . . . (*Gets up as she sings under her breath.*)

OLGA: You're sad to-day, Masha.

MASHA (*puts on her hat, singing*).

OLGA: Where are you going?

MASHA: Home.

IRENA: What a strange thing to do.

TOOZENBACH: What! Going away from your sister's party?

MASHA: What does it matter? I'll be back this evening. Good-bye, my darling. (*Kisses* IRENA). And once again—I wish you all the happiness in the world. In the old days when Father was alive we used to have thirty or forty officers at our parties. What gay parties we had! And to-day—what have we got today? A man and a half, and the place is as quiet as a tomb. I'm going home. I'm depressed to-day, I'm sad, so don't listen to me. (*Laughs through her tears.*) We'll have a talk later, but good-bye for now, my dear. I'll go somewhere or other . . .

IRENA (*displeased*): Really, you are a . . .

OLGA (*tearfully*): I understand you, Masha.

SOLIONY: If a man starts philosophizing, you call that philosophy, or possibly just sophistry, but if a woman or a couple of women start philosophizing you call that . . . what would you call it, now? Ask me another!

MASHA: What are you talking about? You are a disconcerting person!

SOLIONY: Nothing.

    'He had no time to say "Oh, oh!"
    Before that bear had struck him low' . . .
        (*A pause.*)

MASHA (*to* OLGA, *crossly*): Do stop snivelling!
   (*Enter* ANFISA *and* FERAPONT, *the latter carrying a large cake.*)
ANFISA: Come along, my dear, this way. Come in, your boots are quite clean.
   (*To* IRENA.) A cake from Protopopov, at the Council Office.
IRENA: Thank you. Tell him I'm very grateful to him. (*Takes the cake.*)
FERAPONT: What's that?
IRENA (*louder*): Tell him I sent my thanks.
OLGA: Nanny, will you give him a piece of cake? Go along, Ferapont, they'll
   give you some cake.
FERAPONT: What's that?
ANFISA: Come along with me, Ferapont Spiridonych, my dear. Come along.
   (*Goes out with* FERAPONT.)

THE MAIDS

Jean Genet

(*Madame's bedroom. Louis-Quinze furniture. Lace. Rear, a window opening on
the front of the house opposite. Right, a bed. Left, a door and a dressing table.
Flowers in profusion. The time is evening.*)
(CLAIRE, *wearing a slip, is standing with her back to the dressing table. Her
gestures—arm extended—and tone are exaggeratedly tragic.*)
CLAIRE: Those gloves! Those eternal gloves! I've told you time and again to
   leave them in the kitchen. You probably hope to seduce the milkman with
   them. No, no, don't lie; that won't get you anywhere! Hang them over the
   sink. When will you understand that this room is not to be sullied. Everything, yes, everything that comes out of the kitchen is spit! So stop it!
   (*During this speech* SOLANGE *has been playing with a pair of rubber gloves and
   observing her gloved hands, which are alternately spread fanwise and folded
   in the form of a bouquet.*) Make yourself quite at home. Preen like a peacock.
   And above all, don't hurry, we've plenty of time. Go!
(SOLANGE'S *posture changes and she leaves humbly, holding the rubber gloves
with her fingertips.* CLAIRE *sits down at the dressing table. She sniffs at flowers,
runs her hand over the toilet articles, brushes her hair, pats her face.*)
   Get my dress ready. Quick! Time presses. Are you there? (*She turns round.*)
   Claire! Claire!
                    (SOLANGE *enters.*)
SOLANGE: I beg Madame's pardon, I was preparing her tea. (*She pronounces
   it 'tay'.*)
CLAIRE: Lay out my things. The white spangled dress. The fan. The emeralds.
SOLANGE: Very well, Madame, All Madame's jewels?
CLAIRE: Put them out and I shall choose. And, of course, my patent-leather
   slippers. The ones you've had your eye on for years. (SOLANGE *takes a few
   jewel boxes from the closet, opens them, and lays them out on the bed.*) For
   your wedding, no doubt. Admit he seduced you! Just look at you! How big
   you are! Admit it! (SOLANGE *squats on the rug, spits on the patent-leather
   slippers, and polishes them.*) I've told you, Claire, without spit. Let it sleep
   in you, my child, let it stagnate. Ah! ah! (*She giggles nervously.*) May the
   lost wayfarer drown in it. Ah! Ah! You are hideous. Lean forward and look
   at yourself in my shoes. Do you think I find it pleasant to know that my
   foot is shrouded by the veils of your saliva? By the mists of your swamps?

SOLANGE: (*on her knees, and very humble*): I wish Madame to be lovely.

CLAIRE: I shall be. (*She primps in front of the mirror.*) You hate me, don't you? You crush me with your attentions and your humbleness; you smother me with gladioli and mimosa. (*She stands up and, lowering her tone.*) There are too many flowers. The room is needlessly cluttered. It's impossible. (*She looks at herself again in the glass.*) I shall be lovely. Lovelier than you'll ever be. With a face and body like that, you'll never seduce Mario. (*Dropping the tragic tone.*) A ridiculous young milkman despises us, and if we're going to have a kid by him—

SOLANGE: Oh! I've never—

CLAIRE (*resuming*): Be quiet, you fool. My dress!

SOLANGE (*she looks in the closet, pushing aside a few dresses*): The red dress. Madame will wear the red dress.

CLAIRE: I said the white dress, the one with spangles.

SOLANGE (*firmly*): I'm sorry. Madame will wear the scarlet velvet dress this evening.

CLAIRE (*naïvely*): Ah? Why?

SOLANGE (*coldly*): It's impossible to forget Madame's bosom under the velvet folds. And the jet brooch, when Madame was sighing and telling Monsieur of my devotion! Your widowhood really requires that you be entirely in black.

CLAIRE: Eh?

SOLANGE: Need I say more? A word to the wise—

CLAIRE: Ah! So you want to talk. . . . Very well. Threaten me. Insult your mistress, Solange. You want to talk about Monsieur's misfortunes, don't you? Fool. It was hardly the moment to allude to him, but I can turn this matter to fine account! You're smiling? Do you doubt it?

SOLANGE: The time is not yet ripe to unearth—

CLAIRE: What a word! My infamy? My infamy? To unearth!

SOLANGE: Madame!

CLAIRE: Am I to be at your mercy for having denounced Monsieur to the police, for having sold him? And yet I'd have done even worse, or better. You think I haven't suffered? Claire, I forced my hand to pen the letter— without mistakes in spelling or syntax, without crossing anything out—the letter that sent my lover to prison. And you, instead of standing by me, you mock me. You force your colours on me! You speak of widowhood! He isn't dead. Claire, Monsieur will be led from prison to prison, perhaps even to Devil's Island, where I, his mistress, mad with grief, shall follow him. I shall be in the convoy. I shall share his glory. You speak of widowhood and deny me the white gown—the mourning of queens. You're unaware of that, Claire—

SOLANGE (*coldly*): Madame will wear the red dress.

CLAIRE (*simply*): Quite. (*Severely.*) Hand me the dress. Oh! I'm so alone and friendless. I can see in your eyes that you loathe me. You don't care what happens to me.

SOLANGE: I'll follow you everywhere. I love you.

CLAIRE: No doubt. As one loves a mistress. You love and respect me. And you're hoping for a legacy, a codicil in your favour—

SOLANGE: I'd do all in my power—

CLAIRE (*ironically*): I know. You'd go through fire for me. (SOLANGE *helps*

CLAIRE *put on her dress*.) Fasten it. Don't pull so hard. Don't try to bind me. (SOLANGE *kneels at* CLAIRE'S *feet and arranges the folds of the dress.*) Avoid pawing me. You smell like an animal. You've brought those odours from some foul attic, where the lackeys visit us at night. The maid's room! The garret! (*Graciously*) Claire, if I speak of the smell of garrets, it is for memory's sake. And of the twin beds where two sisters fall asleep, dreaming of one another. There (*she points to a spot in the room*), there, the two iron beds with the night table between them. There (*she points to a spot opposite*), the pinewood dresser with the little altar to the Holy Virgin! That's right, isn't it?

SOLANGE: We're so unhappy. I could cry! If you go on—

CLAIRE: It is right, isn't it! Let's skip the business of your prayers and kneeling. I shan't even mention the paper flowers . . . (*She laughs.*) Paper flowers! And the branch of holy boxwood! (*She points to the flowers in the room.*) Just look at these flowers open in my honour: Claire, am I not a lovelier Virgin?

SOLANGE (*as if in adoration*): Be quiet—

CLAIRE: And there (*she points to a very high spot at the window*), that notorious skylight from which a half-naked milkman jumps to your bed!

SOLANGE: Madame is forgetting herself, Madame—

CLAIRE: And what about your hands? Don't you forget your hands. How often have I (*she hesitates*) murmured: they befoul the sink.

SOLANGE: The fall!

CLAIRE: Eh?

SOLANGE (*arranging the dress on* CLAIRE'S *hips*): The fall of your dress. I'm arranging your fall from grace.

CLAIRE: Get away, you bungler! (*She kicks* SOLANGE *in the temple with her Louis-Quinze heel.* SOLANGE, *who is kneeling, staggers and draws back.*)

SOLANGE: Oh! Me a burglar?

CLAIRE: I said bungler; and if you must whimper, do it in your garret. Here, in my bedroom, I will have only noble tears. A time will come when the hem of my gown will be studded with them, but those will be precious tears. Arrange my train, you clod.

SOLANGE: (*in ecstasy*): Madame's being carried away!

CLAIRE: By the devil! He's carrying me away in his fragrant arms. He's lifting me up, I leave the ground, I'm off. . . . (*She stamps with her heel.*) And I stay behind. Get my necklace! But hurry, we won't have time. If the gown's too long, make a hem with some safety pins. (SOLANGE *gets up and goes to take the necklace from a jewel case, but* CLAIRE *rushes ahead of her and seizes the jewels. Her fingers graze those of* SOLANGE, *and she recoils in horror.*) Keep your hands off mine! I can't stand your touching me. Hurry up!

SOLANGE: There's no need to overdo it. Your eyes are ablaze.

CLAIRE (*shocked astonishment*): What's that you said?

SOLANGE: Limits, boundaries, Madame. Frontiers are not conventions but laws. Here, my lands; there, your shore—

CLAIRE: What language, my dear. Claire, do you mean that I've already crossed the seas? Are you offering me the dreary exile of your imagination? You're taking revenge, aren't you? You feel the time coming when, no longer a maid—

SOLANGE: You see straight through me. You divine my thoughts.

CLAIRE (*increasingly carried away*):—the time coming when, no longer a maid, you become vengeance itself, but, Claire, don't forget—Claire, are you listening?—don't forget, it was the maid who hatched schemes of vengeance and I—Claire, you're not listening.

SOLANGE: (*absentmindedly*): I'm listening.

CLAIRE: And I contain within me both vengeance and the maid and give them a chance for life, a chance for salvation. Claire, it's a burden, it's terribly painful to be a mistress, to contain all the springs of hatred, to be the dung-hill on which you grow. You want to see me naked every day. I am beautiful, am I not? And the desperation of my love makes me even more so, but you have no idea what strength I need!

SOLANGE (*contemptuously*): Your lover!

CLAIRE: My unhappy lover heightens my nobility. Yes. Yes, my child. All that you'll ever know is your own baseness.

SOLANGE: That'll do! Now hurry! Are you ready?

CLAIRE: Are you?

SOLANGE (*she steps back to the wardrobe*): I'm ready.—I'm tired of being an object of disgust. I hate you, too. I despise you. I hate your scented bosom. Your ... ivory bosom! Your ... golden thighs! Your ... amber feet! I hate you! (*She spits on the red dress.*)

CLAIRE (*aghast*): Oh! ... Oh! ... But ...

SOLANGE (*walking up to her*): Yes, my proud beauty. You think you can always do just as you like. You think you can deprive me forever of the beauty of the sky, that you can choose your perfumes and powders, your nail-polish and silk and velvet and lace, and deprive me of them? That you can steal the milkman from me? Admit it! Admit about the milkman. His youth and vigour excite you, don't they? Admit about the milkman. For Solange says: to hell with you!

CLAIRE (*panic-stricken*): Claire! Claire!

SOLANGE: Eh?

CLAIRE (*in a murmur*): Claire, Solange, Claire.

SOLANGE: Ah! Yes, Claire, Claire says: to hell with you! Claire is here, more dazzling than ever. Radiant! (*She slaps* CLAIRE.)

CLAIRE: Oh! ... Oh! Claire. ... You. ... Oh!

SOLANGE: Madame thought she was protected by her barricade of flowers, saved by some special destiny, by a sacrifice. But she reckoned without a maid's rebellion. Behold her wrath, Madame. She turns your pretty speeches to nought. She'll cut the ground from under your fine adventure. Your Monsieur was just a cheap thief, and you—

CLAIRE: I forbid you! Confound your impudence!

SOLANGE: Twaddle! She forbids me! It's Madame who's confounded. Her face is all convulsed. Would you like a mirror? Here. (*She hands* CLAIRE *a mirror.*)

CLAIRE (*regarding herself with satisfaction*): I see the marks of a slap, but now I'm more beautiful than ever!

SOLANGE: Yes, a slap!

CLAIRE: Danger is my halo, Claire; and you, you dwell in darkness ...

SOLANGE: But the darkness is dangerous.—I know. I've heard all that before. I can tell by your face what I'm supposed to answer. So I'll finish it up. Now, here are the two maids, the faithful servants! They're standing in front of you. Despise them. Look more beautiful. We no longer fear you. We're merged, enveloped in our fumes, in our revels, in our hatred of you. The mould is setting. We're taking shape, Madame. Don't laugh—ah! above all, don't laugh at my grandiloquence . . .

CLAIRE: Get out!

SOLANGE: But only to be of further service to Madame! I'm going back to my kitchen, back to my gloves and the smell of my teeth. To my belching sink. You have your flowers. I my sink. I'm the maid. You, at least, you can't defile me. But! But! . . . (*She advances on* CLAIRE *threateningly.*) But before I go back, I'm going to finish the job. (*Suddenly an alarm clock goes off,* SOLANGE *stops. The two actresses, in a state of agitation, run together. They huddle and listen.*) Already?

CLAIRE: Let's hurry! Madame'll be back. (*She starts to unfasten her dress.*) Help me. It's over already. And you didn't get to the end.

SOLANGE (*helping her. In a sad tone of voice*): The same thing happens every time. And it's all your fault, you're never ready. I can't finish you off.

CLAIRE: We waste too much time with the preliminaries. But we've still . . .

SOLANGE (*as she helps* CLAIRE *out of her dress*): Watch at the window.

CLAIRE: We've still got a little time left. I set the clock so we'd be able to put the things in order. (*She drops wearily into the armchair.*)

SOLANGE (*gently*): It's so close this evening. It's been close all day.

CLAIRE (*gently*): Yes.

SOLANGE: Is that what's killing us, Claire?

CLAIRE: Yes.

SOLANGE: It's time now.

CLAIRE: Yes. (*She gets up wearily.*) I'm going to make the tea.

SOLANGE: Watch at the window.

CLAIRE: There's time. (*She wipes her face.*)

SOLANGE: Still looking at yourself . . . Claire, dear . . .

CLAIRE: Let me alone, I'm exhausted.

SOLANGE (*sternly*): Watch at the window. Thanks to you, the whole place is in a mess again. And I've got to clean Madame's gown. (*She stares at her sister.*) Well, what's the matter with you? You can be like me now. Be yourself again. Come on, Claire, be my sister again.

HAMLET, PRINCE OF DENMARK

William Shakespeare

(*Flourish. Enter* CLAUDIUS, *King of Denmark,* GERTRUDE, *the Queen; Council, as* POLONIUS, *and his son,* LAERTES, HAMLET *and others.*)

KING: Though yet of Hamlet our dear brother's death
　　The memory be green: and that it us befitted
　　To bear our hearts in grief, and our whole Kingdom
　　To be contracted in our brow of woe:
　　Yet so far hath discretion fought with nature,
　　That we with wisest sorrow think on him,
　　Together with remembrance of ourselves.
　　Therefore our sometimes sister, now our Queen.
　　Th'imperial jointress to this warlike State,

Have we, as 'twere, with a defeated joy,
With mirth in funeral, and with dirge in marriage,
In equal scale weighing delight and dole
Taken to wife; nor have we herein barr'd
Your better wisdoms, which have freely gone
With this affair along, for all our thanks.
Now follows, that you know young Fortinbras,
Holding a weak supposal of our worth;
Or thinking by our late dear Brother's death
Our State to be disjoint, and out of frame,
Colleagued with the dream of his advantage;
He hath not fail'd to pester us with message,
Importing the surrender of those lands
Lost by his father, with all bonds of law
To our most valiant brother: so much for him.
            (*Enter* VOLTEMAND *and* CORNELIUS.)
Now for ourself, and for this time of meeting,
Thus much the business is. We have here writ
To Norway, uncle of young Fortinbras,
Who impotent and bed-rid, scarcely hears
Of this his nephew's purpose, to suppress
His further gait herein. In that the levies,
The lists, and full proportions are all made
Out of his subject: and we here dispatch
You good Cornelius, and you Voltemand,
For bearing of this greeting to old Norway,
Giving to you no further personal power
To business with the King, more than the scope
Of these dilated articles allow:
Farewell, and let your haste commend your duty.
VOLTEMAND: In that, and all things, will we show our duty.
KING: We doubt it nothing, heartily farewell.
            (*Exeunt* VOLTEMAND *and* CORNELIUS.)
And now Laertes, what's the news with you?
You told us of some suit. What is't Laertes?
You cannot speak of reason to the Dane,
And lose your voice. What wouldst thou beg Laertes,
That shall not be my offer, not thy asking?
The head is not more native to the heart,
The hand is more instrumental to the mouth,
Than is the throne of Denmark to thy father.
What wouldst thou have Laertes?
LAERTES: Dread my Lord,
Your leave and favour to return to France.
From whence, though willingly I came to Denmark
To show my duty in your Coronation,
Yet now I must confess, that duty done,
My thoughts and wishes bend again toward France,
And bow them to your gracious leave and pardon.
KING: Have you your father's leave? What says Polonius?

POLONIUS: He hath my Lord, wrung from me my slow leave
  By laboursome petition and at last
  Upon his will I seal'd my hard consent;
  I do beseech you give him leave to go.
KING: Take thy fair hour Laertes, time be thine,
  And thy best graces spend it at thy will:
  But now my cousin Hamlet, and my son?
HAMLET: A little more than kin, and less than kind.
KING: How is it that the clouds still hang on you?
HAMLET: Not so my Lord, I am too much i' th' sun.
QUEEN: Good Hamlet cast thy nightly colour off,
  And let thine eye look like a friend on Denmark.
  Do not for ever with thy vailed lids
  Seek for thy noble father in the dust;
  Thou know'st 'tis common, all that lives must die,
  Passing through nature, to eternity.
HAMLET: Ay Madam, it is common.
QUEEN: If it be,
  Why seems it so particular with thee?
HAMLET: Seems Madam? nay, it is: I know not seems:
  'Tis not alone in my inky cloak, good mother,
  Nor customary suits of solemn black,
  Nor windy suspiration of forc'd breath.
  No, nor the fruitful river in the eye,
  Nor the dejected haviour of the visage,
  Together with all forms, moods, shows of grief,
  That can denote me truly. These indeed seem,
  For they are actions that a man might play:
  But I have that within, which passeth show;
  These, but the trappings and the suits of woe.
KING: 'Tis sweet and commendable in your nature Hamlet.
  To give these mourning duties to your father:
  But you must know, your father lost a father,
  That father lost, lost his, and the survivor bound
  In filial obligation, for some term
  To do obsequious sorrow. But to persever
  In obstinate condolement, is a course
  Of impious stubbornness. 'Tis unmanly grief,
  It shows a will most incorrect to Heaven,
  A heart unfortified, a mind impatient
  And understanding simple, and unschool'd:
  For, what we know must be, and is as common
  As any the most vulgar thing to sense,
  Why should we in our peevish opposition
  Take it to heart? Fie, 'tis a fault to Heaven,
  A fault against the dead, a fault to nature,
  To reason most absurd, whose common theme
  Is death of fathers, and who still hath cried,
  From the first corse, till he that died to-day,
  This must be so. We pray you throw to earth

This unprevailing woe, and think of us
As of a father; for let the world take note,
You are the most immediate to our Throne,
And with no less nobility of love,
Than that which dearest father bears his son,
Do I impart towards you. For your intent
In going back to school in Wittenberg,
It is most retrograde to our desire:
And we beseech you, bend you to remain
Here in the cheer and comfort of our eye,
Our chiefest courtier, cousin, and our son.
QUEEN: Let not they mother lose her prayers Hamlet:
I prithee stay with us, go not to Wittenberg.
HAMLET: I shall in all my best obey you Madam.
KING: Why 'tis a loving, and a fair reply,
Be as ourself in Denmark. Madam come,
This gentle and unforc'd accord of Hamlet
Sits smiling to my heart; in grace whereof,
No jocund health that Denmark drinks to-day,
But the great cannon to the clouds shall tell,
And the King's rouse, the heavens shall bruit again,
Re-speaking earthly thunder. Come away.

(*Flourish. Exeunt all but* HAMLET.)

HAMLET: Oh, that this too too solid flesh, would melt,
Thaw, and resolve itself into a dew:
Or that the Everlasting had not fix'd
His cannon 'gainst self-slaughter. O God, O God!
How weary, stale, flat and unprofitable
Seems to me all the uses of this world!
Fie on't! oh fie, fie, 'tis an unweeded garden
That grows to seed: things rank, and gross in nature
Possess it merely. That it should come to this:
But two months dead: nay, not so much; not two,
So excellent a King, that was to this
Hyperion to a satyr: so loving to my mother,
That he might not beteem the winds of heaven
Visit her face too roughly. Heaven and earth
Must I remember: why she would hang on him,
As if increase of appetite had grown
By what it fed on; and yet within a month!
Let me not think on't: Frailty, thy name is woman.
A little month, or ere those shoes were old,
With which she followed my poor father's body
Like Niobe, all tears. Why she, even she,
(O Heaven! A beast that wants discourse of reason
Would have mournt' longer) married with mine uncle,
My father's brother: but no more like my father,
Than I to Hercules. Within a month!
Ere yet the salt of most unrighteous tears

Had left the flushing of her galled eyes,
She married. O most wicked speed, to post
With such dexterity to incentuous sheets:
It is not, nor it cannot come to good.
But break my heart, for I must hold my tongue.

(*Enter* HORATIO, BARNARDO, *and* MARCELLUS.)

HORATIO: Hail to your Lordship.
HAMLET: I am glad to see you well:
Horatio, or I do forget myself.
HORATIO: The same my Lord, and your poor servant ever.
HAMLET: Sir my good friend, I'll change that name with you:
And what make you from Wittenberg Horatio?
Marcellus.
MARCELLUS: My good Lord!
HAMLET: I am very glad to see you: good even sir.
But what in faith make you from Wittenberg?
HORATIO: A truant disposition, good my Lord.
HAMLET: I would not have your enemy say so,
Nor shall you do mine ear that violence,
To make it truster of your own report
Against yourself. I know you are no truant:
But what is your affair in Elsinore?
We'll teach you to drink deep, ere you depart.
HORATIO: My Lord, I came to see your father's funeral.
HAMLET: I pray thee do not mock me, fellow-student.
I think it was to see my mother's wedding.
HORATIO: Indeed my Lord, it followed hard upon.
HAMLET: Thrift, thrift, Horatio: the funeral baked-meats
Did coldly furnish forth the marriage tables;
Would I had met my dearest foe in heaven,
Or I had ever seen that day Horatio.
My father, methinks I see my father.
HORATIO: O where my Lord?
HAMLET: In my mind's eye, Horatio.
HORATIO: I saw him once; he was a goodly King.
HAMLET: He was a man, take him for all in all:
I shall not look upon his like again.
HORATIO: My Lord, I think I saw him yesternight.
HAMLET: Saw? who?
HORATIO: My Lord, the King your father.
HAMLET: The King my father?
HORATIO: Season your admiration for a while
With an attent ear; till I may deliver
Upon the witness of these gentlemen,
This marvel to you.
HAMLET: For God's love let me hear.
HORATIO: Two nights together, had these gentlemen
(Marcellus and Barnardo) on their watch
In the dead waste and middle of the night

Been thus encounter'd. A figure like your father,
Arm'd at all points exactly, cap-a-pe,
Appears before them, and with solemn march
Goes slow and stately: by them thrice he walk'd,
By their oppress'd and fear-surprised eyes
Within this truncheon's length; whilst they, distill'd
Almost to jelly with the act of fear,
Stand dumb and speak not to him. This to me
In dreadful secrecy impart they did,
And I with them the third night kept the watch,
Whereas they had deliver'd both in time,
Form of the thing, each word made, true and good,
The apparition comes. I knew your father:
These hands are not more like.

HAMLET: But where was this?

MARCELLUS: My Lord upon the platform where we watch'd.

HAMLET: Did you not speak to it?

HORATIO: My Lord, I did;
But answer made it none: yet once methought
It lifted up its head, and did address
Itself to motion, like as it would speak:
But even then, the morning cock crew loud;
And at the sound it shrunk in haste away,
And vanish'd from our sight.

HAMLET: 'Tis very strange.

HORATIO: As I do live my honour'd Lord 'tis true;
And we did think it writ down in our duty
To let you know of it.

HAMLET: Indeed, indeed sirs; but this troubles me.
Hold you the watch to-night?

BOTH: We do my Lord.

HAMLET: Arm'd, say you!

BOTH: Arm'd, my Lord.

HAMLET: From top to toe?

BOTH: My Lord, from head to foot.

HAMLET: Then saw you not his face?

HORATIO: O yes, my Lord, he wore his beaver up.

HAMLET: What, look'd he frowningly?

HORATIO: A countenance more in sorrow than in anger.

HAMLET: Pale, or red?

HORATIO: Nay, very pale.

HAMLET: And fix'd his eyes upon you?

HORATIO: Most constantly.

HAMLET: I would I had been there.

HORATIO: It would have much amaz'd you.

HAMLET: Very like, very like: stay'd it long?

HORATIO: While one with moderate haste might tell a hundred.

BOTH: Longer, longer.

HORATIO: Not when I saw't.

HAMLET: His beard was grizzled, no?

HORATIO: It was, as I have seen it in his life,
A sable silver'd.
HAMLET: I will watch to-night;
Perchance 'twill walk again.
HORATIO: I warrant you it will.
HAMLET: If it assume my noble father's person,
I'll speak to it, though Hell itself should gape
And bid me hold my peace. I pray you all,
If you have hitherto conceal'd this sight;
Let it be tenable in your silence still:
And whatsoever else shall hap to-night,
Give it an understanding but no tongue;
I will requite your loves; so, fare you well:
Upon the platform 'twixt eleven and twelve,
I'll visit you.
ALL: Our duty to your Honour.

(Exeunt.)

ACTION

Derek Bowskill

The play is written for informal production in coffee-bars, youth centres, clubs and public houses—anywhere the audience is not captive but free to respond, participate or leave.

The improvised opening should grow from the environment of the place of performance, with the cast initially taking part in whatever is happening. Producers are free to use any device to gain the intrigue and involvement that will best begin the play.

An opening that has proved successful is this:

The company is dressed in matching or unisex 'gear'. They move, in every way, as one person and embody the essence of the 'groupie'. This unity, which may cause intrigue or mild hostility, grows into the current pop dance idiom.

At the height of the dance one of the company opts out complaining of the lack of 'Action', and saying 'I'm going where the action is'. The rest of the company ask:

'Where's the action, Jack (or Jill)?'
'What's action, Jack?'

The first actor replies by quoting sensational headlines from the day's papers (national or local). These are acted out by the rest of the company. They should be fast, brief and stylised. After two or three quotes JACK 1 (the drummer), speaks:

'That's not action. I'll tell you what action is. I'll give you some action.'
The company respond with a chant 'Give us action' or 'What we want is action'. They advance upon JACK 1. He retreats to a previously set up drum-kit (preferably hidden or disguised) and says:

'I'll give you action.'

He delivers rim shots—slow and isolated at first and later pouring in a torrent—and the company are 'killed' as if by bullets. JACK 1 surveys the scene:

'Cor. That's what I call action.'

He returns to his drum-kit (which he will not leave till the end of the play). After an introductory roll, he leads the company, who jump to life, in a free modern dance/chant rendering of the text.

The text should be delivered with bite and vitality—accompanied by rhythmic percussion throughout.

The part of the drummer is vital—he is leader, commentator, puppetter and support. His drumming guides the stylized, mimetic contemporary dance action which accompanies the text.

JACK 1 and 2   LET'S GET where the action is.
JILL 1, 2 and 3   LET'S GO where the action goes.
(in any combination)   Today—
I saw—
My first—
Major public heart transplant!

Better than a pile-up
On the M.1.
Bigger than a drowning
At sea.
Bigger than the telly,
Better than the telly,
Super (*Long, drawn out*)

LET'S GET where the action is.
LET'S GO where the action goes.
To-day—
I saw—
My first—
Astronaut lost in space!
Whoooooosh
SUPER (*Long, drawn out*)

Slower than a strip (*Long, drawn out*)
And the taste
Lingers
Longer and longer and longer . . .

LET'S GET where the action is.
LET'S GO where the action goes.
To-day—
I saw—
My first—
Mass execution by nerve gas.
Bigger than Bingo,
Cooler than cool;
Better than a trip . . .
With a black girl.

LET'S GET where the action is.
LET'S GO where the action goes.
Here's a man with 17 parts:
>   NOT
>   HIS
>   OWN.

Here's an astro-corpse
Floating, floating (*Long, drawn out*)
Here:
43,000 thalidomide babies—

Nerve gas—It's a gas!
Sniff it, man
Sniff it!
Sniff it—right out.
RIGHT OUT.

Way out.
Freak out.
Fall out.
Drop out.
Way out.
Freak out.
Fall out.
Drop out.
DROP OUT.
Freak out. Freak out. Freak out. FREAK OUT.

(*Free build up to Ritual Climax.*)

JILL 1: The biggest freak out in the history of human endeavour was probably Joan of Arc. Saint Joan. Sent Joan. What a way to get sent! Hey Jill!

JILL 2: Yeah?

JILL 1: Come on. Here. You're on.

JACK 1: (*Drum rolls, cymbals; like a cabaret or circus act.*)

JILL 1: Tonight ladies and gentlemen, for your superior, sophisticated pleasure we are happy to present for its very first performance in this, or any other, country the latest, most experimental step that television technology has yet made. Here to introduce the show itself—the director.

DIRECTOR (JACK 2): Good evening ladies and gentlemen. I have really very little to say except to thank all the back-room boys who have made this step, this leap, this fantastic breakthrough possible. TV transmission from satellites was great. Colour pictures even greater. But tonight for you we have the realist thing—'Pseudo Embodiment'. From fact and fiction we give you the very latest thing in TV—Pseudo Embodiment. Just look at this stereophonic, stereoscopic phenomenon 'Pseudo Embodiment'—a pseudo person.

JILL 2:   (*Enters*)

DIRECTOR: She walks, Show us your walk

(*Drum beats and JILL 2 walks. It is mechanical and self-conscious.*)

She talks. Show us your talk.

(*Drum beats* JILL 2 *talks fast and robot like. She repeats the line 'Let's Get where the action is'*.)

She sings. Show us your singing.

(JILL 2 *as before. Sings 'Let's Get where the action is' to the tune of the National Anthem.*)

She dances. Show us your dancing.

(JILL 2 *accompanied by drums performs a slow erotic dance sequence.*)

DIRECTOR: And now for the freak out. Our pseudo embodiment can go much further—pseudo, pseudo people. Freak into Joan.

(*Drum beats,* JILL 3 *appears.*)

Freak into Joan's mother.
(*Drum beats.*)

Freak off!
(*Drum beats.*)

JILL 2: Mummy.
JILL 3: Yes dear (*very, very soft and loving*).
JILL 2: Mummy; I'm frightened.
JILL 3: Yes dear. So am I.
JILL 2: But Mummy; I hear voices.
JILL 3: Yes dear, so do I.
JILL 2: But Mummy; my voices are *real*.
JACK 1: (*starts quiet drum roll*).
JILL 3: Yes dear, everything's *real*. It's all for Real.
JILL 2: It's all for REAL?
JILL 3: It's ALL for REAL.

(*They chant and dance to the* DRUMS *addressing the Audience.*)

ALL: It's All for real:

The motor-car and the washing machine,
The football pool and the five-day week,
The holiday abroad and the welfare state,
It's ALL for REAL.

And for real too are those voices:

Instant voices.
From Radio One, Two, Three, Four.
Radio Stoke,
Radio Brighton,
Leicester, London, Luxembourg.
Instant voices.
Telling voices.
Promising voices.
JILL 2: Mummy. Listen.

JILL 3: Yes dear, I'm listening.

(JACK 1 *and* JILL 2 *speak automaton like. The rest of the company silently mouth the words hugely and grotesque*).

JACK 1 *and* JILL 2: Joan. Go to see the King. Go to see the King. Go to see the King. I've been to London to see a great Queen. Go to see the King. Ignore your father. Leave your mother. Go to see the King. Take a trip. Make the big time. What have you got to lose? All those demonstrations and all those marches! You're of age. You've got the vote. You're a big girl now. What've you got to lose? Nothing but your virginity. Go to see the King. Go to see the King. Go to see the King.

JILL 2 (*comes out of trance*): Mummy, I'm frightened.

JILL 3: Yes dear, so am I.

JILL 2: Mummy. I've heard my voices again.

JILL 3: Yes dear, so have I.

JILL 2: Mummy, God said I have to go to see the King.

JILL 3 (*interrupting her—vicious*): You little liar. Blaspheming Bitch—go to your room.

JILL 2: But MUMMY. My voices—they're from God.

JILL 3: You little devil—haven't you said enough—Blaspheming Bitch

(CYMBAL)
(*Long silence.*)

JILL 2: Mummy.

JILL 3: Yes dear.

JILL 2: I'm pregnant.

JILL 3: Yes dear. I thought so. (*Loving*)

(CYMBAL)
(*Long silence.*)

JILL 2: Mummy.

JILL 3: Yes dear.

JILL 2: I've had an offer.

JILL 3: Yes dear.

JILL 2: It's a good one.

JILL 3: Yes dear.

JILL 2: 80 a week and all found.

JILL 3: Yes dear. That's very good.

JILL 2: It's to be a 'hostess'.

(*She moves slowly and sexually to emphasize the point.*)

JILL 3: Yes dear. That's very good isn't it? (*interested and sympathetic*)

(CYMBAL)
(*Long silence.*)

JILL 2: Mummy.

JILL 3: Yes dear.

(*A long silence—held as long as possible*)

JILL 2: I hate your guts.

(*Pause*)

FOR REAL.

CHAPTER FOURTEEN

WORKING WITH A PARTNER

Giving and Taking

Giving out is an essential part of the acting process. So is taking in. An actor must find a **proper balance between giving and taking** if he is to work well with the rest of the cast and succeed with an audience. This two-way movement must occur within the cast as well as between cast and audience. Few actors have difficulty in giving out. Some have to be forcibly restrained from their explosive self-expression. Acting means **self-expression disciplined into communication**. Giving balanced with taking. Taking can be put another way—**enabling the rest of the group to give**. This ideal, once established in a company, will encourage creativity during rehearsals and sensitivity during performances.

These notes are no more than an introduction to some steps in giving and taking. That is, working with a partner. It is practical work that will help. Little can be gained by reading about it. The kinetic experience is essential.

You will no doubt have opportunities in class and rehearsal to work in pairs. You will gain additional benefit if you have a friend with whom you can work regularly at home. The example of stage embraces given in Chapter Nine suggested the need to work in harness or as a double body. The principle applies throughout partner work. Embracing may be an extreme case of the partnership at work, but it is exemplary.

Responding

There is no set rule for working with a partner. Different partners require different responses, initiatives and rhythms, but working with a friend on a regular basis will enable you to **sensitize your own responses** and transfer that skill to other partners and other situations. Regular practice will expose the essence of partnership work and you will be able to share comment, criticism and creativity. You will work to increase your personal sensitivity as well as that of your partner. You will learn to respond in a way useful to your partner and also learn how to draw responses from him. You will have a constant check for your rate of growth in sensitivity and flexibility. You will learn how to work in **unison, in harmony and in contrast**; in speech and in movement, separately and together. Some actors have a highly developed sense of rhythm in speech but not in movement, and vice versa. Working regularly with a partner will help you check your development and progress.

If your performance is to offer a full experience to the audience it must be **kinetic** and **three-dimensional**. Working regularly with a partner you can experiment with those areas of eye to eye and body to body contact you may at first find difficult in a class or rehearsal situation. If an audience is to gain the full physical experience to which it is entitled, you must offer them a character and performance that will stimulate it. Regular experiment and exploration with a partner will help. Seize every opportunity and you will find your rate of development and growth will be surprising and pleasing.

The following exercises are specifically designed to be used under the circumstances suggested above. When you have made progress with them, use the exercises from previous chapters. *Do not hesitate to amend them to suit your particular needs.*

EXERCISES

1. **Mirror Work**

    (*a*) Face your partner. Mirror his movements. Work slowly at first and use isolated parts of the body—one hand; the mouth; one foot. Extend the range of movement as you gain confidence and expertise—hands and arms; feet and legs; the whole face. Finally use the whole body. Take it in turns to lead and follow. Progress towards **working together**, neither leading or following.

    (*b*) Repeat the movement patterns from the previous exercise but work side by side in front of a mirror and look only at your reflections.

The aim in both exercises is to build up mutual understanding and advanced routines with continuity of flow and rhythm. Don't rush the exercise. Let your movements and your understanding grow slowly.

2. **Music**

    Use a wide variety of music and interpret it with your partner in different ways: conduct it, accompany it with percussion, march, hop, skip, jump and dance to it.

    At first, use simple music with a strong time beat and an obvious melody. As you progress and gain understanding of your partner's rhythm, choose music with more inner variations. One of you can use one specific instrument and one another; one the main melody and one accompanying percussion. An example of suitable music is 'Goldenburg and Schmuyle' from 'Pictures at an Exhibition' by Mussorgsky. Most records in the Top Ten have easily discernible divisions which can be used in the same way.

    There are three main areas of movement work to use:

    (*a*) Mechanical, repetitive movements with the emphasis on accuracy and exactitude.

    (*b*) 'Modern dance', creative movement, 'free' or 'dramatic' dance with the emphasis on expressing and exploring your natural style of movement.

    (*c*) Ballroom dance.

    The last combines the merits and skills of the first two and is an excellent vehicle for personal discipline and partnership sensitivity.

3. **Puppets**

    (*a*) Control your partner like (i) a small string puppet or (ii) an 'über-marionette'. Begin by using lengths of string or ribbon—use long or short lengths. Later discard the strings but move as if still attached.

    (*b*) Create a voice for your partner to move to—speech, song or abstract vocalization. Your partner will use it as a stimulus for free or controlled movement. Later, your voice can be used as a basis for characterization and after some practice you will be able to use the *stream of consciousness technique* while your partner puts into immediate action the thoughts you are speaking.

4. Timing and Rhythm

Use the 'Question and Answer' or 'Statement and Counterstatement' technique in percussion; body movement and speech. Later combine all three. The essence of the exercises is to create the possibility of a response couched in the same terms as the action itself. It could be a simple rhythm tapped on a table with a pencil (for example, the initial statement 'DAH DAH di DAH DAH' receives the reply 'DAH DAH'); a straight gesture of command which is obeyed or countered; an object moved from one place to another with distinct purpose and/or emotional overtones or a pattern of foot movements across the floor. The point is to **recognize the rhythm of your partner's statement and to make a suitable reply.**

In the early stages it will be best to keep within the range of one question—one answer. Later you will be able to progress to a series of questions.

5. Contrast

(a) Take two characters from a play or create your own. Devise scenes in which one starts as the stronger and is slowly dominated by the other. (*The Maids* is an example of a play where this movement between superiority and inferiority is taking place all the time.) Keep the change-over slow and subtle.

(b) Repeat the exercise using only: (i) movement; (ii) abstract sounds; (iii) one word; (iv) whispers.

(c) Experiment with different ways of achieving dominance. (i) Let the sound of your voice get louder as your dominance grows; (ii) let the sound of the voice get softer; (iii) let the movement become more active; (iv) let the movement reduce to stillness.

When you have mastered the techniques of the process, play the scenes with the dominance alternating between the two characters.

(d) One partner gives detailed instructions in mime. When the instructions are finished, the other partner performs them. (i) Use the exercise at first in isolation to build up vocabulary and understanding; (ii) construct improvised scenes; (iii) use extracts from plays and substitute mimed 'instructions' for the dialogue.

(e) Create a stimulus for partner's improvisation in movement, speech or both. Begin the exercises with movement only. The stimulus can be from drums, cymbals, finger clicks and body noises; abstract voice and words; music—live or recorded; a stage spotlight and dimmer. For example, with this last, a simple exercise could be for the responding partner to be supine on the floor when the light is out and standing tip-toe, with arms fully extended, when the light is at full. When you have practised the method you will be able to work together so that at one moment the dimmer, say, may be **controlling** the actions of the moving partner and at another **responding** to them.

6. Dialogue

(a) Take a sequence similar to the one below and play it with different rhythms, pitch and volume—moving up and down the emotional scale with each response.
   A   I am tired
   B   So am I

A That's good
B Is it?
A Yes
B But I wasn't tired before
A That was different
B How?
A Just different, that's all
B That's all?

(b) Take a simple dialogue scene from a previous chapter and play it with different body relationships:
  (i) Both standing (a) face to face; (b) back to back; (c) close; (d) distant.
  (ii) Both sitting—repeat as in (a) (b) (c) and (d) above.
  (iii) One standing—One sitting (a) face to face; (b) one behind; (c) side by side.
  (iv) One kneeling—one standing.
  (v) Both kneeling.
  (vi) One lying down—one standing: sitting or kneeling.

(c) Tape a similar dialogue and play it with parts of the body in **close contact with partner**—hand to hand; arm to arm; body to body; etc. Vary the parts touching—hand to face; arm to shoulder; etc.

(d) Take a similar dialogue and play it as follows:
  (i) Speak only when touching your partner.
  (ii) Speak only when not touching your partner.
  (iii) Use touch to interrupt partner—or to silence him.

(e) Take a similar dialogue and play it as follows:
  (i) Keep eye to eye contact throughout.
  (ii) Look only at partner's hands, neck, feet, ears.
  (iii) Never look at partner.
  (iv) Look at the floor.
  (v) Look at the ceiling.

Partner varies his playing similarly.

7. Limbering

The following are useful *follow-up exercises* to those in Chapter Nine. They will also help sensitivity in partnership work.
  (a) Stand face to face with your partner, feet together and toes touching partner's. Hold hands, grip fingers or wrists. Slowly bend backwards until arms are fully extended. Keep the body straight and pivot from the ankles. Keep your movements slow and retain balance throughout. Pull back to starting position. Keep eye to eye contact and don't rush. Repeat no more than six times.
  (b) Stand back to back, link hands and wrists and bend forwards until arms are fully extended. Keep your movements slow, retain balance and pivot from ankles. Pull back to starting position. As in the previous exercise keep your body straight. Repeat no more than six times.

With both exercises, when you have mastered the technique repeat with eyes closed.

(c) Sitting back to back—arms not linked. One partner bends forward until chest is on knees. The other partner leans over backwards keeping full body contact. Keep the movements slow and do not lose body contact. Reverse and repeat no more than six times.

(d) Standing back to back, with arms linked at elbows repeat the exercise in (c). Keep your movements slow and do not go too far too soon. Body contact and balance are essential. When you have gained confidence, progress the exercise into back to back dancing. (Exercises (a) and (b) can be used in groups of not more than 5.)

CHAPTER FIFTEEN

WORKING WITH A GROUP

Internal Unity

The principles of sensitivity and response described in the previous chapter obtain even more when working in a group than with a partner. The difference is one of degree not kind. The aim of partner work is to achieve a relationship based upon mutually sensitive responses and shared responsibility—not for one partner merely to reflect or respond to the stimulus of the other. **The aim of group work is to establish a set of internal forces that bind the individuals together for needs and purposes held in common.** If the group is to be fully effective and creative, its dynamic should be internal. A working group is not a unit of ciphers, held together by external disciplines.

Hierarchy?

There are groups led by a single enthusiast; there are those led by a coterie with esoteric tastes; there are groups whose aim is to be leaderless and there are those who function through apparent democracy with complicated protocol, elections, officers and committees. Generally speaking, the administrative organization of a group reflects its artistic aims and standards and there seems as little place for a dictatorship—benevolent or otherwise—as there does for a democracy.

Co-operative?

Since theatre is a co-operative art form bringing together writer, director, cast, stage crew and audience, there would seem to be merit in creating a company based on the **spirit of a creative co-operative**. Out of such a company, leadership can emerge by common consent and continue by the same process. Nominations, ballots and elections should not be necessary in a group trying to establish high standards of personal and group sensitivity, sincerity and creativity. If there are two, three or more who can effectively lead the group in production and/or training, an atmosphere of co-operative flexibility should soon grow.

Group Policy

Some groups come together for a single production, some for a season, some for a single ten-week term and some for three years' training. There are groups with a policy of continuity and permanence.

The more a group is concerned with continuity, the more will it find its *raison d'être* within itself. It must surely hope its productions will create, establish and please a growing audience but it will not set out to please the general public at all costs. It will choose, present and perform plays which reflect the needs and purposes of the group. It is this process that gives a group its style.

Group Style

Ensemble playing is not yet a common thing in the theatre. The move towards it is slowly growing, and the days of the cast hastily drawn together for a single production seem numbered.

The essence of group style lies in the existence of **areas of experience and means of expression common to the members of the group.** The style of presentation—choice of play, casting, rehearsal and production methods—will reflect those common areas of experience and expression. Ideas, thoughts, feelings and interests held in common will emerge and be consolidated. By common consent the group will journey towards certain types of play and production techniques.

When a group places a high priority on the development of personal sensitivity and awareness there will be a natural growth towards group sensitivity and rhythm. It is not possible to graft group sensitivity when individual members have little concern for personal sensitivity. Personal development, partnership sensitivity; and group awareness grow together when each individual member approaches the work with enthusiasm and integrity.

Inside and Outside

Successful group work depends upon individual members balancing loss of identity in the group situation with an intellectual awareness of contribution. The intuitive/animal quality which will encourage the individual to surrender individuality and go with the group is sensitively guided by intellectual assessment and selection. From time to time there may be a special need to surrender totally and unthinkingly to the group situation—perhaps the rehearsal of a physical ritual in which animality is an important quality—but most of the time the intellect should be aware of what is happening and able to select or reject accordingly.

Numbers

The question of numbers is important. The group must be large enough to enable the individual to experience something different from a collection of single units. In a group of four or five each individual will be aware of the others as individuals, and group feeling will have little chance to develop. With more than twenty, the group becomes too large for group work without total loss of identity. Ten to sixteen seems to be an optimum. Fewer than eight seldom transcend individuality and more than twenty become either an anonymous mass or split into smaller groups.

Leaders' Participation

One of the benefits of having more than one person who can lead the group at any one time is that the leaders can join in group work. No matter how experienced or sensitive a leader may be, he is still distanced from the group experience—especially if it is creative. It is important that any leader should have regular opportunities to participate as a student in class work.

Members' Participation

In working towards group effort, rhythm and style a further step is desirable. During the course of a season, or a year, everyone should participate as fully as possible in all the activities that keep the group in existence. It is a principle that applies as much to set design as to sweeping the floor, operating the lights, making the coffee, directing the production or repairing a broken prop. Such co-operation promotes understanding and sympathy and will encourage the growth of strong **group identity**. An awareness of such identity is the most fruitful starting-point for sensitivity, creativity and style.

EXERCISES

The following exercises do not set a course of training. They indicate a method of approach. Use them in any way that meets the needs of the group. (Previous exercises, especially in Chapter Fourteen, can be easily adapted. Other chapters contain some already plotted for group work.)

1. Meet as often as you can, formally and informally. Go to the theatre and cinema as a group. Watch television plays and listen to radio plays. Read plays and talk about them. Above all meet and talk as often as possible.

2. Make one of your priorities a permanent meeting-place. If it can also be suitable for rehearsal and performance so much the better. But aim for a home or headquarters of some kind—if no more than an old garage or attic.

3. Ensure you share out all the tasks of the group. This will help identification with the group's needs.

4. As a full group, in smaller groups, or individually go to football matches, boxing matches, bingo meetings, etc. and submerge your identity with that of the large group.

5. In smaller groups go to restaurants, hotels and other public places. Create your own group identity by the way you dress, speak, move and behave generally. From time to time take this to extremes by everyone in the group behaving **completely in unison**. (This means every single movement and gesture —smoking cigarettes, drinking, combing hair, etc.—will be performed in unison.) Treat it as a technical exercise in movement. Notice particularly the impact such group behaviour has on other people.

The following exercises are designed for use in a rehearsal or class space.

6. Move in a restricted space without touching. Freeze in position when you are touched.

(*a*) Reduce the space at intervals.
(*b*) Speed up the movement at intervals.

7. You are at a cocktail party. You are looking for a *special guest*. You create the identity of the guest—real or imaginary—and by meeting everyone else, asking questions and giving descriptions, you try to find your target. (If your group is new, proper names and genuine curiosity can be capitalized. The party element and the search can operate at different levels of actuality.)

8. You are at a conference. Everyone knows he is the only new member or the only shy member. Everyone adopts a persona to disguise these facts.

9. You are at a meeting or conference and you are a spy. You know there is another spy who is particularly searching for you. The exercise can be left at the general level and progressed under its own energy. Alternatively the leader can prepare it with sufficient detail so that each student is matched with one other. It is then their task to find their particular partner. Everyone is of

course deliberately trying to avoid detection, yet seek out their particular target. Since this applies to all members in exactly the same way it can provide plenty of opportunities for general intermingling, fun and games or a complex exercise in dramatic behaviour.

10. A cocktail party or hotel lounge setting. You change your name, character and behaviour with each new guest you meet.

11. You set out to encounter everyone in the group at least once. Conversation is restricted to the phrase 'I am Fred Smith' (your proper name should be used). In the early stages the exercise will provide much amusement. Later it should grow so that you try to communicate real messages and real information but still using the single sentence.

12. The group forms a circle and one student stands in the middle.

(a) The student in the middle says his name over and over again. It must be spoken loudly enough for everyone to hear and repeated at least once for each member of the circle. The student looks at each member of the circle eye to eye as he says his name.

(b) The student goes round the circle touching each member of the group. As he touches each individual so he says his name at least once.

(c) Repeat the previous exercise using a different manner of touching for each individual student.

(d) Repeat the previous exercise using a different manner of touching and a different phrase or sentence for each individual.

13. The group work together on time-beat, rhythm and climax,—humming, singing, speaking, moving and dancing together: (a) Work towards climax and down from it; (b) work towards an explosive ultimate climax. Exercises from earlier chapters using foot-tapping, finger-clicking, hand-clapping, larger movements; vowels, consonants, words, phrases, sentences, etc. can be used in different combinations. The question and answer—or statement or counter-statement—technique can be used by dividing the group into two. Group dances—mechanical, free, ballroom or disco can also be used.

14. (a) Develop the exercises in 13 with eyes closed.

(b) With eyes closed help pass one another on from person to person slowly and without accident.

(c) Repeat the exercise in 6 above with eyes closed.

(d) Explore and identify other members of the group with eyes closed: (i) concentrate on touch; (ii) concentrate on smell.

15. In a circle, move hands towards the centre of the room or the ceiling, then back again. Move in unison. Repeat the exercise with different parts of the body. Undertake the exercise consciously aiming at unison work in the first place; later attempting to sense group rhythm rather than watching the rest of the group. When the group has had some experience of success the exercise should be tried with eyes closed.

16. The group moves as far away from the centre of the room as possible. The exercise in 15 is repeated. Progress the exercise by moving to the centre of the room and retreating to the edges. Vary by taking to a point of group climax and (a) stopping the exercise at that point; (b) holding for a period of time before retreating. Later combine with the separate parts of the body as in exercise 15. Repeat all the exercises with eyes closed.

Use the pattern of these exercises in improvised scenes with and without dialogue.

17. (a) Using the stronger members of the group for support positions practise group climbing and balancing exercises. Try them first with eyes open and later with eyes closed.

(b) Carry one member of the group shoulder high around the room.

(c) One student stands in the middle of a circle formed by the rest of the group. He has his eyes closed. Keeping his feet still and his body straight he is moved around the circle by the rest of the group.

Repeat the exercises as follows:

(i) With humming and abstract vocalization.
(ii) With real words.
(iii) With improvised speech and characters.
(iv) With improvized characters but leading to an organized dramatic situation.

18. Vary the exercise in 6 above by using:

(a) Big movements and loud sounds.
(b) Small movements and quiet sounds.
(c) Big movements and quiet sounds.
(d) Small movements and loud sounds.

19. Using a rostrum block or small platform about three-feet square with a group of six to eight let each person achieve a standing position on the block **as slowly as possible**. One by one everyone is helped on to the block. The exercise should be performed in **extreme slow motion**. When everyone is on the block the exercise should progress into climbing, twining and balance. After the climbing the retreat from the block to starting positions should use the same slow motion. The group should take **as long as possible** to perform the exercise.

20. A character from a play is chosen. Everyone in the group becomes that character *at the same time*. Everyone encounters everyone else. The dialogue can be taken from the play or improvised.

21. Share out the space in the room or the hall so that everyone is equidistant from everybody and everything. Repeat and go to new positions.

22. At any moment during class work or rehearsal, at a signal from the leader do exactly the same as everyone else in the group. This is a real test of sensitivity and co-operation. Do not be misled by the apparent simplicity or hilarity of the exercise. It requires delicacy and diligence. The exercise can also be prepared for consciously with the group sitting or standing in a circle.

23. Everyone in the group sits or stands in exactly the same way. Try to move and change your position without being noticed by anyone.

24. A short extract from a play is chosen. It should have three or four characters. Everyone in the group learns all the lines. Rehearsals of the extract are conducted with members of the group coming and going from the actual scene and changing the parts they play.

25. Experiment with extracts from plays requiring organized group action. For example *The Silver Tassie* and *Action*.

CHAPTER SIXTEEN

THE DIRECTOR

Comparisons With Actors

Actors and directors have much in common. They need imagination, perception, sensitivity, purpose and charisma. There are two areas not held in common. The differences are important.

Attitude

The first is their main attitude to their craft. An actor needs those qualities which typify an adolescent: an urge towards growth, exploration, explosion, the discovery of important frontiers and a preparedness to leave home. A director needs qualities that are more paternalistic. He needs to guide, foster, encourage, strengthen and be prepared to let his family leave home.

Process

The second difference is closely associated with the first. An actor must be able to respond first and think later—nothing must interfere with the natural movement of his responses. A director needs to think first, controlling his responses until the appropriate moment.

The two differentials have been over-simplified and, to a certain extent, polarized. There must of course be flexibility and interchange in the roles but the essential basis of the relationship is that of the exploding energy of the actor as a growing artist, controlled and fostered by a director as guiding agent.

Qualities of a Director

The term director is something of a misnomer. It suggests a more positive and at the same time narrower method of working than is usually the case. A director's major task is that of a **creator of possibilities**. He is not a dictator, a traffic-warden or a builder. As suggested earlier, he is more a gardener. He is an enabler—not a megalomaniac or a puppeteer. His fulfilment should come through the satisfaction his company gives and receives. A director who is looking for direct and immediate rewards will find frustrations and problems. The director **arranges the forces at work** so that everyone else concerned with the play can do something. His talent lies in **getting them to use theirs.**

A drama adviser once told me a director's most important talent was to be able to make coffee. While this takes the concept of self-effacement to an amusing extreme it does illuminate the principle of service that should motivate a good director.

What a Director Does Not Do

There are many strange views of the director's work. Some actors believe it is his responsibility to go into a kind of trance and emerge with moves, gestures, and inflections ready to pass on for exact execution. The following notes should help to rectify such a view.

Unless the cast is very large and the action fast moving and complex there is no need for the director to plot or block moves, action or business. It is better for him to help the cast discover their needs and their ways of meeting them.

He does not train actors until they are automatons or zombies (thereby giving reality to his fantasy) and faultlessly repeat his detailed instructions.

He does not tell actors what to do. Nor does he tell them how, where or when to do it. (A director who feels a need to give that kind of instruction should himself be told where to go.)

He does not teach acting. There are occasions when a need for such instruction arises. It is best met away from rehearsals—preferably through allied courses of training. In their absence, the director may have to take on the task himself. He should do it away from rehearsals. If not, the two different functions will become confused and the rest of the cast may begin to expect the same kind of instruction to substitute for their own preparation.

He does not demonstrate. There are a number of reasons:

(a) He may not be able to do it well.
(b) He may do it so well that it leaves the actor little chance to use his initiative and imagination.
(c) He may do it so excellently well that the actor feels inadequate.
(d) It unnecessarily illuminates his own acting ability without any guarantee that it will release the actor's.

What may well be right for one actor in terms of expression and communication will not automatically serve another. All a director can achieve by demonstrating is to show the actor what he, the director, feels about a certain part of the role. It is possible that this may be of help in isolated instances, but the risk of uninspired imitation or a dulled imagination is not worth taking.

The director does not actively concern himself with the **tactics** of the production but with the **strategy**. He must know the tactical possibilities so that he can understand and sympathize with the problems of those to whom he has delegated authority. He does not keep all the strings of the operation in his own hands—first, because it is a co-operative creative endeavour and secondly because it would exhaust him. He knows how to delegate, not only actual jobs, but also full responsibility and authority.

Finally, he does not keep to himself the 'master plan' behind the production as if to declare it were to destroy it. He shares his hopes and his intentions with all the members of the cast.

What a Director Does

First Stage: Decisions

The most important thing a director does is to **decide to direct the play**. It may be his choice in the first instance. Even if this is not the case, the responsibility of accepting it is his. The director must find the play an attractive proposition. Nothing but frustration and unhappiness is caused when a director is involved in the production of a play with which he cannot totally identify.

In making this decision there are relevant questions he must ask about the play:

What kind of Play? Is it basically tragic or comic? Frequently these terms are used as synonyms for sad or funny. Tragedy concerns the situation of man, naked and alone against the backcloth of universal eternity. Comedy concerns his situation fully clothed, in company, against a backcloth of his society—domestic, local or national.

Is it a well-made Play? Does it delicately balance scene for scene: character for character; situation for situation? Are both sides of the dramatic question equally weighted? Is each scene and each act symetrically constructed?

Is it a Satire? Does it need apparent total commitment in playing; sophisticated style and biting technique? Does it laugh loudly or smile quietly in its attack? Is its target you, them or us and are the weapons fatal or mildly irritating?

Does it belong to the Theatre of the Absurd—a school which exposes the impossible hope for personal life in the midst of omnipresent death and contrasts man's individual, spiritual ambitions with the reality of the careless yet malevolent universe?

Does it belong to the Theatre of Cruelty—a term much abused and with no necessary connection with violence or visciousness? It refers to the style of total theatre outlined and championed by Antonin Artaud. A style which involves music, song and dance; the plastic arts, dumb show, cries, moans, puppets and film; moving scenery and architecture, flashing lights, travelling sound-sources, incantation and ritual. It has more in common with a psychedelic disco than an ordinary stage play.

Does it belong to the Theatre of Alienation—a style the opposite of the theatre of cruelty? It aims, not to stimulate into near hypnotic participation, but to provoke philosphical and political thought, completely detached from emotional responses and involvement. Bertolt Brecht is the acknowledged leader of this style of play. It is ironic that his plays fail to achieve the intended alienation and succeed in the emotional and experiential.

Does the play fall into the well-known style of Naturalism? There are many varieties of this school—the dramatized documentary; the slice-of-life; ordinary stories of ordinary people—and it is sometimes misleadingly called Realism. (Since the aim of all theatre is to *expose the reality of man's internal or external existence*, 'Realism' is not a useful definitive term). The varieties have in common: the employment of apparently natural behaviour from the characters: the pretence that neither audience nor cast is aware of the other's presence. The main challenge in presenting a naturalistic or behaviouristic play is to **illuminate what is universally significant by the tedious and banal exactitudes of every life.**

If the play does not come into one of the categories already mentioned it will probably fall into one of the apparently more structured schools of **Expressionism, Symbolism, Ritualism** or the **Poetic.** Each of these exposes its structure and does not ask the audience to pretend the experience is not factitious and self-consious.

Ibsen and Strindberg within their own works demonstrate these contrasting approaches. Comparisons of *The Screens* by Genet—one of the greatest and most complex of modern plays, *Strife* by Galsworthy and *The Connection* and *The Apple* by Gelber will exemplify many of the points outlined above.

Is it a good Play? Having decided what kind of play it is, the director must next make up his mind about its quality. Time and the critics are the usual criteria. Time is not on the side of the director—especially if he is dealing with a new play. If his own creative urges are strong, the comments of critics will be irrelevant. At this stage in the assessment of a text, the director is alone.

Here are some notes regarding what a 'good' play usually achieves:

(i) It celebrates the joys and fears of the human condition in ways that are assimilable by an audience at large.

(ii) It gives enrichment, enlightenment and delight.

(iii) It creates situations which require responses, stimulate imagination and provide intense experiences.

(iv) It does not make statements. It asks questions to which there is no easy or even apparent answer. (For example: Not; there is a housing problem. Not; how do we solve the housing problem? But; why do we not solve the housing problem?)

(v) It has a marked rhythm and style. Its dialogue invites speaking aloud.

(vi) It can be seen or read many times with growing understanding and reward. It does not set up a series of unnecessary questions; surround them with an air of mystery; dress them in whimsy or pomp and answer them in a last-minute denouement.

(vi) It does not depend upon the specifics of time, place, characters or story line for its impact. (These may contribute and some authorities stress the need of a strong story line with recognizable characters.) The overall effect transcends these details.

(viii) It carries the ring of truth of one man's view of the human condition. It is genuine, broad and deep—not false or superficial.

Is it Right? Having decided the play is good of its kind, the director must next consider whether it is right for the group he is to work with. The main elements to consider are **casting, conditions of performances, budget and policy**.

The group must have the **appropriate number of players** with the **right distribution of abilities**. There must also be sufficient talent available for the tasks in addition to performing. Nothing is more frustrating than to attempt a production beyond the manpower of the group.

If the financial resources of the group are limited, the play chosen must be capable of being mounted within the available budget. If the play requires heavy expenditure on special costumes, etc., the group must have the funds to provide them or be sure of gaining them at the box office.

Some plays need more living space than others. Some require complex technical facilities. Some can be performed anywhere. If the play uses every inch of the stage, leaving no work space for the stage crew or little access for the cast, troubles are bound to follow.

The group may have a definite policy regarding its audiences. It may be trying to build an audience that appreciates a particular approach. It may be chasing the bubble reputation by trying to please all its customers all the time. The choice of play must reflect the prevailing ethos of the group or the director will find himself defending his choice of play instead of directing it. Antagonisms can creep in even at a late stage of rehearsal.

It is interesting to note that what an audience says it would like a group to perform and what the same audience remembers with greatest pleasure and intensity of emotion are seldom the same.

Second Stage: Reading

Having taken the first step in the process of getting the play off the ground, the director is faced with a long journey of exploration and discovery. His next task is to **abstract the theme of the play**. Every play has a theme. Every play is about something—and the theme is that something.

The best way of abstracting the theme is to read, read, read the play—and then read again. Take plenty of time and let the idea of the theme slowly emerge and grow in your mind. Notice how the details of character, situation, story and setting all reflect the central idea of the play. Get deeply absorbed in the style and rhythm, the external and internal meanings of the text. Expose and visualize the challenges and opportunities.

Let its wholeness grow slowly. Discard any ideas, no matter how brilliant, that do not properly and easily fit into the thematic pattern. Towards the end of the readings your ideas about the play—general feelings or specific details—should seem necessary rather than optional. There will be plenty of time for optional variations later. At this stage you should be concentrating upon the hard core of the author's meaning and method.

Casting. The next step is to cast the play. The group's aims, purposes and habits will be a guiding factor. It may be a permanent group and you may be part of it or you may have been invited to undertake a single production. If the former is the case you will know more or less who you want and what part you wish them to play. If the latter you will need auditions.

There are many ways of conducting auditions—solo readings, prepared readings, solo performances of extracts, duos and trios of possible parts and full group auditions involving group practical work with the text and improvisation. The last method has much to recommend it, but the detailed mechanisms of audition must rest with the director. It is a personal matter.

There are two dangers. The first comes with the **reading audition**—prepared or unprepared. There are many actors who impress at a first reading. Unfortunately, the reading is often the only thing they can do. Some are never able to recapture the expertise and some are incapable of growth or change.

The second danger comes with the **casting committee**. Any director would be foolish to reject helpful comment offered by wise and trusted friends and colleagues. The casting committee, with its frequent internal struggles and emotional tangles, can be a man-trap. Churchill said a camel was a race-horse designed by a committee—and casting committees can overtake that error with ease.

After Casting. Once the cast is assembled and ready to work, the director's first task is to help them get into the body of the play for themselves. Actors need this help to gain a wider vision than their own which, by the nature of their role, focuses on scenes which concern them. They need help to become involved in the possible varieties of meaning and experience to be found in the play. Such help will encourage them to build up affection for the play.

The director needs to be a reservoir of **enthusiasm, sympathy and energy**. He must always be interested in the individuals who make up the company or group. He must be **tolerant** but not **indulgent**; **kind** and **compassionate** but not **soft** or **sloppy**. He must remember at all times that he is the eyes and ears of the audience.

It is the director's job to present the truth to the group in the way they can best take it. The more he can build up a reputation for **sincerity and frankness** the more will the cast respect him. If he can do this without hurting feelings, so much the better. Actors like to know exactly where they stand in the eyes of a director and **frankness married with compassion** will gain their respect, admiration and co-operation.

Above all the director must be **prepared for change**. He is working with a cast who are attempting to undertake a creative process. It is a process involving constant change and growth. It feeds on experiment and innovation. The director must ensure the cast know at all times he is aware of the processes and is sympathetic to them. They will be encouraged to pursue their creativity if they can see the director understands their problems. If the director wishes the cast to work in an atmosphere where **permission to fail is taken for granted,** he himself must show no fear of failure. One of the surest ways of convincing the cast is for the director to admit errors when they have occurred and to do so without tension or strain. In a sensitive area such as creative work—which if it is developing properly will have a high failure rate in the early stages—the theatre director is in a unique position to be leader, peer and camp follower to everyone.

Third Stage: Rehearsals

In the early stages of a rehearsal it is important for the director to create an atmosphere in which the actors can absorb the *elan vital* of the play. It is the director's job to build up the ethos surrounding the production. No one else can do it and the production will not grow effectively without it.

The rest of his task can be divided into two main sections:

(*a*) The working detail of the growth and development of the play.

(*b*) The elements of personal growth and development within the company and the individual members.

No actor can be expected to give of his best if he is **anxious, fearful** or **hostile**. It is the director's job to ensure these qualities do not appear and if they do, to remove them as quickly as possible.

An actor will feel hostile as a result of being bullied, misunderstood, satirized or just hurt. Too often actors are hurt because the director takes a too authoritarian approach. **A director's authority is no more and no less than the cast freely give him.** If he asks for more, he will lose respect. His authority will emerge from the company's faith and respect in his talent and his person.

Some Practical Suggestions

Every director works and must work in his own way to inspire his cast. Most directors would agree with the following suggestions. They help to make rehearsals happier and more productive.

(*a*) Be on time. Start on time. Both habits will soon be followed.

(*b*) Plan rehearsals well in advance. Let the cast know, also well in advance, what the plans are. Actors rely on the director to arrange and organize their creative powers in rehearsal. Allow for contingencies.

(*c*) Accept the need for socializing but prevent it from spilling into actual rehearsal time. Socializing during rehearsals siphons off creative energy.

The funny joke can often let an actor 'off the hook.' Being 'on the hook is an essential part of the rehearsal process.

(d) Don't keep anyone under-employed. It is frustrating and unnecessary. It also encourages unnecessary socializing.

(e) Be on the look-out at all times for inter-personal relationships within the cast. They provide the motivation to keep rehearsals and progress moving along the right lines. They can also be the cause of serious disturbances.

(f) Take note of the *law of diminishing returns* in length of rehearsals. Short intense periods are more fruitful than drawn out leisurely ones.

(g) Know your specific aims for each rehearsal. Be prepared to drop them if better ones appear during practical work, but always be clear about precisely what you are trying to do.

(h) Make sure everyone knows your pattern of working. Share your aims, methods and assessments.

(i) Liaise regularly with all design, costume, lighting and SM staff.

(j) Keep notes—in an interleaved prompt copy if you prefer—of everything decided or agreed. Make it as available as you can to all the cast.

The best way to become a director of talent and sensitivity is not to read about it, but to practise the job itself. Try either to work with a group of friends on a co-operative, exploratory basis or to find a director whose work you admire and ask him to let you help him. Don't be hurt if he refuses!

In the absence of a friendly and co-operative director to train with the following exercises may be useful.

EXERCISES

1. Choose an extract from Chapters Eight or Ten to Thirteen and read and study the whole play.

2. Describe the theme in as few words as possible. Write it down. (You may need to do this at length at first. Cut it down day by day until you are left with an irreducible statement.)

3. Describe in detail how the characters, plot, setting, etc., reflect the theme and provide opportunities to make it clear.

4. Make models and sketches. Use chess pieces or counters to explore possible ways of interpreting an extract and bringing it to life.

5. Cast the extract in your mind from friends; people in the street, TV actors, etc. Listen for suitable voices in a similar way.

6. Choose photographs, sketches and paintings from newspapers, magazines and art galleries for the characters' faces, make-up, bodies, clothing, etc.

7. Do the same for the settings of the extract. In addition, find them in the street, your friends' homes, etc.

8. Above all—experiment with friends. Try out various methods of production and rehearsal—inspiration; innovation; improvisation; suggestion; demonstration; instruction. Find out for yourself the merits and pitfalls of the different approaches.

Judge what you read here against what you experience in practice.

CHAPTER SEVENTEEN

REHEARSALS

Pre-rehearsal

Much of the pre-rehearsal work of the actor has been outlined in previous chapters. It can be summarised as follows:

1. **Read the play** a number of times for overall impact and assessment of rhythm and style.
2. **Research and study** the play for its detailed structure and inner meaning.
3. Undertake practical work, probably privately, to build up a **vocabulary of imaginative inner experience** through creative experiment.
4. From this practical work **reject and select** until the optimum range of modes of external expression has been reached.

By rehearsal time the individual actor should be ready to relate and communicate with the rest of the cast. In the group situation he should be flexible and confident. He will not be rigid in his approach nor will he be without ideas. He will be ready to **grow and develop within the group**—giving and taking from the rest of the cast.

Compare his situation with that of a swimmer who has been training. At the time of the first rehearsal:

there is no competition;
he is not swimming in a race;
he is not drowning nor is he out of his depth;
he is not petrified at the water's edge;
he is floating—easily and freely—with some knowledge of the water, its depth, its temperature and its currents. He is ready at any moment to use the most appropriate strokes.

This state of confident preparedness is what an actor should bring to the first rehearsals. As individuals, the cast will have experimented, experienced and expressed. They will have been thoroughly absorbed in the play and ready to communicate inter-personally with the other members of the cast. The pattern of experience—expression—communication will now be followed by the **group**. No company can hope to begin its corporate experience and expression until its individual members can communicate with one another in terms of the play. No company can hope to communicate through performance unless the processes of group experience and expression have been properly undertaken.

If the group is a permanent one, there is the opportunity for this exploration into the play to continue to an advanced stage before casting takes place. This has the advantage of showing exactly what each member can bring to the particular play and its roles when working with other members of the group. Most groups rely on past performances to make this kind of assessment. There are not many groups with the organization to support such processes, but the merits are worth the effort required.

Rehearsals—Where and When

The final decision regarding the place, length and time of rehearsals is a matter for the Director. It may be a question of free choice or the most acceptable compromise. The Director may wish to take advice from colleagues—especially if he is new to the group. He may wish to work on a fully democratic basis. In the final resort, he is the one who must make the decision and his decision **fundamentally affects the whole rhythm and progress of the rehearsal period** as well as the quality of the finished production.

Place

The best place to rehearse is the stage on which the group is to perform. This is frequently impossible. The next best place is a permanent headquarters, where equipment can be left in safety and members can meet regularly and frequently. If neither of these is possible, an empty attic or disused garage might be found. The rehearsal place should have at best the equipment and atmosphere the group needs. At worst it should have a neutral atmosphere. Public Houses and private homes are unsuitable. Since they offer too many distractions in noise, decorations, furnishings and business. Creative co-operative work cannot easily be achieved if the environment is unsuitable.

Length

The overall length of the rehearsal period will have to fit in the group's planning. This will often be a matter of policy. Within this policy and planning the Director must decide the time he needs, state his case and, if necessary, defend it. He may feel he needs as little as six weeks (weekly and fortnightly rep. still set an example.) He may decide he needs six months. He will be lucky if he finds a group capable of supporting a rehearsal rhythm over such a period—the average time being much less. Whatever his decision, he must be sure the company will not be unduly rushed by his unexpected speed or bored by his apparent lack of it.

Time

The 'little and often' rule applies here, although there are limits. Sufficient time must be allowed on each occasion for the group to establish the right atmosphere, attitude and pattern of work. This obviously affects the minimum period chosen. For example a $1\frac{1}{2}$-hour session is better than three half-hour ones, but six hours will probably not be as good as three two-hour sessions. Each director will have an optimum period for each group and it is wisest not to force a different one. The law of diminishing returns is inexorable.

A General Pattern

Group work will now fall into five main areas. Generally the order will be as follows:

1. Research and creativity.
2. Exploration and discovery.
3. Selection and rejection.
4. Consolidation and continuity.
5. Progress to perfection and/or performance.

The Director may make his first approach to the play through many methods. He may:

1. hold readings.
2. promote discussions.
3. direct or brrange improvisations involving movement and/or speech related to the theme of the play.
4. conduct immediate practical rehearsals.

His initial approach must be governed by the factors of place, length and time already mentioned. It will also be affected by decisions taken regarding the group's or the Director's policy on the learning of lines. This can often be a thorny problem. When there is no dead-line of public performance the group can take a leisurely rate and rehearse with lines learned when they are ready. Most groups will have their first night fixed and the date for lines to be properly learned must reflect it. There is little purpose in actors trying to create, relate and communicate when they have one eye, one hand and one arm involved with a copy of the script.

The Director must decide the length of the units he is going to rehearse in the first stages. The decision is best taken on the grounds of the play's structure and not groupings that reflect personal conveniences. This is a matter of supreme importance for the progress of the production. The Director has a number of choices:

1. Start at the beginning of the play and work through to the end. A simple procedure, likely to get simple results: Act 1, rather good; Act 2, adequate; Act 3, poor. With this method care must be taken to ensure a **proper distribution of energy, care and attention over the whole play.**
2. **Key narrative or plot scenes** are selected and dealt with in depth. Rehearsals then work outwards from them.
3. **Climactic scenes** are selected and treated similarly.
4. **Particular groupings of characters** are selected to build up acting relationships. Rehearsals follow an orthodox pattern or work outwards from the scenes.
5. **Scenes exemplary of the play's rhythm and style** are selected and worked on with rigour, intensity and discipline until they are mastered. Rehearsals follow an orthodox pattern or work outwards from the selected scenes.

The Director must know his purpose in whichever he chooses. There is no panacea and each method is only as good as its purpose and execution. The cast should know and preferably approve of the choice of method.

A Typical Rehearsal

Two and a half to three hours is a period accepted as being well within the reach of most groups. The time might be divided as follows:

1. Introductory socializing; winding down and away from the outside world. Time—10 minutes.
2. Relaxation. Time—5 minutes. These fifteen minutes spent moving from everyday business and domestic matters are time well spent. The change in ethos and pace from the external world to the internal one of imagination and spirit is marked. The cast should be given every opportunity to reorientate.

There is no reason why the first period should not lead easily into the second. It is essential that the period of relaxation offers complete silence and stillness at its conclusion.

3. Physical and vocal limbering. Time—15 minutes.
4. A short scene played and researched in depth. Time—60 minutes.
5. Break. Time—15 minutes.
6. The previous scene expanded outwards—scenes before it and after—and played for continuity and co-ordination.

The above details are only suggestions—particularly 4 and 6. The Director will vary the pattern as the needs arise. He will watch out for signs of **strain and anxiety**. He will also keep an eye open for **over-relaxation**. In trying to correct any or all of these symptoms he may well resort to an improvised approach.

Improvisatory Methods

The Director should at all times be prepared to use a flexible, improvisatory method to help the cast get deeper into the play's theme and its manifestations. It should not, however, be used as a remedy for improperly learned lines. It is not a technique to improve ad-libbing. By its very nature—involving the actors in a deeper understanding of the play's feelings and thought-processes—it will help the cast overcome many of the problems of 'drying'. Such problems are serious only when the actor is not totally in sympathy and empathy with the character and the situation. At no time should the Director allow the cast to confuse a period of improvisatory work with rehearsal to the text. The following are the usual areas for flexible, free-wheeling work:

1. The style of speech of the play and the individual characters.
2. The style of movement.
3. Characters.
4. Situations.

These four areas can be used separately and in different combinations.

Stage Management

The more the members of the cast are involved in the totality of the production, the more they will respect the work undertaken by others. If the stage management crew participate in limbering and improvisations and the cast work on some aspects of stage management there will be a truly co-operative atmosphere—not just pseudo team-work—and give and take will grow more quickly.

The Director will have held preliminary discussions with the lighting, set, costume, properties and general stage management heads and members. Plans should be well under way by this time, and sketches and models should be available for all company members to see and study. There should be plenty of opportunities for interaction and cross-fertilization between all concerned in the production. Under no circumstances should anyone feel that the design and stage management elements are permanently fixed. It should be known that preparatory work is in hand, plans laid, some progress made and everyone ready to receive ideas and comment—about design or execution.

All the elements of stage management—SET, LIGHTING, PROPS, COSTUME, MUSIC and SOUND—should **grow with the production** and should infiltrate it from the first rehearsal. Stage management is not like the icing on a cake, although frequently treated as such. Many companies leave their lighting until the last moment. Indeed, some casts appear in public for the first time with lighting still unknown to them.

A balance is needed between the aesthetic growth of the total unit and the technical preparation and execution that some aspects of stage management work require. Some of this work can only be undertaken on an empty stage. For example, the initial setting of the lanterns. If the separatist technical work can be kept to a minimum, the production will benefit and the whole company be more involved.

The constant feeding in of the stage management side of the production gains rich rewards. Clothes and set will affect, initiate and stimulate interpretation and action, lighting and music will create and affect atmosphere and handling the properties will increase the possibilities open to the actors. If these elements are fed in slowly there will be little of the notorious nervous laughter accompanying first use of costume and make up.

There should be full liaison with the Stage Manager all through the rehearsal period. Ideally, he should be present at all rehearsals—as should the prompter, if there is to be one. Actors who know there is going to be no prompter tend not to need one. If one is used—and it is not necessary to have one—he must be present at *all* rehearsals and know the inner rhythms of the play as well as the actors do. Being a good prompter is one of the most difficult tasks in the theatre.

Throughout the rehearsals there should be constant selection and rejection of the stage management elements. The cast will come to respect the Director and Stage Manager who select and reject on the principle that what supports and stimulates the actors will be used. The stage management side is functional supportive and decorative—with the functional leading at all times. The visual element in a play does not merely relieve boredom or distract from poor acting.

Dress Rehearsals

The most important thing at a dress rehearsal is for the Director to **leave the production in the hands of the Stage Manager, his crew and the cast.** It is not easy just to look and listen but anything more will be a disservice to cast, crew and production.

There should be at least three dress rehearsals and they should all run as such. There is nothing worse to an actor's morale than to have an intended run interrupted. Their function is to give everyone confidence in the smooth running of the production. Minor errors should be corrected—but they should be few. If the process of creative growth suggested throughout this book has been followed there should be little need for correction at the dress rehearsal stage. Everyone should be content with what they are trying to do and the dress rehearsal should set out to help them do it smoothly.

There should be no need for many of the traditional notes. One of the Director's main tasks will have been to encourage a growth of self-awareness in the cast and crew and to foster a development of group awareness.

There should be no need for dress-rehearsal or first-night nerves. If the elements have been slowly fed into the production and regularly consolidated the dress rehearsal should take its place in the general scheme of things as another small step towards final achievement; an achievement which does not occur until after the last performance—not at the end of the first.

The absence of nervous anxiety, lack of confidence, fear of failure or the awareness of inadequacy is a good thing. It is also good for everyone concerned with the production to be in a state of heightened awareness—very different from nervous tension—with their personal and group creative energy working towards a controlled explosion of artistic expression.

Perhaps the Director might allow himself two words before the dress rehearsal or the First Night—'Good Luck'.

CHAPTER EIGHTEEN

THE STAGE

Some Past Stages

The history of the theatre is long and complex. The history of stage—those areas denied to all but the select-elect—is even longer and more complex. It is a complicated story marked by change. Just a few examples will show this.

The Egyptians used open-air stages with casts of thousands and mass public participation. The Chinese performed esoteric rituals in small inner rooms. The Greeks used open-air temples and the Romans had sacrificial amphitheatres. Stages have been in booths, cockpits, and inn-yards; in churches and the entrances to churches. There have been simple carts with bare wooden boards. The Italians invented elaborate closed boxes to parade their newly discovered perspective. The travelling players of the past used village greens and those of the present use pantechnicons. There are circus rings, boxing rings, bingo halls, mannequin parades and football matches—not to mention tennis tournaments, golf tournaments (with peripatetic audiences), water regattas and fireside television.

The Ritual

The shape of the stage always reflects the nature of the dramatic ritual that is to be played out—whether the player is priest, actor, pop-star or sportsman. The essence of the spectacle remains constant—a simulated conflict, with appropriate rituals, between Man and Superman—be it other men, nations, the universe or someone's god. Priest and Actor serve the same purpose and occupy the same platform—a stage, with all its genius loci. The only differential between actor and priest lies in the quality of the texts.

The Proscenium

The stage shape most popular and apparently most suited to the early part of the twentieth century was the closed proscenium arch type. It dominated the theatre for many decades and its grip is only slowly being prised open. Many drama groups with halls perfectly suited to open-stage, arena or end-stage still go to great lengths to build temporary imitations of proscenium stages. It would appear the groups are more pleased with the often rickety, unsafe and ugly constructions built in the image of decadent Edwardian theatre than in the different shapes that could be properly contained in their hall.

Changes in the theatre and in society have occurred side by side. Many free-form writers have been ahead of social change and have played their part in preparing society for what lies ahead. Most theatre directors, designers and architects have been well behind. The notable exceptions of Gordon Craig, Antonin Artaud and Sean Kenny confirm the point. All of them have been dismissed by the majority of their contemporaries as being gifted but unbalanced.

Definitions

A stage can be defined as that area occupied exclusively by the select-elect of the theatre. Bernard Shaw said a miracle was an act that created faith. In a similar way a stage might be said to be a place where drama occurs. It is a location which must meet two major requirements.

Function

The stage must permit the desired relationship between actors and audience —the elected and the electorate.

Symbol

The stage must represent and evoke the events that take place there—the rituals with which we pretend to control the uncontrollable and in which we seek security in the midst of insecurity.

A Place of One's Own

From both functional and symbolic points of view it should be the aim of every drama group to operate and control its own headquarters, stage and theatre. A small, poorly equipped, permanent home is more useful and fruitful to a group's development than a few days in a splendidly furnished palace of varieties. Perhaps a rehearsal and meeting-place might come first and be of modest proportions. Many groups make a lot of money and it is frequently donated to charity. It is possible to claim they would be serving their society better by establishing themselves in a permanent home and offering an improved public service of theatre.

There is no need to seek a large place. In fact, there is merit in a small one. It can be filled with an audience, that feels a united group, for three to four weeks, instead of the usual run of three to four nights in a much larger hall. Cast and audience alike will benefit. The minimum seize of audience to create the right feel is debatable. As I write, I have just received a request from a group to perform a play of mine at a reduced royalty because they will be playing in a theatre where the maximum seating capacity is twenty-six.

Mobility and Flexibility

Many groups perform away from their own or their base theatre. They tour pubs, clubs, hospitals, old people's homes, etc., performing with minimal scenery and props. Often the stage area is no more than six or seven feet square—a challenge or a drawback, dependant upon the point of view. My own plays, *Action* and *Re-action*, were written to be played in youth centres, discotheques, cafes and bowling alleys.

There is a strong move towards regular lunch time and evening presentations in hotels and public houses. Perhaps there is to be a return to the idea of the eating/drinking/smoking concert drama. Such conditions of performance offer easy opportunities for the audience to leave without causing disturbance, and their continued attention is more complimentary than that of the disenchanted individual trapped in the middle of a long row.

Most groups are able to vary their style of presentation without changing halls or theatres, but tradition dies hard, and there are few who move from proscenium to arena to mixed media to total theatre without fuss. Most halls are much more flexible than appears at first—given an open mind, enthusiasm and imagination. The permanent appearance of the proscenium arch and the caretaker's orthodox layout of the seating can be discouraging. If the stage curtains are opened wide and a few rows of chairs put on the stage the impression can soon become exciting.

Arts Centres

With support from the Arts Council and through Regional Arts Associations, the emergence and growth of Arts Centres has become an important factor. They can go a long way towards offering flexibility of performance. Most of them have a multi-purpose neutral area and many have a number of contrastingly shaped rooms. The membership of Arts Centres encourages an enlightened attitude to presentations requiring mixed media or combined arts styles.

In Arts Centres, pubs, clubs or the much abused village hall flexibility is becoming the keynote. Flexibility in the place and methods of staging as well as in design and production style. Opportunities to leave behind uninspired repetitions of past achievements or trifles are plentiful.

Whatever the physical attributes of the hall, stage or theatre, the imaginative use of projection and lighting can transform, easily and quickly, the most dull and drab space into a cave of magic or a palace of mystery. The subject of lighting is dealt with fully in Chapter Nineteen.

Size and Shape

Production style, cast numbers, design and stage management are all affected by the size and shape of the theatre and its stage. These aspects are external and fairly obvious. A fundamental factor, frequently overlooked, is that the size and shape of stage and theatre **affect the nature of the relationship between actor and audience.** Sometimes it is more conscious than others. The main areas are:

1. The vertical relationship between actor and audience.
2. The distance between actors and audience.
3. A closed or open stage.

Vertical Relationships

There are three possibilities. The audience can be situated as follows:

(*a*) **Above the actor.** There will be a tendency for the actors to seem less than human and more like manipulated puppets. In the *Insect Play* the human qualities would appear under emphasized and the insect nature would be uppermost. The Greeks balanced this by providing the actors with built-up boots, padded costumes, large masks and hidden megaphones.

(*b*) **Below the actor.** The actors will appear to be more than life size and more than human. This is seen dramatically at work when wrestlers, boxers and mannequins achieve the stature of gods and goddesses—or the other. (In the *Insect Play* the human qualities would again be under-emphasized and the characters would appear to be strange gods or unusual beasts.)

(*c*) **On the same level.** A balanced relationship is achieved and actors and audience can relate and communicate on a one to one basis. In the *Insect Play* the actors would be free to vary the middle of the road situation set up by the stage relationship to stress the human or the insect aspect as preferred. They would not be able to achieve the qualities in (*a*) or (*b*) above, but they would be able to pursue the ambivalence the satire needs.

Distance

Physical closeness and intimacy stimulate immediate responses through personal involvement. In intimate arena presentations, the sensations of touch and smell come into action as part of the action—in participatory theatre violently so. This can trigger off unexpected over-reactions. **Physical distancing permits a greater degree of objectivity.** A member of an audience can observe from a distance symbols and rituals he may disapprove of. At a distance he may merely register his disapproval intellectually. If the same person is closely and intimately involved, because of physical proximity, the kinaesthetic quality of the experience may precipitate violent disgust and physical rejection.

A major problem regarding vertical relationships and audience proximity is that many productions must cater for some of the audience being on the same level and some above; some close and some distant. There are few halls which ameliorate the problem. Most of them create or exacerbate it. It is seen in its simplest form in the question of make-up, where what is proper for the first five rows may be inadequate for the last five. The points raised above are, unfortunately, even less susceptible of solution than make-up.

There does seem a general move towards a closer relationship between actors and audience, allowing of subtler playing and delicate direction. The move has no doubt been encouraged by the growth of television and its impact on cinema techniques. It is a movement welcomed by most groups.

Closed or Open?

The closed stage offers:
1. the magic and mystery of effects without apparent causes.
2. the microcosm of a self-sufficient sanctum sanctorum.
3. removal. There is no possibility of real or apparent contact between actors and audience.

The open stage offers:
1. An overt dependance of actors upon audience.
2. Involvement and participation.
3. Contact.

It is claimed that some plays are more suited to the Open stage than others and that some can only be effective behind a proscenium arch. There is no such rule and each director must judge for himself the conditions most suited to his company and the chosen play.

The ideas mentioned so far in this chapter can be combined in many ways. The major alternatives are:
1. A permanent stage giving maximum flexibility within a fixed structure.
2. A flat-floored open hall with no permanent stage, equipped with flexible lighting and movable rostrum blocks for building stage and seating.

The architectural design of theatres and stages is well beyond the scope of this book and few readers will be in a position to promote or influence their construction. The second alternative is likely to hold more appeal and the idea can be put into action in halls with permanent proscenium stages, provided the seating is not fixed to a raked floor.

The main types of stages come within two categories—**open** and **closed**. These are now described and illustrated in accordance with the following key:

A = Audience.   → = Line of vision.

X = Acting area.   W = Wing space

ΛΛΛΛ = Curtains.

- - - - = Variable boundaries.

Closed Stages
Proscenium

This is raised above floor level. The audience can be below, above or at the same level as the stage, and generally face all the same way. Seating is often raked to improve sight lines. Its critics claim it is a three-dimensional peep show catering for voyeurs rather than stimulating a shared experience. It is essentially a box, without one side open.

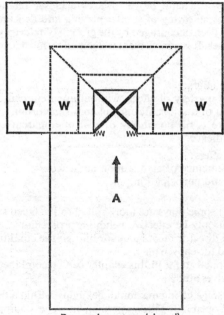

Proscenium stage (closed)

End

This is a variation of the proscenium stage, with the stage opening the full width of the auditorium and level with the first rows of seating. The audience is on one side only, facing the same way. As in the proscenium version, effects can be achieved without the cause being apparent. The action is contained within the stage box although there is an impression of more direct audience contact. The end stage can also be used in an open version (see below).

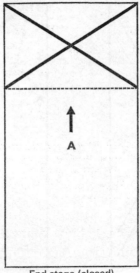

End stage (closed)

Central

This is a special version of the proscenium stage, in so far as there are two prosceniums. The audience sits on two sides, facing one another across the stage area. It can be used in an open version.

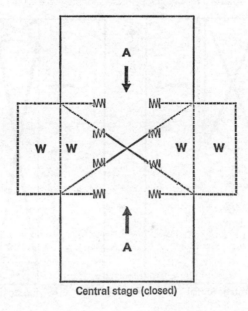

Central stage (closed)

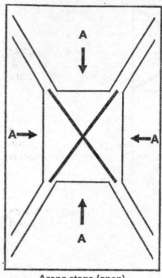

Arena stage (open)

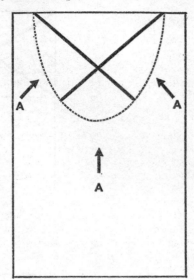

End stage (open)

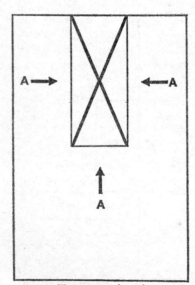

Thrust stage (open)

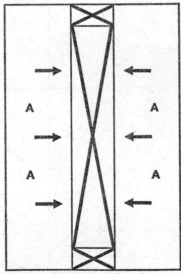

Avenue stage (open)

Open Stages

Arena

The shape of this stage can be square or circular and the seating capacity can be large or small. It is usual for arena theatres to aim for intimacy. The audience completely surrounds the acting area. Stage and auditorium share the same space.

End

Similar to the end stage (closed) except that with the open version, stage and auditorium share the same space. The stage is not contained within a separate box. The audience can partly surround the stage area and variations between this and the closed end stage are easily arranged.

Thrust

Here the audience sits on three sides. The main feature is that the stage area is raised. When it is level with the audience, it becomes a variation of the end stage. In either case stage and auditorium share the same space.

Avenue

This is a special version of the central stage. There is no separate box and the length/breadth relationship is altered. It is most effective with audiences no greater than 300 and with plays requiring two separate locations of contrasting or conflicting interests, with a central no-man's-land. Its critics say it causes serious 'tennis neck'.

Space

These stages are a reversal of all previous patterns. The stage and its action surround and/or interpenetrate the audience. This is accomplished by the use of 'stations', sometimes raised above floor level. Swivel chairs are desirable for the audience. Stage and audience share the same space, although special versions sometimes use surrounding inner stages.

The Total Theatre Stage

This comes in many forms. At its simplest it is represented by productions of plays like *Rose and Crown* by Priestley and *The Man with the Flower in his Mouth* by Pirandello where the layout and furnishing of the auditorium represent the public-house or restaurant where the action occurs. The audience are treated as normal clients and the play is presented naturalistically in the total setting.

In its more experimental form it involves an attack upon the audience from all directions, and in many spaces. It involves the use of all the senses, journeys from hall to hall, and from stage to stage and a constant bombardment from actors, sound sources, lights, films, slides, television and moving scenery. The audience may be invited to participate, to improvise, to spectate, to move freely from place to place or to be taken on a long trip. Presentations involve techniques drawn from the music-hall, ballet, the circus, strip-clubs, encounter groups and political rallies. It owes much to 'happenings' and while it achieves the impact it desires it does not always gain enthusiastic commitment from the

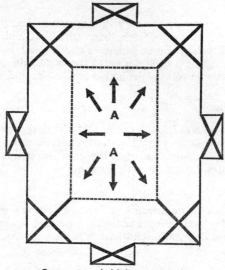

Space stage (with inner stages)

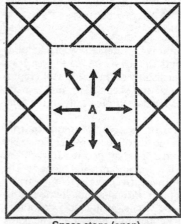

Space stage (open)

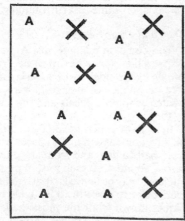

Space stage (scattered or integral)

participants. Its advocates would claim that this latter is part of their aim, since most groups practising this form are extreme in their social or political views. The following extract from *The Guardian* of 20 April 1972 gives some idea of the principles.

MEANWHILE, Londoners, prepare for the arrival of Liquid Theatre. As seen in New York, earning a pat on the back from Clive Barnes, no less, for being not really theatre but 'a marvellous way to use the Guggenheim Museum at night.'

Quite true, it isn't really theatre. The organisers here—some of the same people behind the Cinecenta—call it 'show–event–happening–performance–party.' Which means the audience will pay its money (under three of the Charing Cross arches), deposit a proportion of looser clothing in a plastic sack and be led on a 2½-hour trip through rooms. A gamut of sensations; led by the hand through music, touch, talk, taste (madly participating all the while) until one of the troupe of 42 young performers leads the way into a final happiness party room.

Less than tactfully, the liquid people are announcing that they want to recruit 42 'non-Equity' performers. The show has had union troubles in its six months in New York, and in Paris; the organisers expect some rumblings from Equity here too. But then, as everyone keeps saying, it's not really theatre.

Undoubtedly there is a move to free the theatre from some of its more crippling orthodoxies, but how long it will be before the move towards a psychedelic, kaleidoscopic total theatre gains a large following must remain a matter for conjecture.

Safety

Whatever form of staging is adopted there are certain regulations to be met. **Local requirements vary considerably and groups should take advice from their Fire Officer.** Many of the statutory regulations are out of date and bear little relevance to theatre arts, but they carry the backing of the law and must be respected. Groups should do everything in their power to ensure that outdated requirements are changed, although Local Authorities are slow to understand and slower to change.

Important matters for any group are:

1. Easy entrance and exit to and from all parts of the stage and auditorium —including the case of fire or other emergency.
2. Maximum precautions against accidental fire and in the use of inflammable materials.
3. Areas of special fire risk made separate.
4. Provision of emergency lighting.
5. Provision of ample means of fire extinction.
6. Provision of proper first aid facilities.

These precautions are all necessary and no group would object to them. Local requirements may be well in excess of any or all of them and the Local Authority should be contacted well in time. It is unfortunate if a Fire Officer feels it necessary to intervene on the first night and forbids the production to continue.

In Conclusion

Approach your hall, theatre or stage with a fresh, imaginative and open eye for each production. Assess the conditions of performance and make use of them as they exist—unless you have the opportunity to undertake minor conversions. Consider all possible—and apparently impossible—variations in the use of your space as it exists. Then transform it by the use of lighting, rostrums and ingenuity.

Finally, settle for what you can achieve within your budget and manpower. Wishing for something different is a waste of energy and merely causes depression and dissatisfaction.

CHAPTER NINETEEN

DESIGN

'The essential character of aesthetic modernism arising from the adoption of a modern technique is stylisation. He who says "stylisation"—says "simplification" and "selection". It is not unusual in the stage design of the past twenty years for a single element of décor (a construction, piece of furniture or a property) to represent a complete scene.

'If this element is of good proportion, in a suitable material, and if it is set on the stage in the most visible spot and the most obvious one from the point of view of the action, if its shape offers the largest number of surfaces for the reception of pre-arranged lighting, and according to requirements of changing light, then it has all the qualities of a complete set added to which is a greater power of suggestion and often a special fascination.'

Yves-Bonnat, Stage Design throughout the World since 1950

Design shows itself in the **marriage of form and content**—manner and matter. It covers everything that informs the senses. In theatre terms, it usually means the visual aspects of a production—set; costumes and properties; lighting and make-up. Ideally it should cover a much wider range and include advertisements in the press; posters; tickets; the theatre foyer, the audience area and the seating. Not all these are, however, under the control of every company. But every opportunity should be taken to use these factors to influence the audience's approach to the play.

The Visual Aspects of a Production

There are three main categories to the visual aspects of a production. They are given below in order of priority.

Functional

Includes those things physically required by the play, being essential to the action and necessary for the actors.

Supportive

Includes those things not essential to the action but making it more credible to the audience, facilitating the actors' performance and building up atmosphere. They are desirable for the production and in particular are helpful to the actors.

Decorative

Includes those things not essential to action or atmosphere but adding richness and lustre that will help explore and exploit the experience of the play. They are optional to the production and in particular are helpful to the audience.

The following examples are taken from Scene 11 of *Mother Courage and her Children* by Bertolt Brecht.

'(KATTRIN, *unperceived, has crept off to the wagon, has taken something out of it, put it under her apron, and has climbed up the ladder to the roof.*)

THE PEASANT WOMAN: Be mindful of the children in danger, especially the little ones, be mindful of the old folk who cannot move, and of all Christian souls, O Lord.

THE OLD PEASANT: And forgive us our trespasses as we forgive them that trespass against us. Amen.

(*Sitting on the roof,* KATTRIN *takes a drum from under her apron and starts to beat it.*)

THE PEASANT WOMAN: Heavens, what's she doing?

THE OLD PEASANT: She's out of her mind!

THE PEASANT WOMAN: Get her down, quick!

(*The old peasant runs to the ladder but* KATTRIN *pulls it up on the roof.*)

Functional. Kattrin must drum from a position where she is obvious and inaccessible. The absolute minimum required is Kattrin's isolation and the sound of drumming. This may be achieved as follows:

(*a*) Kattrin can be isolated by a rostrum and/or a pool of light. The rostrum can be as low as 6 in. permitting one step only.

(*b*) Kattrin can drum and be seen to do so.

(*c*) She can appear to do so by performing drumming actions and masking the place where the drum should be with her body.

(*d*) Kattrin can mime the drumming.

In each case the drumming could be created and/or amplified by off-stage effects—live or recorded. Loudspeakers could be placed:

(i) by the drum;

(ii) all over the acting area and/or;

(iii) the audience area.

Supportive. Kattrin uses the drum and ladder. She can be isolated as before by a rostrum block and/or lighting.

(*a*) Rostrum and step-ladder centrally placed. Neither more than 2 feet high —allowing four steps.

(*b*) Rostrum and ladder placed on the edge of the acting area rising to a height of 6 feet or more. (With a closed stage the rostrum could disappear into the wings.)

The variations in drumming mentioned above still obtain. The size of the drum is a matter of interpretation. The higher the rostrum the bigger the drum may need to be. Here are four approaches.

(i) Kattrin as a big girl with a small (toy?) drum. Used to stress incongruity—naïvety.

(ii) Kattrin as a big girl with a large drum. Used to make a solid dramatic statement.

(iii) Kattrin as a small child with a small (toy?) drum. Used to emphasize pathos.

(iv) Kattrin as a small child with a large (huge regimental?) drum. Used to emphasize the symbolism of the situation—Kattrin as a pawn in the game.

Decorative. Kattrin uses the drum, the ladder and roof. The set becomes more architectural.

(a) Building and roof can be built so that Kattrin is as exposed and removed as Ibsen's 'Master Builder' himself perched high on a fully built roof or scaffolding.

(b) Her climb can be that of an agile monkey or exhausted child—using ladder and/or scaffolding.

(c) Natural elements can be brought into play. Wind and rain can threaten her position.

The Designer

A group may have the services of a number of designers and they may be responsible, individually, for set, costumes, props, etc. They must obviously co-operate closely, not only with the director and stage manager but also with one another—and especially the lighting team.

At the other extreme the group may have no designer and the director will have to undertake the work himself. He will need to be: painter, sculptor, architect, draughtsman, engineer, technician and much more.

The following notes outline the approach taken by most designers. At each stage three questions should be asked about all the elements of design:

What do the actors physically need?
What will help them?
What will help the audience?

1. Read the play many times.
2. Discussions with director and author if possible.
3. Read, think and sketch.
4. Discussions with director, stage manager, crew and cast.
5. Read, think, sketch and model.
6. More discussions.
7. Prepare, execute and light in co-operation with director, stage manager, crew and cast.

Many designers always work to scale from earliest sketches to working drawings. There is certainly a need at some time during the early planning period, to provide ground plans, drawings and models made accurately to scale. All working drawings must, of course, be exact in their measurements.

The Set

Most plays can be presented merely with 'bare boards and a passion'. Most benefit from having a special setting created for them. This setting, designed and dressed, is the platform from which the actors work. It is more than a decorative background in front of which they move and speak. It is their launching pad, and the nature of their vehicle—the play—will influence its design. It is also a focus for the audience, affording a dynamic link throughout the performance. There are many considerations affecting the designer's decisions.

The Stage

The stage can be **open or closed.** If it is open, all design elements must be considered from back, front and both sides. If it is a closed box, only some aspects will be seen by the audience.

The Settings

The settings can be as follows:

(a) **Two-dimensional solid.** Made up of drapes and curtains; flats—with or without a ceiling to create a box; a cyclorama.*

(b) **Three-dimensional solid.** Made up of rostrum blocks and/or furniture with or without units from (a) above. These affect the vertical relationships possible for the actors.

(c) **Projected.** Projected light images—representational or abstract—can be used by themselves or in conjunction with (a) and (b) above. For further detail see the later section on lighting.

The settings can also be:

(d) **permanent.**

(i) A neutral unit set. The whole of the set is designed to accept all the scenes. It generally consists of classical/architectural shapes—different levels, flights of steps and pillars.

(ii) A composite set. This accepts all scenes in separate areas and is generally representational.

(e) **semi-permanent.** Similar to (d) above but with some units only, to each scene.

(f) **a number of different sets.** Here settings are created specifically for each scene and have few or no units in common.

Alternatively, the settings can be:

(g) **representational.** No design can be wholly naturalistic. Flowers; forests; blood and corpses; clocks—all pose problems. Some are quite insoluble naturalistically. The aim of the representational method is to create the appearance of external actualities.

(h) **abstract** (symbolic/impressionist/formalist). The essence of this method is that one object shall suggest more objects or other objects. For example a throne suggests a castle; an altar a cathedral; one army pennant, many pennants. Chairs become a taxi; tables become an arc; a bed creates a bedroom. The aim is to fire the imagination of the audience and suggest the presence of external reality.

The Materials

The materials can be as follows:

(a) Standard painted canvas and wood flats with or without stage drapes.

(b) Drawn from the following list. A few examples only are given. They may be used by themselves or in conjunction with (a) above.

Netting	Glass and mirrors
Rope	Cork, leather, hessian, straw
Hosepipe	Foam rubber
Fish or orange boxes	Wire-netting
Egg cartons or other packagings	Composition board and blocks
Bottles and bottle-tops	Iron
Bronze	Alloy
Tin or copper foil	Plastic tubes and sections.

*A permanent backing to the stage, usually a plastered wall.

Floor coverings are particularly important. Not only do they affect the visual aspects of the production they also affect the acoustic qualities. This is important in terms of voice and speech as well as any use made of footsteps, marching and other noises. If floor coverings of any kind are used they must be safely secured.

The Lighting

Lighting will play an important and integral part in the production and should be considered at every stage of the design. In particular, thought should be given in the early stages to the exposure of light (and sound) sources. It is too late when the set is under construction. The subject of lighting is considered separately in a later part of this chapter.

Functions

The set has a number of specific jobs to do. It must:

1. provide a springboard for the cast to move and act. It must be functional, hardwearing and safe;
2. inspire the imagination of the cast;
3. reflect the theme, style and rhythm of the play;
4. lend atmosphere.

It therefore plays a significant part in the total experience of actors and audience alike. It is not an optional-top-dressing-extra.

The set can economically and attractively create time, place and mood. It can also be neutral—allowing, for example, brightly coloured costumes to create the desired effect.

In considering the design, the effect of television and cinema need to be borne in mind. Audiences are now accustomed to quick changes in drama—cuts, quick and slow fades, dissolves—and long intervals, caused by difficult scene changes, are not popular. If the aesthetic and practical aspects of design are always considered together there will be little danger of scene shifting causing such a problem.

Practical considerations of **space, budget and manpower** should be considered at all times, particularly in the early stages of the design. They are factors not to be overlooked since they will inexorably effect the designer's final choice of methods and materials.

For those who may be interested in the practical details of scenery construction, the bibliography lists useful titles. They include standard, well tried methods. Remember at all times to keep an open mind and an open eye for **chance materials**. Everything that appears on stage will mean something to someone in the audience. Let it be there not by accident but by design.

Stage Management

The director may devise artistic possibilities and opportunities but he will get nowhere without a stage manager who can efficiently create the practical conditions for their realization. The following notes cover the main features of stage management.

1. Keep everyone posted of the overall plan, its progress and details of any changes.

2. Feed in the elements of setting, costume, props and lighting as rehearsals progress. Discuss the order and timing with the director so that each element can be best used to help the production grow. All the elements will interact and stimulate the actors.

For example, the sudden appearance of a red sweater may suggest the overall lighting for a scene or the use of a special spot. A particular lighting combination may help an actor to feel himself more deeply into the dramatic situation. This, in turn, may take him on to a rostrum block whereas before he had been undecided. Encourage this interaction and don't be afraid of change.

3. Make accurate notes, sketches, plots and plans of all relevant details—particularly those which cannot be changed.

4. Make sure all the backstage staff know their responsibilities, budgets and deadlines. Give them full responsibility and authority within their own areas.

5. Ensure early preparation is made for every rehearsal. Everything that is to be used should be ready and to hand.

6. Any necessary substitutes used during rehearsals should be of the right size and shape. What an actor will do with a kitchen chair he will not do with a stool or couch.

7. The stage manager is responsible for the safety of everybody and everything. Make sure everything is safe from causing or suffering damage.

Dress Rehearsals and Performances

The stage manager is now in complete charge. His responsibility covers full liaison with all dressing rooms, front of house staff, lighting—including house lights—staff, stage crew and cast. He should:

1. treat all dress rehearsals as performances;
2. check and recheck with all heads of departments;
3. have everything ready well in advance. The acting area should be ready and cleared at least 30 minutes before the performance begins;
4. be calm and confident, don't fuss;
5. keep an eye open for safety at all times.

EXERCISES (The Set)

1. Look at stage designs and reproductions of stage designs (in particular those of Gordon Craig and Sean Kenny). Look at window displays in big stores. Paint, sketch, choose photographs and assemble collage material. Do these with regard to the extracts in Chapters Eight and Ten to Thirteen and with a particular regard for (*a*) time, (*b*) place, (*c*) mood.

2. Design a permanent or semi-permanent set to accommodate three of the extracts in Chapters Eight and Ten to Thirteen.

3. (*a*) Experiment with models, using different materials, colours and textures.

   (*b*) Practise photographing the models. It will be helpful if you have a camera with interchangeable lenses.

4. Arrange the furniture and objects in your room so that they speak in different ways:

(*a*) Reflecting different moods and emotions.

(*b*) Relating and interrelating with one another (or *appearing* to do so).

5. (*a*) Make models using modular units—square, rectangular, triangular, circular.

1. Use only one kind.
2. Use them in different combinations. For example: squares and rectangles; triangles and circles.
3. Use them all together.

(*b*) Whenever possible experiment with full-size rostrum blocks based on the same modular principle.

(*c*) Use a camera as in 3 above.

6. Create basic sets for acting and improvisatory exercises with your group.

7. Work with a stage manager and crew as much as you can. Work with a designer whose style you admire.

8. Keep a notebook at all times for the following: interesting shapes, colours and textures. Ideas for time, place and mood.

Costume and Properties
Functions

Within the overall design, costumes and properties should achieve the following:

1. **Make their own statement** relevant to the scene and the character. In a scene where the overall colour is grey the introduction of a character dressed in bright red will make a dramatic impact. A similar impact will be achieved by a character dressed in black coming into a scene of pale pinks and blues.

2. **Build up the image of the actor**—his own as well as other peoples. The actor and his clothes should be one. He must feel comfortable and good.

3. **Permit and stimulate action**—functional and dramatic. They should allow and encourage appropriate movement patterns. An actress cannot make a sweeping exit wearing a tightly hobbled skirt.

There is a two-way movement between actor and clothes. The character created by the actor will suggest the clothes to be worn. The clothes themselves will suggest variations within that character and dramatic possibilities. Many actors find one particular part of their clothing—hat, boots, gloves, jacket—is a special trigger for their imagination and/or absorption.

Costumes

Costumes can be bought, hired or made. Hiring or buying can be expensive. In either case it is best to use nationally established suppliers and to take great care over the exact specifications they will require—measurements, colour, style, period and/or character.

Making the clothes for each production can be inexpensive, exciting and an excellent way of building up a wardrobe. This involves three major stages:

Aesthetic and dramatic design.
Practical design and pattern-making.
Making-up.

It is not easy to find one person who can undertake all these stages. A group having such a person is indeed lucky. In any case there must be the closest co-operation between designer, director, head of wardrobe and individual actor. The bibliography at Appendix One contains useful books for anyone interested in the practical details of making clothes for the stage.

At all times during the making or selection of costumes, lighting should be considered. Materials will appear to change their colour and texture under different lights (see page 307).

The impressions created by individual costumes vary considerably:

(*a*) when they are still;

(*b*) when moving.

When trying out a costume, be sure the wearer goes through the full range of movements needed. It is wise to allow an additional 10% increase in that range of movement.

A designer of stage clothes will find it helpful to consult current issues of magazines like *Vogue*. They can be an excellent guide to modern trends. Their overall feel and flair can be a helpful influence upon a designer's general approach. Whether the stage clothes are contemporary or historical their impact will depend upon the following:

Line and outline

These will suggest:

(*a*) **period and function**—period costumes being best recognized by their profiles or silhouettes.

(*b*) **character**—vertical lines adding height and horizontal lines adding width.

Colour

Colour influences an audience's response to individual characters; their relationships and the scene or play as a whole. (The subject of colour is treated more fully in the lighting section.) Here it is appropriate to give a reminder that reds and yellows suggest warmth, while blues and greens suggest cold. They have equally strongly associated emotions.

Historically it is important not to use colours obtained from mineral or synthetic dyes in a production set in a period when only vegetable dyes were available.

No definitive attitude to historical costume should be taken. The design emphasis will change from decade to decade as historical fashion is filtered through the eyes of current trends. Pictures of costumes, for the same play set in the same period, over the past two centuries will demonstrate this. The bibliography contains useful titles of specialist books on period costumes.

Material

This will affect the way the clothes hang. Although lighting can affect appearances—making a cheap material look expensive—it cannot disguise discrepancies in weight. The sweep of a heavy cloak cannot be achieved by light taffeta.

Properties

The range is vast—from double beds to drawing pins. Properties can be divided as follows:

1. (*a*) **Practical.** Those actually handled, used and required to work.
   (*b*) **Non-practical.** Additional dressings for the scene.
   For example; a hat stand in a boarding house may need to contain a number of umbrellas. If not used in the action they need not open. If, however, a character actually uses one it must operate easily and look right—open and closed.
2. (*a*) **Stage props.** These stay on stage throughout the action in any scene and may be used by all the characters. For example: a telephone, a teapot or a chair.
   (*b*) **Personal or hand props.** These are used by specific characters only. Some actors prefer to look after their own, but property masters and stage managers tend to distrust this.

Just like the set and costumes, the properties need to be functional, hard-wearing and safe. They can be hired, borrowed, bought from jumble sales or secondhand shops or made. The following list gives some idea of the variety of properties frequently needed:

Food and drink, both hot and cold.
Flowers.
Cigarettes and matches.
Tables and chairs.
Weapons, ornaments, clocks, telephones.
Money, magazines, documents.
Logs, coal and fireplaces.
Hall stands, tallboys and sideboards.
Picture rails, pictures and mirrors.

Picture frames and mirrors must be placed with care so that no reflections—particularly of lights—distract the audience. (It is often best to remove the glass from picture frames.)
The bibliography at Appendix One suggests books for those specially interested in making hand properties.
   For costumes and properties alike the following are important:

Decide what you want and why.
Try to visualise it.
Try to find it.
Make it.

EXERCISES (Costume and Properties)

Costume
   1. Look at historical portraits and fashion magazines. Look at displays in fashion shops and big stores. Sketch, and paint or collect photographs of clothing that suggests period, mood or character.
   2. Choose samples of materials for their special qualities—colour and texture. Build up a wardrobe of samples.
   3. Design a finished costume from an isolated detail that has attracted you. For example: a shoe, a hat, a tie or a bolero.
   4. Design a finished costume for a particular character or to illustrate a specific personality trait, mood or period.

5. Wear unusual clothes from second hand shops.
6. Wear ordinary clothes in an unusual way.
7. Use lengths of cloth (say 36 in. — 48 in. by 6 ft. — 9 ft.) to drape on yourself, a friend or a tailor's dummy.
8. Create or provide unusual costume details to stimulate group acting and improvisatory exercises.
9. Bring a collection of unusual clothes to the group. Discuss individual feelings and reactions. Prepare your own list beforehand describing the impact you think each garment will have.

Properties

1. Repeat the previous exercises substituting properties for costume where possible or appropriate.
2. Paint, sketch and make representational models—from cornflake packets, egg cartons etc.—of properties used in one of the extracts of Chapters Eight and Ten to Thirteen. Make more than one and vary the design to reflect different moods and emotions.

  (a) Keep the representational element accurate and recognizable.
  (b) Extend individual details (for example the handle of a teacup; the ear-piece of a telephone; the lock on a cabinet) so they make a special statement.
  (c) Vary the design of one item (a kitchen chair) so that it represents something different (a machine gun; the prow of a ship; a guitar; a taxi cab.)

3. Collect materials with unusual colours and textures from the home, the street, the countryside and the beach. Build them into a permanent collection for reference.
4. Keep a notebook with full details of any unusual materials you discover and their possible uses.

Make-up

A Personal Matter

Some groups still use a 'make-up expert' to 'do' their faces. At best this can only be superficial or irrelevant and at worst can be disastrous. It is a personal matter—personal to the actor, to the character he is playing and the thoughts and feelings he has about that character. The actor is the best person to do it. Nothing can replace personal experiment and practice.

Make-up should be approached in consultation with a mirror, the director and the designer since costume, set, properties and, in particular, lighting, will all affect the appearance of the make-up. Light sources and their reflections play a large part.

Straight

A straight make-up will compensate for:

  (a) The colour and intensity of the light. Bright light tends to wash out features, leaving a blank face.
  (b) The distance of the audience. An average approach should be taken. What might look excellent from the back row would probably look overdone and dreadful from the front.
  (c) The make-up worn by the rest of the cast.

Women may wear straight day, street or evening make-up—or none at all. They need to consider how much they should *appear* to be using. If this is only a little, their normal make-up may be satisfactory. Generally speaking, men should not appear to be wearing make-up. With the right colour and texture to their skin, they may need none at all.

Character

A character make-up will apparently change the features. This is done to help actor and audience improve the credibility of the character's features. The shape, colour and texture of the face, and other parts of the body, can be apparently transformed—but only within reasonable limits. A very fat face can be made to appear less fat. Ludicrous results would be obtained, however, by trying to make it thin.

The easiest form of make-up for the stage is the stick of greasepaint. Some actors prefer to use a cake or tube. The colours are identified by number or name.

A Basic Approach

The following notes outline a possible approach to the art of stage make-up.
1. Study faces—in natural and artificial light.
2. Study your own face—in pocket mirrors; full length; shaving and distorting. Practise over a long period. Take time and concentrate.
3. Decide on any changes in your own face. Experiment and practise.
(*a*) By yourself.
(*b*) With a friend.
(*c*) In class or rehearsal.
(*d*) Ask for the director's and designer's comments.
4. Reject and select.
5. Consolidate.
Begin to use make-up in rehearsals as soon as possible. Concentrate on those aspects that will transform your features.

Foundation

This is the main remedy for the bleaching effect of strong artificial light. It is usually a combination of greasepaint colours 5 and 9.

Light and shade

These give the features their basic shape and suggest character. They are created by white, grey, black, light and dark brown. (These are the general colours; others can, of course, be used when appropriate). Light areas stand out and dark areas retreat.

Colour

This suggests race, age, and character. It does so by changing the colour and, apparently, the texture of the skin.

Lining

This adds subtle finishing touches. It gives a bonus to the actor himself, the rest of the cast and those close enough in the audience to be able to appreciate it. In general, horizontal lines suggest placidity or neutrality; upward curving lines vitality and downward curving lines depression.

Eyes and mouth

These are the liveliest and most expressive parts of the face. Particular care should be taken when making them up.

Hair

Colour and dressing of the hair can be changed by the use of dye, powder, rinses, hairpieces and wigs. They are all easily obtainable and can achieve startling changes.

Application

The main steps in applying make-up are as follows:

1. Preparation—cleansing the skin.
2. Foundation—basic colouring for race, age and character.
3. Light and shade.
4. Further colouring—character.
5. Lining—details to eyes, wrinkles, lips, ears. etc.
6. Powdering—to set the greasepaint. It should be pressed in firmly but gently and any surplus removed with a soft brush. Some actors like to dab the face gently with a flannel soaked in cold water—or even immerse the face. Further powdering is not essential after the cold water treatment.
7. Hair, eyebrows, eyelids—attention to final details.

A full range of make-up comprises:
    Standard sticks.
    Liners.
    Liquid body make-up.
    Blending powder.
    Hair powder.
    Crepe hair.
    False eyelashes.
    Eyebrow pencils.
    Fixative (for crepe hair) and remover.
    Modelling putty.
    Tooth enamel.
    Blood.
    Astringent.

The make-up charts which follow show some basic make-ups. The charts are provided by Leichner—a firm that supplies comprehensive make-up and that also runs an excellent advisory service for both amateur and professional.

EXERCISES (Make-up)

Visit portrait galleries—look at paintings and sculptures. Collect photographs of interesting faces. Look in photographer's windows. Photograph your friend for close-ups of faces; a Polaroid camera is particularly useful for this. Project slides—holiday snaps are satisfactory but faces that fill the frame are better—to see the features magnified. Carefully inspect masks in museums and art galleries as well as those of stage suppliers. Design and create your own.

Young Woman
Leichner Make-up Chart

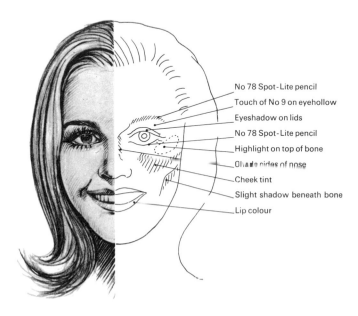

No 78 Spot-Lite pencil

Touch of No 9 on eyehollow

Eyeshadow on lids

No 78 Spot-Lite pencil

Highlight on top of bone

Shade sides of nose

Cheek tint

Slight shadow beneath bone

Lip colour

This is a "straight" make-up. Foundation, highlights and shadows are used to accentuate your own features.

FOUNDATION   Colouring must be selected according to type but No. 2 is a pale "Dresden China" tint, No. 2½ a warm pink, No. 52 Peach Dark is a medium peach shade and No. 53 Peach Special is a very effective deep peach.

SHADING   No. 16 mixed with No. 25 Crimson Lake.

HIGHLIGHTS   No. 5 is generally most effective, but No. 2 or No. 20 (White) may be necessary under strong lighting.

CHEEK COLOURING   No. 9 on cheekbones fading into Carmine 1 or Carmine 2 on fullness of cheeks.

LIPS   Carmine 1, Carmine 2, or Carmine 3, sometimes with a little No. 20 (White) or No. 9 (Brick Red).

EYE MAKE-UP   Add touch of No. 9 to eyehollow (between upper eyelid and eyebrow). Use the Blue, Green, Mauve, Grey or Brown Eyeshadows on upper eyelids. Line eyes along line of lashes with No. 78 Spot-Lite Pencil and use the same pencil on eyebrows. Apply Mascara to lashes or use False Eyelashes.

POWDER   Rose Blending Powder.

Apply Liquid Make-up to neck, hands and limbs.

Young Man
Leichner Make-up Chart
No. 2

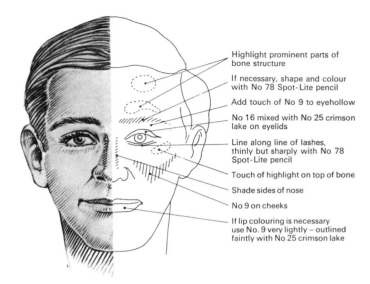

Highlight prominent parts of bone structure

If necessary, shape and colour with No 78 Spot-Lite pencil

Add touch of No 9 to eyehollow

No 16 mixed with No 25 crimson lake on eyelids

Line along line of lashes, thinly but sharply with No 78 Spot-Lite pencil

Touch of highlight on top of bone

Shade sides of nose

No 9 on cheeks

If lip colouring is necessary use No. 9 very lightly – outlined faintly with No 25 crimson lake

This is a "straight" make-up. Foundation, highlights and shadows are used to accentuate your own features.

FOUNDATION   Colouring must be selected according to type but as examples No. 3½ gives a light tan, which can be deepened by adding No. 8 or No. 9, while No. 5 mixed with No. 9 gives a slightly yellow tan. No. 4 is a fairly deep reddish tan.

SHADING   No. 16 Deep Brown mixed with No. 25 Crimson Lake.

HIGHLIGHTS   No. 5 is most effective although No. 20 (White) may be necessary under strong lighting.

CHEEK COLOURING   No. 9 gives the most natural effect.

LIPS   When lip colouring is necessary apply No. 9 lightly and outline with the faintest trace of No. 25 Crimson Lake.

EYE MAKE-UP   Add touch of No. 9 to eyehollow (between upper eyelid and eyebrow). Use No. 16 with No. 25 Crimson Lake on eyelids. Line eyes along line of lashes with No. 78 Spot-Lite Pencil and when necessary use same pencil on eyebrows.

POWDER   Rose or Brownish Blending Powder.

Apply Liquid Make-up to neck, arms and hands.

Middle-aged Woman   No. 3
Leichner Make-up Chart

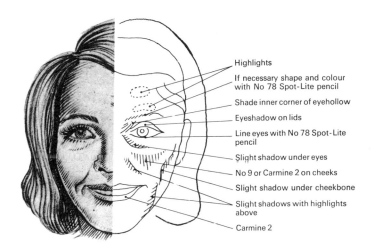

Highlights

If necessary shape and colour
with No 78 Spot-Lite pencil

Shade inner corner of eyehollow

Eyeshadow on lids

Line eyes with No 78 Spot-Lite
pencil

Slight shadow under eyes

No 9 or Carmine 2 on cheeks

Slight shadow under cheekbone

Slight shadows with highlights
above

Carmine 2

This is a mature face, still with some youthful features. Ageing should not be overdone. Facial colouring remains pleasantly warm and alive.

FOUNDATION   Colouring must be selected according to type but as examples, No. 52 Peach Dark and No. 53 Peach Special are sophisticated shades, No. 2½ gives a medium pink complexion, while No. 6 is slightly sallow with a pink undertone.

SHADING   No. 16 Deep Brown mixed with No. 25 Crimson Lake creating subtle pools of shadow accentuated with highlights.

HIGHLIGHTS   No. 5 is most effective although No. 2 or No. 20 (White) may be necessary under strong lighting.

CHEEK COLOURING   No. 9, Carmine 1 or Carmine 2.

LIPS   Carmine 2 or Carmine 3.

EYE MAKE-UP   The Blue, Green, and Mauve Eyeshadows are used on the eyelids when the characters are sophisticated, otherwise the Brown or Grey eyeshadows. Line eyes along line of lashes with No. 78 Spot-Lite Pencil, and apply Mascara to eyelashes, or use False Eyelashes.

POWDER   Rose or Neutral Blending Powder.

Apply Liquid Make-up to neck, arms and hands.

Middle-aged Man   No. 4
Leichner Make-up Chart

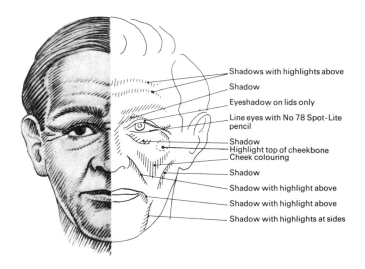

Shadows with highlights above
Shadow
Eyeshadow on lids only
Line eyes with No 78 Spot-Lite pencil
Shadow
Highlight top of cheekbone
Cheek colouring
Shadow
Shadow with highlight above
Shadow with highlight above
Shadow with highlights at sides

This is a mature face, firm, still with some youthful features. Facial colouring remains pleasantly warm and alive.

FOUNDATION   Colouring must be selected according to type but, as examples, No. 3½ with a little No. 9 gives a light normal skin tone, No. 4½ gives a rugged, outdoor tint, while No. 6 with a little No. 8 or No. 9 gives a healthy warm tint, with a slightly sallow undertone.

SHADING   No. 16 Deep Brown mixed with No. 25 Crimson Lake, creating pools of shadow accentuated with highlights, not hard lines.

HIGHLIGHTS   No. 5 is most effective although No. 20 (White) may be necessary under strong lighting.

CHEEK COLOURING   No. 25 Crimson Lake, sometimes also mixed with No. 9.

LIPS   When lip colouring is necessary, apply No. 9 lightly and outline with the faintest trace of No. 25 Crimson Lake.

EYE MAKE-UP   Use shading material at inner corner of eyehollow, No. 16 mixed with No. 25 Crimson Lake, or No. 32 Dark Grey on eyelids. Line eyes along line of lashes with No. 78 Spot-Lite Pencil and if necessary use same pencil on eyebrows.

HAIR   Slightly grey – use White or Light Grey Hair Powder, streak hair at temples with No. 20 (White) Greasepaint or the Eau de Lys Liquid Make-up White.

POWDER   Rose or Brownish Blending Powder.

Elderly Woman
Leichner Make-up Chart

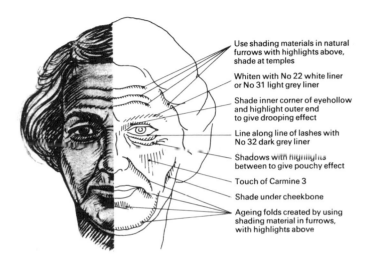

Use shading materials in natural furrows with highlights above, shade at temples

Whiten with No 22 white liner or No 31 light grey liner

Shade inner corner of eyehollow and highlight outer end to give drooping effect

Line along line of lashes with No 32 dark grey liner

Shadows with highlights between to give pouchy effect

Touch of Carmine 3

Shade under cheekbone

Ageing folds created by using shading material in furrows, with highlights above

In the elderly, face muscles and tissues sag, facial hollows deepen and folds of skin become pronounced. The skin tone is often sallow, frequently very delicate.

FOUNDATION   No. 6 gives a sallow appearance with a slight pink undertone. Add No. 2½ for a healthier pink tone, or No. 9 for an outdoor appearance. No. 5 with the addition of No. 59 Chrome Yellow will give a transparent, parchment effect.

SHADING   No. 16 Deep Brown mixed with No. 25 Crimson Lake, or No. 25 Crimson Lake mixed with No. 31 Light Grey.

HIGHLIGHTS   No. 5 or No. 20 (White).

CHEEK COLOURING   Carmine 2 or Carmine 3 lightly applied.

LIPS   Carmine 3 lightly applied.

EYE MAKE-UP   Mauve shades of eyeshadow are most effective, or No. 16 mixed with No. 25 Crimson Lake. Line along line of lashes with No. 32 Dark Grey, or with No. 25 Crimson Lake to give tired effect. Use No. 20 (White) or No. 31 Light Grey on eyebrows.

HAIR   Use White or Light Grey Hair Powder. Streak with No. 20 (White) Greasepaint or Eau de Lys Liquid Make-up White.

Arms, neck and hands must be made up in character.

Elderly Man   No. 6
Leichner Make-up Chart

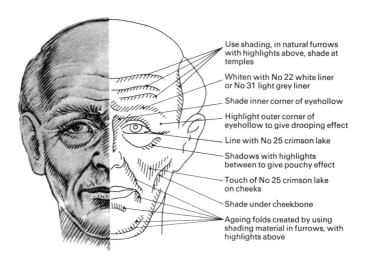

Use shading, in natural furrows with highlights above, shade at temples

Whiten with No 22 white liner or No 31 light grey liner

Shade inner corner of eyehollow

Highlight outer corner of eyehollow to give drooping effect

Line with No 25 crimson lake

Shadows with highlights between to give pouchy effect

Touch of No 25 crimson lake on cheeks

Shade under cheekbone

Ageing folds created by using shading material in furrows, with highlights above

In the elderly, face wrinkles and facial hollows deepen, muscles sag and the skin tone often looks sallow and blotchy.

FOUNDATION   No. 6 is a sallow pink, useful for the ageing skin tone. Add No. 8 or No. 9 for a healthy ageing skin colour or add No. 25 Crimson Lake for a purplish complexion. No. 6½ is a sallow, olive tint.

SHADING   No. 25 Crimson Lake, mixed with No. 16 Deep Brown or No. 32 Dark Grey.

HIGHLIGHTS   No. 5 or sometimes No. 20 (White) when the lighting is very strong.

CHEEK COLOURING   No. 25 Crimson Lake.

LIPS   Light application of No. 25 Crimson Lake.

EYE MAKE-UP   Use deep shadow at inner corner of eyehollow and highlight at outer end of eyehollow to create drooping effect, No. 25 Crimson Lake mixed with No. 16 Deep Brown or No. 32 Dark Grey on eyelids, and line along line of lashes with No. 32 Dark Grey or No. 25 Crimson Lake to give a bloodshot effect. Use No. 20 (White) or No. 31 Light Grey on eyebrows.

HAIR   Use White or Light Grey Hair Powder. Streak with No. 20 White Greasepaint or Eau de Lys Liquid Make-up White.

POWDER   Rose or Neutral Blending Powder.

Remember to make-up hands and neck in character.

Haggard Man
Leichner Make-up Chart

No. 7

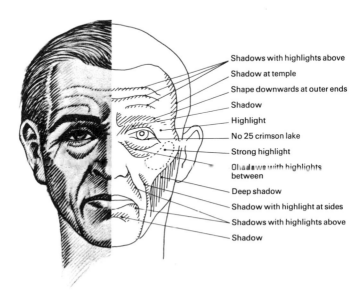

Shadows with highlights above

Shadow at temple

Shape downwards at outer ends

Shadow

Highlight

No 25 crimson lake

Strong highlight

Shadows with highlights between

Deep shadow

Shadow with highlight at sides

Shadows with highlights above

Shadow

This is essentially an exercise in thinning down the face by using very broad highlights on the bone structure, deep shadows, sunken eyes and sagging facial muscles.

FOUNDATION No. 6, or No. 6½ mixed with No. 5 will give a pale, sallow effect.

SHADING No. 25 Crimson Lake mixed with either No. 16 or No. 32 Dark Grey.

HIGHLIGHTS No. 5, or when the lighting is very strong use No. 20 (White).

LIPS Light application of No. 25 Crimson Lake over foundation tint which is carried across the lips.

EYE MAKE-UP Deep shadow at inner corner of eyehollow, highlight at outer end to give drooping effect. Deep shadows beneath eyes – outline along line of lashes with No. 25 Crimson Lake. Shape eyebrows downwards at outer end.

POWDER Rose or Neutral Blending Powder.

Hands, neck and limbs must be made up in character.

Stage Butler

Leichner Make-up Chart

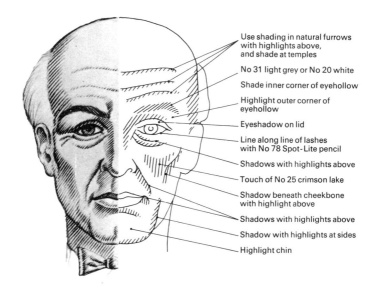

Use shading in natural furrows
with highlights above,
and shade at temples

No 31 light grey or No 20 white

Shade inner corner of eyehollow

Highlight outer corner of
eyehollow

Eyeshadow on lid

Line along line of lashes
with No 78 Spot-Lite pencil

Shadows with highlights above

Touch of No 25 crimson lake

Shadow beneath cheekbone
with highlight above

Shadows with highlights above

Shadow with highlights at sides

Highlight chin

Elderly, benign, impersonal. A strongly-marked face with rather pale, firm, clean looking complexion. Sometimes grey side-whiskers.

FOUNDATION   No. 6 with a little No. 9, or Lit. K with a touch of No. 9 for a more yellowish skin tone.

SHADING   No. 16 Deep Brown mixed with No. 25 Crimson Lake, creating gently curving shadows with highlights to accentuate.

HIGHLIGHTS   No. 5 or No. 20 (White) when the lighting is strong.

CHEEK COLOURING   A touch of No. 25 Crimson Lake.

LIPS   Light application of No. 25 Crimson Lake.

EYE MAKE-UP   Apply a shadow at inner corner of eyehollow and a highlight at outer corner. No. 16 Deep Brown or No. 32 Dark Grey on eyelids and line along the line of the lashes with a No. 78 Spot-Lite Pencil. Use No. 20 (White) on eyebrows.

HAIR   Use White or Light Grey Hair Powder. Streak with No. 20 (White) Greasepaint or Eau de Lys Liquid Make-up White.

POWDER   Rose or Neutral Blending Powder.
   Remember to make-up hands and neck in character.

Italian
Leichner Make-up Chart
No. 10

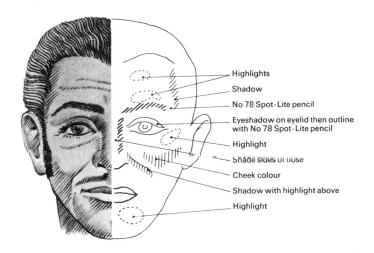

Highlights
Shadow
No 78 Spot-Lite pencil
Eyeshadow on eyelid then outline
with No 78 Spot-Lite pencil
Highlight
Shade sides of nose
Cheek colour
Shadow with highlight above
Highlight

A jovial Mediterranean type, fairly narrow forehead, big jaw, and a straight nose, high bridged, olive sun-tanned complexion.

FOUNDATION   No. 6½ with No. 8, or No. 6 with No. 8 is slightly paler. No. 4½ with No. 8 gives a darker tan.

SHADING   No. 16 with No. 25 Crimson Lake.

HIGHLIGHTS   No. 5 or No. 59 Chrome Yellow.

CHEEK COLOURING   No. 8 or No. 9. Older characters would use No. 25 Crimson Lake.

LIPS   No. 9 lightly applied, then add a touch of No. 25 Crimson Lake.

EYE MAKE-UP   No. 16, or No. 16 mixed with No. 25 Crimson Lake on eyelids, outline eyes with No. 78 Spot-Lite Pencil and use same pencil on eyebrows.

POWDER   Brownish Blending Powder.

Use Liquid Make-up on neck, limbs and body.

Arab

Leichner Make-up Chart

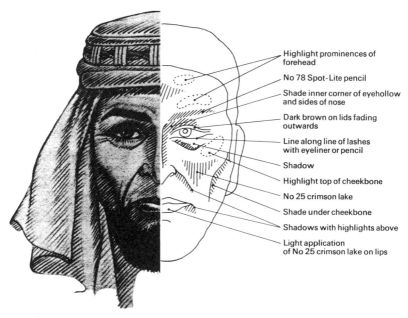

Highlight prominences of forehead

No 78 Spot-Lite pencil

Shade inner corner of eyehollow and sides of nose

Dark brown on lids fading outwards

Line along line of lashes with eyeliner or pencil

Shadow

Highlight top of cheekbone

No 25 crimson lake

Shade under cheekbone

Shadows with highlights above

Light application of No 25 crimson lake on lips

Features firm and clear cut, long face with high cheekbones, aquiline convex nose, black hair, eyes dark brown or hazel.

FOUNDATION   No. 6½ mixed with No. 8, or No. 4½ with No. 8. Add No. 7 if required to be darker. No. 7 mixed with No. 8 gives a very dark effect.

SHADING   No. 16 mixed with No. 25 Crimson Lake.

HIGHLIGHTS   No. 5.

CHEEK COLOURING   No. 8 or No. 25 Crimson Lake.

LIPS   Fairly thick. Use No. 8 lightly then outline with No. 25 Crimson Lake fading this into the No. 8 away from edges of lips. No. 9 is sometimes used in place of the No. 8.

EYE MAKE-UP   Use No. 16 on eyelids and line along line of lashes with the No. 78 Spot-Lite Pencil Black, using the same pencil on the eyebrows.

POWDER   Brownish Blending Powder.

Liquid Make-up should be used on hands and arms.

Clown   No. 12
Leichner Make-up Chart

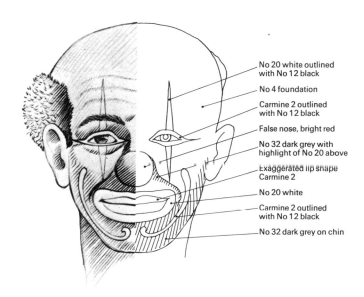

No 20 white outlined with No 12 black

No 4 foundation

Carmine 2 outlined with No 12 black

False nose, bright red

No 32 dark grey with highlight of No 20 above

Exaggerated lip shape Carmine 2

No 20 white

Carmine 2 outlined with No 12 black

No 32 dark grey on chin

Clown Make-up is completely individual (traditionally none is identical) but there are broad categories such as the "White-Faced" clown and the "Tramp" type. The illustration is a combination of both.

FOUNDATION   For the White Clown No. 20 (White) over which the eccentric, decorative markings of brilliant colours such as Red, Blue, Green and Black are painted as required. For the tramp type, No. 3½ and No. 4 are often used.

POWDER   Rose or Neutral Blending Power.

Red Indian
Leichner Make-up Chart
No. 13

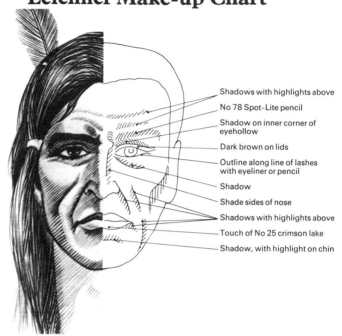

Shadows with highlights above

No 78 Spot-Lite pencil

Shadow on inner corner of eyehollow

Dark brown on lids

Outline along line of lashes with eyeliner or pencil

Shadow

Shade sides of nose

Shadows with highlights above

Touch of No 25 crimson lake

Shadow, with highlight on chin

A basic Mongoloid appearance is discernible. They have a yellow-brown skin, though sometimes reddish, hair is black, coarse and straight, prominent cheekbones. Noses generally hooked.

FOUNDATION   No. 8. No. 4 with No. 8. No. 4½ with No. 8 or No. 9. No. 6½ with No. 8.
SHADING   No. 16 with No. 25 Crimson Lake.
HIGHLIGHTS   No. 5 or No. 59 Chrome.
CHEEK COLOURING   No. 25 Crimson Lake.
LIPS   No. 25 Crimson Lake, sometimes outlined with No. 78 Spot-Lite Pencil Brown.
EYE MAKE-UP   No. 25 Crimson Lake in inner corner of eyehollow, No. 16 on eyelids. Line eyes along line of lashes with No. 78 Spot-Lite Pencil Black.
POWDER   Brownish Blending Powder.

Arms, legs and the body should be made up with liquid make-up. The Eau de Lys No. 7 lightly applied with a damp sponge is fairly dark. The No. 8 is sometimes used or the Tan Klear Liquid Make-up Suntan Dark.

Special Note: For War Paint use streaks of the No. 20 (White) Greasepaint, the No. 12 (Black) and the Carmine 3 Liner.

Oriental
Leichner Make-up Chart
No. 14

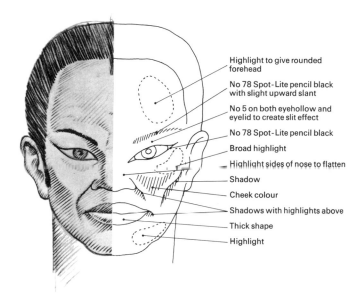

Highlight to give rounded forehead

No 78 Spot-Lite pencil black with slight upward slant

No 5 on both eyehollow and eyelid to create slit effect

No 78 Spot-Lite pencil black

Broad highlight

Highlight sides of nose to flatten

Shadow

Cheek colour

Shadows with highlights above

Thick shape

Highlight

Characteristics are a yellowish skin, coarse straight black hair, a rounded head, large cheekbones, flat face and nose, and a Mongolian fold to the eyelids.

FOUNDATION   Lit. K., No. 6½ with No. 8, No. 5 with No. 9. Sometimes a little No. 59 Chrome Yellow is added to these to give a more yellowish effect.

SHADING   No. 16 mixed with No. 25 Crimson Lake.

HIGHLIGHTS   No. 5.

CHEEK COLOURING   No. 8 or No. 9.

LIPS   No. 9 with a little No. 25 Crimson Lake, rounded shape to upper lip.

EYE MAKE-UP   No. 5 on eyehollow and eyelid to give effect of Mongolian fold, then use triangle of Black (No. 78 Spot-Lite Pencil) sloping downwards at inner corner of eye and upwards at outer corner to give slanting effect. Use same pencil on eyebrows.

POWDER   Brownish Blending Powder.
     Use Liquid Make-up on neck, limbs and body.

Jovial Woman
Leichner Make-up Chart
No. 15

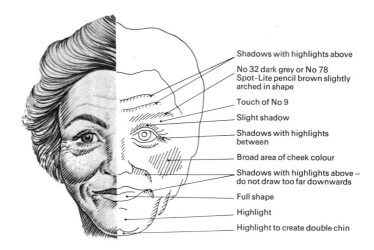

Shadows with highlights above

No 32 dark grey or No 78 Spot-Lite pencil brown slightly arched in shape

Touch of No 9

Slight shadow

Shadows with highlights between

Broad area of cheek colour

Shadows with highlights above – do not draw too far downwards

Full shape

Highlight

Highlight to create double chin

Mainly an exercise in filling out the face with good areas of colour on cheeks, and using shadows and highlights to create softly rounded folds.

FOUNDATION No. 2½, No. 5 with No. 9, No. 6 with No. 9.

SHADING No. 16 with No. 25 Crimson Lake.

HIGHLIGHTS No. 5.

CHEEK COLOURING Carmine 2 or No. 9.

LIPS Full shape, Carmine 2.

EYE MAKE-UP Eyebrows slightly arched. Shadows and highlights at outer corners to give effect of "laugh" lines, use the Blue, Green or Mauve Eyeshadows on the eyelids only and add touch of No. 9 to eyehollow. Outline eyes with No. 78 Spot-Lite Pencil Brown.

POWDER Rose Blending Powder.

Neck, hands and limbs must be made up in character.

Ballet
Leichner Make-up Chart

No 78 Spot-Lite pencil

Touch of No 9 in eyehollow

Dark grey, brown, blue or green on crease

Eyeshadow on lid, fading upwards and outwards

Line along line of lashes, above and below extending upwards and outwards with eyeliner or pencil

Highlight top of cheekbone

Cheek colour

Shadow immediately beneath cheekbone fading downwards

The classical Ballet make-up is pale and ethereal, the face softly and clearly sculptured with the eyes sharply marked. Make-up for the modern and fantasy Ballets permits the use of a wide range of bright colours.

FOUNDATION   No. 2½ with No. 5, Peach and Peach Dark, Peach Special for modern dancing.

SHADING   No. 32 Dark Grey with a little No. 25 Crimson Lake or No. 16 Deep Brown with No. 25 Crimson Lake.

HIGHLIGHTS   No. 2.

CHEEK COLOURING   No. 9 or No. 2½ with No. 9.

LIPS   Light application of Carmine 1 or Carmine 2.

EYE MAKE-UP   Eyebrows clearly defined in an exaggerated upward tilt with No. 78 Spot-Lite Pencil, touch of No. 9 on eyehollow below eyebrows. The Blue, Green and Mauve Eyeshadows are used on the lids with a darker shade in the crease above the eyelids. Line along line of lashes with No. 78 Spot-Lite Pencil. Shadows and linings are extended upwards and outwards. Use False Eyelashes.

POWDER   Rose Blending Powder.

Remember to make-up arms and neck with Liquid Make-up.

Negro   No. 17
Leichner Make-up Chart

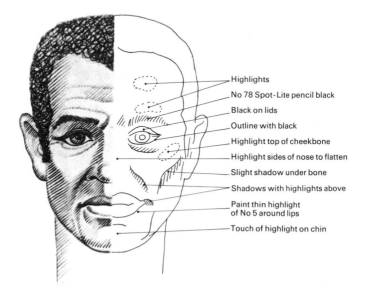

- Highlights
- No 78 Spot-Lite pencil black
- Black on lids
- Outline with black
- Highlight top of cheekbone
- Highlight sides of nose to flatten
- Slight shadow under bone
- Shadows with highlights above
- Paint thin highlight of No 5 around lips
- Touch of highlight on chin

General characteristics are a fairly narrow head, a protruding upper jaw, a very broad nose and thick lips, dark skin ranging from a dark golden brown to almost black.

FOUNDATION   First apply No. 8 (Golden Tan) very lightly then add No. 7, No. 16, or No. 12 to depth of colour required.

SHADING   No. 16, or No. 12 (Black) when the skin tone is very dark.

HIGHLIGHTS   No. 5.

CHEEK COLOURING   No. 25 Crimson Lake.

LIPS   First cover with foundation shade, then add No. 25 Crimson Lake, painting to thicker shape, then outline with No. 5.

EYE MAKE-UP   Outline with No. 78 Spot-Lite Pencil Black and use same pencil on eyelids and eyebrows. Black Mascara.

POWDER   Brownish Blending Powder.

Apply Eau de Lys Liquid Make-up, No. 7, No. 16, or No. 12 to neck, limbs and body.

Special Note: For the "Minstrel" type of make-up apply Negro Black make-up with a damp sponge leaving about ¼ inch around eyes and lips which is covered with No. 20 (White).

Make-up is best applied to the palm of one hand first, mixed with others if necessary, and applied to the face with the fingertips of the other hand. The bibliography suggests specialist books for those interested in further detailed techniques of this fascinating art.

1. Use a dressing table mirror so that you can sit comfortably. Look at your face. Touch it gently with your fingertips and examine its texture and plasticity.

2. Look in a mirror. Grimace and watch for the changing highlights and shadows, shapes and lines.

3. Repeat exercise 2 but pull the face with your fingers.

4. Look to find the shapes you have created in exercises 2 and 3 in other people's faces.

5. Look at your face in a mirror:
(a) in natural light under different conditions and at different times of the day;
(b) in artificial light—tungsten and fluorescent—from pendant, standard and table lamps (above, level and below);
(c) lit by a candle in different positions—above, below, from the sides, etc. Later, use more than one candle. Repeat this exercise substituting battery operated torches for candles, and then by using a filter to change the colour of the light.

6. Experiment with a little make-up. Test its efficiency by going into the street. Discover how much you can change your features without the make-up being discernable to the passer by.

7. Experiment and practise in front of a mirror as follows:
(a) Doodle with the make-up on your hands and face.
(b) Experiment with specific parts of your hands and face: lengthen your fingers; thin your lips; sink your eyes; lengthen your nose.
(c) Use the charts as a guide and experiment within their frameworks.

Lighting

Lighting is probably the one most singularly effective device available to the designer and director. Its impact on mood and atmosphere is well known: in industry; factory; office; dance-hall; restaurant; bowling alley; and discotheque. In the home, too, its skilful use can transform a mediocre room into a place of delight. Church architects have always given it special consideration. Its impact is in no way lessened when used in the theatre. But its employment, like the other design factors, must spring from the text and action of the play. It must also be fully integrated with the other elements of design.

The emphasis upon lighting will vary with the form of the play and the director's needs and, although noticeable lighting changes may (or may not!) be a proper part of a production, they should never obtrude.

Equipment

The fixtures and fitting—lanterns, stands, barrel, brackets, cable, switchboard—may be permanent and inflexible. They may be semi-permanent, flexible or fully mobile. They may have to be hired for each production. The control panel may be hidden somewhere inaccessible on stage allowing the operator no view of the action or it may be well sited and permit a full view of the stage. Conditions will vary from group to group and from theatre to theatre, but whether the production is to be mounted on a proscenium stage with a comprehensive range of modern equipment or in arena style in a bare hall with four spots on stands and a portable home-made switchboard, the following principles remain constant:

1. There must be sufficient lighting intensity to allow the audience to see clearly all action and expression.

2. Colour filters help to create a realistic picture and build up atmosphere.

3. Brighter areas of light attract the audience's attention. This suggests that it should be on the most important parts of the scene or the action. Related to this is:

4. Control of the intensity of light. This also enables changes in time and conditions to be simulated and scenes to change (with appropriate fades) from one to another without distraction.

Lighting can only be evaluated by the finished picture and the audience's reaction to it, not by measurement from a light meter or other scientific instrument. Therefore, lighting techniques for the stage must be developed through practical experience and audience reaction.

Equipment to achieve the above can be simply broken down into:

Floodlights. These are devices which have a single fixed reflector to control the spread of light with no variation. Their function is to illuminate the stage evenly from a given position. These lanterns are available as individual units (see Fig. 1) or linked together to form a batten or trough (see Fig. 2). In this

Fig. 1. Floodlight (batten type)   Fig. 2. Cyclorama trough

category, a very useful item is the cyclorama trough, where, due to the semi-circular shape of the colour filter, an 180° beam angle is produced so that light is evenly spread across the area to illuminate at very close range. This is most effective where a general wash of colour is required, although the multiplicity of the light sources will tend to create a 'flat' effect. For lighting back scenery and cyclorama cloths, however, this type of trough achieves excellent results. The effectiveness of the colour mixing enables it to be positioned at close range—two to three feet from the backcloth. This leaves maximum space for the acting area not possible with any other form of batten or trough. Individual lanterns are more useful in a box set to illuminate door or window backings.

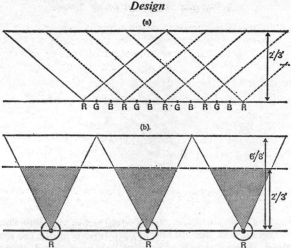

(a)

R G B R G B R G B R G B R

(b).

6'/8'

2'/3'

R   R   R

Fig. 3. Cyclorama – backcloth lighting: (a) 6' twelve compartment (100W 6CY) trough giving wide beam angle; (b) SFL floods with fixed reflector – these reduce beam angle but increase light output.

Spotlights. These are designed to concentrate the light on a given area at high intensity and consist of an optical system with focusing that can be varied so the spread of light is controlled. The intensity of the source and the size of the area covered depend upon the lantern design. Spotlights are available in two distinct categories.

Profile. Where a highly efficient optical system is provided incorporating a wrap round reflector to ensure all light is thrown forward through an apperture producing a hard clear cut edge to the spotlight beam (see Fig. 4).

Fig. 4. SPR Profile spotlight.

Fresnel. Where a simple dish type reflector is used with a Fresnel lens producing a soft edge beam (see Fig. 5). This lantern is easily recognisable by the ribbed formation of the Fresnel lens.

Both types play their part in any well planned lighting scheme and care must be taken in selecting the right type. For general acting area work on the

Fig. 5. SFR Fresnel spotlight.

stage; for lighting from front of house positions or at any time when the build up of light levels must be smooth and almost imperceptible, the Fresnel range should be used. When a strong, dominant light is required, then the Profile version will be more effective.

However, due to the greater efficiency of the Profile lantern in relation to light source rating, this unit is often used in the front of house position where the distance between acting area and lantern is too great for the Fresnel.

Spotlights range from small units with 250/500w. lamp bulbs to the larger lkw. and 2kw. versions. In every case the principle remains the same, with the focusing and size of the lantern increased to cater for the larger light sources.

Recently introduced by the lamp manufacturers has been the tungsten halogen light source. This increases the light output at a given rating by approximately 10%. Because of its higher operating temperature, a better colour response is available and colour balance can be improved. The lamp's life is longer than standard Tungsten—400 hours compared with 200 hours for tungsten, but the units incorporating these are more expensive due to the problems of higher operating temperatures. Two lamp bulbs 650w. and 1000w. are available in the tungsten halogen version, for use in Fresnel and Profile units (providing these are designed to ensure the heat is dissipated correctly). It is possible to use pre-focus cap versions in some of the older, more conventional spotlights, but because of the heat generated, the life may be considerably reduced. A lantern typical of the profile type, showing the increase in size and the possible arrangements of shutters is illustrated in Fig. 6.

Fig. 6. Medium profile tungsten halogen spotlight.

Proper positioning of stage lanterns is essential in avoiding unwanted shadow(s) and creating the optimum effect and such positions *must* be related to the light output and performance of the units to be used.

There is a limit to the effective throw of any spotlight and reference should be made to the manufacturer's specifications.

Practice

A theatre audience sees **by contrast** and therefore from a darkened auditorium, even dim lamps can appear bright. This can be an advantage but by the same token illusion of shadow can be created if proper balance is not achieved between the intensities of light from different positions. The question of balance is most important—particularly with a conventional proscenium stage where it is necessary to light the set and also the front of the stage. Figure 7 shows that lighting to a proscenium or thrust stage is available from two positions:

(*a*) The auditorium.

(*b*) Behind the proscenium arch or directly overhead.

Generally speaking, apart from professional installations, lighting is concentrated on (*b*) at the expense of (*a*) usually to permit the lanterns to be hidden away (see earlier note on exposure or masking of equipment P.) Fig. 7 shows that over-emphasis in either direction will create shadow, particularly noticeable from too much overhead lighting. There are times, of course, when this balance can be properly used to make a player appear larger than life to the audience or to melt him into the background—depending on the scene and the director's interpretation. For general purposes however, the problem is to avoid shadow across the front part of the stage, and care should be taken to ensure that overhead lighting is reduced to enable front lighting to operate at maximum efficiency.

In bigger theatres and with raked auditoria the use of a footlight (marked C in Fig. 7) assists in achieving the right balance. However, where there is a lack of stage depth, or where there is no raked auditorium, the obstruction

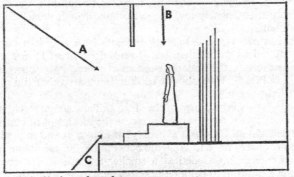

+B—A=Shadow at front of stage
—B+A=Balance in relation to set
—B+2A=Players stand out against background set
+2B—A=Players become dominated by background
A+C—B=Ideal balance where scheme allows use of footlight
2C+A+B=Bad shadow on set and background

Fig. 7. Lighting sources.

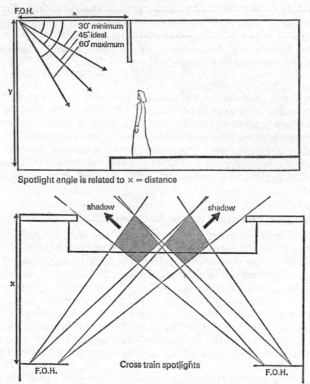

Fig. 8. Lantern positions.

from this light source and the shadows it causes, prohibit its use. But it should not be ruled out completely and the cyclorama trough described earlier can help restore balance.

The position of overhead lighting presents little problem and they can usually be placed where needed, but from the Front of House position, to obtain the best results, the lanterns need exact mounting—approximately 45° as indicated in Fig. 8. They should be crosstrained so that the units on the actor's left light the area on the actor's right and vice-versa. This ensures intensity is built up in the centre of the stage and any shadows created tend to be thrown away at the sides. This represents the ideal, but of course position is related to height and width, ('x' and 'y' in Figure 8) and in actual practice the user will probably have to arbitrate between the 30° minimum and the 60° maximum. Lanterns positioned at a smaller angle than 30° create a 'flat' effect and the backgrounds behind the actors tend to be full of shadow.

Shadow can be a difficult problem but can be minimised by positioning the lighting fittings so that any shadow is cast where it is not distracting (as Fig. 8), or by the balance achieved between the various lighting positions. It is not possible to overcome the problem of shadow merely by increasing the number of light fittings—every light creates its own shadow.

Eliminating shadow by adding lights results in high loading and is virtually self-defeating.

In arena and 'in the round' presentations, the same problems of angles and positioning lanterns apply. In order to provide even lighting it is necessary to light from all sides of the arena, and there is the additional problem of preventing light from spilling into the eyes of the audience on the opposite side of the spotlights, but at the same time covering the acting area and the heads of the actors. With Profile units this problem is overcome by a mask in the aperture or shutters. In the case of the Fresnel units, the soft edge beam results in spill, but this can be overcome by barn door shutters interrupting the beam.

It is not essential to use professionally designed equipment to obtain the best results, a combination of home built floodlights and professional spotlights can achieve the desired effect. Specialist lighting equipment manufacturers can usually produce the most effective optical systems at minimum expense due to the quantity of materials involved. However, simple floodlights or battens are well within the capabilities of the 'do-it-yourself' enthusiasts. But remember the equipment must be **electrically safe**. With a box set and little space on a small stage, bare lamps and lamp holders can be used, screwed behind scenery, to light door or window backings. Pearl lamps should be used to obtain diffused light. Care should be taken to ensure that such lamps do not represent a fire hazard and they should not be in danger of contact with scenery or props.

Colour

In order to create a realistic setting and effective atmosphere, consideration must be given to the use of colour mentioned as the second principle at the beginning of the section. There are, of course, stage designers who have produced excellent settings in black and white. These are special cases, and as a general rule, colour is an essential part of the stage lighting design. Switch on any bulb and it will produce 'white light'. Put in front of it a piece of colour media, and the light will be coloured. Colour media are filters allowing only certain of the colours present in white light to be transmitted—all other parts being absorbed by the filter and converted into heat.

Take two light sources and place a red colour filter in front of one and green in front of another. Direct both light sources towards a white surface, the resulting reflection from the surface is yellow. This happens because our eyes have a mechanism which interprets colour sensations by means of receptors which respond to the **primary colours** in light: **red, green and blue**. Every colour is sensed by this simple function. In the experiment above, the white surface reflects red wavelengths and green wavelengths together and the red and green receptors in our eyes indicate a yellow sensation. If a third source with a blue media is added to the two above the reflection will be near white. White energizes all three parts of our colour mechanism. In other words, white is a complete reflection of all the primaries and we see the additive effect. It is interesting to note that from a painters point of view, the reverse occurs. If paints are mixed together, the result is black—the subtractive effect.

Applying coloured light to a coloured pigment increases the facility of the pigment to reflect **if the light is of the same colour as the pigment, or if it contains some of that colour.** If, however, the light and pigment have no common factor, the pigment will absorb the coloured light e.g. red pigment under blue light looks black; blue pigment under red looks black etc. Colours in costume and scenery can be enhanced, modified or even destroyed in their power to reflect, on the basis that **like enhances and unlike destroys** the reflection of colour.

It is, therefore essential to consider lighting, costume and scenery together and relate all three factors to the required effect. Simple experiments carried out with light sources, material and coloured posters will enable you to gain experience with coloured light.

Strong colours have a **considerably reduced light output** and are generally useful only for lighting backcloths etc. Normally they are not acceptable over the general stage area, and it is wise to consider lighter colours which allow greater light output and can simulate sun, moonlight, or candlelight etc. more realistically. These lighter colours are called tints, and are produced by mixing primary colours. Take for example the red and green—producing yellow—and add a little blue by means of a dimmer, the yellow will immediately appear to be paler, because it is approaching whiteness. This principle is represented

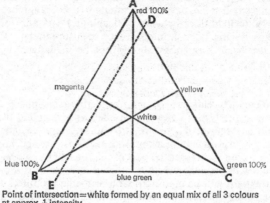

Point of intersection=white formed by an equal mix of all 3 colours at approx. ⅓ intensity.
Addition of colour C on any colour formed along line AB produces a paler tint (line DE)

Fig. 9. Colour mixing triangle.

diagrammatically in Fig. 9. The three primary colours of light are the points of a triangle, and the perpendiculars from the apexes represent the individual colours with 100% light output at the apex and 0% where the perpendicular meet the opposite side. The point of interception of all three perpendiculars represents white—an equal mixture of all three colours at approximately third intensity. Along each side, a range of colours can be produced by mixtures of any two of the primaries. At the centre point of each side (approximately half the intensity of each colour) further colours occur: **magenta, yellow and blue-green** which represent **secondaries**. All colours can be shown as parts of the triangle and it is interesting to note that the introduction of a third colour (**C**) along with any mixture of (**B**) and (**C**) will draw the line closer to white i.e. (**D**) and (**E**), and produce a paler tint of the original mixture.

A wide variety of colour filters is available and although useful to the experienced professional the full range can be confusing to the beginner. It is possible to reduce the range to a basic minimum which will fit the majority of requirements:

COLOUR CHART
Minimum Range of Colours

No.	Colour	No.	Colour
1	Yellow	19	Dark Blue
2	Light Amber	20	Deep Blue (primary)
3	Straw	21	Pea Green
4	Medium Amber	22	Moss Green
6	Red (primary)	23	Light Green
7	Light Rose	24	Dark Green
8	Deep Salmon	29	Heavy Frost
9	Light Salmon	34	Golden Amber
10	Middle Rose	39	Primary Green
11	Dark Pink	40	Pale Blue
13	Magenta	45	Daylight
14	Ruby	51	Gold Tint
16	Cyan (blue-green)	53	Pale Salmon
17	Steel Blue	54	Pale Rose
18	Light Blue	67	Steel Tint

For general front of house lighting, a pale rose or gold tint will generally soften the whiteness of light and complement make-up. For a cold or night scene, steel blue tint will generally work well.

One of the biggest problems is the lack of blue in the normal spectrum range of the tungsten lamp bulb (it has a predominant yellow base) whereby blue intensities are considerably reduced. For sky effects, backcloths are often painted blue to increase the reflective factor. The tungsten halogen light sources operate at a much higher colour temperature, give a more even colour response and reduce the problem.

Obviously there are times when strong colours and alternative treatments are necessary, but the details given form a basis for experimental work and enable the stage lighting tyro to build up his experience from simple colour mixing.

Emotional response to colour is highly subjective, but, in general terms we can state the following:

Warm colours tend to advance.
Cold colours tend to recede.
Reds and oranges are powerful and strong,
assertive, aggressive and warm.
Yellow is gay, happy and cheerful. It stimulates.
Blues and greens are tranquilizing, restful and cold.
Purple and magenta are pompous, regal, powerful and stimulating.
White stimulates (easily over stimulates).
Black depresses (easily over depresses).
Grey neutralizes.

Effects

Many effects are available for projection on the bare wall of a cyclorama or backcloth. They are equally suited for symbolic scenery, naturalistic support or the training exercises for spontaneity, imagination and movement mentioned in earlier chapters.

The following are available for use with standard effects projectors:

Naturalistic: Fleecy clouds; storm clouds; rain; snow; running water; smoke; fire.

Abstract: Dissolving colours.

In addition there are casette projectors in the Kinematic range; liquid wheel projectors in the Liquinatic range and those using the special qualities of polaroid in the Polomatic range. There are also units for cross-fading the images and pulsating them to reflect vocal or musical stimuli.

The following selection from the wide range available will give some suggestion of the experiences to be expected:

Feathery moire; kaleidoscopic tunnel; reverse spiral; spectrum waves; magic eye; catherine wheel; haloscope; scintillating flower.

The above ranges are all made up of moving effects, but experiment with an ordinary slide projector and treated media will open up a wide selection of still projection opportunities—naturalistic and abstract.

Intensity

The heart of any stage lighting scheme is the control system, the fourth basic principle mentioned earlier. The ability to vary any intensity of light source is essential to obtain balance and mix colours.

Control of lamp brightness is through a dimmer. For many years the basic form has been a variable resistance, designed to limit the current to the lamp bulb. Dimmers of this type are designed to carry an intended load with little tolerance. They are usually robust in construction, durable and give little trouble in operation. While more sophisticated types of dimmer have been introduced into the professional theatre from time to time, resistance dimmers, due to their low prices and simple construction, have remained an essential part of any small switchboard. Unfortunately, they suffer from two basic draw-backs:

1. The current consumed by the resistance is dissipated in the form of heat. This can prove troublesome and at the same time costly, through wasted electricity.

2. To obtain an even dimming characteristic so the lamp will smoothly drop from full intensity to blackout over the travel of the dimmer, the design must be carefully related to the lamp load, e.g. a 1000w. resistance dimmer will only accurately dim a 1000w. load. Tolerance of up to a third can be allowed, but efficiency falls off as the differential increases. The former disadvantage has been tolerated over the years and the latter often overcome by ingenious devices in the form of dummy loads, rigged up by enthusiastic electricians.

The application of electronic systems to the control of light intensity means it is now possible for the small stage user to obtain an economically priced electronic dimmer unit giving:

(i) smooth variable load dimming.

(ii) minimum heat loss and therefore a saving in the cost of electricity consumed (the device controls the voltage of the lamp.)

The basic element in this type of dimming is a **silicon controlled rectifier** (SCR) a device which acts as a very high speed switch without moving parts.

It chops the AC wave form and can be considered to act like a rectifier. Two such devices, operating one in each half of the AC cycle (back to back), control the voltage to the lamp load. SCR's are provided with a gate device biased to pass a greater or lesser part of their own half cycle. Thus, by limiting this bias, variable control of the lamp voltage can be established—resulting in 'dimming' or fading. SCR's (commonly referred to as **Thyristors**) are small components looking rather like nuts and bolts mounted through aluminium plates which are referred to as **heat sinks** and which dissipate any heat generated. Because dimming is effected through control of the lamp voltage the device is load independent and therefore proportional dimming is obtained throughout the full range of the unit from approximately 60 watts to the rated load of the device which may be two or even five kilowatts.

When the lamp load is dimmed it is in effect being fed intermittently at high speed by short pulses which result in interference to sound and television

Fig. 10. Typical 2kw electronic dimmer strip.

systems (and perhaps vibration of the lamp filament known as 'sing'). It is therefore necessary to provide a filter circuit to clean up these symptoms. In stage lighting control, allowance must be made for current surges associated with the operation of high wattage Tungsten projection lamps. It is the degree of 'clean up' and suppression which dictates cost and care should be taken when considering purchase to ensure that the dimmer offered incorporates the correct amount of suppression for the application. Many of the smaller, less expensive dimmers on the market today are only intended for domestic use and their SCR's are not rated high enough nor is the circuit sufficiently comprehensive for stage lighting control.

Because of the load independent factor, it is possible to use one or two dimmers in conjunction with a number of circuits through 'patch' systems—a collection of socket outlets (with or without switches) which enable one or more of the incoming stage circuits to be linked in turn or collectively to the dimmer unit. A 2kw. module will cater for the majority of lighting loads enabling two or three stage circuits to be connected at any one time—assuming no lamp load exceeds 1000w. Electronic dimmers are much more compact, a typical strip being illustrated (Fig. 10) and can be purchased singly for building into the user's own control system or purchased complete in the form of a simple switchboard. A typical example of the latter would be eight circuits linked to four 2kw dimmers providing a portable unit-light in weight and catering for simple requirements in a small area (see Figs. 11 and 12).

All stage circuits must be fused correctly to suit the rating of the designed load and a switch should be fitted to every control channel. Over-riding a master blackout switch is also essential. If possible, master dimming should be incorporated and the variable load electronic dimmer could be used in conjunction with resistance dimmers to provide such a facility. Alternatively, with the considerable reduction in size, six or eight electronic dimmer levers grouped together can easily be mastered by a pencil or a finger of one hand.

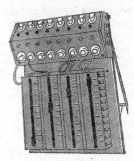
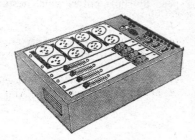

Fig. 11. Portable resistance switchboard   Fig. 12. Portable electronic switchboard
(SRD–T8)   (ET8)

The design and manufacture of dimmer units should be left in the hands of the specialist supplier. The actual cabinet and switches, however, can be made by the enthusiast, provided that such designs are electrically safe and conform to the regulations introduced by the Institute of Electrical Engineers. **Adequate earthing is essential in all parts of a stage lighting installation.** If in doubt, seek advice from an electrical specialist.

In its simplest form, stage lighting can be broken down into a simple dimmer, stand and light source, adequate for experimentation or lighting a small area. Alternatively, it can be built up by the correct selection of equipment into a sophisticated arrangement of spots and floodlights for the full stage. However, in all cases, the principle remains the same and the final result will be the audience's response to the picture presented. 'No Comment' means the lighting plot has fitted smoothly into the overall presentation and played its proper part in the production.

EXERCISES (Lighting)

1. Watch sun-rises and sun-sets.
2. Watch the same panorama through the changing lights of night and day.
3. Look for restaurants, disco's, hotels, shops and shop windows that make a feature of lighting.
4. Take every opportunity to use a camera and look at the work of professional photographers.

5. Experiment with room lighting—candles, torches, fire-light, matches and mirrors, as well as table, standard and pendant lamps.

6. Look carefully at streets at night—noting the effect of the different colours of street lighting and house windows.

7. Practise with a friend, lighting his face:

(a) with different single light sources (candle; torch; spotlight; floodlight) used in different positions—particularly from immediately above; below and each side;

(b) with a number of light sources;

8. Practise with a number of friends, lighting them as a group as in 7 (a) and (b).

9. Practise on a blacked out stage or large space, lighting rostrum blocks; steps; curtains; ropes; ladders; clothing; brickwork; wood etc.

10. Create and execute lighting plots for some of the extracts in Chapters Eight and Ten to Thirteen.

11. Create lighting settings as a basis for improvised group work. Later improvise lighting changes to accompany the group's practical work.

12. Light a matt-white and a glossy-white sphere in as many ways as possible.

13. Practise colour mixing on a white wall.

14. Learn about electricity. TAKE CARE. TAKE ADVICE.

CHAPTER TWENTY

MUSIC AND SOUND

'The man that hath no music in himself,
Nor is not moved with concord of sweet sounds,
Is fit for treasons, stratagems and spoils;
The motions of his spirit are dull as night
And his affections dark as Erebus:
Let no such man be trusted.'

The Merchant of Venice.

The Creation of Atmosphere

Music—the considered arrangement of organized sounds and silences—surrounds us wherever we go. It accompanies us in restaurants, supermarkets, churches and cinemas. Its commercial exploitation is well known in these places and on radio and television.

Music is a major weapon in the theatre and can be put to powerful use. It can blatantly and dramatically arrest the attention of the audience. It can also work with such skilful subtlety that the audience can be unaware not only of the music but also of the effect it is having upon them.

Before, During and After the Performance

Before. Groups may or may not be able to change the look of the entrance foyer and audience area to suit each production. Well chosen music will more than compensate. Music can work on the audience from the moment they arrive at the theatre to the time the performance actually begins. The music should reflect, in particular, the mood of the play. It is much more than mere background music. It can infiltrate the thoughts and feelings of the audience, clearly signalling something of the experience of the play. Some directors plot this introductory music for as long as 45 minutes before the performance is due to begin. Time and care invested in such preparation will be repaid handsomely by the preparedness of the audience to receive the play.

During. American films of the 30's and 40's are extreme examples of music being used at moments of dramatic tension. They are also examples of music creating or substituting for dramatic tension. The cliché conventions behind the use of film music at this time were so strict, it is almost possible to tell the storyline merely by listening to the music.

Music can create or underline atmosphere in a scene. It can add its own dramatic points or ironic comment. It can prepare for dramatic action, reinforce it or elongate its impact. It may be a necessary part of the dramatic action—as in trumpet calls, military drumming or ballroom music—or it may be used symbolically by a director to make a particular point. (For example, if Romeo and Juliet meet for the first time to the accompaniment of a special melody, the director will be able to use that melody at any later moment in the play to summon up appropriate responses. Again: if a character enters once or twice with a musical theme, later use of that theme will place him directly in the stage action although he, in fact, may not be on the stage).

After. Music can help an audience retain the mood, meaning and atmosphere of a play long after the last word has been spoken. It can quietly pursue their thoughts and feelings until they are outside the theatre. This use is not restricted to the conclusion of the performance. It can be used between acts and scenes to retain or change the mood and atmosphere.

Many directors refuse to have a curtain call because it can easily destroy the atmosphere of the play. If there is a curtain call—and it is not necessary—suitable music can accompany the appearance of the cast and help make it a meaningful activity. It can be a number of set group poses or silhouettes. It can be a series of vignettes reminding the audience of particular moments or characters. Whatever the method, music can help its effect by *signalling* the audience. In this way the curtain call will be a continuing reminder of the experience of the play and not a disruption.

Functional, Supportive and Decorative

In plays like *Still Life* and *A Streetcar Named Desire* the music and naturalistic sound effects are so complex and important that they require equal consideration with the text. In fact, they become an integral part of it.

In plays like *The Brig* and *The Quare Fellow* the sounds of chains, locks, bolts and boots are essential to the total dramatic experience and need to be treated as music.

Take a scene set in a factory. The choice of accompanying music and sound is wide. Here are just a few examples:

(*a*) Quiet naturalistic effects to support atmosphere.

(*b*) Loud naturalistic effects to promote a psychedelic experience.

(*c*) Electronic music to suggest a futuristic or abstract effect.

(*d*) Strong, lively 'Music While You Work' to make a political point.

(*e*) Cliché/romantic, sweeping strings for irony.

(*f*) Russian 'Music of the Machines' for additional dramatic impact.

(*g*) Drum beat, metronome or similar to reinforce an idea of automation.

(*h*) Classical/romantic music for incongruity.

(*j*) Absolute silence.

There is no rule of thumb and each director must come to his own decisions about the style of music and sound he is to use. He may choose classical music, popular, jazz, 'Top of the Pops', electronic music or musique concrete. Whatever his choice the *power of silence should not be under-estimated*.

The cast should be allowed plenty of time to work with the music and sound. The more complicated the plot the more time the cast will need. They will need to learn and practise the mechanics of cues as well as to absorb the atmosphere of the music and use it creatively. Time will also be needed to balance sound levels against the use of the actors' voices.

Plenty of time should be allowed for listening, rejecting and selecting music. There should be no reluctance to change the music if it does not achieve the hoped for result. It is just as important that the music should work for the cast as well as the audience.

In a play set in a jungle, the director may have to use loud jungle noises at frequent intervals to help the cast. These should not be allowed to stay in the sound plot unless they are necessary and sufficient. In such a play the director may wish to use jungle noises throughout at background level only, as an atmospheric reminder. He may wish to use them from time to time to heighten the intensity of the scene. He may wish to use them sparingly but pointedly to help or create dramatic climax. He may decide not to use them because they would be a distraction. However they are used, it is easy for cast and director alike to get accustomed to them. Since the audience will be hearing them for the first time it is wise to bring in a friend or colleague with a fresh ear to check.

The sense of hearing is organized to detect change. Music, sounds and silences gain their optimum effect when carefully balanced against one another. It may be the sudden intrusion of heavy thunder, loud drumming or trumpets. It may be the equally sudden stopping of a ticking clock, a dripping tap or dance music. Either will arrest the attention and make an impact.

Live or Recorded?

Live music and sound effects are generally used only when the musicians or operators can be screened from the audience. This usually means a closed stage. Unless the musicians and effects men are part of the dramatic action, they can be a serious distraction if visible.

Nowadays, tape recorders and record players are mechanically quite reliable. Some directors still object to the mechanical reproduction of effects and prefer to have them made 'live'. They claim there is less likelihood of failure; greater exactitude of cueing and more flexibility during performance. Their reasons may be valid but there are few companies able to afford the time, effort and manpower needed to manage all the music and sound effects live.

Recorded music and effects can be played back through speakers placed anywhere in the acting or audience area. They can be exactly placed and made to travel—not only around the acting area but also the audience area. When needed they can totally embrace the audience. Placing and travelling are much more difficult when using live sounds or music.

When recorded sounds and music are chosen, it is essential that any electrical or mechanical unit should be handled with the greatest care. Bad connections, faulty starts, over-abrupt fading or poor recordings irritate an audience. The effect can be worse than no music or sound at all.

D.I.Y.

Tape recorders and record players are easily and cheaply available. So are electronic echo chambers and copycat units. This makes the creation of noises, sounds and music an attractive proposition for any group. Using recorders at half or double speed and playing tapes backwards are techniques that allow groups to experiment, practise and create exactly the effects needed. The original sounds may come from microphones, tapes or discs and their treatment can be an exciting and intriguing experience for all concerned.

Sound Effects

Unless there are particular reasons for using live effects, most companies will find the range of effects available on disc are well in excess of their needs A list of them includes the following:

Thunder.
Wind.
Rain.
Avalanches.
Traffic—cars, trains, aeroplanes, horses' hooves.
Animals—wild and domestic.
Bells—telephone, door, church.
Explosions—revolver shots, machine guns and bombs.

The effects listed above—and they are only a few of those available—are accurately reproduced and are easy to use. A well tried method is to re-record from disc to tape and separate the particular effects with lengths of leader tape so that each can be quickly and easily identified.

The music and sound effects bug can bite. It is just as virulent as the make-up bug. Many groups who have previously relied on others to provide their effects have become carried away into a life long hobby or even obsession. A note of caution is, therefore, appropriate. On each occasion when proposing to use music or sound, the following questions should be asked:

Is it necessary?
Is it sufficient?
Is it right?
Does it work?

EXERCISES

Introductory

If you are not already experienced in handling record-players and tape recorders, practise recording, splicing, editing etc. until you are proficient. Lack of technical expertise will frustrate your creative ambitions. It is only overcome by practice. The bibliography provides suggestions for helpful books on tape recording as well as the practical details involved in 'live' sound effects such as wind, rain, fire and thunder.

1. Listen to the sounds you hear in different environments. Decide what emotional overtones they carry and what moods they readily suggest.

2. With a group of friends play a short scene—improvised or from one of the extracts—against a background of different types of music:
   (*a*) keeping the volume of the music constant.
   (*b*) varying the volume.

3. Play Scene 1 or Scene 3 from Act I of *Macbeth* against a variety of sound effects: wind; drumbeats; top of the pops music; a tap dripping; thunder; gun fire.

4. Using contrasting pieces of music:
   (*a*) begin improvisatory work using the music to create mood. (This should be a dialogue scene and not dramatic dance);
   (*b*) interrupt the music or slowly cross fade to another piece during the middle of the scene.

5. Use sound effects—live and recorded—in a similar way. Choose a wide range of effects. Don't restrict yourself to the orthodox or naturalistic.

6. Listen to radio plays and the special use they make of sound effects and music.

7. Create music and sound plots for some of the extracts. Work with a small group of friends and try different plots for each scene.

8. Make your own sound picture from vocalization, body noises and household objects. Then:

(*a*) make a tape recording;

(*b*) create a similar sound picture recording from discs.

9. Individually, and in groups, work on a short extract with a piece of continuous music where the cueing for every phrase is exact. You may find it helpful to use a stopwatch.

CHAPTER TWENTY ONE

DRAMA WITH YOUNG PEOPLE

Playing Up or Growing Up?

Drama has always been popular with the young; and with the very young it is almost impossible to distinguish factual life from fantasy play. This interest in fantasy, dressing up, 'playing out' or 'creative drama' seems to stem from two basic needs:

1. **To flex the muscles of the growing personality** and, by involved imitation, try out **who they would like to be** and, even more important, **who they would not like to be.**
2. **An unconscious urge to associate with the myths that underpin our culture.**

It is easy to dismiss the first as hero worship and the second as liking story telling. Easy, but deceptive, since these two drives, uninhibited in the young, have been responsible for much of our social development and aesthetic growth.

Both form and content in young people's drama change markedly as they grow older. The major differentials seem to occur as follows:

(a) under 11   (b) 11–14   (c) 14 and over.

Under eleven the interest is in **archetypal figures** of the size and proportion found in the Old Testament. From eleven to fourteen the style is more that of the New Testament and its **parables**. Over fourteen there appears a conscious commitment to the **smaller scale figures of today's world.** It is interesting to note the correlation between these themes and the methods best employed by those leading the groups. The youngest group generally requires of its leader an **authoritarian role**; the middle group asks for intelligent and **friendly paternalism** while the last group demands a kind of **creative co-operative.** Form and content in all three contain something of the other two but the major element in each can be clearly identified.

In and Out of School

A factor which strongly affects the nature of a young people's drama group is the connection there may be with school. The drama class may take place on school premises (in or out of school time), or it may have no connection with the school, taking place, for example, in a club or youth centre. **But no matter how formal the club or how informal the school, the three types of group have persistent differences which regulate the methods to be used in taking the classes.** What will work in the school will not work in the club and, surprisingly, what will work in the club will not work in the school. The young people themselves decide what is appropriate and what can be permitted. The 'free structure' that many of them seek, they themselves change, only too soon, into 'structured freedom.'

Numbers

The number of members is an important question in young people's drama groups. Good groups, because of their scarcity, are very attractive and large numbers tend to enrol. This is always pleasing but, in my experience, the law of diminishing returns starts to work as soon as there are more than eighteen students in one group and inhibitions tend to appear when the numbers fall below twelve. This means that the tutor, aiming to keep his numbers between twelve and eighteen, cannot afford the luxury of a large class or fluctuating numbers—although the members themselves may vary. This can be difficult in an area of work that, for many, already seems to have more than its fair share of challenges.

A Meeting Place

Temporary?

Many young people's drama groups face the serious problem of finding a a place where they can meet regularly and work reasonably. There are many reasons why private or public houses are not suitable, the main ones being the social atmosphere and surrounding furniture. The obvious traffic that is associated with private dwellings and the even more obvious conviviality that permeates public ones offer too many distractions for the concentration and absorption that drama needs. Even if the social life can be by-passed there is still the insurmountable obstacle of the furniture likely to be present. **Furniture designed for family or hotel use is not conducive to a self or body image preparing for creative activity.** From the depths of an armchair it is most difficult not to fall into the attitude for which it was built. True, it is possible, but it is also a waste of effort—effort that should be going into the activity itself—not used to overcome unnecessary obstacles.

Or Permanent?

An alternative to these unsuitable venues is an old garage, loft or shed—even if unheated and draughty. It is far better to have to cope with a bleakness of environment than with the busy trimmings and disturbances of some entirely different activity. An old garage is likely to offer **isolation and space**, both important for drama with young people. Such places are not difficult to find and the cost is not likely to be unreasonable. There is the added advantage that if the place needs attention to make it properly usable, this can be an **excellent way of developing group sensitivity.**

A Place for Everything and Everything . . .

Isolation and space for practical work are needed for many reasons. Here are one or two:

In the early stages with the group it is unlikely that many of the young people will have had any previous experience in drama or theatre. The first step, therefore, must be to gain their **trust and confidence** in this new experience. An excellent way is to make use of the sort of music they are accustomed to and enjoy. In any case, song and dance are not only good for drama, they are also important ingredients of the theatre of today. The music itself can come from tape or disc and cover such extremes as 'greaser beat' and 'progressive'. It should, however, be closely associated with the world of the 'Top Twenty' and the 'Hit Parade'. If it is possible to tempt into the group a live drummer, a guitar player or a group, so much the better.

Music, Dance and Noise

Whatever the music, the necessary concomitant for young people—a high decibel rating—will be present. Hence the first reason for isolation—NOISE. There are those who seriously object to it and can, in fact, be put to considerable inconvenience. There are also those who find it a seductive attraction for its own sake, and although from time to time it is a good ploy to use this as bait for new members, on most occasions it will mean inquisitive visitors. Whether the end-product is attraction or repulsion is irrelevant—either can cause a distraction to the group and is therefore highly undesirable. Isolation guarantees the group against this kind of disturbance.

Noisy music from the charts, although justifiable in its own terms for prospective and new members, has additional merits. Such plays as *The Sport of My Mad Mother* by Ann Jellicoe and *Sweeney Agonistes* by T. S. Eliot, to name but two, demand by their very nature the use of popular music, song and dance. For the members to see that there is an easy transition from their culture to a theatre culture encourages and excites them as well as being a relief to those who had reservations about 'arty-crafty' drama.

The theatre performances of such groups as 'Pink Floyd', the appearances of 'The Who' at the Young Vic, the constant mixing of contemporary poetry with 'jazz' and 'pop' and the whole of the 'West Side Story' idiom make an approach to drama from such music a natural and appropriate one. If the group is to try improvised movement or dance drama, then such an approach becomes almost essential.

Those young people likely to attend will already be used to 'Sound and Light' discos, so the provision and use of stage lighting will be of no great shock to them. As with music, this has the added advantage of speaking to them in their own terms—terms which are also those of the contemporary theatre. The uses of lighting and music are the subjects of other chapters, and their close connection with the theatre does not need to be stressed here. What is important in the early stages with a young people's group is the kind of atmosphere given by the imaginative use of lighting: with the added advantage of the shadows and dark areas that give such comfort and security to the shy and inhibited.

Lights

It is clearly advantageous to leave such lighting in place from night to night and the regular use of one space facilitates this. If the lighting is to be used to full advantage, there must be some form of adequate black-out. Here again regular use makes the proposition easier—exclusive use makes it simple.

Space

If the music and lighting have been used to good effect, it will not be long before the slightly hesitant style of dance preferred by many young people will have grown into something more vital—using more energy and requiring more space. Once this growth has started it is important that there should be sufficient space to allow the young people to progress without bumping and rubbing shoulders at every turn. Fifty to sixty square feet per person is reasonable.

Blocks

It should not be long before the group is ready to use some kind of movable platform, block or rostrum. If these can become the 'furniture' of the place, there is every chance that the group will get used to moving on, over and around them with the greatest expertise. Such unconscious habits are clearly valuable in rehearsal and performance and should be encouraged as soon as possible.

Drapes

It is also useful to hang lengths of cloth—drapes—of contrasting textures and colours on the walls. In time, these will be used quite naturally by the group to change the atmosphere for a special piece of dance or drama, to dress the rostrum blocks or to be 'worn' by group members. It is advantageous if the drapes have been present from the beginning so there is no conscious 'special' event when they are used. If they are fixtures and fittings the members will turn to them without hesitation when they are ready.

Combined Arts

If the group is to have the benefit of paints, materials, chalks, charcoal, polystyrene, etc. to help stimulate their search for self-expression then the need to be able to leave their things about without fear of their being moved (by a 'Landlord' who does not 'understand') is a reasonable one. The current move to the mixing of the arts is a healthy one and it is likely that the members of the group will have nothing but enthusiasm for **combining practical theatre work with creative collage and montage.** If the facilities and finances allow the provision of projectors then the marriage of all these forms becomes a possible and exciting project.

Mirrors

A final suggestion to reinforce the idea of the group needing isolated space: I have found that members of youth drama groups are intrigued by the use of mirrors. If the walls can be hung with large—preferably full length—mirrors from the beginning of the group's formation there are many merits that accrue. For many young people, mirrors are an attraction in themselves and much time is 'wasted' in just looking at the images—probably of themselves and friends. (The fact that this can be excellent training for drama is unthought of by them and is neither here nor there!) After an initial introductory period, the surrounding mirrors become aids to overcoming shyness—not the opposite, as one might expect. Provided the initial 'peacock type' interest is allowed to burn itself out, the mirror does not encourage inhibitions, as most might expect, but in fact becomes a major agent in destroying them. The mirrors will, of course, be of considerable use in later stages as well. Masks, make-up, clothing and acting exercises are all stimulated and helped by the presence of full-length mirrors.

Ethos

My experience in many areas of the country, when starting the idea of a drama group with young people, has been that when the premises can be made available as suggested above, there is every hope of success—in fact I have never come across a group which has failed to establish itself with such popularity that it soon outgrew the available space. The investment of large finances is not necessary. What is crucial is the provision of an ethos so strong that the *genius loci* speaks to the young people as soon as they enter it—and speaks to them in language they understand.

Performance

It will now be clear that a **free form** approach to drama is one that is most likely to succeed with young people. The use of contemporary music, movement and improvisation, allows the group to make its own statement in its own dramatic terms. These principles are still valid when it comes to the questions:

1. Shall we give a performance?
2. What shall we perform?
3. Where shall we perform it?

If the group has been allowed to develop its own natural rhythm of progress and has not been rushed into a too early consideration of performing in public, the need to share what they have created will make a simple and natural appearance. (Too many groups are pressured into, or even formed for, giving public performances for good causes—most of them financial. In my opinion, money is best raised for these good causes by the old stand-by of a jumble sale or what have-you. At least then, the motives are not confused!)

At one time the only answers to the three questions posed above would be 1. 'Yes'; 2. 'Three one act plays (or sketches or a revue)'; 3. 'On the local stage.' At that time the one act plays would probably be pseudo 'high-society' or pseudo 'working-class' comedies, set in the near past, of little intelligence and no style. The stage would have been an imitation of the nearest proscenium type and in a poor state of repair.

Social and dramatic conventions have changed. Movement and improvisation are acceptable for performance; plays are permitted to ask significant questions about the human condition and a stage can be of the shape and dimensions best suited to the nature of the group and its work. Television has done much to broaden minds about length, format and content of plays.

It is likely that the group will have been working on material (its own or a text) for some time before the need to share emerges. I suggest that the best starter for public performance is precisely that material the group was already preparing. Should this happen not to be suitable, there are texts now available that are written for performance in a very free way. Some are written for performance in youth centres where there is no stage; some for open-air performance. Most provide creative opportunities for the groups to build on the text and all have an ear for adolescent sub-culture. Some plays are written for and have been professionally produced in, discotheques, dance halls, restaurants and coffee bars as well as clubs and youth centres.

Young people gain much satisfaction from presenting their work in environments that are more in touch with the living community than the average local or church hall. Hospitals, Homes and Prisons all offer exciting opportunities for staging and, generally speaking, audiences for whom the performances are something more than just a night out.

The Place for Experiment

It is the responsibility and privilege of the adult generation to offer to the young an opportunity to discover, create and establish their own forms of drama and their own ways of presenting them. It is nothing less than indulgence on the part of that adult generation to attempt to preserve its own culture by structuring the practices of the young. Any merit in that culture will emerge from the free experiment and relaxed growth of the next generation— provided it is encouraged to work in its own way at its own pace and not forced underground.

There are more young people than ever before, in real and comparative terms, who are finding an interest in drama and theatre. While that interest is imaginatively fostered there is every reason to believe that our theatre will progress from its post-war re-birth into a healthy, lusty child.

CHAPTER TWENTY TWO

FESTIVALS

All Kinds of Festivals

At one time, drama festivals were almost exclusively competitions for productions of one act plays. Now, there is tremendous variety in scope and shape.

There are competitive festivals, training festivals and even *festive* festivals. There are festivals of the same work; the same author; the same theme. There are festivals of short plays; experimental plays; new plays; improvisations, home-made plays and work in progress. There are festivals for open and closed stage presentations—some separate and some combined.

Drama festivals sometimes exist on their own, sometimes side by side with music festivals and sometimes as part of a large combined arts event.

There may be competition or co-operation. Audience participation and or involvement may be in the productions, adjudications or discussions.

For many groups, drama festivals represent an opportunity to expand an experiment in an atmosphere of sympathy and understanding; for some, an opportunity to use their new recruits, and for others, a chance to indulge their need to win.

Whatever the needs of the group, there is every chance that each year there will be a festival to meet them.

Adjudicators

Adjudication—the judging of standards, of achievement, and even of the aims of a company or an individual—has long been established in the world of the amateur theatre. It should not be confused with the practice of writing articles, critical and appreciative, of productions presented in the professional theatre. It is a completely different matter, where the festival adjudicator is not merely a critic, but where he is inevitably expected to evaluate the merits of a production and suggest ways and means of improving the total result of the work. He has to be more than a man of the theatre. He must know the whole process of play-production, be aware of the whole range of drama from the earliest pre-theatre days to the very latest development of arena work, have a sound knowledge of lighting, make-up, costume, furnishing, scene painting, stage-management and so on and be able to produce, speak, move and act. In addition, he must be able, in a limited time, to assemble his thoughts and evaluations concerning a production, and be ready to make an authoritative comment and judgement, in not more than fifteen or twenty minutes, immediately at the end of a production. In short, he must have a wide practical knowledge of the theatre, enabling him to express his opinions clearly, logically and in such a way that the audience is kept interested, alert and analytical, and that the cast, while listening to the adjudication, learns something from his comments.

Praise or Blame?

This is obviously no easy task for an adjudicator. Too much praise may result in self-satisfaction and unwarranted self-esteem on the part of the cast. Too much criticism may damage the confidence of the amateur actor or producer, creating in them an utter dislike of the theatre with the result that they may be lost to the amateur stage for ever. In other words, as a neutral assessor he has to be helpful to his amateur actors, and yet skilfully guide and stimulate the cast to better work and the audience to a more critical—and therefore more knowledgeable—understanding of what they have seen. The adjudication itself must be a real part of the programme and in the best festivals this is always the case. The adjudicator is chosen with a thought to that very situation, for a dull adjudication, at the end of any play which has been either badly or brilliantly presented, can reduce the evening to a very low level. That is not to say that the adjudicator must be facile or facetious; his is not the moment for the big laugh, nor for that matter, the scholarly-lecture. His task is simply to illuminate the work that has just been performed so that the audience and cast may the more readily understand and appreciate it.

Awards

The task of adjudication does not always follow the same pattern. Some festivals want only comment, others ask for comment and the arrangement of teams in descending order of merit. Whilst some festivals want marks to be announced, others are opposed to this. But all festivals want knowledgeable assessment and practical advice, and most require, in addition, the selection of the festival's best production. Some festivals want even more than that. They want the 'runner-up' to be selected, the best production from a company never having won before, the best actor, the best actress, the best comedy, the best stage decor—and so on. Indeed, some festivals are overburdened with awards to the extent that even the worst losers may receive a special consolation award!

History

This over-abundance of awards dates back, for the most part, to some years ago—even to pre-1939. In the early days of the amateur-theatre festivals, standards (apart from an honourable few) were not always high. But, as the drama festival idea became accepted all over the country, so that no part of the country was without one, standards became higher. The festival movement became a part of the British way of life, and the war of 1939–45 was merely a pause, during which time the amateur theatre got ready to make a fresh onslaught on the British public when hostilities ceased. The British Drama League, which had been the main organization for the fostering of amateur drama, was joined by a whole body of other independent festivals. The enthusiasm for having festivals, and joining in them, was not always matched by an equal understanding of the arts of presentation, production and acting, so that festival standards were often very mixed, and sometimes low.

So many festivals were started at this time that the available adjudicators were quite unable to do all the work, and, in many cases local enthusiasts were often called upon to adjudicate, and often, alas, with some dire results. Sometimes professional actors were called upon, and though they probably might be very good actors, it did not follow that they were also good adjudicators. Rarely, and indeed in only a few cases, were they really helpful to amateurs. Standards they were asked to judge upon were often far below what they considered as a norm, and outlook and aims were different, in many cases, from what they regarded as normal in the professional theatre.

Guild of Drama Adjudicators

It was in 1947 that a number of experienced adjudicators, with the blessing of the British Drama League, established the Guild of Drama Adjudicators. At that time, in the Guild, there were some forty-six founder members, all of them having become well-experienced in the art of adjudicating drama festivals during the previous twenty-five years or so. To day there is a membership of two hundred and fifty, with an independent branch in New Zealand, and contacts in Canada, Australia and the U.S.A.

Aims

The Guild exists in the interests of amateur drama, its main object being to *raise the standards of both amateur performance and adjudication*. It has established recognized principles of practice in the work of adjudication to which members of the Guild are expected to conform. Admission of new members is carried out by Entrance Conferences, held at a week-end from Friday to Sunday, twice a year, for the purpose of instructing candidates for membership in the nature and method of adjudication. All candidates for membership are required to have considerable professional or amateur stage-experience (preferably both) and to possess a thorough knowledge of all aspects of drama. The admissions' conferences are held under the supervision of an Approval Board composed of experienced adjudicators plus one other person who is not an adjudicator but who is closely connected with the amateur theatre and the drama festival movement. During the week-end there are lectures and discussions on subjects ranging from the nature and method of adjudication, and the marking-system, to sessions devoted to talks to performers and the writing of reports. There is also a written paper and, following on a visit to a good amateur company's production on the Saturday night, the final day is devoted to the delivery of adjudications on the production by the candidates. A report on each candidate is then made to the Council of the Guild by the Approval Board, and they either accept the candidates Associate Members, or ask them to come forward again to a later Conference under a new panel, or reject them. New Associate Members are admitted to full membership after not less than six public engagements have been satisfactorily carried out. All full members, and associate members, are bound to observe not less than the minimum conditions of engagement, and are bound to abide by the rules of any festival at which they undertake to adjudicate. Disciplinary action may be taken by the Council against any member who fails to follow the code.

Members

Very many members of the Guild have professional stage-experience as actors, stage-managers or producers. Some are still engaged in the professional theatre, among whom are highly distinguished members of the acting profession. All of them have had experience of the amateur stage and the conditions under which amateur productions are performed, and they are all interested in the furtherance of amateur drama. Many members are engaged in some form of teaching the techniques of the stage, in voice production and so on. Indeed the ability to impart instruction is regarded as a necessary qualification for membership of the Guild, as well as the possession of sound judgment.

Marks

Opinions differ as to whether marks should or should not be awarded at festivals. There are those who are unequivocally set firmly against them, while others regard them as a desirable feature of a festival. Some festival organizers wish marks to be kept for the information of the adjudicator and the committee. Others ask for the public announcement of marks. The Guild has given much attention to the question, and scales of marks have been evolved which are generally accepted at drama festivals everywhere. Some festivals have their own marking schemes, but generally one or other of the following scales is used:

(1) Acting	40	(2) Choice of play	10
Production	35	Acting	40
Presentation	10	Production	30
		Presentation	10
Dramatic achievement	15	Dramatic achievement	10
	100		100

Obviously it is extremely difficult—some say impossible—to attach a mark to something so personal as acting, or so difficult to assess as dramatic achievement. Because it is difficult, however, this is no reason why the idea should be abandoned. When adjudicating twenty or more plays over the period of a week's festival, without some sort of marking standard, it is difficult to carry in one's mind for a full week the real level of achievement, attainment, presentation, and production of any one play. Some sort of marking system is therefore essential to an adjudicator. This means, of course, that he must discipline himself rigidly to adhere to the same standard throughout the run of a festival. Many adjudicators are very busy, and move on from one festival to another, and so carry with them an even set of standards. Others work only occasionally at the task, but the need for a standard is just as pressing, just as demanding.

One often hears a team declare, having received (say) seventy marks at a festival: 'Oh! We got seventy-nine for the same production last week'. They immediately decide that the first adjudicator was the better of the two. They forget to take into account the way their own achievements may differ from week to week. It is often the case that the standard of an amateur production may vary from night to night. Quite often the team may feel very thrilled with their final performance, when in fact it has been loose, over-acted and played to an audience of friends, with no real sense of balance and artistic development. They allow the occasion to inject wrong emphases, forcing laughs, or the over-acting of dramatic moments. The same thing can and does happen with a team which travels a show from festival to festival. Rarely are amateur companies able to repeat the same level of performance, and the same balance, night after night.

An adjudicator reacts to what he sees, and he awards a mark to evaluate that result. This requires a discipline of marking, and so, whatever marking system is used, the Guild recommends that the following scale should be kept in mind:

A total of 81–90   Excellent.
A total of 71–80   Very good.
A total of 61–70   Good
A total of 51–60   Fair.

A total of less than fifty marks would indicate a bad performance. In the opinion of the Guild, only rarely, and when a performance is of quite outstanding merit, should a total of 91 marks or more be given.

Reports

Many drama festivals ask the adjudicator to supply a written report on the plays at the festival, when details concerning choice of play, stage-presentation, production and so on may be considered at length. But the best form of adjudication is probably the occasion when, either immediately after the performance, or at the latest on the following day, it is possible for the cast and adjudicator to meet and talk over, re-act and even reproduce parts of the production. It is through such encounters that a team can more easily achieve the aims which should guide the entrants to a festival in the arts of presentation, the technique of acting and the whole machinery of production.

Specific Festivals

There are many kinds of festival all of which would claim to have the main aim of the festival movement as their guide. The B.D.L. Festival, held annually, results in the selection of a production as the best in the British Isles. There are many companies however which do not enter the B.D.L. Festival, but which are regarded as of the very highest standard. They perhaps do not enter any festival at all, but choose to work within their own area, putting on as many as six or eight plays a year. But there are many other amateur companies which compete in the many 'Independent' festivals. The various women's organizations such as the Women's Institutes, the Townswomen's Guilds and so on, have their own area and national festivals. Many factories, especially those which have a national coverage, hold their own festivals; business firms, the Army, the Navy and the Air Force, the churches, the Scouts and Guides and youth services, the boys' clubs and the girls' organizations are all busy organizing their own festivals. Of recent years the local Education Authorities, the Colleges and the Universities have developed the idea, so that hardly any aspect of business, industrial or educational activity is without its own drama Festival.

Organization

The success of a festival depends a great deal upon the skill and care devoted to the organization of the event. A local festival is just as important in this respect as the national festival. Behind the national festivals there is almost certain to be some existing organization to organize the event. But in the case of a local festival the event must rely on the enthusiasm and skill of local committees.

The idea of holding a festival may seem attractive, and certainly it helps enormously to raise the standards of production, presentation and acting, quite apart from the way in which it can stimulate the interest and understanding of the general public. But to achieve a successful festival, many things are essential, and the first big problem is that of finance. Not only is a theatre to be hired, but there are many other items which have to be paid for, such as tickets, publicity, the adjudicator's fee, expenses, and so on. We will deal with these items in greater detail as we discuss the organization of a festival.

Once a committee has been formed and is satisfied that sufficient money is available to run the festival, or guarantors have been found either through official sources such as local councils or local cultural organizations, or by means of private support, preparations can go ahead. It is first of all necessary to make sure that a suitable theatre or hall is available on the dates when it is proposed to hold the festival. The seating capacity of the building is a matter for the local committee to consider. Some festivals require very large theatres, whilst others can make do with a school-hall or similar place having seating accommodation from two to four hundred people. Next, the stage must be checked to see what is available in the way of lighting equipment, curtains and general stage facilities.

At this point the committee will have to decide whether the festival is to be staged using drapes, or if scenery will be allowed. If a full-length play festival has been decided on, scenery will normally be required, whilst a one-act play festival is more likely to be staged using curtain sets. At this stage the festival staff will be appointed—the stage-manager and his helpers, whose responsibility will entirely be concerned with matters connected with the stage and the presentation of the plays. They will endeavour to get whatever furniture and properties are required during the festival, and arrange for adjustments to the lighting when once the lighting-plots are known to them.

Competing teams will submit their lighting-plots, and their property and furniture requirements, well in advance of the date of the festival.

The front-of-house staff will be appointed—stewards, programme-sellers, door-keepers, box-office staff and the like, bearing in mind that the adjudicator is likely to need one person to whom he can refer, and whose main duty is to attend to any problem which may arise within this field. Arrangements should be made for the adjudicator to be seated in a good position, fairly central, from where it is possible to get a clear view of the stage. In the case of festivals devoted to theatre-in-the-round it may be that the adjudicator may decide to sit in a different place either each night, or even during the performance of a single full-length play. He will normally require a table on which to keep his papers, and a shaded light which will adequately illuminate his notes, but which will not dazzle the rest of the audience.

The committee will have appointed a publicity officer, if they wish to give, as they surely must, a wide coverage of information about the festival. In the first place the main publicity will be directed to societies, either locally, or, as is the case with many festivals, on a much wider basis. This can be done either by directly circularising societies, or through the press (for local companies), or by using the advertisement columns of *Amateur Stage*.

Once the entries have been received, the programme can be arranged, and the main publicity for the festival can begin. Posters, hand-bills, car-stickers, form an important part of this function, and an enthusiastic, imaginative publicity committee will think up all kinds of schemes to help to make local people aware of the project. Most areas are fortunate in having local newspapers willing to print information concerning forthcoming events, especially when the items have an interesting story about, for example, the festival, the teams, the plays, the adjudicator, or, in fact, any topic of special interest relative to the forthcoming festival. If it is possible to illustrate such items with photographs, this always adds a great deal to the impact of the news item.

When the festival itself is taking place, there should be no diminution of effort on the part of any department. The event should be kept as one of local interest, a talking-point for the public at large, and as such it should be made to run smoothly, with every department working flat-out to make a success of its own special responsibilities. As for the adjudication, this is a matter which is solely in the hands of the adjudicator appointed to undertake the job, but who works always in close consultation with the festival officers through his personal steward. The final adjudication itself is entirely a matter for the adjudicator. It is his considered opinion, based on wide experience, and not swayed by personal bias, or local preferences. The Guild of Drama Adjudicators sets high standards for its members to follow, and this is invariably honoured by the adjudicator. There are very rare occasions when disagreements arise between a festival and its adjudicator. Usually all goes happily, but if a dispute should arise, it is better for all parties to refer the matter to the Council of the Guild of Drama Adjudicators, who will consider the whole case, and invariably reach a conclusion satisfactory to all sides.

Finale

As decisions concerning the awards which have to be made are solely a matter for the adjudicator, so, too, are decisions concerning the final announcements, the climax even, at the end of the festival. The only exception to this is when a festival has a special trophy awarded by the audience itself to a team of their own choice. It can happen that a play which has not been selected by the adjudicator is considered by the audience to be the one which they themselves have most enjoyed, and they are sometimes given the opportunity of selecting and voting for the performance they thought was the best. If their choice is different from that of the adjudicator, it should not be assumed that they were right and the adjudicator was wrong. Their decision is based very largely on sheer enjoyment. The adjudicator, on the other hand, has had to consider the whole range of items in the presentation and performance, and he must therefore take into account a far wider, deeper and all-embracing assessment in coming to his conclusion.

Every festival will have its own local problems, not necessarily repeated in like pattern elsewhere. Experience and local knowledge are the best means of achieving the success one hopes for. If special problems arise, it is well to refer such matters to the Guild of Drama Adjudicators, 26, Bedford Square, London, W.C.1, which exists to serve not only its members, but anyone connected with the organization of drama festivals.

The great thing to remember is that in a drama festival, a very large number of individuals must work together to present a stage-experience which will be demanding on all concerned, but which can be rewarding to everyone, cast, staff, and audience. The festival is not a competition with other actors so much as a striving to achieve standards which should be higher and higher as experience is gained. This is true whether the festival be competitive or non-competitive. 'The play's the thing' should be the guiding rule for every drama festival.

CHAPTER TWENTY THREE

AUDITIONS AND EXAMINATIONS

Auditions—Professional and Amateur

'It is no sin to sell dear, but a sin to give ill measure.'

Some groups work together on a continuous basis throughout the year. They cast their plays and recruit new members exclusively through their training schemes. Not all groups are able to work this way and so use auditions to cast or recruit. Other establishments, such as schools and colleges, require some kind of selection system and auditioning is still the most common method of recruiting casts or company members to the theatre, be it professional or amateur.

The purpose of the audition is to enable you to sell yourself and your abilities in an economic way. Some auditions may appear to invite the demonstration of flash-in-the-pan techniques, and much can be learned about an establishment or company from the way it conducts its auditions. It is an opportunity for you to show something of the range of your capabilities.

Group auditions are becoming more frequent in schools, colleges and theatre companies. You should be prepared, however, for exclusively solo work, as this is still common.

The following notes outline the main features:

1. Your audition begins with your preparation and your attitude to it. Take time and care.

2. Your audition proper begins the moment you enter the building and does not stop until you leave. The auditioners will be interested in you as a person as well as a performer.

3. You may be asked to take part in solo and/or improvisatory exercises involving speech and movement. There may also be some abstract vocalization and dance.

4. You may be asked to present prepared pieces—poetry, prose, dramatic dialogue—classical and/or modern. You should always have a full range of such extracts ready to present.

5. You may expect to be given specific instructions regarding what to prepare. Be careful to do exactly what is asked. Be prepared also to do much more.

6. Provide the auditioners with copies of everything you use, including cuts. They need to know how exact you can be.

7. For solo extracts you may choose a long speech, a dialogue sequence in which you play one part only or a scene in which you play more than one part. Only you can decide which will suit you best. You may wish to show your ability to grow and absorb yourself into a scene; your mercurial quick change style; your talent for filling an empty area with imagined people. You are best advised to present as much contrast as possible, in every way, in the material you choose.

8. You may also be invited to a viva-voce with a small group of auditioners

333

or an informal chat with just one. Remember it is all part of the audition process. Be composed but responsive.

9. There is no excuse for presenting material that is not properly committed to memory. You merely waste the auditioners time and do yourself a disservice.

10. Above all take every opportunity to demonstrate your sensitive flexibility as well as your dramatic intensity. This is particularly relevant when you are involved in group work.

Examinations

Examinations in almost anything are becoming more suspect day by day. Ironically the more suspect they become, the more they seem to prosper and proliferate. The gulf between theory and practice appears to be widening.

Anyone taking an examination does so for individual reasons, and there are many of them. If the examination you have in mind is optional and not part of a course of training, only you can tell whether you need to take it or not. You may wish to qualify yourself better for part time or full time employment, to build up your confidence, to test your knowledge and skill or to assess your progress. Paper qualifications are no substitute for direct experience, and process and progress are often more important to you than a performance on a particular occasion. Be aware of those examinations which do not seem to recognize this.

Whether you are preparing for an audition or an examination—individual or group—you should approach all the tasks as if they were for performance. Indeed, **auditions and examinations are performances** and should be approached with the same rhythm as for an opening night. Although the audition or examination may be brief and concentrated there is no reason why you should undertake your preparation in a similar way.

Remember the importance of your initial impact and balance that against your need to give a sincere, absorbed and sustained performance. All good auditioners and examiners will go to great lengths to find out what you can do rather than to expose what you cannot. Take every opportunity to demonstrate your ability to progress and grow as well as to impress with your current talent.

Examinations are becoming increasingly less formal and literary and are moving closer to a practical/group approach. Examinations in the fields of speech, drama and theatre are many and varied. They range from short, introductory tests of speech, through the Certificate of Secondary Education to University degrees. The two outlined below indicate current trends. They are provided by the Drama Board and appear in their present form after many years of practical experience, research and amendment.

The Drama Board
The situation on 21st March, 1972.

Associate of the Drama Board—A.D.B.
There have been: 185 examinations with 1,981 candidates, of whom 968 have passed.

There are running: 10 courses with 168 students, of whom 90 have registered to take the examination.

A.D.B. (*Education*)

The first examinations took place in the Summer of 1971.
There have been: 7 courses with 152 students, of whom 86 have taken the examination. 35 have passed, 11 have been referred.
The Secretariat has already been notified of 25 courses which will start in September.

Diploma

This first pilot course is due to end in July 1972.
23 students have attended of whom 16 were eligible to take the Diploma. 9 have passed and 7 have been referred.

Totals

680 students are attending a Drama Board course.
434 students have registered to take an examination.
Of the 27 A.D.B. (Ed.) courses, the students on 10 are having their examination fee paid by their Local Education Authority.

The Board exists to raise the standard of teaching drama and it considers that courses of training are the most important means of achieving this. It has consequently specified that a course is an essential pre-requisite for the A.D.B. (Ed.) examination and strongly recommended for the A.D.B.

The Board itself does not run courses. They are usually run by drama advisers, college of education lecturers, further education lecturers, etc., with or without additional tutors. No general guide can be laid down as to the optimum number of tutors beyond that there should be more than one person involved in the tuition and that too many part-time tutors might lead to the organizers losing overall control of the course and to confusion in the minds of the students.

Courses are financed by local education authorities through either the drama adviser, the further education department, the youth department, or (for A.D.B. (Ed.)) the in-service training department. Alternative sources of finance are; Technical Colleges, Colleges of Further Education, Colleges of Education, Institutes of Education, Teachers' Centres, Residential Adult Education Centres, Polytechnics. County Drama Committees or Rural Community Councils may be able to help for A.D.B. courses and Extra-mural Departments or the Workers' Educational Association have been known to co-operate with another body. The British Drama League also runs a 10 week full-time course for the A.D.B.

Generally, A.D.B. (Ed.) courses are provided free for teachers and they may claim a percentage of expenses in attending such courses. The fee payable by those attending A.D.B. courses is often in accordance with the fees payable for any other further education class.

Patterns of courses and lengths vary according to the geography of the centre and the standard of students attending. For the average 120 hour course, the following schemes have been used:

1 evening per week for 6 terms.
1 evening per week for 3 terms plus 3 residential weekends.
2 evenings per week for 3 terms.
6 residential weeks ends over 12, 18 or 24 months.
1 summer school plus 1 evening per week for 3 terms.
Part of and complementary to a full-time course at a College of Education or Drama School.

The A.D.B.

Examination Scheme

1. The examination will consist of five sections:
   (a) One three hour written paper.
   (b) A personal project on a topic of the candidate's choice.
   (c) Practical drama—i.e. working with a group for a maximum of one hour.
   (d) Technical aspects.
   (e) A viva-voce.
2. The written paper [Section (a)] will be taken at least a month before the practical [Sections (c) and (e)] which will normally be taken over a weekend. The topic for the personal project [Section (b)] must be stated at the time of registration and handed in at a time to be specified when it has been approved. The project is normally handed in at the time of the written examination [Section (a)].
   The technical aspects [Section (d)] will be locally assessed on the course of training and by arrangement with the Board for independent candidates.
3. The course tutor will submit a confidential report on each candidate to the Board and this report will be given full weight by the examiners. It is recommended that the report be based on a continuous assessment of the candidate on the course of training. In the case of independent candidates, the Board will ask for the names of two people familiar with the candidate's work and these references will be taken up before the practical examination.
4. The preceding represents the Board's examination scheme, but the Board is prepared to consider alternatives to this pattern if they are proposed by a sponsoring authority. In such cases, the Regulations may be modified to suit but any alternative examination scheme must be concerned with the syllabus content as stated below.

Method of Examining

1. The written work and the personal project [Sections (a) and (b)] will be marked by the Board's national examiners.
2. The practical examination [Sections (c) and (e)] will be examined by two examiners, one of whom will be a national examiner and the other, where possible, a local examiner.
3. The technical aspects [Section (d)] will be examined by the local examiner.

Gradings are used (A = outstanding, B = very good, C = pass, D = borderline fail, E = fail) and each candidate is required to achieve a minimum of C in each section (including each section of the written paper) in order to pass. Examiners, however, have discretion to pass a candidate who has one 'D' grade provided that his success in other sections of the examination, especially the viva, warrant it. Failure to pass in either the written work or the project or the technical aids may be referred. Any candidate who fails the practical session is required to take the whole examination again.

Syllabus

The Board hopes that, where candidates have attended a course of training, the resultant examination will be related directly to that course. Provision has therefore been made for considerable individual contributions, both from the tutor by means of the list of plays studied and the nomination of a suitable local examiner, and from the candidate who chooses his own production scene and topic for his project. The method of examining the technical aspects will be devised locally by tutors and local examiners and approved by the Board. The Board believes that drama is a continuing process and hopes that it will be seen that the A.D.B. (Ed.) and A.D.B. examinations are complementary to each other. In order to stress the overlap, it has allowed the project to be common to both.

A. WRITTEN WORK

Each candidate will be required to answer under supervision and within a time limit of three hours, four questions. (Fifteen minutes will be allowed beforehand for candidates to read the paper).

The question paper will be divided into four sections from each of which one question must be answered. The sections will be arranged as follows:

1. The art of production and the methods and techniques used; the organization and planning of a production; the choice of play and the conditions which influence this.
2. The art of acting, including the uses and techniques of improvisation, speech and movement.
3. Theatre history; dramatic literature; critical appreciation.
4. Drama and society; the pattern and aims of drama in the community, in schools, youth organizations and adult groups.

Candidates may bring with them copies of the plays studied and may refer to these if they so desire. Where there is a course, the organizer will be asked to suggest two questions in each of the four sections from which the Board may select one. Questions set by the Board may well be based upon those plays which have been studied on the course. Texts will be available in the examination room for reference.

B. THE PERSONAL PROJECT

Each candidate will select an aspect of drama or theatre which has an especial interest for him and produce a study on this. The topic for the project must be submitted to the Board for approval, and the candidate is advised not to proceed with the work until this approval has been received.

Any subsequent modifications to the topic or method of presentation must be notified to the Board. The project may be in any media the candidate chooses. At all times during the preparation of the project, reference to books and other material will be permitted, but the completed project must show that the candidate's approach and opinions are intrinsically his own.

As a general guide, candidates are advised to choose an original angle to a worth-while topic. Original thinking and research are essential and this must be carried out with the A.D.B. examination in mind. A mere documentary record is not acceptable as a project neither is work submitted for other examinations or courses.

The approximate length of the project should be between 6,000 and 10,000 words exclusive of illustrative material.

Practical considerations are that the project must be recorded in some way (e.g. written, tape, film, etc.) so that the Post Office will accept it for delivery to the examiner. Any references should be listed and illustrative work should be linked to the main body of the project.

It is recommended that the project should not duplicate those areas covered by other sections of the examination, and a duplication of actual material submitted will not be accepted.

C. PRACTICAL DRAMA

Each candidate will work with a mixed group of players for a maximum of one hour. In this time he will be expected to show his awareness of the problems which occur when working on a text and that he is capable of interpreting a text creatively. He must also show that he is capable of using improvisation for dramatic and/or educational purposes. No set procedure is laid down for the session other than this, and the candidate may conduct the work in his own way.

This session basically represents the situation which a part-time tutor is likely to meet in his work and throughout it the examiners are looking for a candidate's ability to create a sympathetic and inspiring relationship with the group. The relative times to be spent on improvisation and production are immaterial provided that the requirements of the syllabus are met.

The Board is anxious that candidates should work in their own accustomed way on both improvisation and production and should not manipulate the group in some way which *they think* will be acceptable to the examiners.

All candidates should have a clear reason for their improvisation and know what they are hoping to achieve by it. The examiners are more concerned with the candidate's awareness in this part of the session than with its success or failure.

The text to be used by the candidate for this session must be a short extract selected from a play of the candidate's own choice.

The candidate is required to provide sufficient copies of the text for the players and the examiners.

It is desirable that tutors advise candidates as to the nature of the extract and certain guide lines can be laid down; the usual length of a scene may be one or two foolscap sides, but there is no reason why a shorter extract should not be chosen and worked on in greater depth; any extract selected should occupy the characters in it, i.e. two active characters with six onlookers would usually not be satisfactory; the last scene of a play could involve so much explanation as to what has led up to it that little time would be left for practical work.

The candidate must present at this session a model and/or scale plan of the set for the extract together with a lighting plot.

The model or stage plan should be based upon a hall, space or stage known to the candidate, and adapted by him to suit his particular production.

D. TECHNICAL ASPECTS

Each candidate will show that he has a competent practical knowledge of two or more of the technical aids listed below. In the case of candidates who are on a course of training, the method of examination will be determined through consultation between the course tutor, the local examiner and the Board. It will be locally assessed. In the case of independent candidates, the Board will make the necessary arrangements.

1. **Lighting.** Adjusting lanterns and operating a small switchboard; knowledge of the colour filters available, their use and effect; designing a production within the limits of the available equipment.
2. **Sound.** How to use and record on a tape-recorder; a knowledge of mechanical sound effects and their operation.
3. **Costume.** Designing and making an effective costume from materials which are readily and cheaply available.
4. **Make-up.** As a character; a knowledge of the various types of stage make-up and their application.
5. **Property making.** A knowledge of the materials available and their use in practice.
6. **Stage settings.** Scenic construction and painting; an understanding of the basic principles of stage design.
7. **Film and television.** How to use either of these two media, especially in mixed-media productions; their contribution to dramatic work.

E. VIVA-VOCE

Each candidate will discuss with the examiners his approaches to and interests in drama as well as the work done in the previous sections. Opportunity will be given for the candidate to clarify or amplify any of this work. Thirty minutes will be allowed for this discussion.

This is intended to be an informal discussion and it will usually follow on from the practical session [Section (*c*)]. Should the technical aspects not have received its own viva-voce, queries will be included on these aspects. All candidates to date have found this a most valuable session enabling them to discuss approaches, opinion, stating interests, etc., with their examiners.

The A.D.B. [Ed.]
Examination Scheme

1. The examination will consist of four sections:

   (*a*) Written work.
   (*b*) A personal project.
   (*c*) Practical work.
   (*d*) A viva-voce.

2. The written work [Section (*a*)] occurs throughout the course of training. The subject for the personal project [Section (*b*)] must be stated at the time of registration and handed in at the time of the supervised written paper, which is normally 4 weeks before the Practical examination [Sections (*c*) and (*d*)].

3. The course tutor will submit a confidential report on each candidate to the Board and this report will be given full weight by the examiners. It is recommended that the report be based on a continuous assessment of the candidate on the course of training.
4. The above represents the Board's examination scheme but the Board is prepared to consider alternatives to this pattern if they are proposed by the sponsoring authority. In such cases, the regulations may be modified to suit the proposed scheme.

Anyone in possession of the A.D.B. Certificate obtained after March 1971 is exempt from the project [Section (*b*)]. This should be stated at the time of registration and a reduction is made in the fee payable.

Method of Examining

1. The supervised written paper and the personal project will be marked by the Board's national examiners, one of whom will attend the practical work [Sections (*c*) and (*d*)].
2. The second examiner will be nominated by the course tutor and approved by the Board. He will mark the unsupervised written work and attend the practical examination [Sections (*c*) and (*d*)].
3. The second examiner shall not be the course tutor, organizer, or local secretary.

The second examiner should not be an interested party in the course or the examination and, if he is not known by the Board, the course organizer will be asked for a brief curriculum vitae before his appointment is approved.

The second examiner's marking of the unsupervised written work will be moderated by a national examiner. The second examiner has authority to conduct a tutorial session with the course on their work but he must not divulge the grades awarded; any arrangements for this tutorial session are entirely between the course and the examiner and the Board cannot be responsible for any costs other than the payment for marking.

The gradings A, B, C, D and E are used (A = very good, B = good, C = pass, D = fail with promise, E = fail) and each candidate is required to achieve a minimum of C in each section in order to pass. Failure to pass in either the written or the project or the practical may be referred. If, however, the practical is referred, it may be necessary for the candidate to re-take this at another centre as the Board cannot run practical examinations for less than 5 candidates.

Syllabus

The syllabus that follows is an outline only as the course tutor will be responsible for the programme of work on the course. This will have relation to the individual needs and work of the students and the local conditions.

In view of the above statement, the syllabus for the A.D.B. (Ed.) examination has deliberately been left as flexible as possible, but the Board hopes that every candidate will know what he is doing and why he is doing it and that this knowledge will be related directly to the children and their needs.

A. WRITTEN WORK

Each candidate will be required to answer in essay form four questions. These questions will be set by the Board after consultation with the course tutor and one will be set in each of the first two terms and two in the third term. Two weeks will be allowed for candidates to write their answers to each of the first two questions; the remaining two questions will be answered under supervision. The written work will be based on a consideration of the following:

1. The nature of drama in education.
2. The aims and objectives of drama in education.
3. Teaching approaches.
4. Drama and the development of the child.

Text books and reference material may be used freely for the first two questions. The examiners may specify books which are permissible for the supervised answers.

Experience has shown that the first term may be too early for the first question; in such cases, the two unsupervised question may be answered together during the second term and a month will be allowed for this. Unsupervised answers may be any length but the examiners are obviously more concerned with quality than quantity. Any books referred to should be listed.

B. PERSONAL PROJECT

Each candidate will produce a piece of work, which need not necessarily be written, showing that he has an interest in, and some knowledge of a particular aspect of drama and/or theatre which should reach beyond the area in which he normally works. The project may be in any form the candidate chooses, i.e. written, tape, film or a combination of any or all three. Any further illustrative material which the candidate wishes to use to support his project should be available at the time of the practical work [Sections (c) and (d)] and may be used as a stimulus for his work with the class if he so wishes. At all times during the preparation of the project, reference to books and other material will be permitted but the completed project must show that the candidate's approach and opinions are intrinsically his own.

All candidates *must* obtain approval before commencing work on their project and must notify the Board of any major change occurring during their preparation. Work submitted for other examinations or courses will not be accepted and, as a general guide, between 6,000 and 10,000 words would be an appropriate length for a written project, exclusive of illustrative material. The quality of supporting material should be satisfactory and it must be relevant to the main body of the project.

The project must be recorded in some way (e.g. written, tape, film, etc.) and the Post Office must accept it for delivery to the examiner.

C. PRACTICAL WORK

Each candidate will work with a class or group for a maximum of one hour. The group will be not less than fifteen in number and of an age range chosen by the candidate. The candidate will be expected to show he is capable of using drama in any way which is educationally valid and that he can use and develop ideas which the group produces. Subject matter, approach and sensitivity to the group will be the main concern of the examiners. No set procedure is laid down for the session but it is hoped that some work in both movement and vocalization will be covered; beyond this, the candidate is entirely in charge and may conduct the work in his own way. Any visual, tactile or aural aids which the candidate feels might act as a stimulation for drama will be allowed and credit given for their imaginative use.

Note: The maximum of one hour may be adjusted by the candidate to suit the age range with which he is working, e.g. 30 minutes might well be more than sufficient time to work with a class in the five to seven years age range.

The class should be handled as a class and not manipulated in a way which the candidate thinks will be acceptable to the examiners.

The examiners are more concerned with the candidate's awareness than with the success or failure of the lesson.

The age range is chosen by the candidate and may include adults. The schedule for the practical examination will be drawn up using the normal lesson length of the age range chosen unless the candidate particularly wishes the full hour. There is no reason why candidates may not work on a text but they should be reminded that this is not the main object of the A.D.B. (Ed.) syllabus.

Attention is drawn to the word 'vocalization' (sound) which may or may not cover 'verbalization' (speech).

D. VIVA-VOCE

The examiners may discuss with the candidate:

1. his written work [Section (*a*)],
2. his personal project [Section (*b*)],
3. his practical work [Section (*c*)],
4. his knowledge and experience of drama and theatre in general.

Up to 45 minutes will be allowed for this section, in order that the aspects may be discussed in reasonable depth.

This is intended to be a friendly discussion and, depending on the schedule, will normally follow straight on from the practical work [Section (*c*)]. All candidates to date have found this a most valuable session enabling them to discuss approaches, opinions, stating interests, etc., with their examiners.

SUGGESTED FURTHER READING

Initial Reading

Brochures

The following contain much useful introductory reading. They are currently available from Stacey Publications who also carry many titles on Drama and Theatre in Education.

Stage Make-up.
Your Problems Solved.
The Play Produced.
Stage Lighting for Clubs and Schools.
Plays of 1966–1971. (Six separate brochures.)

General

Clark, Brian. *Group Theatre.* Pitman, London, 1972.
Hamilton, Peter *Amateur Stage Handbook.* Pitman, London, 1957.
Joseph, Stephen. *New Theatre Forms.* Pitman, London, 1968.
Morley, Sheridan (Ed.). *Theatre 71.* Hutchinson, London, 1972.
Newton, Robert. *Exercise Improvisation.* J. G. Miller, London, 1960.
Rendle, Adrian. *Everyman and his Theatre.* Pitman, London, 1968.
Sweeting, Elisabeth. *Theatre Administration.* Pitman, London, 1969.
White, Edwin. *Problems of Acting and Production.* Pitman, London, 1966.

Specialist

Asser, Joyce. *Historic Hairdressing.* Pitman, London, 1970.
Bentham, Frederic. *The Art of Stage Lighting.* Pitman, London, 1968.
Bullard, Audrey. *Improve Your Speech.* Blond, London, 1967.
Cole, Wilton. *Sound and Sense.* Allen & Unwin, London, 1942.
Colson, Greta. *Voice Production and Speech.* Pitman, London, 1963.
Kenton, Warren. *Stage Properties and How to Make Them.* Pitman, London, 1967.
Kidd and Long. *Projecting Slides.* Focal Press, London, 1963.
Kostelanetz, Richard. *The Theatre of Mixed Means.* Pitman, London, 1970.
Napier, Frank. *Noises Off.* Muller, London, 1962.
Tompkins, Julia. *Stage Costumes and How to Make Them.* Pitman, London, 1969.
Truman, Nevil. *Historic Costuming.* Pitman, London, 1969.

Further Reading

General

Artaud, Antonin. *The Theatre and its Double.* Calder & Boyars, London, 1970.
Bentley, Eric. *The Theatre of Commitment.* Methuen, London, 1968.
Bentley, Eric. *What is Theatre?* Methuen, London, 1969.

Braun, Edward. *Meyerhold on Theatre*. Methuen, London, 1969.
Brustein, Robert. *The Theatre of Revolt*. Methuen, London, 1970.
Burton, Peter and Lane, John. *New Directions*. Methuen, London, 1970.
Ellis-Fermor, Una. *The Frontiers of Drama*. Methuen, London, 1964.
Esslin, Martin. *The Theatre of the Absurd*. Penguin, London, 1970.
Grotowski, Jerzy. *Towards a Poor Theatre*. Methuen, London, 1969.
Hartnoll, Phyllis (Ed.). *The Oxford Companion to the Theatre*. Oxford University Press, London, 1967.
Hodgson, John and Richards, Ernest. *Improvisation*. Methuen, London, 1966.
Marowitz, Charles and Trussler, Simon (Eds.). *Theatre at Work*. Methuen, London, 1967.
Pronko, Leonard. *Avant Garde: The Experimental Theatre in France*. Cambridge University Press, London, 1962.
Stanislavski, Constantin. *Building a Character*. Methuen, London, 1968.
Taylor, John Russell. *Anger and After*. Methuen, London, 1969.
Williams, Raymond. *Drama in Performance*. Muller, London, 1968.
Williams, Raymond. *Drama from Ibsen to Brecht*. Chatto & Windus, London, 1968.

Specialist

Hainaux, Rene (Ed.). *Stage Design throughout the World since 1935*. Harrap, London, 1957.
Hainaux, Rene and Bonnett, Y. (Ed.). *Stage Design throughout the World since 1950*. Harrap, London, 1967.

The following titles are all published by Studio Vista, London.

Angeloglou, Maggie. *A History of Make-up*. (1970.)
Aspden, George. *Model Making in Paper, Board and Metal*. (1964.)
Cunnington, Phillis. *Costume in Pictures*. (1964.)
d'Arbeloff, Natalie. *An Artist's Workbook: line, shape, volume, light*. (1969.)
d'Arbeloff, Natalie and Yates, Jack. *Creating in Collage*. (1967.)
Evans, James Roose. *Experimental Theatre*. (1970.)
Hobbs, William. *Techniques of the Stage Fight*. (1967.)
Jackson, Sheila. *Simple Stage Costumes*. (1968.)
Motley. *Designing and Making Stage Costumes*. (1964.)
Oliver, Charles. *Anatomy and Perspective: the fundamentals of figure drawing*. (1971.)
Percival, John. *Modern Ballet*. (1970.)
Pilbrow, Richard. *Stage Lighting*. (1971.)
Portchmouth, John. *Creative Crafts for Today*. (1969.)
Warre, Michael. *Designing and Making Stage Scenery*. (1966.)

SUPPLIERS, PUBLICATIONS AND ORGANIZATIONS

Suppliers

The following have a well established reputation of service to individuals, drama groups and theatre companies, and are particularly sympathetic to the needs of amateurs:

SAMUEL FRENCH LTD: 26, Southampton Street, Strand, London WC2 7JE Tel: 01–836 7513.

Books and plays—acting editions.
Sound effects—disc and tape.
Guides to play selection—free on request.

They are well known for their acting editions, but their bookshop—offering an unrivalled selection of general and specialized theatre literature—also deserves a high reputation. Their advisory support service is excellent.

W. J. FURSE & CO. LTD: Theatre Division, Traffic Street, Nottingham, NG2 1NF. Tel: 0602–868213.

Stage lighting and other equipment—for sale or hire. Not only will they create, supply and service equipment but they also offer a first class advisory service and will prepare notes, schemes, technical drawings and specifications for clients. No enquiry is too small.
They have branches at:

Bramcote, Brene Knoll, Highbridge, Somerset
61–63 Park Road, Glasgow G4 9JE
The Slat, Atcombe Court, South Woodchester, Stroud, GL5 5ER
15 Moss Carr Avenue, Long Lee, Keighley, West Yorkshire

CHARLES H. FOX LTD: 25, Shelton Street, London, WC2H 9HX. Tel: 01–240 3111.

Next to the stage door of the Cambridge Theatre is a headquarters for make-up, costumes, wigs, armour and jewellery (sale and hire), with an excellent advisory support service. Richard Blore, Leichner's creative director, is available, by appointment, at the centre, for make-up advice and demonstration. The full range of Leichner make-up is always in stock.

PUBLICATIONS

Amateur Stage: available from 1 Hawthornedene Road, Hayes, Bromley, Kent, BR2 7DZ. Tel: 01–462 6461. 35p per copy; £4.50 annual sub. All aspects of amateur theatre—adult, youth, educational.

Broadsheet: available from London Schools' Drama Association, 31 Wyatt Rd., London E7 9ND. 20p.

Creative Drama: available from Educational Drama Association, Drama Centre, Rea St., Birmingham, 5. Twice yearly. £1.20 annual sub.

Drama: Published by the British Drama League, 9 Fitzroy Square, London, W1P 6AE. Quarterly, 60p (free to members).

Noda Bulletin: Published three times a year by the National Operatic and Dramatic Association, 1 Crestfield St., London, W.C.1. £1.00 annually (free to members).

Plays and Players: available from 75 Victoria St., London, S.W.1. Monthly. For the general playgoer, 60p. P.O. Box 294, 2 & 4 Old Pye St., off Strutton Ground, Victoria St., SW1P 2LR.

S.C.D.A. Scene: Published Feb. and Sept. by the Scottish Community Drama Association, 53 Manor Place, EH3 7EG.

Stage and Television Today: 19/21 Tavistock St., London WC2E. Published weekly (Thur), 12p. Professional theatre newspaper.

Theatre Directory: An Amateur Stage Handbook, listing services, suppliers and organizations: available at 80p from Stacey Publications, 1, Hawthornedene Road, Hayes, Bromley, Kent. Tel: 01–462 6461.

Roy Stacey is also the publisher of *Amateur Stage* and *Amateur Stage Handbooks* covering all aspects of amateur theatre—adult, youth and educational.

British Theatre Directory (annual): A guide to theatres in London and the Provinces also listing services, suppliers and organizations. Future editions will include greater cover of material of interest to amateurs and educationalists. Annually (1978 £5.75) from John Offord Publications, P.O. Box 64, Eastbourne, East Sussex BN21 3LW Tel: 0323–37841 or 638945

Organizations

Amateur Drama Council of Ireland, 34, Beech Park, Athlone.

Amateur Drama League of Ireland, Tuam, Co. Galway, Eire.

Arts Council of Great Britain, 105 Piccadilly, London, W1V 0AU.

Arts Council of Northern Ireland, Bedford House, Bedford St., Belfast, BT2 7FX.

British Amateur Drama Association, Orbis, Youlgrave, Nr. Bakewell, Derbys.

British Children's Theatre Association, B. R. Whiteley, 41 Church Lane, Normanton, Yorks., WF6 1EZ.

Drama Association of Wales, Mrs. E. V. Williams, First Floor, Chapter Arts Centre, Canton, Cardiff.

Drama Board, 20 Beaumont St., Oxford OX1 2NP.

Educational Drama Association, Drama Centre, Rea St., Birmingham, 5.

Guild of Drama Adjudicators, Priests' House, Smallhythe, Tenterden, Kent.

International Theatre Institute, British Centre, 44 Earlham St., London WC2 H9LA.

Little Theatre Guild of Great Britain, 19 Abbey Park Road, Grimsby, DN32 0HJ.

National Drama Festivals Association, J. Baker, 3 Laird Drive, Sheffield, 6.

National Federation of Women's Institutes, 39 Eccleston St., London, SW1 W9NT.

National Operatic and Dramatic Association, 1 Crestfield St., London, WC1H 8AV.

National Union of Townswomen's Guilds, 2 Cromwell Place, London, SW7 2JG.

Radius, Religious Drama Society of Great Britain, St. Paul's Church, Covent Garden, Bedford St., WC2E 9ED.

Scottish Arts Council, 19 Charlotte Square, Edinburgh EH2 4DF.

Scottish Community Drama Association, 53 Manor Place, Edinburgh EH3 7EG.

Society for Theatre Research—The Secretary, 14 Woronzow Road, London NW8.

Society of Teachers of Speech & Drama, 82 St. John's Road, Sevenoaks, Kent.

Welsh Arts Council, 9 Museum Place, Cardiff, CF1 3NX

STATEMENTS OF AIMS AND PURPOSES
FROM SOME NATIONAL DRAMA ORGANIZATIONS

The British Theatre Association. (Formerly The British Drama League)
Director: Walter Lucas, 9 Fitzroy Square, London W1P 6AE.
Tel: 01–387 2666.

'To assist the Development of the art of the Theatre and to promote a right relation between Drama and the life of the community'.

The British Drama League is, essentially, an association of theatre-lovers and unites those, professional and amateur alike, who desire to support the Living Theatre. Its membership includes the National Theatre, the Royal Shakespeare Theatre, West End managements and British Actors Equity; distinguished scholars, dramatic critics, leading actors, and most Repertory Companies; amateur dramatic societies here and abroad—in banks and schools, universities and community centres, industry and commerce, youth clubs, Women's Institutes and Townswomen's Guilds, hospitals and prisons, and the armed services of the Crown. The B.B.C. and major ITV companies are members of the League, as are also many public libraries, education authorities and youth committees.

The League has always been active in campaigning for matters of national importance to the Theatre—the preservation of famous theatre buildings, the National Theatre, the abolition of Entertainments Duty. It has secured recognition for drama as an essential factor in education, is in the forefront of new ideas and trends in the theatre and is particularly concerned in protecting the interest of its members and member groups. It works in association with the Theatres' Advisory Council, which is housed in the League's premises at Fitzroy Square.

Services

The Library contains approximately 200,000 volumes, including more than 5,000 sets of plays, and a unique collection of press-cuttings, play programmes, costume designs, which provide an invaluable source for information, reference and research.

The Information and Advisory Service is available to all Library subscribers and covers choice of plays, rights and royalties, artistic and technical aspects of play production, and history and criticism of the theatre. There is also an Information Bureau attached to the Training Department. This deals with non-Library queries and its services are available to all members of the League.

Drama, the illustrated Quarterly Theatre Review, has been published continuously since 1919 and is issued free to members (80p post free per annum to non-members in Great Britain). It carries articles by eminent writers on all aspects of the theatre and a special Members' Supplement is enclosed with each issue.

Services to playwrights include written criticisms of members' scripts (for a fee of £1.05 for a one-act play and £1.50 for a full-length play) and Festival Awards for original one-act plays.

Critics, adjudicators and lecturers may be recommended to member societies for their productions, festivals and general programmes.

The dialect survey provides examples of the main forms of British and American speech on gramophone records, on sale at H.Q.

The B.D.L. Bookshop enables members to obtain any published book easily and quickly.

The Practice Theatre and other rooms at Headquarters are available for hire for rehearsals and meetings.

All members are cordially invited to use the premises at B.D.L. headquarters when in London and to visit the Library, whether a Library member or not, although library privileges of reading and borrowing books there are naturally restricted to library subscribers.

Activities

The Training Department, which is supported by an annual grant from the Department of Education, specializes in training leaders in the amateur theatre, and its past students hold key positions in many parts of the world, Summer Schools and Courses of varying lengths are arranged for producers, actors, students and teachers on artistic and technical subjects related to productions. Weekend Courses on specialized subjects are held in London throughout most of the year.

The Festival of Community Theatre, organized annually by the League since 1926, incorporates many local festivals. It provides opportunities for analysis, comparison of achievement and publicity.

The Annual Conference brings theatre-lovers together for visits to productions in different parts of the country, and for discussions with leading personalities from the professional and amateur theatre on the varied aspects of drama and allied arts.

The Theatregoers' Club is established in London. Regular visits to plays are sometimes followed by meetings with members of the casts for discussion of their productions.

The Junior Drama League, with its lectures and special courses for children, enables young people to appreciate and enjoy the arts of the theatre and so helps to create the perceptive audience of the future.

The Overseas Department works in active co-operation with leading theatre organizations all over the world, through which it arranges exchanges and tours of companies and individuals. It assists overseas members with their problems, and helps students and visitors to this country to see the best of Britain's theatre. The League has given life to branch organizations in Australia and New Zealand, and is a founder of the International Amateur Theatre Association.

The British Drama League will be known as the British Theatre Association with effect from October 1972.

This change is the result of much consideration during the past years and is largely the result of the recognition that the majority of the work is of a practical nature directly concerned with theatre as such. Academic connections will, of course, continue as strongly as before and the change in title has been recognized and agreed not only by the Department of Education and Science but also the Arts Council of Great Britain and the British Council.

It is hoped at the time of the change to institute further services and plans on how this can be accomplished are now being worked out.

List of Organizations at B.D.L. Headquarters

Association of British Theatre Technicians.
British Children's Theatre Association.
National Council of Theatre for Young People.
Society of Theatre Consultants.
Theatres' Advisory Council.

Organizations Using B.D.L. Headquarters as Accommodation Address

National Association of Drama Advisers.
Little Theatre Guild of Great Britain.

THE NATIONAL ASSOCIATION OF DRAMA ADVISERS

The National Association of Drama Advisers was formed in 1960. Its policy is to serve its members by keeping them informed of national developments and by providing national courses. To this end the Association is represented on a number of other bodies, including the Council of Regional Theatres, the National Council of Theatre for Young People, the British Drama League, the Drama Board and the National Conference.

The majority of the Association's members are officers to Local Education Authorities, and although there are variations in their individual responsibilities they are generally concerned with the development of drama at child, youth and adult levels. Much of a drama adviser's time is taken up in schools, where he is primarily concerned with the educational applications of drama. This section of his or her work steadily increases as creative drama becomes more and more an integral part of the school curriculum.

In youth and adult areas, drama advisers work towards the improvement of standards of theatre as an art form, and to this end they are available to advise on all aspects of theatrecraft. In addition, they organize or direct courses to cater for all levels of experience, often in the form of youth and adult theatre workshops. A direct result of their efforts in this field is the increasing number of drama centres that are appearing in various parts of the country. These are usually in the form of fully-equipped studios, which facilitate experiment by all who wish to further their art. The provision of such facilities and expertise can be of considerable help to any group that wishes to develop its resources.

Most County and some County Borough Education Authorities possess a drama adviser. If you are in any doubt of the existence of one in your area, contact your Local Education Office, or write to:

> The Secretary,
> N.A.D.A.,
> British Theatre Centre,
> 9 Fitzroy Square,
> LONDON W1P 6AE

DRAMA IN THE NATIONAL FEDERATION OF WOMEN'S INSTITUTES

The NFWI Drama Sub-committee operates in an adult education capacity. As such it seeks to raise the standard of drama within the WI movement, and, by the contacts of its trainees, outside the movement.

NFWI Drama Producers' Training Scheme

This commenced in 1961 to raise the standard of production/drama training within the movement and to give members the opportunity for personal development through drama in the art of communication, lively speech, self-confidence, etc. The scheme is geared towards an examination—the NFWI Drama Producers' Certificate. Courses are run in conjunction with LEAs, and tutors' reports are called for. Also, courses are held at Denman College, the Women's Institute Further Education College, for prospective candidates.

The examination is almost entirely practical and candidates are examined in solo and group improvisation, script rehearsal, lighting and other technical aspects, design, including costume and make-up, and there is also a final interview with the examiners. The only theoretical part is the comprehensive written work required on the chosen play.

Successful examinees are exempt from the practical part of the ADB, and if recommended by the NFWI examiners, may take the theoretical part of the ADB to obtain this nationally recognized diploma in further education drama teaching.

The NFWI Drama Training Scheme has been outstandingly successful and has raised drama standards to an amazing extent. Successful candidates undertake splendid teaching and production work throughout England and Wales, not only in WIs but for LEAs, Youth Groups, Mental Hospitals, etc.

Effective Speech Courses

These courses are designed to help in everyday communication, as well as actual public speaking, and are based on the premise that speech difficulties are generally psychological rather than technical. So often an inborn hesitancy prevents people from playing as full a part in life as they would like. These carefully designed courses, using the most modern training methods, commence with physical and vocal relaxation exercises using music, and lead up to prepared and spontaneous speech.

WI members, whatever their interests, take part in these courses. Members attending the courses have found them enormously helpful. The effects spread well outside the movement through students' contacts with family and friends and social groups. Early courses trained NFWI Drama Producers' Certificate holders to teach effective speech in their areas. Many are now doing this, not only with WIs, but for LEAs and outside organizations.

Other Courses

Apart from those already mentioned, courses are held at Denman College on other aspects of drama training. For example 'The Teaching of Acting Course' which is designed to give full opportunity for studying dance/drama and the improvisational methods of building character and situation. Other courses deal with production methods other than proscenium. The greatest encouragement is given to experiment, especially in using village halls. A new course is planned on documentary drama, training students to make use of all media available and encouraging original themes and scripts.

Conclusion

As will be seen from the foregoing, the NFWI pursues a drama programme using the most modern teaching methods. It aims not only at raising the level of drama and improving communication between people, but also at providing an outlet for the ever increasing leisure problem, which with progress will increase. With these points in mind, it hopes to give a very real service to the community.

THE NATIONAL OPERATIC & DRAMATIC ASSOCIATION

The association was established in 1899 for the express purpose of bringing together members of amateur operatic and dramatic societies for their mutual assistance and combined benefit. The only organization of its kind devoted exclusively to the amateur stage, it now has over 1,400 affiliated Societies and nearly 1,600 individual members. In January 1968 the association was registered as a Charity under the Charities Act 1960, and its services are now available to all.

Library Services

NODA offers a unique lending library service, comprising the finest collection of vocal scores, libretti, reference books, periodicals and specially prepared production copies of marked stage books. Hiring, say, vocal scores shows a big saving compared with the cost of outright purchase—and this forms a widely-used part of the service. The library is open throughout the year.

Noda Bulletin

The Bulletin, which is published three times a year, contains pages of information of vital interest to all concerned with the amateur stage. Reports on new professional productions from the amateur point of view, announcements of the latest amateur releases, articles on important aspects of the theatre, reports of societies' activities all over the country—these items make the Bulletin a 'must' for every keen and progressive amateur society. It is issued to every affiliated society and individual member, and can be supplied to individual subscribers at a small cost.

Show Publicity

Forthcoming productions of every member-society can be given free publicity in the *Fixture List* forming part of the *Noda Bulletin*. Thus you can keep your eye on production trends and can attract other societies to your shows. Many members find that this additional support covers the cost of their NODA subscription many times over.

Year Book

This annual contains a wealth of information and guidance on all aspects of the amateur theatre. Advice on legal matters, special insurance facilities, specially-negotiated contract terms with costume and scenery firms—plus a complete list of all affiliated societies, with addresses, rehearsal nights and details of recent productions.

Supplies and Services

Whatever you need for your show, NODA can either supply it or advise you where to get it. Scores or libretti to purchase, programme blocks, theatrical make-up, perruquiers, stage properties, sound effects, printing, etc., etc.,—truly a complete service.

Producers and Shows

NODA has an extensive panel of professional producers available to work in any part of the country. They include many of the finest and most successful producers of amateur shows available today.

NODA also acts as agents for the rights of many popular musicals and pantomime scripts.

Conferences

NODA's Annual Conference, at a different centre each year, is a highlight in the amateur theatre world. Representatives from societies all over the country meet to discuss matters of common and special interest, also to help NODA further its activities and services to its members.

In addition there are Sectional Conferences held annually in each area.

Summer School

The NODA Summer School held each August provides first class training under highly qualified professional instructors.

Overseas

Wherever English-speaking communities perform plays, musicals, light or grand opera, NODA is known, respected and represented. Many Overseas Societies—from the West Indies to New Zealand, from the Middle East to South Africa, find it useful to call upon the many services offered by NODA.

Organization

Head Office has an experienced and dedicated permanent staff who with the Director and Secretary give prompt, efficient service and advice to all. Their accumulated specialist knowledge is invaluable. They are supported by a Council comprising an elected councillor from each of the 11 major areas into which NODA divides the British Isles. Each area is further covered by Regional Representatives who form an area committee under the councillor. Thus NODA reaches out to provide a local and personal service wherever there is an amateur society.

Membership

The best and most economical way of enjoying all the services offered by NODA is to become a member—at the very low rates of subscription which are made possible by the very large membership. Most Societies agree that it is the best investment they ever made, and so it can prove to be for you.

Inclusion on the NODA mailing list ensures that you receive the first notice of any announcement of interest to the amateur stage.

Members also have the privilege of nominating and electing the members of the Council and Regional Representatives, and thus of taking part in the democratic process by which NODA is run.

Enquiries should be made to:

> The Director,
> National Operatic & Dramatic Association,
> 1, Crestfield St.,
> London WC1H 8AV
> Tel: 01–837 5655.

DRAMA IN THE NATIONAL UNION OF
TOWNSWOMEN'S GUILDS

In towns and cities throughout Great Britain, Northern Ireland and the Channel Isles, there are active groups of women who are members of the National Union of Townswomen's Guilds. Their interests are many and varied, but their aims and objects are the same:

'To serve as a common meeting ground for women irrespective of race, creed and party; to enable them through study and the pursuit of educational, cultural and social activities to fulfil their responsibilities as citizens'.

It is more than forty years since the movement was started by a few pioneers who wanted women to have opportunities for better education. The Carnegie Trust made a number of grants, including one in 1937 which made it possible for a part-time Adviser in Drama and Music to be appointed. It was at about this time that the National Union headquarters was set up at 2 Cromwell Place, London S.W.7, where it is still situated. Every Guild member pays a subscription, part of which is an affiliation fee to the National Union. A Guild will have between 50 and 150 members, and its activities are arranged by an executive committee elected by the members. Each Guild is affiliated to a Federation and is entitled to send delegates to the Federation Council. The Federation comprises 20 to 40 Guilds in an area which is geographically viable. A representative from the Federation executive committee sits on the Central Council, which meets in London and is responsible for electing the National Executive Committee.

This committee is responsible for the management of the N.U.T.G., including the Education Department, and for carrying out the policy decided by the National Council. The Annual General Meeting is held at the Royal Albert Hall each year when 300 delegates vote on major issues.

Many Guilds have Drama as a popular activity. The members who perform are well supported by those who form enthusiastic audiences. Original sketches and topical pantomimes and revues are frequently the entertainment for special celebrations. Both one and three act plays are perhaps the most usual choice and some Guilds reach a very high standard, receiving high marks in festivals, often in competition with mixed groups. There have been winners and runners-up in the British Drama League Festival.

A great deal is also done to entertain local organizations, such as the handicapped, the blind, or senior citizens.

Federations are able to tackle more ambitious productions, with several thousand members to call on for support, the standard reached being frequently very high. Documentaries on social and historic subjects are researched and written—these often have a local interest. Costumes are made, properties and scenery constructed, all with great historic accuracy and care.

Music and dancing are often incorporated, and these sometimes include national and international themes. Productions of three act plays and other full scale works are undertaken. These include musical plays, light opera such as Gilbert and Sullivan, and more serious opera. Dido and Aeneas, Hiawatha and The Jackdaw of Reims, among others, have been successfully produced, with the stage presentation mimed to orchestra and choir.

Competitive and non-competitive festivals are organized by Federations. These range from one act plays to speech and mime festivals. Experiments have been made with theatre-in-the-round, arena and open stage, and the more traditional proscenium stage. Some Guilds and Federations invite men and children as guests to take part in their dramatic productions.

National Union has periodically arranged Drama Conferences, which have been attended by Federation Drama chairmen at National Union expense. Some of the subjects covered at the Conferences have been, 'Women in the Theatre', 'The Impossible Hall', 'Minimum Stage Equipment', 'Tackling the Problems of an Open-air Set', 'The Possibility of Putting on a Costume Play Quite Inexpensively', and 'Theatre in the Round'. At the Drama Conference, 'Let's Pool Ideas', teams from different parts of the country demonstrated some of the more out-of-the-ordinary ventures that T.G.s had attempted.

National Union arranges activities which concern the individual Guild member. A study visit was arranged to the Festival of Music and Drama at Salzburg, and one to the Oberammergau Passion Play. Two study tours were arranged to Greece, members visiting Hungary en route. The itinerary included sightseeing tours and theatre performances.

Members attended residential courses at the Shakespeare Study School held at Westham House Residential College, Barford, Warwick. They visited productions at the Royal Shakespeare Theatre, toured back-stage, and studied various aspects of Shakespeare's works.

At the same time, students had the chance to experiment in widely contrasting methods of group work, including practical activities.

Several theatrical productions have been organized nationally, and these have involved Guild members from all parts of the country.

A modern masque, entitled *With this Sword*, was presented at the Royal Festival Hall. In this, 550 players from 24 Federations took part. Most of the Federations held mime classes throughout the year in preparation for the production. The theme was a social one to cover the work and place of women from the eighteenth century to the mid-twentieth century. The presentation was in dramatic episodes, which were cameos of a changing social structure, and it ended with a challenge, 'Thus far have we come; what shall we do to progress still further?'.

Another venture was the first production on television—a new mime, *The Word*, by Marion Jay. This was a joint effort by drama and music sections. The production was outstanding for its novelty of style—costumes, set, lighting and some of the grouping were entirely modelled on Rembrandt's paintings.

Combining drama with music, social studies and art and crafts sections, a documentary play, *Pleasure or Pain in Education*, was presented in London. The Middlesex Education Authority supported this venture by granting two L.E.A. classes, one on documentary production (for drama members) and the other on the making of theatrical costumes (for drama and art and crafts members combined). From this, a demonstration of *The Basic Wardrobe* was given. These costumes were made on the principle of a limited number of simple basic dresses adaptable to different periods by the addition of the appropriate sleeves, petticoats, aprons, collars, etc. Demonstrations of *This Adaptable Wardrobe* were given all round the country at Area Conferences and proved very helpful and popular. They were shown several times on one day at the National Union of Teaching Exhibition, 'Education and Careers', at Olympia, when a performance of 'Pleasure or Pain in Education' was given too.

During the Silver Jubilee Year, music and drama joined to give two performances at the Scala Theatre, London, of a choral mime, *The Gifts*, specially composed for Townswomen's Guilds by Armstrong Gibbs and Benedict Ellis. About 100 performers from near-London Federations took part.

Marking the 40th anniversary of the formation of the first Guilds, the spectacular production of the *Miracle*, by Engelbert Humperdinck, was produced at the Royal Albert Hall. A cast of over 600 actors and singers, male guest actors and singers, and children were drawn from the near-London Federations. Mime and movement were at first practised in three centres, one in North West London, one in Central London and the other south east of the Thames, and then in combined rehearsals at a large central hall. The whole cast was finally assembled with the 60 strong Pro Arte Orchestra, with only one rehearsal at the Royal Albert Hall. This mime set to music was a tremendously exciting and ambitious undertaking, and was generally voted a great success.

Drama members of the Townswomen's Guilds have taken part in Radio and T.V. After the conference on 'Let's Pool Ideas', the Open Forum was recorded for the B.B.C. *Dropping-in* programme in Woman's Hour. Members took part in the B.B.C. Television programme, *I mean to say*, which dealt with problems of personal communication.

Much of the drama work which goes on at National Union is, naturally, administrative, and some of it is concerned with public relations. The monthly magazine of the National Union, *The Townswoman*, includes regular play reviews and photos, and reports of Guild or Federation accounts of plays performed. A survey on *Live Theatre and the next Generation* was carried out by N.U.T.G. for the British Drama League. It was given considerable publicity and aroused great interest, not only among amateur drama societies and organizations, but also in the professional theatre.

The Education Adviser of the National Union of Townswomen's Guilds acts as a liaison with the Department of Education and Science, Local Education Authorities, Extra-mural Departments, and County Drama Advisers on Drama matters concerning members throughout the country.

Initiating a new look at drama, the national headquarters have arranged to mount a conference at Bedford College under the title 'Linking the Performing Arts'. By this, it is hoped to encourage Guilds and Federations to experiment with sound and movement, in developing group work which will include choral and group speech, verse speaking, mime, dramatic discussion, documentary and theme programmes.

A publication bearing the same title as the Conference has been written by Mr. James Dodding, giving practical examples on this fresh approach to drama. This should help Guilds and Federations, where drama and music sections have worked independently, to combine to improve their standard of work in the performing arts.

The future policy is to encourage members to attend residential seminars organized by the Education Department of N.U.T.G., where subjects can be studied in depth, thus enabling the ideas formulated and developed to be spread throughout the movement.

INDEX

(Page numbers in **bold type** refer to substantial extracts)

359